Communications in Computer and Information Science 918

Commenced Publication in 2007
Founding and Former Series Editors:
Phoebe Chen, Alfredo Cuzzocrea, Xiaoyong Du, Orhun Kara, Ting Liu, Dominik Ślęzak, and Xiaokang Yang

More information about this series at http://www.springer.com/series/7899

Ioannis Stamelos · Rory V. O'Connor
Terry Rout · Alec Dorling (Eds.)

Software Process Improvement and Capability Determination

18th International Conference, SPICE 2018
Thessaloniki, Greece, October 9–10, 2018
Proceedings

Springer

Editors
Ioannis Stamelos
Department of Informatics
Aristotle University of Thessaloniki
Thessaloniki
Greece

Rory V. O'Connor
School of Computing
Dublin City University
Dublin
Ireland

Terry Rout
Software Quality institute
Griffith University
Brisbane, QLD
Australia

Alec Dorling
Impronova AB
Askim
Sweden

ISSN 1865-0929 ISSN 1865-0937 (electronic)
Communications in Computer and Information Science
ISBN 978-3-030-00622-8 ISBN 978-3-030-00623-5 (eBook)
https://doi.org/10.1007/978-3-030-00623-5

Library of Congress Control Number: 2018954492

This Springer imprint is published by the registered company Springer Nature Switzerland AG
The registered company address is: Gewerbestrasse 11, 6330 Cham, Switzerland

These proceedings are dedicated to the memory of Fabrizio Fabbrini, our dear friend, colleague, and member of the Program Committee, who was an active member of the SPICE community since its inception. The SPICE community has lost a dear friend.

Preface

On behalf of the SPICE 2018 Conference Organizing Committee we are proud to present the proceedings of the 18th International Conference on Software Process Improvement and Capability Determination (SPICE 2018), held in Thesssaloniki, Greece, during October 9–10, 2018.

The SPICE project was started in 1993 to support the development of an international standard for software process assessment. The work of the project eventually led to the finalization of ISO/IEC 15504 – Process Assessment, and its complete publication represented a climax for the work of the project. The standardization effort continues, with the publication of the first documents in the new ISO/IEC 330xx family of standards on process assessment.

As part of its charter to provide ongoing publicity and transition support for the emerging standard, the project organized a number of SPICE workshops and seminars, with invited speakers drawn from project participants. These have now evolved to a sustaining set of international conferences with broad participation from academia and industry with a common interest in model-based process improvement. This was the 18th in the series of conferences organized by the SPICE User Group to increase knowledge and understanding of the International Standard and of the technique of process assessment.

The conference program featured invited keynote talks, research papers, and industry experience reports on the most relevant topics related to software process assessment and improvement; a significant focus this year was on detailed studies of aspects of process implementation, assessment, and improvement, and the expansion in the range and variety of relevant process models. Members of the Program Committee selected the papers for presentation following a peer review process.

SPICE conferences have a long history of attracting attendees from industry and academia. This confirms that the conference covers topics that are up to date, important, and interesting. SPICE 2018 offered a unique forum for industry and academic professionals to discuss their needs and ideas in the area of process assessment and improvement and in related aspects of quality management.

On behalf of the SPICE 2018 Conference Organizing Committee, we would like to thank all participants. Firstly all the authors, whose quality work is the essence of the conference, and the members of the Program Committee, who helped us with their expertise and diligence in reviewing all of the submissions. As we all know, organizing a conference requires the effort of many individuals. We also wish to thank all the members of our Organizing Committee, whose work and commitment were invaluable.

October 2018

Ioannis Stamelos
Rory V. O'Connor
Terry Rout
Alec Dorling

Preface

[illegible] Greece, during October 9–10, 2018.

[illegible] to the fifth part of ISO/IEC 15504 – Process Assessment, and an exemplar [illegible] of the project. [illegible]

[illegible]

[illegible] and improvement and related aspects of software development.

On behalf of the SPICE 2018 Conference Organizing Committee, we would like to thank [illegible] experts [illegible] conference requires the effort of many individuals. We also wish to thank all the members of the Organizing Committee, whose work and commitment were invaluable.

October 2018

Ioannis Stamelos
Rory V. O'Connor
Terry Rout
Alec Dorling

Organization

General Chair

Alec Dorling	Impronova AB, Sweden

Program Co-chairs

Terry Rout	Griffith University, Australia
Rory V. O'Connor	Dublin City University, Ireland

Local Organizing Chair

Ioannis Stamelos	Aristotle University of Thessaloniki, Greece

Industry Chair

Tomas Schweigert	SQS, Germany

Proceedings Chair

Rory V. O'Connor	Dublin City University, Ireland

Program Committee

Apostolos Ampatzoglou	University of Groningen, The Netherlands
Béatrix Barafort	Luxembourg Institute of Science and Technology, Luxembourg
Stamatia Bibi	University of Western Macedonia, Greece
Luigi Buglione	Engineering Ingegneria Informatica SpA, Italy
Gerhard Chroust	University of Southern Queensland, Australia
Paul M. Clarke	Lero, Dublin City University, Ireland
François Coallier	Ecole de technologie Superieure, Canada
Antonio Coletta	Qual. IT. Consulting, Italy
Onur Demirors	Middle East Technical University, Turkey
Fabrizio Fabbrini	Italian National Research Council, Italy
Panos Fitsilis	University of Applied Sciences of Thessaly, Greece
Vassilis Gerogiannis	Technological Education Institute of Thessaly, Greece
Dennis Goldenson	Software Engineering Institute, USA
Christiane Gresse von Wangenheim	Federal University of Santa Catarina, Brazil
Victora Hailey	VHG Corporation, Canada
Linda Ibrahim	Enterprise SPICE, USA

Ho-Won Jung	South Korea University, South Korea
George Kakarontzas	Technological Educational Institute of Thessaly, Greece
Panagiotis Katsaros	Aristotle University of Thessaloniki, Greece
Elia Kouzari	European University Cyprus, Greece
Apostolos Kritikos	Aristotle University of Thessaloniki, Greece
Giuseppe Lami	National Research Council, Italy
Marion Lepmets	SoftComply, Ireland
Catriona Mackie	BT, UK
Antonia Mas Pichaco	Universidad de les Illes Balears, Spain
Fergal McCaffery	Dundalk Institute of Technology, Ireland
Tom McBride	University of Technology Sydney, Australia
Antoni Mesquida	Universidad de les Illes Balears, Spain
Antanas Mitasiunas	Vilnius University, Lithuania
Nikos Mittas	Aristotle University of Thessaloniki, Greece
Takeshige Miyoshi	Miyoshi Art of Software Process Inc., Japan
Risto Nevalainen	FiSMA Association, Finland
Rory V. O'Connor	Dublin City University, Ireland
Saulius Ragaisos	Vilnius University, Lithuania
Alain Renault	Luxembourg Institute of Science and Technology, Luxembourg
Patricia Rodriguez-Dapena	SoftWcare SL, Spain
Clenio Salviano	CenPRA, Brazil
Anup Shrestha	University of Southern Queensland, Australia
Jean-Martin Simon	CGI Business Consulting, France
Fritz Stallinger	Software Competence Center, Austria
Timo Varkoi	Spinet Oy, Finland
Bharathi Vijayakumar	Wipro Technologies, India
Larry Wen	Griffith University, Australia
Murat Yilmaz	Çankaya University, Turkey

Local Organizing Committee

Ioannis Stamelos	Aristotle University of Thessaloniki, Greece
Lefteris Angelis	Aristotle University of Thessaloniki, Greece
Alexander Chatzigeorgiou	University of Macedonia, Greece

Acknowledgments

The conference organizers wish to acknowledge the assistance and support of the SPICE User Group and the SPICE 2018 Program Committee and reviewers in contributing to a successful conference.

ARISTOTLE
UNIVERSITY
OF THESSALONIKI

SPICE
USER GROUP

Contents

SPI Education and Management Issues

SPI Knowledge and Change Processes

SPI Compliance and Configuration

SPI and Agile

SPI Systematic Literature Reviews

Characterizing DevOps Culture: A Systematic Literature Review

Mary Sánchez-Gordón and Ricardo Colomo-Palacios(✉)

Østfold University College, 1757 Halden, Norway
{mary.sanchez-gordon, ricardo.colomo-palacios}@hiof.no

Abstract. Time and quality pressures are affecting software process in all its stages. One of the proposed solutions to these pressures is DevOps. DevOps is aimed to increase the frequency, quality and speed of deploying software from development into production by means of new organizational structures and processes with a high degree of automation. Several authors underlined the fact, that beyond the tool chain, DevOps is a culture shift. However, to date the characterization of DevOps culture remains unclear. In this paper, authors tackle this problem by means of a Systematic Literature Review. Results provide a deeper understanding of the phenomena from human factor´s perspective.

Keywords: DevOps · Culture · Empathy · Systematic Literature Review
Human factors

1 Introduction

For software makers, one way to gain a sustainable competitive advantage is to deliver products and new features to customers considerably faster than before, if not near to real-time [1]. In this scenario, continuous software engineering (CSE) is a new approach aiming at establishing strong connections between software engineering activities in order to accelerate and increase the efficiency of the software process [2]. CSE can be related to DevOps [2, 3], which has risen to the fore as a prominent trend in the software engineering community and attracted growing attention from researchers in the last years, especially since 2014 [3]. For instance, Bosch [4] provides an overview of the adoption of CSE practices at large companies producing software-intensive systems. More recently, Fitzgerald and Stol [5] have proposed a roadmap and agenda for CSE. The findings in [6] have confirmed that DevOps is as an evolution of agile software development and is informed by a lean principles background. However, according to [1], research on continuous deployment is still in its infancy, despite the industrial relevance of the topic. In support of that, the results of a recent systematic mapping study [3] emphasizes both continuous practices and the term DevOps are vaguely defined and loosely used in the software engineering community. Likewise, other mapping [7] points out that there is no standard definition for DevOps. By reviewing the published literature, one can see that DevOps efficiently integrates development, delivery, and operations, thus facilitating a lean, fluid connection of these traditionally separated silos [8]. DevOps integrates also any technique aiming to

I. Stamelos et al. (Eds.): SPICE 2018, CCIS 918, pp. 3–15, 2018.
https://doi.org/10.1007/978-3-030-00623-5_1

decrease the time between changing a system and transferring that change to the production environment, including continuous deployment but also practices like continuous monitoring [9]. But the most common interpretation is that DevOps is about culture [3]: DevOps means a culture shift toward collaboration between development, quality assurance, and operations [8], or DevOps is about aligning the incentives of everybody involved in delivering software [10] where its success is based on four principles:

- Culture. Joint responsibility for the delivery of high quality software.
- Automation. Automation in all development and operation steps towards rapid delivery and feedback from users.
- Measurement. All process must be quantified to understand delivery capability and setting goals to improve the process.
- Sharing. It is crucial the sharing of knowledge enabled by tools.

Furthermore, a novel perspective is the notion of DevOps as a superset of values, principles, methods, practices —including continuous practices— and tools [3]. This proposal is based on the point of view several forefront figures of the movement [10–12], but is focused on what one might consider a "meta definition" of the concept. In this scenario, it is not surprising that human aspects are taken in account by DevOps because software is a product of human activities that incorporates our problem solving capabilities, cognitive aspects, and social interaction [13]. In other words, software is intensive in human capital [14, 15]. Indeed, in DevOps, tools are important but people are an integral part of any human-designed complex system [16, 17]. Therefore, how we grow DevOps culture and practices in our organizations needs more attention [16]. In fact, [8] highlights that a key lesson for companies which embraced DevOps was not to underestimate the needed culture shift. In support of that view, a more recent study [18] reveals that DevOps is more a cultural shift for IT than a process or tools shift.

In the light of that, a key question, which will facilitate the understanding of the current status of research and address further investigation, is "How the scientific literature is characterizing DevOps Culture?". To the best of authors' knowledge, there are not published secondary studies about this topic. This paper is aimed to bridge this gap by conducting a systematic literature review (SRL) on the cultural side of DevOps.

The structure of the paper is as follows. The remainder of this section analyzes the works related with our proposal. Section 2 presents the design of this SRL. In Sect. 3 reports on the results of the SRL. Finally, Sect. 4 summarizes a conclusion and future research.

1.1 Related Works

This SLR focuses on DevOps culture. Before performing this study, an initial study was conducted to identify the existing secondary studies related to the topic. In order to obtain the maximum information about this topic, we searched the following two major online search academic article search engines: Scopus and Google Scholar. Given that, both of them cover all major publisher venues —e.g. Elsevier, Springer, ACM and IEEE—, they were estimated as enough for this initial purpose.

The searches were conducted in May 2018 using the search string ("*Culture*" AND "*DevOps*") AND ("*Systematic review*" OR "*Systematic literature review*" OR "*Systematic mapping*" OR "*Mapping study*" OR "*Multivocal review*" OR "*Multivocal literature review*"). When the searches were performed, 19 results were found in Scopus while Google Scholar showed 221 results. However, most of them were not actually a secondary study. After reviewing the literature on secondary studies for similar research objectives, it can be identified that there is no previously published search on the topic.

2 Research Methodology

This study was carried out following Kitchenham and Charters guidelines on Systematic Literature Review (SLR) [19]. In what follows, an overview of this SLR is presented.

2.1 Planning

In this stage, a SLR protocol was adapted to define the plan for the review. The protocol comprises research background, research questions, search strategy, study selection criteria and procedures, data extraction, and data synthesis strategies to make sure that the study is undertaken as planned and reduce the possibility of researcher bias. In this review protocol, the whole study timetable was not decided from the beginning, but rather the actual timetable of the study and results produced were recorded as the study progressed.

Objectives and Research Questions. To get an explicit view of the current definition of DevOps culture, this SLR is conducted with the following specific objectives in mind. The objectives of this study are threefold. First, we would like to understand the attributes that define DevOps culture. Second, authors would like to investigate and find out the emotional phenomenon behind DevOps culture. Finally, we would like to see if there is a growing interest in the field or not.

In order to achieve these goals, the research objectives were translated into specific research question as follows:

1. What are the documented attributes of DevOps culture?
2. What emotional phenomenon could be experienced by people in the DevOps culture? and
3. What is the trend of studies related to DevOps culture in the scientific literature?

The keywords used to find an answer to the research questions were two: "DevOps" and "Culture". Therefore, the search string was *"Culture" AND "DevOps"*.

Search Strategy and Search Process. The search strategy includes search resources and search process. Each one of them is detailed as follows:

Search Resources. In order to find the scientific literature available about DevOps culture, the search was performed on five electronic databases: (i) ACM Digital Library

(ii) IEEE Xplore Digital Library, (iii) ScienceDirect, (iv) Wiley Online Library and (v) SpringerLink.

Search Process. The overall search process is depicted in Fig. 1 and is explained in what follows.

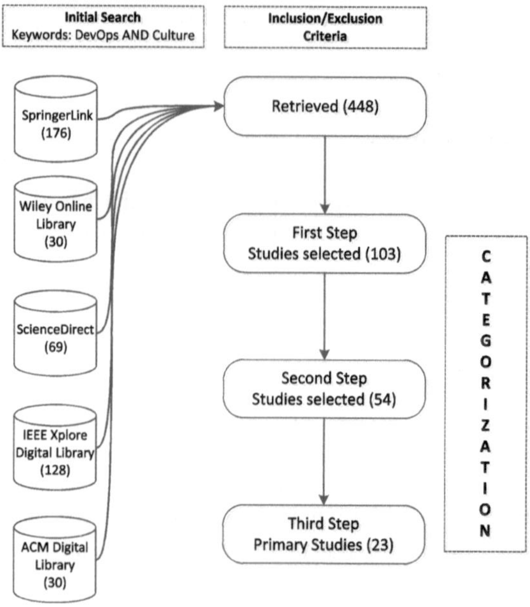

Fig. 1. Search process description

First step, the search string was applied in May 2018, returning 448 papers (in total). By manual inspection of abstract and the keywords in text context, the irrelevant studies were removed and a set of 103 unique papers remained. If multiple studies with the same title by the same author(s) were found, the most recent one was included and the rest were excluded. Moreover, only studies written in English language and electronically available were included.

Second step, all 103 papers were reviewed based on full text, and then were classified into two types:

- Relevant papers: if the paper satisfies the two inclusion criteria (explained in what follows).
- Excluded papers: other papers, which are not relevant to the topic.

A paper is kept in this study if it satisfies one of the two criteria:

- The paper is explicitly related to the DevOps and reveals some cultural aspect.
- The paper is relevant to software engineering research.

Some of the reasons for elimination were:

- The short versions of studies (with less than 4 pages).
- Book chapters. As it is generally difficult to determine how robust their findings are and if they have been subjected to peer review. However, chapters from books that are compiled as scientific articles or conference proceedings were included in this SLR.

This list was reviewed in order to check for inconsistencies. When there was doubt or disagreement about the classification of a paper, it was included in the relevant group, leaving the chance of discarding the paper during the next phase when the full texts of the papers were studied again. As a result, 54 papers were classified as relevant.

Third step, each full paper was retrieved and read to verify its inclusion or exclusion. But this time, we attempt to identify the cultural aspect in the results or discussion. The reason for exclusion or inclusion in this third phase was documented. The result of this step was that 23 papers were classified as relevant.

Fourth step, in order to check the consistency of the inclusion/exclusion decisions, a test-retest approach and re-evaluation of a random sample of the primary studies was made. However, there is a risk that some papers have been missed. Therefore, this study cannot guarantee completeness, but it can still be trusted to give a good overview of the relevant literature on DevOps culture.

2.2 Data Extraction

The data extracted from each paper was documented in a spreadsheet and kept in a reference manager. The bibliographic details for all the 23 primary studies are available in appendix A. In this paper, the primary studies are referred in the form of [S01],..., [S23] and these labels are the same as in the appendix. After selection of the primary studies, the following data was extracted: (i) Source (journal or conference), (ii) Title, (iii) Authors, (iv) Publication year (v) Classification according to a set of categories (see Table 1), (vii) Summary of the research. Based on (at least) the title, abstract and introduction of each study, a set of initial categories was created and assigned to them. When the assignment of studies to categories could not be clearly determined in this way, more about the study was considered. This process was inspired in open coding, memoing and constant comparison techniques proposed by Ground Theory. Thus, the categories were emerged and they were updated or clarified during the classification process as necessary. Moreover, both the categories and the assignment of studies to the categories were further refined. That means that an attribute generalization and iterative refinement was done. We used a spread sheet to record this process and a whiteboard and post-it notes to get a visual representation of the categories. As a result, a characterization of DevOps culture was built. Though we did not a-priori develop a categorization scheme for this research, we were broadly interested in: (i) Collaboration (ii) Sharing knowledge, and (iii) Communication.

Table 1. Characterization of DevOps culture.

ID	Attribute	Frequency	%	Primary studies
1	Communication	22	14,10	[S02]–[S23]
2	Collaboration	19	12,18	[S01]–[S05],[S07],[S09],[S10],[S12],[S13],[S15]–[S23]
3	Feedback (Continuous and immediate)	17	10,90	[S02]–[S10],[S12],[S15]–[S20],[S23]
4	Responsibility (personal/mutual)	17	10,90	[S01],[S02],[S04],[S05],[S07],[S09],[S12]–[S16],[S18]–[S23]
6	Sharing knowledge	15	9,62	[S01],[S02],[S06],[S07],[S10],[S12],[S13],[S16]–[S23]
5	Improvement cycle	15	9,62	[S03]–[S05],[S08],[S09],[S12],[S15]–[S23]
7	Transparency	12	7,69	[S01],[S02],[S05],[S07],[S15]–[S20],[S22],[S23]
8	Commitment and agreement	9	5,77	[S01],[S05],[S08],[S09],[S14],[S16],[S17], [S20],[S23]
9	New personnel and ideas	8	5,13	[S03],[S05],[S06],[S07],[S08],[S16],[S18],[S22]
10	Leadership	7	4,49	[S05],[S06],[S13],[S16],[S19],[S20],[S21]
11	Blameless	6	3,85	[S05]–[S07],[S12],[S13],[S16]
12	Experimentation	5	3,21	[S01],[S07],[S16],[S18],[S19]
13	Trust	4	2,56	[S05],[S18],[S21],[S22]
	Total	**156**	**100,00**	

2.3 Study Quality Assessment

In this study, each paper was assessed for quality at the same time as the data extraction process was performed. This process provided information about author and source, as well as the minimum information required to establish credibility. 22 of the 23 selected studies satisfied the quality questionnaire: (i) Does the paper introduce any aspect of culture? (ii) Is there a clear statement of the aims of the research? (iii) Does the paper provide relevant data related the research topics?, (iv) How adequately is the research results documented? (v) Does the paper allow answering the research questions?. The remaining paper [S14] was kept although it was identified as an expert opinion because it is focused explicitly on the topic and allowed us to answer the second question.

3 Results

From the initial set of 448 publications (see Fig. 1), 23 studies were identified as contributing to DevOps culture. This section presents an overview of this topic according to the research questions.

3.1 What are the Attributes of DevOps Culture Confessed to?

Bearing in mind that this study is focused on culture as a human factor in SE processes and particularly DevOps, a full review of the 54 publications in the second step was done. At this stage, the findings revealed that some actually do not address — much less discuss the meaning of — culture at all. That is the reason why we attempt to identify the cultural aspect into the sections of results and discussion of each paper during the third step of this SLR (23 publications). The final classification scheme was developed after applying the process described in Sect. 2.2. Table 1 lists the attributes, Columns 1 and 2 are self-explanatory. Column 3 denotes the number of publications related to the attribute while Column 4 denotes the percentage of average weighted by attribute. Finally, Column 5 indicates the list of primary studies related to the attribute.

To summarize, 13 attributes were identified in the primary studies. 7 of the attributes are up to 75% out of the total. These attributes are: (i) Communication, (ii) Collaboration, (iii) Feedback (Continuous and immediate), (iv) Responsibility (personal/mutual), (v) Improvement cycle, (vi) Sharing Knowledge, and (vii) Transparency. However, taking into account the number of primary studies (23) it seems that there is a consensus of more than 70% of them in which DevOps culture is primarily seen as Collaboration, Communication, Feedback and Responsibility.

3.2 What Emotional Phenomenon Could Be Experienced by People in the DevOps Culture?

This is not an easy question to answer because there is not one standard emotion word hierarchy [20]. Even more, according to [21], Kleinginna et al. reported more than 90 definitions have been produced for this term, and no consensus in the literature has been reached. Therefore, from a comprehensive literature review of this topic in SE, we focus on the Parrott's emotion framework which was previously chosen to conduct an exploratory analysis of emotions in software artifacts [22]. Table 2 shows as this framework classifies human emotions into a tree structure with three levels. Each level refines the granularity of the previous level, making abstract emotions more concrete. Taking into account that structure, the statements associated to the attributes during the data extraction were read again to identity the emotions of practitioners. Furthermore, although, that structure allowed us to understand these emotions at different levels during the characterization process we chose the use of think-aloud as a strategy to enhance the ability to think critically. In this way, eventually, the answers were "*compassion*" and "*empathy*". The first clue was found in the article *"Containers Will Not Fix Your Broken Culture (and Other Hard Truths)"* [S14] which points out that *"We have to live it [DevOps]; change for the better is a choice we make every day through our actions of listening empathetically and acting compassionately"*. However, such an idea was not clear at the beginning. During the third step of this review, the idea was growing as the same time that the empirical evidence related to the attributes was identified. At the end, we built a schema of attributes (for DevOps culture) where *"empathy"* seemed to fit well. Thus, empathy *"dissolves the barriers between self and other"* [23] as DevOps dissolves the barriers between developers and operators. This is certainly accepted by practitioners and researchers as part of the essence of DevOps despite that the term DevOps is vaguely defined.

Table 2. Parrott's emotion framework.

Primary emotions	Secondary emotions	Tertiary emotions
Love	Affection	Adoration, Sentimentality, Liking, Compassion, Caring, …
	Lust	Desire, Passion, Infatuation
	Longing	
Joy	Cheerfulness	Amusement, Enjoyment, Happiness, Satisfaction, …
	Zest	Enthusiasm, Zeal, Excitement, Thrill, Exhilaration
	Contentment	Pleasure
	Optimism	Eagerness, Hope
	Pride	Triumph
	Enthrallment	Enthrallment, Rapture
Surprise	Surprise	Amazement, Astonishment
Anger	Irritability	Aggravation, Agitation, Annoyance, Grumpy,. . .
	Exasperation	Frustration
	Rage	Outrage, Fury, Hostility, Bitter, Hatred, Dislike,. . .
	Disgust	Revulsion, Contempt, Loathing
	Envy	Jealousy
	Torment	
Sadness	Suffering	Agony, Anguish, Hurt
	Sadness	Depression, Despair, Unhappy, Grief, Melancholy,. . .
	Disappointment	Dismay, Displeasure
	Shame	Guilt, Regret, Remorse
	Neglect	Embarrassment, Humiliation, Insecurity, Insult,. . .
	Sympathy	Pity, Sympathy
Fear	Horror	Alarm, Shock, Fright, Horror, Panic, Hysteria,. . .
	Nervousness	Suspense, Uneasiness, Worry, Distress, Dread,. . .

Figure 2 depicts our schema, however, it is a little different of the list of attributes in Table 1. As one can see, the attribute *"New personnel and ideas"* was divided in order to facilitate the understanding. The two new attributes are *"Hiring"* and *"New ideas"*, the first one describes the attribute *"New personnel"* and the second one *"New ideas"* allows us to think not only in new personnel.

This scheme is consistent with the findings of a previous empirical study in software development about collective empathy [24]. According to [24], collective empathy prevents team dissolution by facilitating the development of bonds among team members, as well as creating and affirming a sense of groupness.

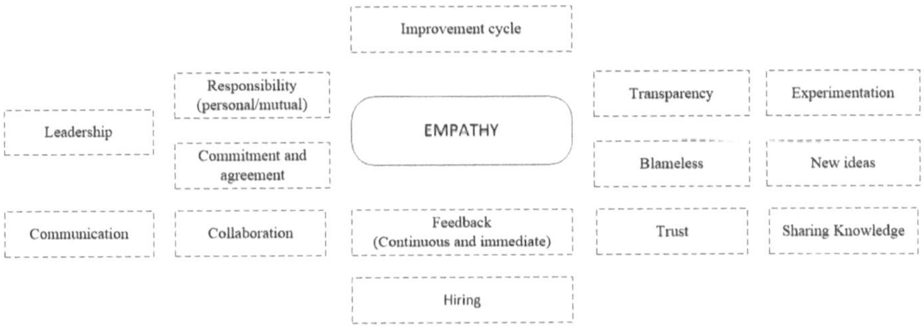

Fig. 2. Characterizing DevOps culture

3.3 What is the Trend of Studies Related to DevOps Culture in the Scientific Literature?

Figure 3 presents the number of publications over time per source. A quick look at the compiled data shows that the research field of Culture DevOps is slowly growing. Moreover, IEEE Xplore Digital Library is the source that more primary studies (13) has provided.

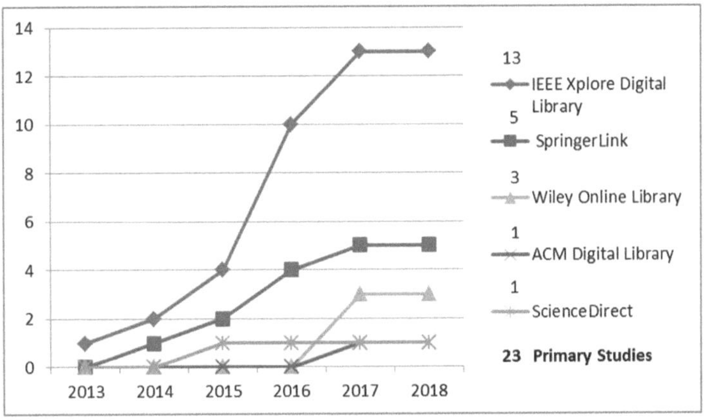

Fig. 3. Number of publications over time per source.

3.4 Limitations of Results

The limitation to academic search engines represents the state-of-the art of academic DevOps research. Therefore, future research should focus on the gap between professional research and the academic research on the topic, maybe using a multivocal literature review. The inclusion of English-only papers might mean that relevant studies in other languages are missed out, but this study is focused on the academic field and English is the most common language on this field. Another major limitation is possible selection bias, but the protocol is a way to reduce this threat. Finally, it is worth noting that the categorization was also reviewed by another researcher in order to minimize the threat's risk of do that in a wrong way.

4 Conclusions and Future Work

In spite of the literature presents an increasingly interest on DevOps, a comprehensive systematic review about DevOps culture does not exist. Even more, the definition of DevOps remains unclear in the scientific literature despite the previous efforts, such as [3, 7], made in this direction. Therefore rather than define "DevOps culture", we prefer to characterize it in order to understand its current status and address further research.

This review reveals that the soft side of DevOps is not always confessed among practitioners and researchers but it is always presented in software development [17]. It seems that culture is a term that everyone thinks they understand and it has become a powerful aspect of identity. In fact, culture is very related to human factors [25]. As a result of the characterization process, we identified 13 attributes. The most frequently attributes in the 23 primary studies were 7: (i) Communication, (ii) Collaboration, (iii) Feedback (Continuous and immediate), (iv) Responsibility (personal/mutual), (v) Improvement cycle, (vi) Sharing Knowledge, and (vii) Transparency. However, there is a relatively scarce number of primary studies related to this topic, although it is slowly growing in the scientific literature. Therefore, there is a need for empirical research.

Another aspect in the soft side of DevOps is the emotional phenomenon experienced by people. At the end of this review, empathy seems to be behind DevOps culture because, as already mentioned, *"dissolves the barriers between self and other"* [23] as DevOps dissolves the barriers between developers and operators. Bearing in mind that idea, we also built a scheme which is consistent with the findings of a previous empirical study in software development about collective empathy [24]. However, further research is needed in order to validate and enhance the schema and study the phenomenon itself.

Appendix A: Primary Studies

[S01] de Bayser, M., Azevedo, L. G., & Cerqueira, R. (2015). ResearchOps: The case for DevOps in scientific applications. In *Integrated Network Management (IM), 2015 IFIP/IEEE International Symposium on* (pp. 1398–1404). IEEE.

[S02] Ebert, C., Gallardo, G., Hernantes, J., & Serrano, N. (2016). DevOps. *IEEE Software, 33*(3), 94–100. https://doi.org/10.1109/MS.2016.68

[S03] Soni, M. (2015). End to end automation on cloud with build pipeline: the case for DevOps in insurance industry, continuous integration, continuous testing, and continuous delivery. In *Cloud Computing in Emerging Markets (CCEM), 2015 IEEE International Conference on* (pp. 85–89). IEEE.

[S04] Lwakatare, L. E., Kuvaja, P., & Oivo, M. (2015). Dimensions of devops. In *International Conference on Agile Software Development* (pp. 212–217). Springer.

[S05] Farroha, B. S., & Farroha, D. L. (2014). A framework for managing mission needs, compliance, and trust in the DevOps environment. In *Military Communications Conference (MILCOM), 2014 IEEE* (pp. 288–293). IEEE.

[S06] Kamuto, M. B., & Langerman, J. J. (2017). Factors inhibiting the adoption of DevOps in large organisations: South African context. In *Recent Trends in Electronics, Information & Communication Technology (RTEICT), 2017 2nd IEEE International Conference on* (pp. 48–51). IEEE.

[S07] Feitelson, D. G., Frachtenberg, E., & Beck, K. L. (2013). Development and deployment at facebook. IEEE Internet Computing, 17(4), 8–17.

[S08] Furfaro, A., Gallo, T., Garro, A., Sacca, D., & Tundis, A. (2016). ResDevOps: a software engineering framework for achieving long-lasting complex systems. In *Requirements Engineering Conference (RE), 2016 IEEE 24th International* (pp. 246–255). IEEE.

[S09] Punjabi, R., & Bajaj, R. (2016). User stories to user reality: A DevOps approach for the cloud. In *Recent Trends in Electronics, Information & Communication Technology (RTEICT), IEEE International Conference on* (pp. 658–662). IEEE.

[S10] Diel, E., Marczak, S., & Cruzes, D. S. (2016). Communication Challenges and Strategies in Distributed DevOps. In *Global Software Engineering (ICGSE), 2016 IEEE 11th International Conference on* (pp. 24–28). IEEE.

[S11] Camacho, C. R., Marczak, S., & Cruzes, D. S. (2016). Agile team members perceptions on non-functional testing: influencing factors from an empirical study. In *Availability, Reliability and Security (ARES), 2016 11th International Conference on* (pp. 582–589). IEEE.

[S12] Perera, P., Silva, R., & Perera, I. (2017). Improve software quality through practicing DevOps. In *Advances in ICT for Emerging Regions (ICTer), 2017 Seventeenth International Conference on* (pp. 1–6). IEEE.

[S13] Hussain, W., Clear, T., & MacDonell, S. (2017). Emerging trends for global DevOps: a New Zealand perspective. In *Proceedings of the 12th International Conference on Global Software Engineering* (pp. 21–30). IEEE Press.

[S14] Kromhout, B. (2017). Containers Will Not Fix Your Broken Culture (and Other Hard Truths). *Queue*, *15*(6), 50:46–50:56. https://doi.org/10.1145/3178368.3185224

[S15] Gupta, V., Kapur, P. K., & Kumar, D. (2017). Modeling and measuring attributes influencing DevOps implementation in an enterprise using structural equation modeling. *Information and Software Technology*, *92*, 75–91.

[S16] Colomo-Palacios, R., Fernandes, E., Soto-Acosta, P., & Larrucea, X. (2017). A case analysis of enabling continuous software deployment through knowledge management. *International Journal of Information Management.*

[S17] Hussaini, S. W. (2015). A Systemic Approach to Re-inforce Development and Operations Functions in Delivering an Organizational Program. *Procedia Computer Science*, *61*, 261–266. https://doi.org/10.1016/j.procs.2015.09.209

[S18] Erich, F. M. A., Amrit, C., & Daneva, M. (2017). A qualitative study of DevOps usage in practice. *Journal of Software: Evolution and Process*, *29*(6).

[S19] Riungu-Kalliosaari, L., Mäkinen, S., Lwakatare, L. E., Tiihonen, J., & Männistö, T. (2016). DevOps adoption benefits and challenges in practice: a case study. In *International Conference on Product-Focused Software Process Improvement* (pp. 590–597). Springer.

[S20] Lwakatare, L. E., Karvonen, T., Sauvola, T., Kuvaja, P., Olsson, H. H., Bosch, J., & Oivo, M. (2016). Towards DevOps in the embedded systems domain: Why is it so hard? In *System Sciences (HICSS), 2016 49th Hawaii International Conference on* (pp. 5437–5446). IEEE.

[S21] Nybom, K., Smeds, J., & Porres, I. (2016). On the Impact of Mixing Responsibilities Between Devs and Ops. In *International Conference on Agile Software Development* (pp. 131–143). Springer.

[S22] Erich, F., Amrit, C., & Daneva, M. (2014). A mapping study on cooperation between information system development and operations. In *International Conference on Product-Focused Software Process Improvement* (pp. 277–280). Springer.

[S23] Myrbakken, H. avard, & Colomo-Palacios, R. (2017). DevSecOps: A Multivocal Literature Review. In *International Conference on Software Process Improvement and Capability Determination* (pp. 17–29). Springer

References

1. Rodríguez, P., et al.: Continuous deployment of software intensive products and services: a systematic mapping study. J. Syst. Softw. **123**, 263–291 (2017)
2. Ameller, D., Farré, C., Franch, X., Valerio, D., Cassarino, A.: Towards continuous software release planning. In: 2017 IEEE 24th International Conference on Software Analysis, Evolution and Reengineering (SANER), pp. 402–406 (2017)
3. Stahl, D., Martensson, T., Bosch, J.: Continuous practices and DevOps: beyond the buzz, what does it all mean?. In: 2017 43rd Euromicro Conference on Software Engineering and Advanced Applications (SEAA), pp. 440–448. IEEE (2017)
4. Bosch, J.: Continuous software engineering: an introduction. In: Bosch, J. (ed.) Continuous Software Engineering, pp. 3–13. Springer, Cham (2014). https://doi.org/10.1007/978-3-319-11283-1_1
5. Fitzgerald, B., Stol, K.-J.: Continuous software engineering: a roadmap and agenda. J. Syst. Softw. **123**, 176–189 (2017)
6. Lwakatare, L.E., Kuvaja, P., Oivo, M.: Relationship of DevOps to agile, lean and continuous deployment. In: Abrahamsson, P., Jedlitschka, A., Nguyen Duc, A., Felderer, M., Amasaki, S., Mikkonen, T. (eds.) PROFES 2016. LNCS, vol. 10027, pp. 399–415. Springer, Cham (2016). https://doi.org/10.1007/978-3-319-49094-6_27
7. Jabbari, R., bin Ali, N., Petersen, K., Tanveer, B.: What is DevOps?: a systematic mapping study on definitions and practices. In: Proceedings of the Scientific Workshop Proceedings of XP2016, p. 12. ACM (2016)
8. Ebert, C., Gallardo, G., Hernantes, J., Serrano, N.: DevOps. IEEE Softw. **33**, 94–100 (2016)

9. Balalaie, A., Heydarnoori, A., Jamshidi, P.: Microservices architecture enables DevOps: migration to a cloud-native architecture. IEEE Softw. **33**, 42–52 (2016)
10. Humble, J., Molesky, J.: Why enterprises must adopt DevOps to enable continuous delivery. Cut. IT J. **24**, 6–12 (2011)
11. Debois, P.: DevOps Areas - Codifying DevOps practices. http://www.jedi.be/blog/2012/05/12/codifying-devops-area-practices/
12. Mueller, E.: What Is DevOps? (2010). https://theagileadmin.com/what-is-devops/
13. Capretz, L.F.: Bringing the human factor to software engineering. IEEE Softw. **31**, 104 (2014)
14. Colomo-Palacios, R., Gomez-Berbis, J.M., Garcia-Crespo, A., Puebla-Sanchez, I.: Social Global Repository: using semantics and social web in software projects. Int. J. Knowl. Learn. **4**, 452–464 (2008)
15. Colomo-Palacios, R., Casado-Lumbreras, C., Soto-Acosta, P., Misra, S., García-Peñalvo, F. J.: Analyzing human resource management practices within the GSD context. J. Glob. Inf. Technol. Manag. **15**, 30–54 (2012)
16. Kromhout, B.: Containers will not fix your broken culture (and other hard truths). Queue **15**, 50:46–50:56 (2017)
17. Capretz, L.F., Ahmed, F., da Silva, F.Q.B.: Soft sides of software. Inf. Softw. Technol. **92**, 92–94 (2017)
18. Colomo-Palacios, R., Fernandes, E., Soto-Acosta, P., Larrucea, X.: A case analysis of enabling continuous software deployment through knowledge management. Int. J. Inf. Manag. **40**, 186–189 (2018)
19. Kitchenham, B., Charters, S.: Guidelines for performing Systematic Literature Reviews in Software Engineering. School of Computer Science and Mathematics, Keele University, Keele (2007)
20. Sailunaz, K., Dhaliwal, M., Rokne, J., Alhajj, R.: Emotion detection from text and speech: a survey. Soc. Netw. Anal. Min. **8**(1), 28 (2018)
21. Graziotin, D., Wang, X., Abrahamsson, P.: Understanding the affect of developers: theoretical background and guidelines for psychoempirical software engineering. In: Presented at the 7th International Workshop on Social Software Engineering, pp. 25–32. ACM (2015)
22. Murgia, A., Tourani, P., Adams, B., Ortu, M.: Do developers feel emotions? An exploratory analysis of emotions in software artifacts. In: Proceedings of the 11th Working Conference on Mining Software Repositories, pp. 262–271. ACM, New York (2014)
23. Pavlovich, K., Krahnke, K.: Empathy, connectedness and organisation. J. Bus. Ethics **105**, 131–137 (2012)
24. Akgün, A.E., Keskin, H., Cebecioglu, A.Y., Dogan, D.: Antecedents and consequences of collective empathy in software development project teams. Inf. Manag. **52**, 247–259 (2015)
25. Sánchez-Gordón, M.-L.: Getting the best out of people in small software companies: ISO/IEC 29110 and ISO 10018 standards. Int. J. Inf. Technol. Syst. Approach **10**, 45–60 (2017)

Techniques Based on Data Science for Software Processes: A Systematic Literature Review

Alvaro Fernández Del Carpio[1](✉) and Leonardo Bermón Angarita[2]

[1] Software Engineering Department, Universidad La Salle, Av. Alfonso Ugarte 517, Arequipa, Peru
alfernandez@ulasalle.edu.pe
[2] Computing Department, Universidad Nacional de Colombia, Campus La Nubia, Manizales-Caldas, Colombia
lbermona@unal.edu.co

Abstract. Software quality is an important topic for software practitioners in order to guarantee how the system is built and performed. In last years, techniques related to data science have been utilized in software engineering field as sup-port for building mainly prediction models. These approaches focused on trying to minimize software problems during the development and performance of software, helping to make right decisions. This systematic literature review (SLR) aims at investigating the significant techniques of data sciences used in software processes, identifying their major impacts and problems/challenges of use. This review will be of interest for software practitioners concerned on software quality.

Keywords: Data analysis · Data science · Software quality
Software processes

1 Introduction

Improving software quality aspects has been an increasing concern topic in the software industry. Some problems such as cost overruns, code defects and faults arisen during software development due to the complexity of projects can affect software product quality. Data science has emerged as a new inter-disciplinary field concerning topics in statistics, data mining, machine learning, and data analytics [1]. Data Science leads to use a variety of approaches related to recommender systems, exploration of data, predictive analysis, graph analytics, natural language processing (NLP), among others. Techniques used are addressed mainly to prediction, classification, and clustering which have quickly integrated into software engineering. From data science viewpoint, such techniques give new opportunities to software engineering discipline aiming to translate data into insight and knowledge. That allows to get better results and achieve improvements in quality aspects.

Data mining derives from machine learning, classical statistics and artificial intelligence [2]. Data mining centers on making predictions and descriptions (patterns

I. Stamelos et al. (Eds.): SPICE 2018, CCIS 918, pp. 16–30, 2018.
https://doi.org/10.1007/978-3-030-00623-5_2

discovery and data behavior) with the data extracted and analyzed. Data mining has been proposed in a number of research works as support for software engineering processes, analyzing and extracting knowledge from artifacts and data repositories. Techniques are centered on: predictive analysis (Regression Analysis, Bayesian Networks, Neural Networks, etc.); classification (Decision Trees, Naives Bayes, Support Vector Machine, Association Rules, etc.); and clustering (K-Means, Self-Organizing Map, etc.). Moreover, the Mining Software Repositories (MSR) is used as a way for discovering valuable and actionable information and knowledge addressed to: reported bugs, software defects and effort predictions, class change patterns, detection of code clones [3].

This systematic review seeks to identify, evaluate and synthesize the data-science based techniques used more frequently by software practitioners. We think that extracting from empirical findings the advantages, impacts, challenges, handicaps or problems of using them will be of interest for software community.

The paper is organized as follows. First, the method is presented and developed. Then, the results obtained from final studies are described and discussed. After, some limitations of this review are shown. Finally, conclusions and future work are presented.

2 Research Methodology

This study follows the guidelines proposed by [4] for conducting systematic literature reviews in software engineering. This section describes the stages to conduct our review: defining research questions, designing the search strategy, selecting the studies, assessing the quality, extracting and synthesizing data.

2.1 Research Questions

We have formulated the following research questions that this review tries to answer:

A. **RQ1: What methods or techniques have been used to analyze data in software processes?**

RQ1 aims at identifying the more usual data analysis techniques for getting insightful information from engineering software processes to improve the software quality and get useful information and knowledge to software practitioners for making decisions.

B. **RQ2: What problems or challenges have been observed by practitioners when applying data analysis techniques to software processes?**

RQ2 aims to identify possible difficulties, constraints or limitations presented by data analysis techniques being applied in particular software processes. Application of such techniques does not come without problems considering the variety of features surrounding them.

C. **RQ3: What kinds of impacts have produced the use of data analysis techniques in software processes?**

RQ3 tries to determine the benefits and advantages of using data analysis techniques. Certain techniques can become referential elements for improving software quality. Understanding the technique's impacts will provide software practitioners important chunks of background for future software projects.

2.2 Study Protocol

In this subsection, based on the research questions, the search strategy was formulated and defined the selection and extraction of studies.

Search Terms. The search string was elaborated based on "software processes" and "data science" terms. Therefore, the search expression is defined as follows:

(("software process" OR "software engineering" OR "software model" OR "software development" OR "software method" OR "software construct") AND ("data science" OR "data analytics" OR "data-drive science" OR "data mining" OR" data processing" OR "big data" OR "big data analytics"))

Selected Sources. For this SLR we used the following electronic databases to find relevant literature: ACM Digital Library, IEEE Xplore Digital Library, Science Direct, Springer Link, Web of Science and Scopus. The search string was fit according to the features provided by each of these databases.

Inclusion and Exclusion Criteria. Studies were eligible for inclusion in the re-view if they presented empirical, case study and experimental information of data analysis techniques on software processes. Only studies from journal or conferences publications written in English were included in the list, as well as those with publication year between 2008 to 2018.

Studies were excluded if they presented duplicated publications, being only included the first one found; techniques not related to the purpose of this SLR; and those that not were directly relevant and related to any software process.

Study Selection. A set of stages were defined for selecting relevant studies (see Fig. 1).

In stage 1, papers recovered from databases were stored in an Excel template containing title, authors, publication title, abstract, keywords, publication year and publisher.

At stage 2, both authors decided jointly the inclusion or exclusion by article's title according to its alignment with some of the topics of the review.

At stage 3, papers were excluded by abstract. The measurement of agreement between the two reviewers was determined by applying the Kappa coefficient. For the 739 abstracts assessed we obtained a percentage value of 0.83 as observed agreement. The Kappa coefficient calculated for this stage was 0.56 (moderate agreement). As result, we had 681 papers for the next stage.

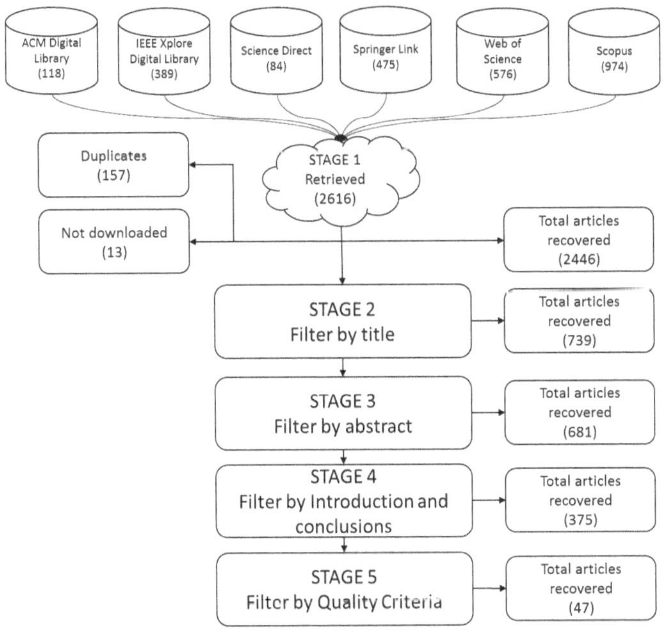

Fig. 1. Study Selection Process

At stage 4, papers were excluded by introduction and conclusion, and type of data. The percentage of the observed agreement was of 0.87 with a Kappa coefficient of 0.61 (substantial agreement). We obtained 375 papers for the next stage.

Finally, at stage 5, papers were assessed on a set of quality criteria. The percentage of the observed agreement was of 0.89 and a Kappa coefficient of 0.62 (substantial agreement).

The papers equal or greater than threshold were taken as final studies (see Table 1) for the review. A total of 47 studies were obtained in the last stage. We set the threshold in 11 in order to present the most relevant studies and besides, because values minor to 11 presented a large number of papers.

Review Quality Assessment. Each of the 47 studies obtained after stage 5 was assessed independently under 6 assessment criteria. These criteria were formulated adapting [52] and taking recommendations of [4] to the scope of this review. The first of these criteria represents the minimum quality threshold and was used to exclude studies not addressing any of the research questions. We formulated the following quality assessment criteria:

- QA1. Is the topic addressed in the paper related to the research questions?
- QA2. Is it clear in which context the research was carried out?
- QA3. Is the research methodology adequately described?
- QA4. Is the process of the data collection methodology or data analysis technique clearly explained in the paper?

Table 1. Study selection process results

Publisher Sites	Initial Results	Final Results	Percentage	Relevant Studies
ACM Digital Library	118	0	0%	
IEEE Xplore	389	9	19.15%	[13–16, 19, 34, 35, 37, 44]
Science Direct	84	4	8.51%	[5–8]
Springer Link	475	9	19.15%	[11, 12, 17, 19, 20, 29, 30, 39, 42]
Web of Science	576	8	17.02%	[9, 10, 13, 14, 16, 18, 22, 25, 26, 28, 31–33, 36, 38, 40, 41]
Scopus	974	17	36.17%	
Summary	2616	47	100%	

- QA5. Is the data analysis approach accurately evaluated in the paper?
- QA6. Is there a clear statement of the findings?

Both authors rated each criterion independently. If some discrepancies arose, there were discussed and the study was reread again in order to get an agreement of score for each criteria. The score of each criterion had 3 possible values: 2 (yes), 1 (partly) and 0 (no). Only studies rated with 2 or 1 in the first criteria were included in this review. The total score for each study was calculated with the sum of individual criterion scores.

Data Extraction. Data was extracted from final studies and stored in a form containing information as: SID, Authors, Year of publication, Study title, Publisher, Objective, Research Method, Context, Software Process, Technique, Artifact, Problem/Challenge, Impact, and Findings.

Data Synthesis. Firstly, we grouped findings to identify the main topics of the review, and then we conduct a comparative analysis on the characteristics obtaining relevant data in order to seek answers to the research questions. Some data synthesis approaches were taken: (1) Narrative synthesis: a narrative summary of the findings of the selected papers was elaborated; (2) Reciprocal translation: it was used in this review to analyze and synthesize the qualitative data extracted from the selected papers.

3 Results and Discussion

In this section we presented the results obtained from analyzing each study as answer to the research questions:

A. Methods and Techniques (RQ1)

RQ1: What methods or techniques have been used to analyze data in software processes?

The results of the study show that the majority of techniques are applied to the project effort estimation and software-testing phases (see Table 2). Techniques mostly used are Artificial neural networks, Association rules and Bayesian networks. Techniques are used for building mostly prediction models related to cost, effort, defect, assignment of requirements, structure of software teams, risk, decision making, techniques skill factors for software projects, among others [6, 8–10, 12, 13, 17, 19, 24, 27, 39, 40, 49]. The predictive models were validated by metrics such as Area Under the Receiver Operating Characteristic (AUROC), Area Under Curve (AUC), Recall, Precision, Mean Relative Error (MRE), Magnitude of MRE (MMRE), Prediction (PRED), Balanced Relative Error (BRE), cross-validation, etc. [10, 11, 15–17, 19, 23–25, 38].

Table 2. Techniques of Data Analysis used in Software Processes

Software Process: Techniques
Process Management: Association Rules [49]
Software Project Management: Decision Trees [8, 21], Bayesian Network [9, 24], Case-Based Reasoning [34], Data Farming [34], J48 [44]
Project Effort Estimation: Analogy-Based Estimation [29, 32], Association Rules [26], Artificial Neural Network [14, 16, 27, 29, 32, 33, 38], Bayesian Network [23, 46], Bayesian Regression [41], Case-Based Reasoning [14], Clustering [35, 37], Fuzzy Analogy [31], Fuzzy Clustering [33], Genetic Algorithm [33], K-means [43], Linear Regression [27, 29, 41], Log Linear Regression [38], Radial Basis Function Networks [27], Regression Analysis [7, 18], Regression Trees [27, 41], Support Vector Machines [27], Support Vector Regression [41], CART [14, 26, 29], Fuzzy Logic [38], OLS Regression [43]
Software Requirements: Genetic Algorithm [12]
Programming: Sequential pattern mining algorithm: MG-FSM [48]
Software Testing: Artificial Neural Network [45], Association Rules [50], C4.5 [11], Clustering [39, 40], Decision Trees [6, 11, 17], Linear Discriminant Analysis [20], Genetic Algorithm [13, 25], J48 [17], Logistic Regression [11, 15, 17], Naive Bayes Classifier [11, 15, 17, 20, 28], N-gram [50], Random Forest [15, 20, 45], Support Vector Machine [17, 20, 45], Time-Series Analysis [42], K-Nearest Neighbor [20, 28]
Software Maintenance: Stacked Generalization [19], C4.5 [22], AdaBoost [36], Artificial Neural Network [36], Bagging [36], Bayesian Network [22, 36], J48 [36], LogitBoost [36], Naive Bayes Classifier [20, 22, 30, 36], Nnge [36], Random Forest [20, 36], Regression Analysis [36], Support Vector Machine [20, 22], K-Nearest Neighbor [20], Decision Tree [20]
Software Development/Team communication: Clustering [5]
Software Quality: Bayesian Network [10], Random Forest [10], Subgraph Mining [51], C4.5 [10], Naïve Bayes Classifier [10]
Software Reuse: Association Rules [47]

B. Problems and Challenges (RQ2)

RQ2: What problems or challenges have been observed by practitioners when applying data analysis techniques to software processes?

Table 3 presents a list of problems/challenges detected by applying data analysis techniques in software processes. The problems of the techniques are related to the dependence of the datasets [18, 20, 27, 29, 31–33], defined parameters of the software project (i.e. amount of projects, project size, development effort) [20, 33, 34, 38, 39, 41, 51], some techniques require combined techniques to improve performance [27, 29, 36, 43], inaccurate performance estimates if model validation techniques are wrongly selected [15], training data selection [17, 22, 36], building of specialized models [24], low performance compared to other techniques [19, 22, 33, 48], performance of defect prediction models by scattered datasets [15, 18], prediction ability [14], and evaluations of some techniques by a set of metrics when assignment bugs automatically [19].

Table 3. Problems detected by applying Data Analytic Techniques in Software Processes

Problem/Challenge (Techniques involved): Studies
It can be used with other machine learning algorithms to improve the efficiency and performance of the model. (AdaBoost): [36]
It assumes that similar instances of the dataset have similar dependent variable values, into SEE domain is that similar projects have similar effort values. (**Analogy-Based Estimation**): [33]
Neural nets perform much worse than other learners such as analogy learners for SEE predictors; low population datasets and reliability in dataset. Multilayer Perceptron (MLP) require adjust properly the number of hidden nodes and not to get training errors (**Artificial Neural Network, MLP**): [14, 29, 32, 33, 38]
Low performances can be obtained if the number of test projects is large with missing data. (**Bayesian regression**): [41]
As sampling is carried out with replacement, some instances may appear more than once in the same training set, while others may not be present at all. (**Bagging**): [36]
It does not always perform better than methods as Naïve Bayes and Bayesian Networks. (**C4.5**): [22]
Use CBR when data are scarce or noisy or when project data cannot be expressed in the required form. (**Case-Based Reasoning**): [34]
Fitting the variations in the distribution of predictors among projects of diverse contexts, and categorize bug reports with labels without prior knowledge of the data. (**Clustering**): [39, 40]
Data farming method will likely to make incorrect decisions if it generates elaborated extrapolations of very small software process data sets. (**Data farming**): [34]
Explore whether more attributes from the reports lead to better classification, tuning the classifiers to a greater degree, and expanding the datasets and classifiers. (**Discriminant Analysis**): [20]
Investigate other combination rules especially the non-linear ones. Moreover, replication studies using other datasets are required. (**Fuzzy Analogy**): [31]
Membership function is not always accurately defined. (**Fuzzy Clustering**): [33]
Calibration of parameters, choice of sampling methods and reliability in dataset. (**Genetic Algorithm**): [33]
Results of classifying bugs from issue reports can vary if datasets are changed (**Linear Discriminant Analysis, NB, KNN,SVM, DT, RF**): [20]

(continued)

Table 3. *(continued)*

Problem/Challenge (Techniques involved): Studies
A multi-layer perceptron (MLP) neural network model can be used as an alternative to relevant regression models to estimate projects of effort less than 3000 person-hours. (**Log-linear regression**): [38]
These techniques are not significantly outperformed by Log + OLS when estimating software effort (in large datasets, nonlinear techniques did not perform well). (**Median squares regression, Ordinary least squares regression, CART**): [27]
The classifier performance for bug assignment is heavily dependent on the quality of bug reports. For bug assignment, computationally-intensive classification algorithms such as C4.5 and SVM do not always perform better than their simple counterparts such as Naïve Bayes and Bayesian Networks. (**Naive Bayes, BN, C45, SVM**): [22]
Predictive models based on Naïve Bayes are worse than those based on a decision tree or a logistic regression in terms of the convergence for cross-project defect prediction. Analyzing data streaming for building predictive models with J48 can result in an inconsistent set of decision trees. (**Naive Bayes, J48**): [6, 28]
Neural nets and simple linear regression perform much worse than other learners such as analogy learners. Moreover, Linear Regression can incur in high computational cost by building a learning model (**Neural Networks**, **Linear Regression**): [12, 29]
Estimation of effort obtained in case of OLS Regression is more scattered resulting in instability as compared to the values obtained of K-means clustering (**OLS Regression, K-means**): [43]
Least Square Regression is a method used for software effort estimation, but this model usually shows poor performance if the dataset is scattered. (**Regression analysis**): [18]
Few of sequential pattern mining algorithms are capable of even producing maximal patterns. (**Sequential patterns mining**): [48]
Existing call-graph-based techniques can only localize defects which affect the call graph of a programme execution and if the value affects a control statement. Although this happens frequently, it might occur in methods which are actually defect-free, leading to erroneous localizations (**Sub graph mining**): [51]
SG is not enough to ensure good results; some care must be taken when doing the ensemble selection, especially when older training sets are used. (**Stacked generalization**): [19]

Based on the results, we can identify that although some techniques have been combined in order to achieve high accuracy for identifying defects, that has not yet been achieved in a complete way. It is required to make improvements in categorizing bugs (retaining its nonparametric and non prior knowledge properties), minimize the effect of scattered data in datasets for building software effort estimation predictive models, and determine causal relationships between metrics and types of failures for building specialized models, just for mention some of them.

C. Level of Impact (RQ3)

RQ3: What kinds of impacts have produced the use of data analysis techniques in software processes?

The use of data analysis techniques had a broad spectrum in software process improvement. Main improvements produced in specific stages of the software process were:

- Software Project Management: Improvements on assigning human resources to teams, risk identification at each phase of the software process simulating the probability and the impact being ranked by importance.
- Project Effort Estimation: Analysis of productivity in software teams, improving the predictive accuracy of software effort estimation compared to traditional estimation models such as COCOMO and the Function Point Analysis, estimation accuracy based on data partitioning approach. Moreover, selecting highly predictive attributes such as project size, duration and development can increase significantly the estimation accuracy. Data mining techniques can make a valuable contribution to the set of software effort estimation techniques and should be complementary to expert judgment.
- Software Requirements: Determination of requirements based on the Next Release Problem (NRP) alongside the Decision Maker (DM) subjective knowledge.
- Software Testing: Proposals for defect prediction, fault localization with models trained in Events Per Variable (EPV) context, bug assignment, detection and categorization, and identifying duplicate bug reports applying similarity criteria.
- Software Maintenance: Prediction & Assessment of change management and technical debt management, improving bug assignment to a development team or an individual developer.

Table 4 presents a list of the relevant impact by data technique:

Table 4. Impact of Data Analysis Techniques in Software Processes

Technique: Impact: Studies
AdaBoost: It is less susceptible to the overfitting problem than most other learning algorithms. It helps developers in performing effective regression testing at low cost and effort: [36]
Analogy-Based Estimation: The accuracy of software development effort estimation improved in the datasets used: [29, 33]
Artificial Neural Network: Building change-prone class prediction model, constructing software effort estimation models, performing effective regression testing and defect prediction. The ANN estimate results presented better accuracy indices than those obtained with multiple regressions, and simple linear regression to estimate effort from software size: [14, 16, 27, 32, 33, 36, 38, 45]
Association Rules: It can assist to developers in the proper identification of reusable classes, in prediction for software effort estimation, software defect prediction by discovering patterns, and software fault localization: [26, 47, 49, 50]
Bagging: It is considered good for predicting change-prone classes: [36]
Bayesian Network: It improves software development effort estimation, risk identification, fault prediction, change-prone classes and decision-making: [9, 10, 22–24, 36, 46]
Bayesian Regression: It is supported by maximum likelihood estimates in probabilistic models using incomplete data. It helps to produce better performances when the percentage of test projects is small with missing data: [41]

(*continued*)

Table 4. (*continued*)

Technique: Impact: Studies
C4.5: It is suited for bug assignment: [10, 22]
CART: Classification and regression Tree manages to estimate cost of projects more satisfactory than Association Rules (AR), since CART offer a coarse grain estimation model, into which new projects fit easily, estimating a high productivity value: [14, 25, 26, 29]
Case-Based Reasoning: It generally achieves the best overall performance in terms of average accuracy, and it is suitable when are scarce or noisy: [14, 34]
Clustering: It can provide valuable information regarding the distribution of the effort and defect prediction, building promising predictor models by clustering similar projects, and categorizing bug reports: [5, 35, 37, 39, 40]
Data Farming: Use it in data rich domains and when the data are not noisy and when the project data can be expressed in the same form as the model inputs: [34]
Decision Trees: It improves the performance of bug-report deduplication, it can flexibly evaluate different team makeups, it obtains good prediction accuracies and it identifies useful rules for forming software project teams. Predictors based on DT learning algorithm provide suitable prediction results.:[6, 8, 11, 17, 21]
Discriminant Analysis: Identify topics in a corpus and is hence useful in categorizing bug reports: [20]
Fuzzy Analogy: It help to estimate effort when software projects are described by linguistic values such as low and high: [31]
Fuzzy Logic: This technique provides more accurate results for predicting software effort estimation with large projects, managing successfully the abrupt change in productivity levels, adjusting the values of the productivity factor: [38]
Fuzzy Clustering: The accuracy of software development effort estimation improved in the datasets used: [33]
Genetic Algorithm: Good decision maker in architecture and estimating the requirements for the next cycle, defect proneness of a software module, accuracy in predicting defects by analyzing subdomains..:[12, 13, 25, 33]
J48: It can provide suitable defect prediction results. The predictors models based on J48 may provide acceptable prediction results in an average level. Besides, it can identify the employee's performance patterns: [17, 36, 44]
K-means: For threshold calculating to predict fault-proneness, K-means seems to give slightly better results as compared to OLS Regression technique in case of Norm Data preprocessing: [43]
K-Nearest Neighbor: This technique, used for predicting software quality, outperforms in imputation accuracy when analyzing datasets with missing data, identify bug reports supported by contextual features: [10, 11, 18, 20]
Linear Regression: The ordinary least squares regression with logarithmic transformation is a suitable technique for Software Effort Estimation: [27, 29, 41]
LogitBoost: It helps developers in performing effective regression testing at low cost and effort providing a suitable performance, similar to Bayes Net and RF: [36]
Logistic Regression: It could make considerable enhancement in identifying duplicate bug reports compared to others techniques: [11, 15, 17]
Naïve Bayes Classifier: It is useful in predict the change prone classes. Naives Bayes coupled with product-component features perform best by automating bug assignment to fixers in order to reduce software evolution effort and cost. Evaluate the performance of defect prediction models: [10, 11, 15, 17, 20, 22, 28, 30, 36, 39]
N-gram: The algorithm successfully find faults especially for large programs: [50]
Nnge: It helps developers in performing regression testing at low cost and effort: [36]

(*continued*)

Table 4. *(continued)*

Technique: Impact: Studies
Random Forest: It is used for classifying issues reports from software development processes: [10, 15, 20, 36, 45]
Sequential pattern mining algorithm: MG-FSM: Sequential patterns from large-scale datasets are used as a means of identifying deficiencies in IDE usability by mining frequent usage patterns, due to flaws in design, gaps in developer knowledge in using the IDE: [48]
Stacked Generalization: It can yield a higher prediction accuracy than using individual general purpose classifiers when classifying bug reports, especially if it is trained with more recent data, reaching prediction accuracies from 50% to 89% [19]
Subgraph Mining: It promises a strong reduction of time spent on defect localization in software engineering projects: [51]
Support Vector Machines: The predictors models based on SVM algorithm trend to detect more defect-prone modules, and analyze issue reports achieving accuracy of 75–83% depending on the project. SVM with certain kernels can achieve high performance: [17, 20, 22, 27, 45]
Time-Series Analysis: It allows studying temporal evolution of source code activity, issue tracking repositories activities, and release dates: [42]

As priorities for future research we can mention: to replicate the results of data mining of software processes to other contexts (different repositories, different parameters, different training data, etc.); selection of the most appropriate machine learning methods according to the context of the process problem and the quality of the data, generalization of results of techniques application, include other types of datasets, application of results to large projects or teams, improve the selection of training data, inclusion of expert judgment and comparison with other data mining techniques.

The knowledge gaps are mainly focused on: the information does not represent all the activities of the software process, some studies do not have representative data of the industry, adding context data does not improve the prediction, improving the selection of attributes of the models and the elimination of outliers. In addition, the works must be consistent in their processes of data selection training and data preprocessing.

4 Limitations of This Review

We considered the following threats to validity for this SLR:

a. Internal validity: this study was carried out by two researchers following the SLR procedure. Both researchers worked together to perform properly the SLR protocol. The replication of results done by others researchers could vary depending on each one's criteria. This SLR presents useful findings about the implications of using data analysis techniques related to software processes.
b. External validity: The results of this SLR can are not generalized because of using a specific range of studies due to space restrictions of this paper and for including a determined set of research databases.

c. Construct validity: At the beginning of this research was difficult to define the aspects that this study should include in order to recover relevant studies. These aspects were established in Sect. 2.
d. Conclusion validity: Studies just with a high-quality assessment were presented in this review. Due to the representative number of them, this study establishes a reference about the applicability of those techniques.
e. Results validity: We considered the most representative searching terms in the context of data analysis techniques in software processes and used 6 databases. Hence, the results are based only on these specifications

5 Conclusions and Future Work

In this review, different studies were investigated in order to understand the current research status of data science techniques in software processes. We conducted a literature review searching for the relevant studies available from 2008 - 2018. Our review considered 47 primary studies. The results can be summarized as follows:

- RQ1: A lot of techniques have been used to analyze data on software processes. The most used techniques are Artificial neural networks, Association rules and Bayesian networks. Moreover, the software process more applied are project effort estimation and software testing.
- RQ2: The studies considered showed that the main problems are related to the dependence of the datasets used, defining parameters, combining of techniques, training data selection and building of specialized models.
- RQ3: The studies have shown wide improvements on aspects of software process such as: assigning human resources, risk identification, decision-making, effort prediction, productivity and cost estimation, fault localization, bug assignment, detection and categorization, issue reports, prediction and assessment of change management, and technical debt management. Data preprocessing is a fundamental factor in the accuracy of effort estimation models. Training data is important for machine learning based defect prediction. Obtaining accurate estimations can have a direct impact over remuneration of staff.

The majority of the research works were based on empirical studies (73%), case studies (19%) and comparative studies (6.39%). In regards to research questions, only 47% of the works defined them. The vast majority of the works included stages related to data preprocessing, training, prediction and evaluation model. The experimental works were mainly based on data collection from large data repositories of software projects. The most used repositories were PROMISE (23.4%), ISBSG (10.63) and Eclipse (8.5%).

This SLR aims at investigating the significant techniques of data sciences used in software processes, identifying their major impacts and problems/challenges of use. This study will be of interest for software practitioners concerned on software quality.

As future work, our study can be extended by considering more data sources and we can perform more in-depth studies on specific data science techniques in software processes.

References

1. Cao, L.: Data science: a comprehensive overview. ACM Comput. Surv. (CSUR) **50**(3), 43 (2017)
2. Han, J., Kamber, M.: Data Mining: Concepts and Techniques. Morgan Kaufmann, San Francisco (2000)
3. Godfrey, M.W., Hassan, A.E., Herbsleb, J., Murphy, G.C., Robillard, M., Devanbu, P., et al.: Future of mining software archives: a roundtable. IEEE Softw. **26**, 67–70 (2009)
4. Kitchenham, B.: Procedures for performing systematic reviews. Keele, UK, Keele University **33**, 1–26 (2004)
5. Licorish, S.A., MacDonell, S.G.: Communication and personality profiles of global software developers. Inf. Softw. Technol. **64**, 113–131 (2015)
6. Finlay, J., Pears, R., Connor, A.M.: Data stream mining for predicting software build outcomes using source code metrics. Inf. Softw. Technol. **56**(2), 183–198 (2014)
7. Rodríguez, D., Sicilia, M.A., García, E., Harrison, R.: Empirical findings on team size and productivity in software development. J. Syst. Softw. **85**(3), 562–570 (2012)
8. André, M., Baldoquín, M.G., Acuña, S.T.: Formal model for assigning human resources to teams in software projects. Inf. Softw. Technol. **53**(3), 259–275 (2011)
9. Li, J., Li, M., Wu, D., Dai, Q., Song, H.: A Bayesian networks-based risk identification approach for software process risk: the context of chinese trustworthy software. Int. J. Inf. Technol. Decis. Making **15**(06), 1391–1412 (2016)
10. Madera, M., Tomoń, R.: A case study on machine learning model for code review expert system in software engineering. In: 2017 Federated Conference on Computer Science and Information Systems (FedCSIS), Prague, pp. 1357–1363 (2017)
11. Alipour, A., Hindle, A., Stroulia, E.: A contextual approach towards more accurate duplicate bug report detection. In: 2013 10th Working Conference on Mining Software Repositories (MSR), San Francisco, CA, pp. 183–192 (2013)
12. Araújo, A.A., Paixao, M., Yeltsin, I., et al.: An architecture based on interactive optimization and machine learning applied to the next release problem. Autom. Softw. Eng. **24**, 623 (2017)
13. Murillo-Morera, J., Castro-Herrera, C., Arroyo, J., Fuentes-Fernández, R.: An automated defect prediction framework using genetic algorithms: a validation of empirical studies. Intel. Artif. **19**(57), 114–137 (2016)
14. Huang, J., Li, Y-F., Xie, M.: An empirical analysis of data preprocessing for machine learning-based software cost estimation. Inf. Softw. Technol. **67**, 108–127 (2015)
15. Tantithamthavorn, C., McIntosh, S., Hassan, A.E., Matsumoto, K.: An empirical comparison of model validation techniques for defect prediction models. IEEE Trans. Softw. Eng. **43**(1), 1–18 (2017)
16. Barcelos-Tronto, I.F., Simões da Silva, J.D., Sant'Anna, N.: An investigation of artificial neural networks based prediction systems in software project management. J. Syst. Softw. **81**(3), 356–367 (2008)
17. He, Z., Shu, F., Yang, Y., et al.: An investigation on the feasibility of cross-project defect prediction. Autom. Softw. Engi. **19**, 167 (2012)

18. Seo, Y.-S., Bae, D.-H., Jeffery, R.: AREION: software effort estimation based on multiple regressions with adaptive recursive data partitioning. Inf. Softw. Technol. **55**(10), 1710–1725 (2013)
19. Jonsson, L., Borg, M., Broman, D., et al.: Automated bug assignment: ensemble-based machine learning in large scale industrial contexts. Empir. Softw. Eng. **21**, 1533 (2016)
20. Pandey, N., Sanyal, D.K., Hudait, A., et al.: Automated classification of software issue reports using machine learning techniques: an empirical study. Innov. Syst. Softw. Eng. **13**, 279 (2017)
21. Vargas-Baldrich, S., Linares-Vásquez, M., Poshyvanyk, D.: Automated tagging of software projects using bytecode and dependencies (N). In: 2015 30th IEEE/ACM International Conference on Automated Software Engineering (ASE), Lincoln, NE, pp. 289–294 (2015)
22. Bhattacharya, P., Neamtiu, J., Shelton, C.R.: Automated, highly-accurate, bug assignment using machine learning and tossing graphs. J. Syst. Softw. **85**(10), 2275–2292 (2012)
23. Mendes, E., Mosley, N.: Bayesian network models for web effort prediction: a comparative study. IEEE Trans. Softw. Eng. **34**(6), 723–737 (2008)
24. Misirli, T., Bener, A.B.: Bayesian networks for evidence-based decision-making in software engineering. IEEE Trans. Softw. Eng. **40**(6), 533–554 (2014)
25. Mauša, G., Galinac-Grbac, T.: Co-evolutionary multi-population genetic programming for classification in software defect prediction: an empirical case study. Appl. Soft Comput. **55**, 331–351 (2017)
26. Bibi, S., Stamelos, I., Angelis, L.: Combining probabilistic models for explanatory productivity estimation. Inf. Softw. Technol. **50**(7–8), 656–669 (2008)
27. Dejaeger, K., Verbeke, W., Martens, D., Baesens, B.: Data mining techniques for software effort estimation: a comparative study. IEEE Trans. Softw. Eng. **38**(2), 375–397 (2012)
28. Ryu, D., Baik, J.: Effective multi-objective naïve Bayes learning for cross-project defect prediction. Appl. Soft Comput. **49**, 1062–1077 (2016)
29. Keung, J., Kocaguneli, E., Menzies, T.: Finding conclusion stability for selecting the best effort predictor in software effort estimation. Autom. Softw. Eng. **20**, 543 (2013)
30. Huang, Q., Shihab, E., Xia, X., et al.: Identifying self-admitted technical debt in open source projects using text mining. Empir. Softw. Eng. **23**, 418 (2018)
31. Idri, A., Hosni, M., Abran, A.: Improved estimation of software development effort using classical and fuzzy analogy ensembles. Appl. Soft Comput. **49**, 990–1019 (2016)
32. Bardsiri, V.K., Jawawi, D.N.A., Hashim, S.Z.M., Khatibi, E.: Increasing the accuracy of software development effort estimation using projects clustering. IET Softw. **6**(6), 461–473 (2012)
33. Kaushik, A., Tayal, D.K., Yadav, K., Kaur, A.: Integrating firefly algorithm in artificial neural network models for accurate software cost predictions. J. Softw. Evol. Process **28**(8), 665–688 (2016)
34. Menzies, T., et al.: Learning project management decisions: a case study with case-based reasoning versus data farming. IEEE Trans. Softw. Eng. **39**(12), 1698–1713 (2013)
35. Menzies, T., et al.: Local versus global lessons for defect prediction and effort estimation. IEEE Trans. Softw. Eng. **39**(6), 822–834 (2013)
36. Malhotra, R., Jangra, R.: Prediction & assessment of change prone classes using statistical & machine learning techniques. J. Inf. Process. Syst. **13**(4), 778–804 (2017)
37. Mittas, N., Angelis, L.: Ranking and clustering software cost estimation models through a multiple comparisons algorithm. IEEE Trans. Softw. Eng. **39**(4), 537–551 (2013)
38. Bou-Nassif, A., Ho, D., Capretz, L.F.: Towards an early software estimation using log-linear regression and a multilayer perceptron model. J. Syst. Softw. **86**(1), 144–160 (2013)
39. Zhang, F., Mockus, A., Keivanloo, I., et al.: Towards building a universal defect prediction model with rank transformed predictors. Empir. Softw. Eng. **21**, 2107 (2016)

40. Limsettho, N., Hata, H., Monden, A., Matsumoto, K.: Unsupervised bug report categorization using clustering and labeling algorithm. Int. J. Softw. Eng. Knowl. Eng. **26**(07), 1027–1053 (2016)
41. Zhang, W., Yang, Y., Wang, Q.: Using Bayesian regression and EM algorithm with missing handling for software effort prediction. Inf. Softw. Technol. **58**, 58–70 (2015)
42. Rossi, B., Russo, B., Succi, G.: Analysis of open source software development iterations by means of burst detection techniques. In: Boldyreff, C., Crowston, K., Lundell, B., Wasserman, A.I. (eds.) OSS 2009. IFIP, vol. 299. Springer, Heidelberg (2009). https://doi.org/10.1007/978-3-642-02032-2_9
43. Sehra, S.K., Kaur, J., Bra, Y.S., Kaur, N.: Analysis of data mining techniques for software effort estimation. In: 2014 11th International Conference on Information Technology: New Generations, Las Vegas, NV, pp. 633–638 (2014)
44. Gupta, S., Suma, V.: Data mining: a tool for knowledge discovery in human aspect of software engineering. In: 2015 2nd International Conference on Electronics and Communication Systems (ICECS), Coimbatore, pp. 1289–1293 (2015)
45. Han, W., Lung, C.H., Ajila, S.A.: Empirical investigation of code and process metrics for defect prediction. In: 2016 IEEE Second International Conference on Multimedia Big Data (BigMM), Taipei, pp. 436–439 (2016)
46. Karna, H., Gotovac, S.: Estimating software development effort using Bayesian networks. In: 2015 23rd International Conference on Software, Telecommunications and Computer Networks (SoftCOM), Split, pp. 229–233 (2015)
47. Parashar, A., Chhabra, J.K.: Mining Class Association Rules from Dynamic Class Coupling Data to Measure Class Reusability Pattern. Tan Y., Shi Y., Chai Y., Wang G., (eds.) ICSI 2011. LNCS, vol. 6729, pp. 146–156. Springer, Heidelberg (2011). https://doi.org/10.1007/978-3-642-21524-7_18
48. Damevski, K., Shepherd, D. C., Schneider, J. Pollock, L.: Mining sequences of developer interactions in visual studio for usage smells. IEEE Trans. Softw. Eng. **43**(4), 359–371 (2017)
49. Chang, C-P., Chu, C-P.: Software defect prediction using intertransaction association rule mining. Int. J. Softw. Eng. Knowl. Eng. **19**(06), 747–764 (2009)
50. Nessa, S., Abedin, M., Wong, W.E., Khan, L., Qi, Y.: Software fault localization using N-gram analysis. In: Li, Y., Huynh, D.T., Das, S.K., Du, D.Z. (eds.) WASA 2008. LNCS, vol. 5258, pp. 548–559. Springer, Heidelberg (2008). https://doi.org/10.1007/978-3-540-88582-5_51
51. Eichinger, F., Krogmann, K., Klug, R., Böhm, K.: Software-defect localisation by mining dataflow-enabled call graphs. In: Balcázar, J.L., Bonchi, F., Gionis, A., Sebag, M. (eds.) ECML PKDD 2010. LNCS (LNAI), vol. 6321, pp. 425–441. Springer, Heidelberg (2010). https://doi.org/10.1007/978-3-642-15880-3_33
52. CASP, Critical Appraisal Skills Programme. https://casp-uk.net/. Accessed 15 Mar 2018

A Systematic Literature Review on the Gamification Monitoring Phase: How SPI Standards Can Contribute to Gamification Maturity

Manuel Trinidad(✉), Alejandro Calderón, and Mercedes Ruiz

University of Cádiz, Cádiz, Spain
{manuel.trinidad, alejandro.calderon, mercedes.ruiz}@uca.es

Abstract. Gamification is a novel concept that has attracted the attention of many research fields, including software engineering, software process improvement or software process standards education as an approach to increase productivity, engagement, and motivation of participants involved in a system, site or business. However, gamification is a relative new concept that needs to deal with many problems in order to consolidate and mature its understanding and process. The main goal of this study is to explore the gamification scope with the goal to identify its problems and needs, focusing on the monitoring process of gamification strategies. A systematic literature review was performed following a predefined procedure that involves automatically searching in scientific digital databases. 383 papers were found by the automatic searches in the digital databases and only 2 papers were selected as primary studies. Outcomes show that there is a clear scope of research on the road to provide tools for monitoring high-scalable gamified systems that support gamification experts on gamification analytics and end-users on getting real-time feedback, as well as, a need to mature the gamification process that can be supported by taking advantages from other disciplines, especially from the scope of process capability and maturity.

Keywords: Systematic literature review · Gamification · Monitoring Assessment · Gamification analytics · SPI standards

1 Introduction

Software process improvement (SPI), software engineering (SE), software process standards or software project management are fields of interest under the SPICE conference that have begun to re-think and transform the traditional ways to foster engagement, increase productivity, promote motivation and change behavior through the development, design, integration or/and adaptation of new approaches such as gamification [1–3].

The emerging and popular approach of gamification [4] has attracted the attention of both practitioners and researchers as a promising approach to motivate actions,

I. Stamelos et al. (Eds.): SPICE 2018, CCIS 918, pp. 31–44, 2018.
https://doi.org/10.1007/978-3-030-00623-5_3

increase end-user engagement and change behaviors in many contexts [5]. However, despite the promising advantages of the use of gamification and the high studies published in recent years, we can observe a high level of misunderstanding about the concept of gamification, where lots of studies that claim to deal with gamification for education, in fact, deal with game-based learning.

In this context, we can observe how gamification is a relative new concept that needs to deal with many problems in order to achieve its full potential and consolidate its design, implementation and monitoring process [6–8]. For that reason, in this study, we conducted a systematic literature review (SLR) to explore the gamification scope with the goal to identify its problems and needs, focusing on the monitoring process of gamification strategies. Moreover, we briefly discussed how taking advantage of the guidelines and processes of SPI frameworks and standards such as the ISO/IEC 33000 family of standards can help to mature the gamification monitoring process.

The structure of the paper is as follows: Sect. 2 exposes the background of this work and Sect. 3 analyzes the works related to our proposal. Section 4 provides the methodology used for conducting our SLR. Section 5 shows and analyzes the results of this review. Section 6 discusses how SPI standards can contribute to the problems identified. Finally, Sect. 7 summarizes the paper and presents our conclusions and future works based on the findings obtained.

2 Gamification Process

Gamification, or the use of game elements and game design techniques in non-game contexts [4], is a novel topic which aims at the improvement of the user's engagement, motivation, and performance when carrying out a certain task. By means of incorporating game-based mechanics, aesthetics and game thinking user's tasks are more attractive [2]. However, gamification does not mean to turn our processes, sites and systems into a game, but it means to apply game mechanics (status, challenges, connections, competition, rewards, etc.) to motivate the users and encouraging the right behavior, which is aligned with the business goals [9].

Considering the studies published by Herzig [10–12], the gamification process can mainly be summarized into the following four high-level phases:

(1) *Business modeling and Requirements*, where the application context is analyzed and the business general goals are identified.
(2) *Design*, where the gamification design is developed and play tested.
(3) *Implementation*, where the design is implemented as software artifacts and it is functionally tested.
(4) *Monitoring and Adaptation*, where business goal achievement is measured and subsequent design adaptations are conducted.

Although, many guidelines and frameworks have been published to deal with the gamification process, the majority of the published studies aim to cover particular problems. As a consequence, new proposals continue appearing in the literature, and therefore, the deviation towards the consolidation and understanding of a common framework to design, implement and monitor gamification strategies go on increasing [13].

Bearing in mind this issue and the four high-level phases previously described, in this study, we have focused on the analysis of the main problems and needs existing in the Monitoring phase of the gamification process. This phase implies a continuous track of the participants involved in the gamification strategy and deals with providing end-user feedback and gamification experts analytics to assess, improve and adapt the gamified system [6, 8, 11]. We have focused on the monitoring phase since it is a crucial phase within the gamification process that allows the assessment, improvement and adaptation of the gamification experiences. Moreover, the consolidation of the monitoring phase will contribute to the maturity of gamification research and applications [14].

3 Related Works

An initial study that involves automatic searches in several digital databases was conducted in order to observe if there exists any previous secondary study that aims to identify the problems and needs of the monitoring phase of the gamification process. Seven different digital databases (ACM Digital Library, IEEE Xplore, SpringerLink, ISI Web of Science, Scopus and Science Direct) were analyzed by applying the search string "(A **AND** B **AND** (C1 **OR** C2) **AND** (D1 **OR** D2 **OR** D3 **OR** D4))", where the search terms are shown in Table 1.

Table 1. Search terms to identify related secondary studies.

A. Gamification	B. Monitor	C1. Review	D1. Systematic
		C2. Study	D2. Mapping
			D3. Literature
			D4. Multivocal

As a result, we retrieved a total of 121 papers. Figure 1 shows the number of studies retrieved from each digital database.

However, although some of the retrieved studies involve a review of the use of gamification in different fields such as SPI [1], SE [2], or provide a study of the current state of the art related to the frameworks for design gamification [8], none of them focus on providing a complete overview regarding the existing problems and needs of the gamification monitoring process.

For that reason, in this study, we have conducted a SLR to identify the main problems and needs which the gamification monitoring process deals with, and at the same time, provide a basis for new lines of research.

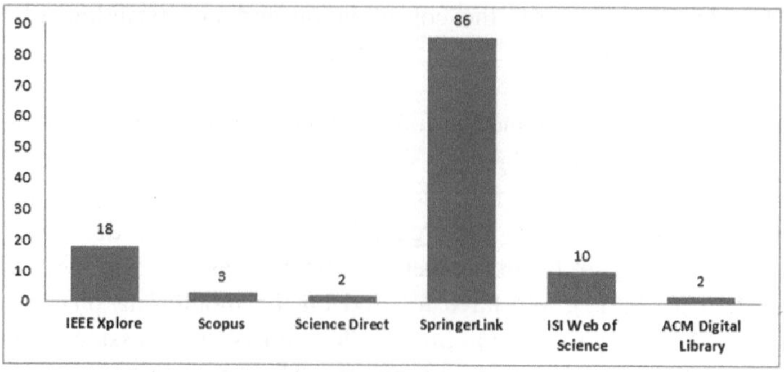

Fig. 1. Number of studies retrieved from each digital database.

4 Method

The objective of this work is to analyze the current studies that deal with the gamification monitoring process with the goal of identifying the main existing problems and needs in this field. To do this, we conducted a SLR based on the guidelines proposed by Kitchenham et al. [15, 16] and the review procedure described by Calderon et al. [17]. Figure 2 shows the SLR process followed to conduct this SLR.

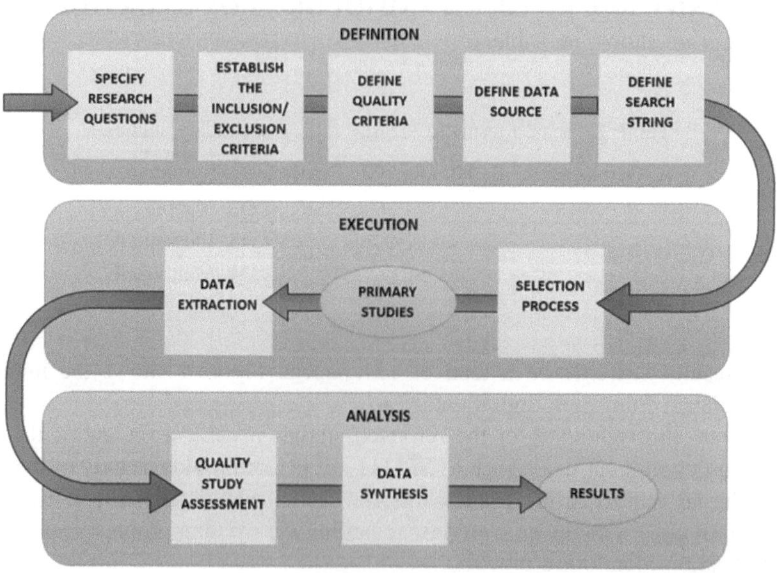

Fig. 2. SLR process.

4.1 Specify Research Questions

In order to achieve the goal of this study, the following two research questions have been defined.

- RQ1: What works focus on the scope of the gamification monitoring process?
- RQ2: What are the main problems and needs that require to be addressed regarding the monitoring of gamified experiences?

4.2 Establish the Inclusion/Exclusion Criteria

This SLR identifies the papers that deal with the field of gamification monitoring process, introduce a tool for supporting the gamification monitoring process, or add value in any sense to this field. In order to select only relevant studies for answering these research questions, we established the inclusion and exclusion criteria shown in Table 2. In addition, to get an overview of the whole state of the art of our topic under review, we have not limited the start of the publication period.

Table 2. Inclusion/Exclusion criteria

Inclusion criteria	• The retrieved study deals with the field of gamification monitoring process • The retrieved study introduces a tool for supporting the gamification monitoring process • The retrieved study adds value to the field of gamification monitoring process • The study is written in English
Exclusion criteria	• The retrieved study does not focus on gamification process • The retrieved study presents a specific application of gamification but does not deal with the gamification monitoring process • The retrieved study only has its abstract available and it is not possible to find its full-text • The retrieved study does not provide the required information clearly • The retrieved study is written in a language different from English • The retrieved study does not provide information included in other retrieved study or in other digital database (duplicates studies)

4.3 Define Quality Criteria

The quality factors were established and evaluated regarding the main topic of our study and the information that the retrieved studies were able to provide. A questionnaire consisting of three quality assessment questions (QA) was defined as the quality instrument. The three questions used were the following:

QA1. Does the study deal with the gamification monitoring process?
QA2. Does the study introduce a tool for supporting the gamification monitoring process?
QA3. Does the study allow retrieving the information related to the main problems and needs existing in the road to monitor gamified experiences?

Each question was answered YES (Y) or NO (N). The scoring procedure was Y = 1 an N = 0. Thus, the total number of Ys defined the quality assessment score of each study.

4.4 Define Data Sources

IEEE Xplore, ISI Web of Science, SpringerLink, ACM Digital Library and SCOPUS were selected as the scientific digital databases in where we conducted our searches. The main reason for selecting these digital databases was that they are the main ones using in the majority of the published secondary studies related to our research [17].

4.5 Define Search String

To construct the search string, we first need to identify the search terms of this work. For that reason, we performed some initial searches to test and calibrate the search string. Finally, we defined the search string as the following Boolean expression: *gamification* ***AND*** *monitor*. Although this search string was very generic, we decided to apply it to ensure that no relevant works were missed since no previous secondary studies related to our topic had been published.

4.6 Selection Process

The SLR was executed regarding the studies published until June 2018. The selection process that we followed to conduct our review was based on the scientific selection process proposed by Calderon et al. [17]. This process is composed of four phases. During the first phase of the selection process (*P1. Initial search*), the search string was applied to the selected digital databases. As a result, we found a total of 383 papers (see Fig. 3).

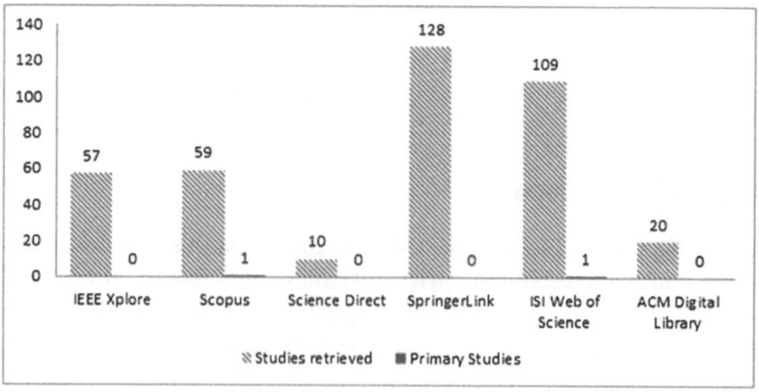

Fig. 3. Retrieved studies from each digital database and primary studies.

After removing the duplicates (*P2. Remove duplicates*) and checking the title and abstract of each paper according to the inclusion and exclusion criteria (*P3. First selection process*), in the fourth phase of the selection process (*P4. Second selection process*), the full text of the papers was analyzed against the inclusion and exclusion criteria. As a result, two papers were considered for data extraction. These two papers defined the primary studies of our SLR.

Figure 3 shows firstly, the retrieved papers from each digital database, and secondly the number of papers that were included as primary studies in our review.

4.7 Data Extraction

During the extraction process, the primary studies were thoroughly analyzed to collect all the needed information and ensure that the data were accurate. All the collected data were stored in a spreadsheet to place all the information of our study in the same location, and to facilitate the analysis and comparison of the collected data during the synthesis process. In this review, the data of the primary studies was classified according to the research questions addressed, as Table 3 shows.

Table 3. Extracted data classification.

Data	Research question addressed
The main topic of the study	RQ1
Authors of the study	RQ1
Publication year	RQ1
Source of publication	RQ1
Description of tools that support the gamification monitoring process	RQ1
Problems and needs that require to be addressed regarding the gamification monitoring process	RQ2

5 Results

In this section, we discuss our outcomes and answers to the research questions that addressed this SLR, as a result of the study quality assessment and the data synthesis process.

5.1 Study Quality Assessment

Considering the quality criteria defined in Sect. 4.3, we assessed the quality of the primary studies. The two primary studies covered 100% by Yes answer the three defined QA since both studies deal with the monitoring phase of the gamification process, comment tools for supporting the gamification monitoring process, and provide information related to the main problems and needs existing in the road to monitor gamified experiences.

5.2 RQ1: What Works Focus on the Scope of the Gamification Monitoring Process?

The objective of this question was to identify the current studies that focus on providing knowledge and tools to the field of gamification, concretely those studies that deal with the monitoring phase of the gamification process.

Although, during the development of this review many studies have been found regarding different lines of research within the gamification scope, the majority of them introduce a specific application of gamification but none of them deal with the gamification monitoring process with the exception of two works. The study titled 'Tools for Gamification Analytics: A Survey' that focusses on the identification and assessment of relevant software solutions for gamification analytics domain as an importance requirement of the gamification monitoring process [12], and the study titled 'MEdit4CEP-Gam: A model-driven approach for user-friendly gamification design, monitoring and code generation in CEP-based systems' that proposed a tool based on Complex-Event Processing (CEP) and Model-Driven Engineering (MDE) technologies to support the design, implementation and monitoring of gamification strategies [13]. Both studies share similarities since both present tools for supporting the gamification process, both identify problems and needs regarding the gamification monitoring process and both assess the ability of the presented tools for supporting gamification experts with analytics. They also share the evaluation procedure which is based on the analysis of the coverage of the set of 22 requirements for gamification analytics tools provided by Heilbrunn et al. [12]. These requirements are classified into five categories regarding the ability of the environment to provide support to for gamification experts to: (a) define and monitor Key Performance Indicators (KPIs) (6 requirements), (b) monitor the gamification elements state (8 requirements), (c) define and analyze groups of users (4 requirements), (d) adapt gamification designs (3 requirements), and (e) validate gamification design ideas by using simulation (one requirement).

In Table 4, we show the main data of these studies regarding their authors, source where the studies have been published and the year of publication.

Table 4. Data of the primary studies.

Primary study	Authors	Source of publication	Type of publication	Year of publication
[13]	Calderon, A.; Boubeta-Puig, J.; Ruiz, M.	Information and Software Technology	Journal	2018
[12]	Heilbrunn, B.; Herzig, P.; Schill, A.	IEEE/ACM 7th International Conference on Utility and Cloud Computing	Conference	2014

From these studies, a total of four tools for supporting the gamification monitoring process were identified. These tools were described and assessed in those studies. The tools are the following:

- **Badgeville** is a commercial engine that allows to gamify from objectives and personalized rewards [18]. It has not been evaluated according to the requirement for gamification analytics tools provided by Heilbrunn et al. [12].
- **BunchBall** is a commercial gamification platform that offers a set of pre-defined gamification-related reports and a user segmentation feature [12]. It satisfies one out of 22 requirements for gamification analytics tools provided by Heilbrunn et al. [12].
- **Gigya** is a gamification platform whose target is the online communities. It offers a set of predefined reports for social metrics [12]. It satisfies one out of 22 requirements for gamification analytics tools provided by Heilbrunn et al. [12].
- **MEdit4CEP-Gam** is a tool developed at the University of Cadiz for supporting the gamification process that automates controlling and monitoring of gamification strategies on highly scalable and heterogeneous environments [13]. It satisfies 10 out of 22 requirements for gamification analytics tools provided by Heilbrunn et al. [12].

5.3 RQ2: What Are the Main Problems and Needs that Require to Be Addressed Regarding the Monitoring of Gamified Experiences?

The objective of this question was to identify the existing problems and needs in the field of the gamification process regarding the monitoring phase of gamification experiences. To answer this question, we analyzed the primary studies and collected all the problems and main necessities that authors reported along their works. Moreover, we categorized them according to the following main topics:

- ***General:*** The monitoring phase of the gamification process requires to be consolidated in order to help the gamification concept to achieve its maturity.
- ***Metrics:*** The gamification process needs to be supported by tools that allow the design and analysis of gamification metrics in order to evaluate, change and improve gamification strategies.
- ***Participants:*** The gamification process needs to be supported by tools that allow the analysis of the behavior of the participants involved in a gamification experience for adapting them.
- ***Environment:*** The gamification process needs to be supported by tools that allow the monitoring of gamified systems in real-time with a high number of participants.
- ***Testing:*** The gamification process needs to be supported by tools that allow the testing of gamification strategies during the design phase.
- ***KPIs:*** The gamification process needs to be supported by tools that allow the definition and monitoring of KPIs of gamified applications aligned with critical success factors and business goals.

Considering this conclusions, Table 5 shows the main problems and needs identified regarding this issue according to each statement and primary study.

From this analysis, we can state that the monitoring phase of the gamification process is a crucial step in the lifecycle of a gamification experience that needs to be supported by appropriate tools that support gamification experts to evaluate, improve on/and adapt gamification experiences.

Table 5. Main problems and needs found in the gamification monitoring phase.

Topics	Problems and needs
General	The non-consolidation of a common gamification framework for monitoring gamification strategies in heterogeneous environments [13]
General; Environment	Gamification monitoring is especially complex when there exists a huge number of participants, the strategy is not well designed or there is an inadequate tool support [13]
General	There is still an unsatisfied demand for tools that support the monitoring phase of the gamification process [12]
General	The adoptions of the majority of the existing gamification analytics tools involve an integration effort that creates a new data-silo which not allow expert to take the control of the gamification data [12]
General	The existing tools for supporting the monitoring gamification process do not offer considerable support for the monitoring and adaptation phase of gamification projects [12]
Metrics	There is a need of tools that offer gamification analytics to measure the success of gamification strategies and gamification design changes [12]
Environment	There is a need of highly-scalable monitoring tools [13]
Environment	There is a need of monitoring tools that provide gamification design experts with real-time analytics that help them to assess, improve, adapt or redesign the gamified experience [13]
Environment; Participants	There is a need of monitoring tools that process gamification end-users' data in real-time and provide immediate feedback to the participants involved in the gamified experience [13]
Participants	There is a need of gamification analytics tools for better understanding the user behavior [12]
Testing	There is a need of gamification analytics tools for learning when a gamification design requires adjustment [12]
Metrics; KPIs	There is a lack of appropriate solutions that helps gamification experts to define and monitor KPIs which operationalize business goals in context of the gamified application [12]
Metrics	There is a lack of appropriate solutions that supports gamification experts in monitoring the game state [12]
Participants; Metrics	There is a lack of appropriate solutions that allows experts to discover and define different groups of gamification users [12]
Testing	There is a lack of appropriate solutions that enables experts to simulate gamification designs to early validate gamification design ideas [12]
Testing	There is a lack of appropriate solutions that enables gamification experts to create and analyze experiments that test the impact of gamification design changes on user behavior [12]

6 Gamification Process Capability and Maturity

Implementing a gamification strategy within an organization needs necessarily to follow a well-defined and structured process to achieve success [19]. Initiatives such as Herzig's [10] are interesting contributions towards the definition of the gamification process that includes explicitly a monitoring task. Nevertheless, this monitoring task is generally aimed exclusively at tracking the activity of the user of the gamified applications so that they can receive adequate feedback and the responsible of the gamification initiative can get information about the results of such initiative. Therefore, tracking users' activities to provide feedback and analytics to the responsible of the gamification initiative are mentioned in the two relevant works found in this SLR. The small number of works retrieved together with the narrow scope of the measuring and monitoring activities introduced in the proposals analyzed, lead us to conclude that gamification has still much to learn from other disciplines, especially from the scope of process capability and maturity.

One of the signs of a mature discipline is the interest in measuring and monitoring its progress, quality and effectiveness. The crucial role of measuring and monitoring in the area of process improvement has been highlighted by many process improvement frameworks, standards or families of standards, such as ISO 9000 [20], CMMI [21], ISO/IEC 330xx [22] or TIPA [23].

Generally, in the previous mentioned frameworks and standards, process quality is defined as the ability of a process to satisfy stated and implied stakeholder needs when used in a specified context. Process quality is measured based on a series of relevant process attributes. The monitoring and measurement of process outcomes is essential to determine the process quality level according to a process measurement and assessment framework.

For this reason, we believe that, for example, the definition of an ISO/IEC 33000 compliant measurement framework can significantly help to the measurement of the extent the gamification process is performed and to perform gamification process assessment that guides a continuous process improvement. Moreover, counting with a set of best practices to address the development and maintenance of gamification strategies along their complete lifecycle, from their conception to their execution and maintenance, can significantly contribute to the maturity of the field.

In that sense, one effective strategy for ensuring that gamification process design, execution, and assessment efforts are in line with best practices and have enough quality could be the use of Process Reference Models (PRMs), Process Assessment Models (PAMs) or frameworks for measuring processes. For that reason, it will be important to define a gamification PRM, PAM or measurement framework that: (a) offer a starting point for formalizing the practices within the gamification process; (b) provide common practices to be adopted by gamification experts that can help gamification field benefit from the experiences of others; and (c) provide a common language for gamification process elements that may be used to standardize the design, execution, and monitoring of gamification strategies, as well as, to train stakeholders in the field.

Concretely, the structure of levels, process attributes and rating scales used in ISO/IEC 33002 [24] and ISO/IEC 33003 [25] can be applied to set the requirements for the definition of a gamification measurement framework and performing process assessment. The gamification PRM can be based on well-known process proposals such as Werbach and Hunter's [4], Herzig's [10] and Morschheuser et al.'s [26] and defined according to the requirements established in ISO/IEC 33004 [27]. This last standard can serve also to define the gamification PAM.

Counting with a gamification measurement framework, a PRM and a PAM can set the basis towards the solution of the problems of gamification monitoring identified in Table 5, as well as serve as the starting point on the road to the definition of gamification process capability and the maturity of the field.

7 Conclusions

As many authors state, gamification is still a rather novel development that suffers from growing pains, and therefore, it has still been under significant conceptual chaos and theoretical turbulence [28]. For that reason, before starting to promote the use of gamification within our expertise fields such as SE, software process, software process standards or SPI, it is necessary to provide knowledge and tools to consolidate the gamification concept and process for ensuring that its use will help in the success of our business goals.

In this paper we have presented a SLR related to the analysis of the state of the art of the monitoring phase of the gamification process in order to identify the main problems and needs of the gamification monitoring phase for providing the basis for future research lines. We selected 2 from 383 papers found in 6 digital databases until June of 2018. We organized and categorized the information obtained to provide an answer to each of the two research questions that addressed our review in order to locate the main studies that deal with the monitoring phase of the gamification process, as well as to identify the main deficiencies of this topic. From these studies we collected the necessary data to identify each study, the tools for supporting the gamification monitoring process that these studies introduce, and the main problems and needs that their authors expose.

The analysis of the collected data shows that there is a lack of tools for monitoring high-scalable gamified systems that offer gamification experts with real-time analytics that support the evaluation, improvement or adaptation of gamification strategies, allow the gamification end-users' data processing in real-time, and provide immediate feedback to participants.

Moreover, taking into account the outcomes of the conducted SLR, we have discussed how considering the guidelines and processes of SPI frameworks and standards such as the ISO/IEC 33000 family of standards can help to mature the gamification process. Therefore, there is a clear scope of research in which several new lines can be established regarding the different needs found.

Acknowledgments. This work has been carried out during a post-doctoral contract, funded by the Program of Promotion and Impulse of Research and Transfer at University of Cádiz 2018–2019, and a pre-doctoral contract for the training of research personnel, funded by the University of Cádiz through the University Research and Transfer Plan (UCA/REC01VI/2017).

This work was funded by the Spanish National Research Agency (AEI) with ERDF funds under projects BadgePeople (TIN2016-76956-C3-3-R) and the Andalusian Plan for Research, Development, and Innovation (grant TIC-195).

References

1. Dorling, A., McCaffery, F.: The gamification of SPICE. In: Mas, A., Mesquida, A., Rout, T., O'Connor, Rory V., Dorling, A. (eds.) SPICE 2012. CCIS, vol. 290, pp. 295–301. Springer, Heidelberg (2012). https://doi.org/10.1007/978-3-642-30439-2_35
2. Pedreira, O., García, F., Brisaboa, N., Piattini, M.: Gamification in software engineering - a systematic mapping. Inf. Softw. Technol. **57**, 157–168 (2015)
3. Orta, E., Ruiz, M., Calderón, A., Hurtado, N.: Gamification for improving IT service incident management. In: International Conference on Software Process Improvement and Capability Determination, Palma de Mallorca, Spain (2017)
4. Werbach, K., Hunter, D.: For the Win: How Game Thinking Can Revolutionize Your Business. Wharton Digital Press, Philadelphia (2012)
5. Hamari, J., Koivisto, J., Sarsa, H.: Does gamification work? — a literature review of empirical studies on gamification. In: 47th Hawaii International Conference on System Sciences, Hawaii, USA (2014)
6. Andrade, F.R., Mizoguchi, R., Isotani, S.: The bright and dark sides of gamification. In: International Conference on Intelligent Tutoring Systems (2016)
7. Dichev, C., Dicheva, D.: Gamifying education: what is known, what is believed and what remains uncertain: a critical review. Int. J. Educ. Technol. High. Educ. **14**, 9 (2017)
8. Mora, A., Riera, D., Gonzalez, C., Arnedo-Moreno, J.: A literature review of gamification design frameworks. In: 7th International Conference on Games and Virtual Worlds for Serious Applications (2015)
9. GIGYA, Gamification: five plays for winning the game (2012)
10. Herzig, P.: Gamification as a Service: Conceptualization of a Generic Enterprise Gamification Platform. Dresden, Technische Universität Dresden, Ph.D. Dissertation (2014)
11. Herzig, P., Ameling, M., Schill, A.: A generic platform for enterprise gamification. In: Joint Working IEEE/IFIP Conference on Software Architecture (WICSA) and European Conference on Software Architecture (ECSA) (2012)
12. Heilbrunn, B., Herzig, P., Schill, A.: Tools for gamification analytics: a survey. In: 2014 IEEE/ACM 7th International Conference on Utility and Cloud Computing (UCC) (2014)
13. Calderón, A., Boubeta-Puig, J., Ruiz, M.: MEdit4CEP-Gam: a model-driven approach for user-friendly gamification design, monitoring and code generation in CEP-based systems. Inf. Softw. Technol. **95**, 238–264 (2018)
14. Nacke, L.E., Deterding, S.: The maturing of gamification research. Comput. Hum. Behav. **71**, 450–454 (2017)
15. Kitchenham, B., Charters, S.: Guidelines for performing Systematic Literature Reviews in Software Engineering. Keele University and Durham University Joint Report (2007)
16. MacDonell, S., Shepperd, M., Kitchenham, B., Mendes, E.: How reliable are systematic reviews in empirical software engineering? IEEE Trans. Softw. Eng. **36**(5), 676–687 (2010)

17. Calderón, A., Ruiz, M., O'Connor, R.V.: A multivocal literature review on serious games for software process standards education. Comput. Stand. Interfaces **57**, 36–48 (2018)
18. Badgeville. https://badgeville.com/products/badgeville-enterprise-plus/. Accessed 14 June 2018
19. Gartner, Gartner says by 2014, 80 percent of current gamified applications (2014) http://www.gartner.com/newsroom/id/2251015
20. ISO, ISO 9000:2015 - Quality management systems – Fundamentals and vocabulary (2015)
21. ISO/IEC, ISO/IEC 330xx Information Technology – Process Assessment, 2013 (2017)
22. Capability Maturity Model Integration (CMMI). http://www.sei.cmu.edu/cmmi/. Accessed 15 June 2018
23. Luxembourg Institute of Science and Technology, TIPA, 21 June 2018. http://www.tipaonline.org/
24. ISO/IEC, ISO/IEC 33002:2015 Information Technology - Process Assessment - Process measurement framework for assessment of process capability (2015)
25. ISO/IEC, ISO/IEC 33003:2015 Information Technology - Process Assessment - Requirements for process measurement frameworks (2015)
26. Morschheuser, B., Hassan, L., Werder, K., Hamari, J.: How to design gamification? a method for engineering gamified software. Inf. Softw. Technol. **95**, 219–237 (2018)
27. ISO/IEC, ISO/IEC 33004:2015 Information Technology - Process Assessment -Requirements for process reference, process assessment and maturity models (2015)
28. Hamari, J., Parvinen, P.: Introduction to gamification: motivations, effects and analytics minitrack. In: 49th Hawaii International Conference on System Sciences (HICSS) (2016)

SPI and Assessment

Towards a Taxonomy of Process Quality Characteristics for Assessment

Anup Shrestha(✉)

School of Management and Enterprise, University of Southern Queensland, Toowoomba, Australia
Anup.Shrestha@usq.edu.au

Abstract. Previous assessment of process quality have focused on process capability (i.e. the ability of a process to meet its stated goals). This paper proposes a taxonomy of alternative process quality characteristics based on intrinsic and extrinsic quality attributes. The ultimate goal of this taxonomy is to provide a framework to conduct process assessments using different process quality aspects. Such a framework would considerably broaden process quality perspectives beyond the primary measure of process capability. It would also allow practitioners to identify and evaluate relevant quality characteristics for processes based on specific contexts and implications. For the process assessment model developers, it offers a list of process quality characteristics that could be used to develop relevant process measurement frameworks.

Keywords: Process assessment · Process quality characteristic
Process measurement framework · Taxonomy · Process quality

1 Introduction

The roots of process quality may be traced back to the 1900s from the Industrial Engineering discipline when Henry Ford managed to build cars at a significantly reduced price by changing his manufacturing process [1]. The focus on process quality led to a major shift in quality control where processes were measured with statistical techniques. The quality control movement led to the development of Total Quality Management (TQM) principles in the 1970s, Six Sigma in the 1980s and Lean techniques are being used more recently [2]. The quality control movement entered the software engineering discipline with the development of the Capability Maturity Model (CMM) in the 1990s where process quality was measured in maturity levels of process capability [3]. The successor of CMM, the CMM Integration (CMMI) was progressively made abstract to cover development, management and acquisition aspects beyond software and into the areas of product, service and overall business processes. However, CMMI maturity levels that determine process capability are the only key representation of process quality characteristics in process assessments.

The initial standard for process assessment ISO/IEC 15504, also termed Software Process Improvement and Capability Determination (SPICE) was also based on, *inter alia*, CMM. The ISO/IEC 15504 standard series were initially focused on software development processes but it had been expanded in other business areas including

I. Stamelos et al. (Eds.): SPICE 2018, CCIS 918, pp. 47–59, 2018.
https://doi.org/10.1007/978-3-030-00623-5_4

management, engineering and service operations. The reference models based on ISO/IEC 15504 defined the capability aspect as the only process quality characteristic. While the scope of processes has expanded in terms of its types (i.e. development, management, governance, and so forth) and its application (i.e. software, IT service management, automotive, space, medical devices, and so forth), the quality characteristic of processes is limited to process capability. There is a need for a common vocabulary and conceptual framework to recognize and categorize other process quality characteristics for assessment.

It is understandable why process capability is the widely adopted measurable aspect of process quality. According to ISO/IEC 33001, process quality is defined by the "ability of a process to satisfy stated and *implied* stakeholder needs when used in a specific *context*". When a process is described, the stakeholder needs of a process are often listed as outcomes that the process needs to achieve to meet its purpose. It then implies that process quality is the ability of the process to meet its purpose – which is defined as process capability. Based on this rationale, one might incorrectly conclude that process quality is process capability. However, if one reviews the definition of process quality, there are two caveats:

(a) How can one be certain that "all" stakeholder needs of a process are listed as outcomes to achieve?
(b) How can the "implied" stakeholder needs, and the "context of use" considered for assessment?

Process capability determines the ability of a process to meet business goals [4]. Since meeting process goals is the major quality check for a process, there is no doubt that process capability is the major process quality characteristic. However, the two questions raised above introduce the need for other quality aspects of a process during assessments. Currently the scope of process capability is limited, so it does not determine the overall process quality. The ISO/IEC 33000 standards series released in 2015 recognized this challenge and used the generic term "process quality characteristics" to develop generic process measurement frameworks for assessment [5].

Specific examples of process quality characteristics beyond process capability are provided, such as process security, process agility and process safety [5]. However, there is only a single process measurement framework for assessment of process capability published as ISO/IEC 33020 [4], paving a way for other process measurement frameworks to be built. Recent studies on the adoption of ISO/IEC 33000 assessment framework still relate to process capability as the sole process quality characteristic, e.g. [6]. Other process quality characteristics have been proposed, e.g. for safety [7] and sustainability [8], however a holistic list of constructs (theoretical concepts) for process quality characteristics have not been proposed for assessment.

In this paper, a comprehensive view of process quality is undertaken, by focusing on the intrinsic and extrinsic quality attributes associated with a process. This focus is used to propose a taxonomy of process quality characteristics. The exemplar studies where the proposed process quality characteristics have been used for the determination of process quality are also included.

The purpose of this taxonomy is twofold: (1) to provide a framework for representing and combining process quality characteristics; and (2) to ultimately enable process assessment using multiple process quality characteristics. Both purposes are critical, given the importance of process assessments to understand quality attributes of a process internally (intrinsic factors) as well as quality surrounding the process environment that are influenced by extrinsic factors.

2 A Proposal of Characteristics as Intrinsic and Extrinsic Quality Attributes

Table 1 identifies the proposed aspects of the taxonomy and defines, for each of these aspects, whether it is something that the process can control (intrinsic quality attribute) or the process cannot control (extrinsic quality attribute) or both. It is important to recognize that the taxonomy should not be considered exhaustive or a final list. In this first instance, all possible aspects of process quality characteristics have not been considered and the taxonomy itself is subject to continuous revisions. The elements that classify process quality continue to evolve due to context-dependent scenarios and implications surrounding process execution, management and environment during assessment.

Table 1. Aspects for process quality characteristics

Process aspect	Section	Intrinsic quality	Extrinsic quality
Effectiveness	3.1.1	*	
Efficiency	3.1.2	*	
Satisfaction	3.2.1	*	*
Usability	3.2.2	*	*
Compatibility/Variability	3.2.3	*	*
Reliability	3.3.1	*	*
Flexibility/Agility	3.3.2	*	*
Sustainability	3.4.1		*
Security	3.4.2		*
Culture	3.4.3		*

In determining the aspects that characterize process quality for assessments, two simple heuristics were followed. The first was to review the extant literature to determine the aspects and its application in process assessments across different disciplines, mainly software engineering and business process management. For example, the process attributes in system and software quality models from ISO/IEC 25010 [9] and BPM principles [10] were considered to determine initial aspects for process quality characteristics.

The second heuristic was to put the aspects in a simple sentence of the form: "*<aspect> is what the process can or cannot control*". If an aspect can be controlled by the process, i.e. it is mainly related to process activities and outcomes, it is classified as an intrinsic quality attribute. By intrinsic quality, it refers to "quality something has in itself, apart from its relations to other things" [11]. For example, because one can say that "process must meet its purpose by fulfilling its outcomes", the "effectiveness" is an intrinsic quality attribute. In a similar way the aspects of "culture" and "security" are classified as extrinsic quality attributes, i.e. these are quality aspects outside of process control but still belong to the environment where the process is executed or managed.

Note that being an intrinsic quality attribute and being an extrinsic quality attribute are not mutually exclusive. For example, the aspect "reliability" described in Sect. 3.3.1, is employed as an intrinsic quality attribute because it is something a process can improve by making changes within its activities, but also an extrinsic quality attribute since there are other environmental and contextual factors to consider reliability of a process (e.g. availability of technology to support process execution). All aspects are discussed in detail in Sect. 3.

3 A Taxonomy for Process Quality Characteristics

Beyond a process's core focus on its activities, outcomes and resources, it is apparent that the process is affected by its relationship with its stakeholders and other processes; operating environment; and management environment. This paper will discuss each of the aspects in Table 1 under the following four logical themes: *core attributes* (activities and resources of a process); *relationship attributes* (association of a process with stakeholders, other processes and reference models); *operating environment* (operational context for a process); and *management environment* (management context for a process).

Figure 1 illustrates these themes and the aspects that each contains. However, it should be noted that this represents only one of a number of ways that process quality characteristics can be categorized. The themes and their aspects are discussed in detail in the following subsections.

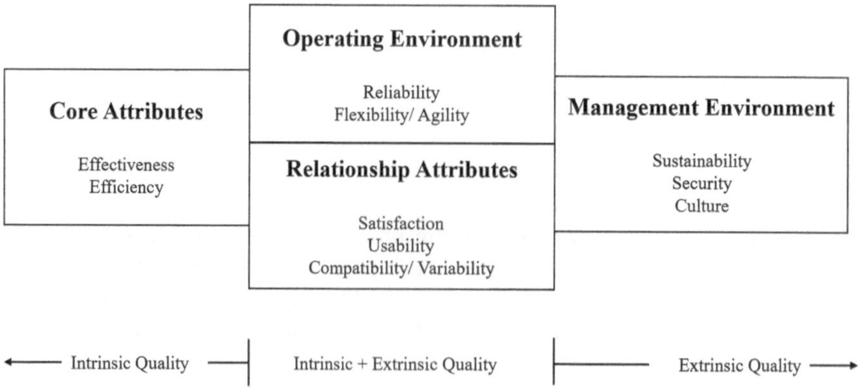

Fig. 1. Themes & aspects of process quality characteristics

3.1 Core Attributes

The first logical theme in the taxonomy addresses the core attributes of process quality. Aspects discussed in this grouping describe the intrinsic quality features of a process – its ability to meet the stated goals and the usage of resources.

3.1.1 Effectiveness

Process effectiveness, also referred to as efficacy, defines the quality feature of a process to meet its purpose by fulfilling all stated outcomes. The major constituent of a process is a series of activities; therefore, it is important to measure that the activities are performed as intended. When one considers process assessment, they are primarily interested to find out the effectiveness of a process. Consequently, it is the most widely accepted process quality characteristic. This aspect is primarily defined as the metric of "process capability" and it has been used since early days of maturity models for processes. A formalization of Process Effectiveness was included in the Maturity Model proposed by Humphrey [12]. The process measurement framework for assessment of process capability published in ISO/IEC 33020 [4] also provides the metric for process effectiveness.

3.1.2 Efficiency

The second most important process quality characteristic deals with resource utilization, primarily in terms of time and cost involved. Efficiency determines that the process makes optimal use of the resources available to it while performing its activities effectively. Effectiveness and efficiency are often contradictory since highly effective processes typically require costly resources. Nevertheless, a balance between these two quality attributes is needed so that the process productivity is promoted, while deadlines are achieved and costs are reduced [3]. A typical example of process efficiency is the metric of "process cycle time" to measure the duration of a process. Since optimal resource utilization is a core objective of a process, this quality attribute may be listed as a key outcome for a process and measured in terms of overall process capability.

3.2 Relationship Attributes

The second logical theme in the taxonomy addresses the relationship of a process with its stakeholders. Aspects included in this theme describe a process's relationship with its customers, process team members in the role of managers or performers, and with other processes and process reference models. Since these aspects focus on the relationship of a "process" with other stakeholders, both intrinsic and extrinsic quality attributes can be relevant for process assessment.

3.2.1 Satisfaction

Every process has at least one customer – internal or external. Process satisfaction defines the relationship of a process with its customers. Customer satisfaction may not be defined at the process level, however once the relationship of a process with its immediate customer(s) is determined, the usefulness, value, trust and service level of a process can be ascertained based on the customer satisfaction indicator.

Consumer satisfaction can be a process metric describing customer emotions resulting from process assessments (including perceived performance of a process) based on their experiences dealing with the process as a stakeholder external to the process [13]. The value perceived by a customer is usually determined by the utility and warranty of the underpinning service [14]. The utility and warranty parameters of a process are typical candidates of process outcomes, therefore achieving the outcomes of a process, i.e. process effectiveness may cover this aspect. However, process satisfaction considers value and usefulness *from the eyes of the customer.* One useful metric for this aspect is "service level", which enables customers to report their degree of satisfaction (or dissatisfaction) within the agreed service levels (also referred to as service level agreements or SLA) [15].

3.2.2 Usability

While satisfaction represents quality characteristics in terms of a process's relationship with its customers, the quality characteristic of usability portrays its relationship with the process team members – typically in the roles of process owner, process manager and process performer. Usability is about user experience same as satisfaction for customer experience.

Since activities and involvement of process team members vary widely, process usability is challenging to monitor [16]. Process usability can be determined from the assessment of the appropriateness of the process in terms of its ease of use, accessibility and operability. Accessibility and usability are closely related, as they both enhance user experience. Operability can be measured in terms of users' perceived difficulty of performing process activities. A useful metric for process usability could be related to its learnability measured in terms of the metric of "learning time" needed by users to understand and train to use the process, as being undertaken in a study for user requirements elicitation [17].

3.2.3 Compatibility/Variability

A process rarely executes in isolation. For any process, it may depend on other processes or there could be other processes that depend on it (inter-dependencies). It is also possible for a process to co-exist with other processes in parallel. Therefore, the process in use must be "compatible" with its reference models that explains the relationship with other processes. The aspect of compatibility (or variability as the opposite measure) of a process refers to its relationship with other processes and process reference models.

Compatibility with process models also determines the quality attribute of maintainability and testability of a process. By compatibility, a process must be a good fit with a process model so that the model can be used for assessments, estimations and testing to determine the quality state of the process itself [18]. Another quality attribute that is useful to check is interoperability – typically highly capable processes contributes towards better process interoperability across enterprises [19]. A practical metric for process compatibility could be evaluating "process tailoring guidelines". While process variations may be necessary, such variations are typically managed using tailoring guidelines [20]. Therefore, a review of tailoring guidelines can help to determine process compatibility (or lack thereof – i.e. process variability).

3.3 Operating Environment

This logical theme concerns the operating environment where the process executes. It should be noted the aspects in this grouping can relate to both intrinsic and extrinsic quality attributes since these process quality characteristics can be improved by actions within the process parameters and also other operational factors beyond the process.

3.3.1 Reliability

Under realistic operating environment, a process cannot be expected to be perfectly capable, i.e. there cannot exist a process with 100% process capability, that means a process is directly affected by its reliability [21]. A reliable process is typically characterized by its availability. A highly capable process that is not available when it is needed is of no use. Therefore, process reliability is a very important aspect of process quality that depends on the operating environment of the process.

Process assessments determine process quality at a specific point of time. Therefore, measuring reliability is challenging during process assessments because process reliability is a dynamic aspect that requires active monitoring [22]. Therefore, real-time process reliability assessment may not be possible unless the process is fully automated and support real-time decision support, for example, online sales process. For other processes, historical process performance data can be used to ascertain reliability. For example, it may be possible to undertake a historical trend analysis from active monitoring systems to assess reliability. A review of other proactive measures that ensure high availability of a process can also demonstrate a strong process reliability. A process that can *regularly* fulfil its intended outcomes is one that is considered "reliable". Therefore, a useful intrinsic quality metric to test process reliability is check historical data of its "failure rate", i.e. how much a process has failed per unit time in the current operating environment. An example of extrinsic quality metric for process reliability is identifying the "knowledge level" of operating environment for a process, i.e. the number of inventive problem-solving knowledge for executing the process. Using knowledge-based methodology to develop new systems and solutions to resolve process problems during its operations has been proposed to improve process reliability, for example, using the principles of Theory of Inventive Problem Solution (TRIZ) to check existing knowledge if the problem has been solved already [23].

3.3.2 Flexibility/Agility

Processes must be able to accommodate changes in the environment in which they operate. To determine this attribute of a process, two closely related aspects of flexibility and agility are useful. Flexibility relates to adaptability of a process to respond to changes; while agility focuses on the speed of response to the changes (how quickly can a process change) in the process operating environment. Process flexibility and agility are determined by intrinsic quality attributes as well as context-dependent operating environment of the process.

Internally, process flexibility can be determined by evaluating "process tailoring guidelines" against the capability of a process to meet its outcomes; i.e. how capable is a process given the number of adaptations. Likewise, process agility can be measured using tailoring guidelines against the time efficiency of a process; i.e. how quickly can a process change given the number of adaptations. A number of quantitative and qualitative metrics to determine process flexibility and agility use the aspects of process effectiveness and efficiency along with the measure of tailoring guidelines or actual process changes [24].

Four process flexibility configurations as extrinsic quality metrics to improve the process operating environment have been proposed in the area of business process management [25]: flexibility by design (handling anticipated changes with defined supporting strategies); flexibility by deviation (handling simple occasional unanticipated changes); flexibility by under-specification (handling anticipated changes where supporting strategies are not defined); and flexibility by change (handling complex but occasional or permanent unanticipated changes). When the process flexibility metrics are compared against the speed of response to changes, they provide useful metrics for operating environment that support process agility.

3.4 Management Environment

During process assessments, the overall management environment under which the process operates plays a critical role in determining process quality and performance. In ISO/IEC 33020 [4], the proposed process measurement framework for process capability recognizes the importance of management environment for quality levels beyond level 1, i.e. regarding process management, standardization, control and innovation. The progression from capability levels 2 to 5 demonstrate maturity of the management systems under which individual processes or process areas operate. Since key aspects of management activities affecting process quality are covered by the process measurement framework for process capability, the focus of this theme is on the management areas where processes operate.

This logical theme describes three key management areas as aspects for process quality characteristics. This list is not exhaustive as a large number of management areas can be relevant for different processes based on their context of use and implied objectives. These are extrinsic quality attributes as processes have little to no influence towards these aspects. However, a process is significantly dependent and affected by these management environment aspects.

3.4.1 Sustainability

Sustainable growth and environmental impact of human activities are significant areas of research in all areas. The evolving green ICT initiatives are an indication of the recognition of process sustainability as a quality metric.

Research by Lami et al. [26] have presented sustainability aspect in software processes by evaluating the culture of green IT in software organisations. This research discussed process sustainability and initially related the concept of sustainability with process capability so that sustainability can be measured as part of process capability. This is only feasible when sustainability goals are explicitly included in the expected outcomes of a process. Given the broader implication and extrinsic nature of sustainability beyond processes, the researchers proposed a new measurement framework for process sustainability assessment [8] that comply with ISO/IEC 33000 series. A practical metric for process sustainability is "carbon emissions and energy costs". While it appears sustainability is only significant for manufacturing industries, one must realise ICT carbon footprint in terms of energy use by data centers and by ICT consumers. Therefore, recognizing sustainability as a process quality characteristic will encourage promoting a sustainable culture and activities at a process level.

3.4.2 Security

Process security as a quality characteristic for assessment can be undertaken from various perspectives: *information security* relating to confidentiality, integrity, authenticity and non-repudiation of data associated with process work; and *safety* and *risks* associated with process environment. This aspect is related to extrinsic quality attribute since most of control activities fall beyond the boundaries of a typical process.

While security is important and has its own set of processes for maintaining information safekeeping, what is important is the content of security measures undertaken during process work [27]. Since processes are information-intensive and increasingly prone to automation in the digital era, evaluating information security at a process level is critical so as to determine data access requirements and data integrity. A useful metric to evaluate security environment for a process is "number of information security breaches" in relevant process environments.

Beyond information security, security can be viewed from the perspective of process risks. An integrated risk management process model has been proposed to operate within IT settings based on the foundations of ISO standards on risk management and process assessment [28]. While the researchers provided a useful process model and harmonized with a focus on process assessment, there is an opportunity to extend this research so that process risk determination perspectives can be a foundation towards process security as a process quality characteristic. In a similar vein, process safety has been proposed as a potential process quality characteristic [7]. In this research, safety integrity levels have been proposed to determine process dependability that is measured in terms of reliability, maintainability and availability – some of these aspects are already covered earlier in this paper.

3.4.3 Culture

Process culture is an extrinsic quality attribute that is proposed as a single aspect in this paper but it is determined by multiple organizational factors. Some key factors that may facilitate process culture are: leadership buy-in, governance of process actions, continuous improvement, communication support, knowledge management, documentation, IT architecture and innovation. Process culture elements are adopted from the management environment at an organisational level.

There is a large body of research on process culture in the discipline of business process management as culture is considered a key element in BPM practice [29]. Cultural assessment in terms of process quality has been undertaken at an organisational level in areas of customer service, organisational structure, continuous improvement, commitment, innovation and accountability [30]. Current BPM researchers and practitioners treat culture as a manageable enabler of process initiatives rather than a barrier. In software engineering discipline, use of technology to improve process culture in software development teams have been researched [31]. In this light, process culture can be used as a process quality characteristic to monitor culture environment conducive for process activities. A relevant process metric for process culture can be "number of improvement actions" for a process.

4 Discussion

Section 3 presented a discussion on the potential process quality characteristics for process assessments. Table 2 outlines the proposed taxonomy of process quality characteristics (represented as "process aspects") with example process quality metrics and exemplar research references on the relevant process quality.

Table 2. Taxonomy of process quality characteristics

Theme	Process aspect	Example metric	Exemplar studies
Core attributes	Effectiveness	Process capability	Humphrey (1989) [12] ISO/IEC 33020 [4]
	Efficiency	Process cycle time	Paulk (1993) [3]
Relationship Attributes	Satisfaction	Service level	Babin and Griffin (1998) [13]
	Usability	Learning time	Feiler and Humphrey (1993) [16]
	Compatibility/Variability	Process tailoring guidelines	Staron (2006) [18]
Operating Environment	Reliability	Failure rate knowledge level	Tripathy, Wee and Majhi (2003) [21]
	Flexibility/Agility	Process tailoring guidelines flexibility by design	Gong and Janssen (2010) [24]
Management Environment	Sustainability	Carbon emissions & Energy costs	Lami, Fabbrini and Buglione (2014) [8]
	Security	Number of information security breaches	Varkoi (2013) [7]
	Culture	Number of improvement actions	vom Brocke and Sinnl (2011) [29]

Figure 2 illustrates the ten process quality characteristics represented as "process aspects" based on the four themes to provide a framework for process assessment.

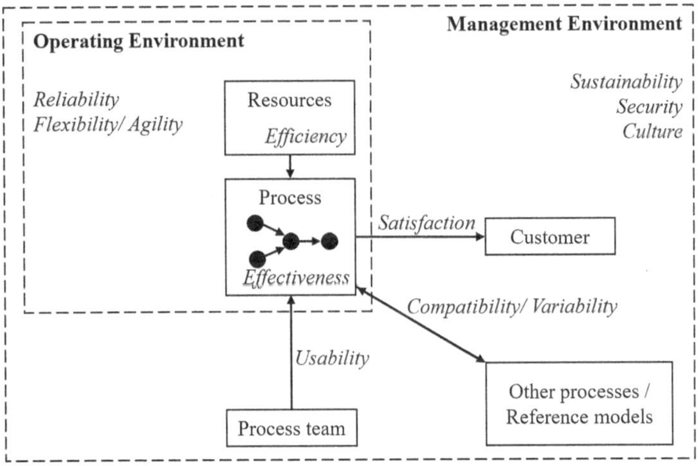

Fig. 2. A framework for assessment areas based on process quality characteristics

5 Conclusion

In this paper a taxonomy of process quality attributes is proposed based on ten aspects mapped to intrinsic and extrinsic quality attributes. The discussion of these aspects subdivides them into four logical themes: core attributes, relationship attributes, operating environment and management environment. While assessment areas have expanded in different areas, the process quality metric is limited to process capability, even with the recent movements towards automation to determine process quality during assessments, for e.g. [32, 33]. The proposed taxonomy can be used to evaluate processes with a wider view based on different contexts and implications during process assessments. There is currently no discussion of theoretical underpinnings and limited justification for the proposed process quality characteristics. In the future the taxonomy can be used as a platform to justify broader aspects of process quality measurement. Consequently, this research serves as a foundation to develop process measurement frameworks and ultimately to evaluate different process quality aspects during process assessments.

References

1. Frederick, T.: The Principles of Scientific Management. Harper Brothers, New York (1911)
2. Barney, M., McCarty, T.: The New Six Sigma: A Leader's Guide to Achieving Rapid Business Improvement and Sustainable Results. Prentice Hall Professional (2003)
3. Paulk, M.: Capability maturity model for software. In: Encyclopedia of Software Engineering (1993)
4. ISO/IEC, ISO/IEC 33020:2015 Information technology – Process assessment – Process measurement framework for assessment of process capability. International Organization for Standardization, Geneva (2015)

5. ISO/IEC, ISO/IEC 33003:2015 Information technology – Process assessment – Requirements for process measurement frameworks. International Organization for Standardization, Geneva (2015)
6. Del Carpio, A.F.: Visualizing composition and behavior of the ISO/IEC 33000 assessment framework through a multi-layer model. Computer Standards & Interfaces (2018)
7. Varkoi, T.: Safety as a process quality characteristic. In: Woronowicz, T., Rout, T., O'Connor, Rory V., Dorling, A. (eds.) SPICE 2013. CCIS, vol. 349, pp. 1–12. Springer, Heidelberg (2013). https://doi.org/10.1007/978-3-642-38833-0_1
8. Lami, G., Fabbrini, F., Buglione, L.: An ISO/IEC 33000-compliant measurement framework for software process sustainability assessment. In: Software Measurement and the International Conference on Software Process and Product Measurement (IWSM-MENSURA), pp. 50–59. IEEE, October 2014
9. ISO/IEC, ISO/IEC 25010:2011 Systems and software engineering – Systems and software Quality Requirements and Evaluation (SQuaRE) – System and software quality models. International Organization for Standardization, Geneva (2011)
10. Harmon, P.: The scope and evolution of business process management. In: vom Brocke, J., Rosemann, M. (eds.) Handbook on Business Process Management 1. IHIS, pp. 37–80. Springer, Heidelberg (2015). https://doi.org/10.1007/978-3-642-45100-3_3
11. Harman, G.: The intrinsic quality of experience. Philos. Perspect. **4**, 31–52 (1990)
12. Humphrey, W.: Managing the Software Process. Addison Wesley, Reading (1989)
13. Babin, B.J., Griffin, M.: The nature of satisfaction: an updated examination and analysis. J. Bus. Res. **41**(2), 127–136 (1998)
14. Cannon, D., Wheeldon, D., Lacy, S., Hanna, A.: ITIL Service Strategy. TSO, London (2011)
15. Lewis, L., Ray, P.: Service level management definition, architecture, and research challenges. In: Global Telecommunications Conference, GLOBECOM 1999, vol. 3, pp. 1974–1978. IEEE (1999)
16. Feiler, P.H., Humphrey, W.S.: Software process development and enactment: Concepts and definitions. In: Second International Conference on the Software Process-Continuous Software Process Improvement, pp. 28–40. IEEE, February 1993
17. Azadegan, A., Papamichail, K.N., Sampaio, P.: Applying collaborative process design to user requirements elicitation: a case study. Comput. Ind. **64**(7), 798–812 (2013)
18. Staron, M.: Adopting model driven software development in industry – a case study at two companies. In: Nierstrasz, O., Whittle, J., Harel, D., Reggio, G. (eds.) MODELS 2006. LNCS, vol. 4199, pp. 57–72. Springer, Heidelberg (2006). https://doi.org/10.1007/11880240_5
19. Guédria, W., Naudet, Y., Chen, D.: Interoperability maturity models – survey and comparison –. In: Meersman, R., Tari, Z., Herrero, P. (eds.) OTM 2008. LNCS, vol. 5333, pp. 273–282. Springer, Heidelberg (2008). https://doi.org/10.1007/978-3-540-88875-8_48
20. Hallerbach, A., Bauer, T., Reichert, M.: Capturing variability in business process models: the Provop approach. J. Softw. Evol. Process **22**(6–7), 519–546 (2010)
21. Tripathy, P.K., Wee, W.M., Majhi, P.R.: An EOQ model with process reliability considerations. J. Oper. Res. Soc. **54**(5), 549–554 (2003)
22. Mendibil, K., Turner, T.J., Bititci, U.S.: Measuring and improving business process reliability. Int. J. Bus. Perf. Manag. **4**(1), 76–94 (2002)
23. Arcidiacono, G., Bucciarelli, L.: TRIZ: engineering methodologies to improve the process reliability. Qual. Reliab. Eng. Int. **32**(7), 2537–2547 (2016)
24. Gong, Y., Janssen, M.: Measuring process flexibility and agility. In: Proceedings of the 4th International Conference on Theory and Practice of Electronic Governance, pp. 173–182. ACM, October 2010

25. Schonenberg, H., Mans, R., Russell, N., Mulyar, N., van der Aalst, W.M.: Towards a taxonomy of process flexibility. In: CAiSE forum, vol. 344, pp. 81–84, June 2008
26. Lami, G., Fabbrini, F., Fusani, M.: Software sustainability from a process-centric perspective. In: Winkler, D., O'Connor, R.V., Messnarz, R. (eds.) EuroSPI 2012. CCIS, vol. 301, pp. 97–108. Springer, Heidelberg (2012). https://doi.org/10.1007/978-3-642-31199-4_9
27. Siponen, M.: Information security standards focus on the existence of process, not its content. Commun. ACM **49**(8), 97–100 (2006)
28. Barafort, B., Mesquida, A.-L., Mas, A.: Developing an integrated risk management process model for IT settings in an ISO multi-standards context. In: Mas, A., Mesquida, A., O'Connor, R.V., Rout, T., Dorling, A. (eds.) SPICE 2017. CCIS, vol. 770, pp. 322–336. Springer, Cham (2017). https://doi.org/10.1007/978-3-319-67383-7_24
29. vom Brocke, J., Sinnl, T.: Culture in business process management: a literature review. Bus. Process Manag. J. **17**(2), 357–378 (2011)
30. Schmiedel, T., vom Brocke, J., Recker, J.: Culture in business process management: how cultural values determine BPM success. In: vom Brocke, J., Rosemann, M. (eds.) Handbook on Business Process Management 2. IHIS, pp. 649–663. Springer, Heidelberg (2015). https://doi.org/10.1007/978-3-642-45103-4_27
31. Araujo, R., Borges, M.: Extending the software process culture - an approach based on groupware and workflow. In: Bomarius, F., Komi-Sirviö, S. (eds.) PROFES 2001. LNCS, vol. 2188, pp. 297–311. Springer, Heidelberg (2001). https://doi.org/10.1007/3-540-44813-6_26
32. Barafort, B., Shrestha, A., Cortina, S., Renault, A.: A software artefact to support standard-based process assessment: Evolution of the TIPA® framework in a design science research project. Comput. Stand. Interfaces **60**, 37–47 (2018)
33. Shrestha, A., Cater-Steel, A., Tan, W.G., Toleman, M.: Software-mediated process assessment for IT service capability management. In: European Conference on Information Systems (ECIS), Tel Aviv (2014)

Process Risk Determination Supporting Data Protection Impact Assessment

Stéphane Cortina(✉), Philippe Valoggia(✉), Alain Renault(✉), and Béatrix Barafort(✉)

Luxembourg Institute of Science and Technology, Avenue des Hauts-Fourneaux. 5, 4362 Esch/Alzette, Luxembourg
{Stephane.Cortina, Philippe.Valoggia, Alain.Renault, Beatrix.Barafort}@list.lu

Abstract. This paper explores the opportunity to consider the process-risk determination approach (presented in the upcoming ISO/IEC 33015 standard) as a means to determine the level of risk associated to personal data processing activities. It outlines how the rights and freedoms of individuals are impacted by the risks related to the organizational processes supporting the new citizens' rights introduced by the General Data Protection Regulation (GDPR), which requires performing Data Protection Impact Assessment on data processing activities, in some specific circumstances.

Keywords: Data subject's right to data protection
Data protection impact assessment · Process risk determination
ISO/IEC 33015 · GDPR

1 Introduction

For many years, process assessment has been used for several purposes such as: conformity assessment, performance improvement, process-related risks evaluation and performance benchmarking. The usage of a Gap Analysis as a mean to make the link between process and conformity assessment and to prepare for compliance has been studied in [1]. Performance improvement has been extensively performed in various domains such as software engineering, but also in IT Service Management, and many more. Process-related risks evaluation have been performed in specific applications for supplier selection with process capability determination (i.e. in the space domain [2] and in the automotive industry [3]) and specifically for Governance, Risk management and Compliance (GRC) application in the financial sector [4]. For process-related risks evaluation, a new standard is currently being developed[1], which focuses on process risk determination (PRD): the ISO/IEC NP PDTR 33015[2] Guide to process-related risk determination [5]. This document gives additional guidance on the application of the results of process assessment to the determination of process risk.

[1] New proposal introduced on 2018-03-08, awaiting ballot results when writing this paper.
[2] ISO/IEC NP PDTR 33015 will be mentioned ISO/IEC 33015 in the rest of the paper to make reading easier.

I. Stamelos et al. (Eds.): SPICE 2018, CCIS 918, pp. 60–72, 2018.
https://doi.org/10.1007/978-3-030-00623-5_5

In the current GRC landscape, more and more regulations are coming into force and are requiring enterprises to organize themselves to meet regulatory requirements. The latest and most famous one in Europe is the General Data Protection Regulation (GDPR), entered into force on May 25th, 2018 [6]. GDPR is expressed in terms of rights with Article 1 stating that the Regulation «protects fundamental rights and freedoms of natural persons and in particular their right to the protection of personal data». Companies are required to implement appropriate measures in order to satisfy the exercise of the rights of the citizen. Each enterprise has to be able to demonstrate that the right and freedoms of the data subject are fulfilled at any time. In case of processing activities resulting in a high risk, Article 35 of GDPR requires to carry out a Data Protection Impact Assessment (DPIA) for these processing activities.

Several approaches have arisen in the industry in order to guide and achieve a DPIA of personal data processing [7, 8]. These approaches do however focus on privacy aspects centered on information security issues only. But privacy is just one of the values underpinning data protection as a fundamental right, so assessing the impact of a personal data processing on the protection of personal data should not be limited to privacy. It should also include an assessment of the risks related to rights of the data subject to control his or her personal data. Enabling individuals (data subjects) to control their personal data supposes dedicated organizational processes are implemented in enterprises. These processes contribute to protecting the data subject's rights.

In this context, a process risk determination of the processes contributing to the rights and freedoms of data subjects can bring a valuable complementary contribution to the classical privacy risk assessment based on information security issues. The research question is "*how to use process risk determination to support GDPR Data Protection Impact Assessment?*" The paper explores to which extent PRD as described in the new standardization project ISO/IEC 33015 might help carrying out an assessment of the impact of personal data processing activities on the protection of personal data.

The paper is structured as follows. In Sect. 2, we depict how to determine process-related risk according to ISO/IEC 33015. Then in Sect. 3, we present the DPIA and the management of the risk to right to data protection, before explaining in Sect. 4 how to apply process-related risk determination to DPIA. Section 5 presents the conclusion including perspectives.

2 Determining Process-Related Risk According to ISO/IEC 33015

ISO/IEC 15504-4 "Guidance on use for process improvement and process capability determination" [9] explains that "*Process-related risk arises from inappropriate process management, i.e. not deploying appropriate processes, or from deploying them in a way which does not achieve required process attribute ratings.*" It further states "*Process-related risk can be inferred from the existence of gaps between a target process profile and an assessed process profile.*"

"*Process-related risk is assessed from the probability of a problem arising from an identified gap, and from its potential consequence, should it occur.*" In this approach, process-related risk is one component to take into account when considering process improvement or process capability determination.

The ISO/IEC 330xx new series of standards [10] replaces the ISO/IEC 15504 and reflect the current state of the art for process assessment. They however offer a wider range of applicability as the ISO/IEC 330xx set of International Standards, as a whole, addresses process quality characteristics of any type. Results of such assessments can be applied for improving process performance, benchmarking, or for identifying and addressing risks associated with application of processes. Addressing risks has become an objective in itself whereas it was but a means to support higher-level goals in ISO/IEC 15504-4. ISO/IEC 33015 "Guide to process risk determination" is a new JTC1/SC7 draft document resulting from the evolution of the previous ISO/IEC 15504 series of standard. This document gives additional guidance on the application of the results of process assessment to the determination of process risk. Identified process-related risks can then feed into an organization's risk management process together with other types of risks, including strategic, organizational, financial, personnel and many others.

The ISO/IEC 33015 defines *process-related risks* as "*risks resulting from weaknesses in the performance, management or deployment of a process*".

The objectives of the process-related risk determination are defined by particular requirement or set of requirements, which may involve deploying an organization's processes for a new or an existing task, a contract or an internal undertaking, a product or a service, or any other business requirement. An organization may then need to identify risks and determine the significance associated with application of the processes for a particular requirement or set of requirements.

ISO/IEC 33015 defines a number of steps to support process-related risk determination (PRD). The resulting process suggested by the standard can be summarized as in Fig. 1.

1. Define PRD Project

The project definition phase is critical, as it is where the assessment input (i.e. the information required before a process assessment can commence) and target process profile (i.e. the process attributes required and the rating necessary for each of them) are prepared based on a sound understanding of the processes that are relevant for the particular requirement or set of requirement that are at stake. The types of risks to be identified are defined by the objectives of the process-related risk determination and associated with application of the processes for a particular requirement or set of requirements. This will influence the selection of processes subject to the assessment and the target process profile with indication of the target process attribute achievement judged to be adequate, subject to an acceptable process risk, for meeting the specified requirement. The target process profile sets the process attributes that will serve as a basis to determine the risks related to the processes.

2. Assess process

A traditional (ISO/IEC 33002 compliant [11]) assessment is then performed on the processes, based on the target process profile defined previously. The objective being to understand the potential risks related to the processes (and not improving these

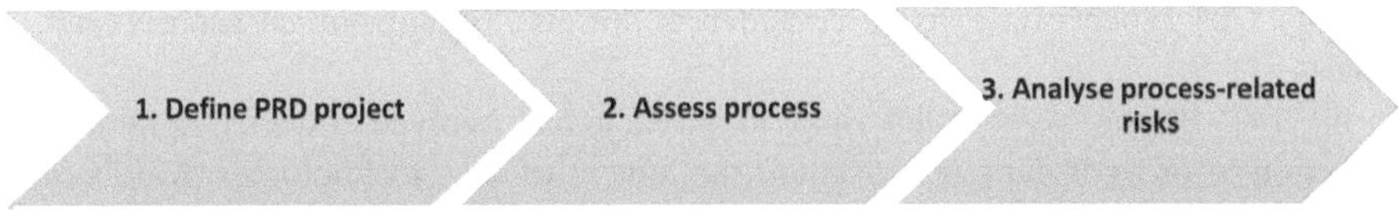

Fig. 1. Process-related risk determination steps

processes), a particular attention will be paid to make sure that the quantity and type of objective evidence collected will serve the initial purpose, considering the process context and class of assessment retained.

3. Analyze process-related risks

The set of process profiles produced as output of the assessment of the evidence collected will serve to identify the process attributes for which achievements are actually lower than the expectations set in the target process profile. The analysis of these gaps infer process-related risk. Annex B of the ISO/IEC 33015 gives an example of how to analyze process-related risks.

Ensuring data protection and understanding GDPR readiness of an organization are the set of requirements at the origin of the definition of the objectives of the process-related risk determination discussed in this paper.

3 DPIA: Managing the Risk to Right to Data Protection

Article 35 of the GDPR provides that "*where a type of processing [...] is likely to result in a high risk to the rights and freedoms of natural persons, the controller shall, prior to the processing, carry out an assessment of the impact of the envisaged processing operations on the protection of personal data.*" DPIA under the GDPR is a tool for managing risks to data protection. Managing such risks implies to clarify what these risks are and how they could be managed.

The Article 29 Working Party (A29WP), now known as the European Data Protection Board (EDPB), initially considered that "*the scope of the rights and freedoms of the data subjects primarily concerns the right to privacy*" as stated in [12]. Consequently, several Data Protection supervisory authorities (Commission Nationale de l'Informatique et des Libertés[3] in France, Agencia Española de Protección de Datos[4] in Spain...) have offered guidelines and tools focused on the right to privacy. These guidelines and tools encourage the data controllers to assess and treat risks that could affect confidentiality, integrity, and availability (CIA) of the personal data processed as performed in an information security context. Three years later, the position of A29WP has slightly evolved: henceforth the reference to the "rights and freedoms of data subject "primarily concerns the rights to data protection and privacy [13]. It means that

[3] https://www.cnil.fr.

[4] http://www.agpd.es.

not only CIA aspects have to be considered, but also organizational aspects such as processes.

In [14], Blume argues that right to privacy has evolved towards right to data protection in order to take into account the advent of new technologies. Mc Dermott [15] however considers that right to privacy is only a sub-right to the right to data protection, which covers three additional rights: the right to autonomy of the data subject regarding the control over his or her personal data, the right to transparency and the right not to be discriminate.

Carrying out an assessment of the impact of the processing activities on the protection of personal data (i.e. performing a DPIA) should thus not be limited to analyzing the risks to data privacy, but also those related to the three others principles that also make up the right to data protection: the autonomy, the transparency, the non-discrimination.

Third chapter of GDPR introduces the "rights of the data subject". Article 12 to 23 specify eight rights: right to be informed (article 12, 13, 14, 23), right of access (article 15, 23), right to rectification (article 16, 19, 23), right to erasure (article 17, 19, 23), right to restriction of processing (article 18, 23), right to data portability (article 20 and 23), right to objection (article 21, 23), right to contest a decision based on automated processing (article 22, 23). Effectiveness of the right to be informed contributes to the transparency of the processing activities, while others allow data subject to have control over his/her personal data. These rights can be exercised by any individual against the data controller. Therefore, in any organization, the controller has to implement suitable *Data Control* processes that enable data subject to control over his/her personal data. These processes are however risk sources because they have "*the intrinsic potential to give rise to risk*", as defined in [16]. Indeed, a flaw in these processes can have an impact on the ability of the data subject to control over his/her personal data and on the transparency of the processing activities. That is why determining the risks related to the *Data Control* processes is key for managing the risks to the rights of the data subjects.

In the following section of this paper, we will describe how the PRD process (described in Sect. 2) can be adapted and then applied to assess the risks associated to the eight *Data Control* processes, in order to support the performance of a DPIA.

4 Applying Process-Related Risk Determination to DPIA

There is no specific methodology required to carry out a DPIA. GDPR only sets out the minimum mandatory features. Thus, Article 35(7) states that "*the assessment shall contain at least*:

- *systematic description of the envisaged processing operations and the purposes of the processing*;
- *an assessment of the necessity and proportionality of the processing operations in relation to the purpose;*
- *an assessment of the risks to the rights and freedoms of data subjects;*
- *the measures envisaged to address the risks".*

This section describes how the generic PRD process is developed in order to contribute to the "*assessment of the risks to the rights and freedoms of the data subject*", required in any DPIA.

4.1 Adapting the Generic PRD Process to the DPIA Context

Defining a PRD project in the context of a DPIA have some consequences on some of the activities related to the initiation of the process (step 1.1), the selection of the assessment input (step1.2), the determination of the target profile (step 1.3), as well as to the analysis of the process-related risks (step 3), shown on Fig. 2.

Defining the Purpose of the PRD and Identifying the Key Roles
In the context of a DPIA, the purpose of the PRD process is to assess the risks to the rights and freedoms of natural persons resulting from the processing of personal data by assessing them and determining the measures to address them. As stated in Article 35 of GDPR, the controller is accountable of carrying a DPIA assessment, and consequently he or she will be the sponsor of the PRD project.

Selecting the Process Assessment Method to Be Used
The process assessment method to be used for performing the PRD process should satisfy the requirements of ISO/IEC 33002. The TIPA framework [17] is a widely used method that complies with these requirements.

Selecting the Process Quality Characteristic and the Measurement Framework
In the context of a DPIA, the selected Measurement Framework is the "Process measurement framework for assessment of process capability". Published in ISO/IEC 33020 [18], it allows the assessment team to determine the "*ability of a process to meet current or projected business goals*".

Selecting the Process Reference Model and the Process Assessment Model
The selected Process Reference Model is the GDPR PRM currently under development at Luxembourg Institute of Science and Technology (LIST[5]). The construction of this PRM is ongoing and follows the documented transformation process described in [19]. At the time of writing this paper, this GDPR PRM is composed of two process groups: 'Data Control processes' and 'Other Data Protection processes' as depicted in Fig. 3.

The selected Process Assessment Model is composed of the eight processes defined in the Data Control process group of the GDPR PRM, combined with the Process Attributes defined in the capability Measurement Framework described in ISO/IEC 33020, and enriched with the appropriate capability level 1 indicators (base practices and work products). Each of the eight processes relates to one of the eight rights of the data subject.

Defining the Type of Risk and the Target Profile
GDPR does not only require that data subjects' rights are effective, it also defines expected timeline and minimum required information for the exercise of these rights. The risks to be identified for performing a DPIA are the ones impacting the rights and

[5] https://www.list.lu/.

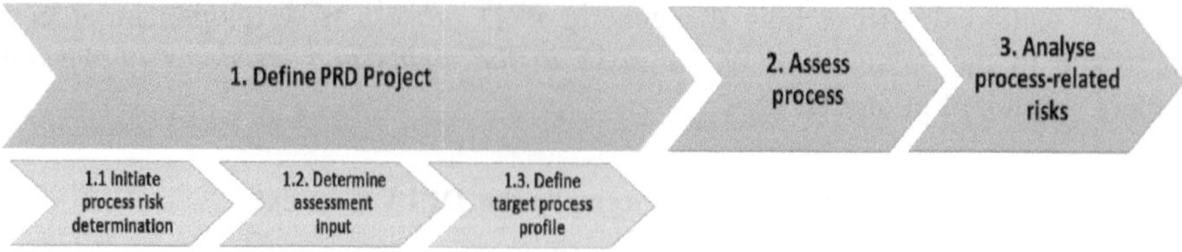

Fig. 2. Process-related risk determination detailed steps

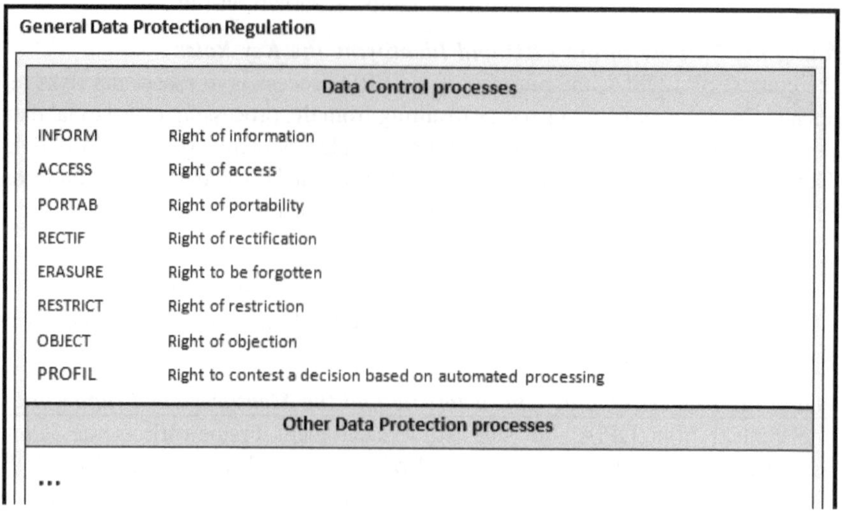

General Data Protection Regulation
Data Control processes
INFORM Right of information
ACCESS Right of access
PORTAB Right of portability
RECTIF Right of rectification
ERASURE Right to be forgotten
RESTRICT Right of restriction
OBJECT Right of objection
PROFIL Right to contest a decision based on automated processing
Other Data Protection processes
...

Fig. 3. Draft of GDPR process map

freedoms of the data subjects. When assessing the Data Control processes, we propose that the PRD team should focus on the following consequences:

- Risk to not achieve process purpose: for instance, if a data subject's request to erase his/her data cannot be performed; this means that the data subject right to erasure is not fulfilled: the process purpose for the Right to erasure process purpose is not achieved.
- Risk to not achieve process purpose in due time: for instance, where personal data have not been obtained from the data subject, the data controller shall provide information to the data subject within a reasonable period after obtaining the personal data, but at the latest within one month.
- Risk to not provide data subject with expected information: for instance when the data subject requests to have access to his/her personal data, the data controller shall provide a well-defined set of data, in a well-defined format.

We made the assumption that these consequences (listed above) are supported by the three process attributes Process Performance, Performance Management and Work Product Management from ISO/IEC 33020 if they are fully achieved.

The purpose of a DPIA is to "*assess the risks to the rights and freedoms of data subjects*". Thus, when setting the target profile for the eight Data Control processes (presented on Fig. 3), the main objective of the authors was to retain process attributes if and only if their non-achievement would directly impact the end users of these processes (in other words, the citizens). Consequently, only thc "Process Performance (PA1.1), the "Performance Management" (PA2.1), and the "Work Product Management" (PA2.2) attributes were kept. Indeed, a gap in these attributes implies respectively a risk that the data control process does not reach its purpose (PA1.1), a risk for the citizens that their requests are not handled in due time (PA2.1), or a risk for the citizens that the responses to their requests do not contain all the expected personal data (PA2.2).

On the other hand, a gap occurring in one of the others (higher) attributes of the capability measurement framework (i.e. PA3.1, PA3.2, PA4.1, PA4.2, PA5.1, or PA5.2) would result in a risk for the organization (such as a risk of inconsistency in the process performance or an inability to quantify the process performance) without any direct impact on the data subjects.

Based on these assumptions, we suggest the target profile presented in Fig. 4 below for performing a PRD based DPIA.

Analyzing the Process-Related Risks

The analysis of the process-related risks consists in determining the risk level of the assessed processes, based on the profiles resulting from a process assessment. For that, the assessors identify the process attribute gaps and the process capability level gaps, determine the risk level associated with each process capability level and finally the process risk level.

Determination of the process attribute gap is done by a comparison between the 'required process attribute rating' and the 'assessed process attribute rating' as in Fig. 5 below where one can see that a process attribute that is largely achieved is considered as a minor gap compared to a "*Fully*" target, whereas *partially* or *not* are considered as major gaps.

Then, the process capability level gap is determined based on the number and types of process attribute gaps for each process capability level where these gaps occurred (Fig. 6).

The final level of risk for the process is then determined through combining the process capability level gaps with the capability level at which the gap occurred.

Figure 7 below shows that a significant gap in process performance will result in a high risk for of the process, whereas a slight gap would result in medium risk. This would be different at capability level 2 where a slight gap would result in a low risk only.

The final process risk level is then deduced by taking the highest level of process quality risk.

Level 1 Performed	Level 2 Managed	
Process Performance	Performance Management	Work Product Management
F	F	F

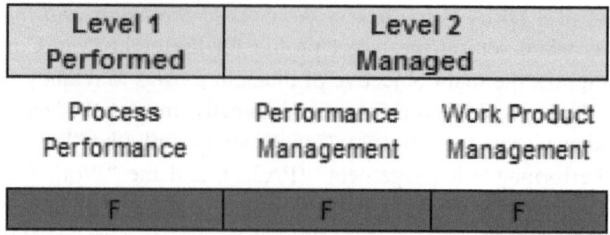

Fig. 4. The selected target profile

Target process attribute rating	Assessed process attribute rating	Process attribute gap
Fully achieved	Fully achieved	None
	Largely achieved	Minor
	Partially achieved	Major
	Not achieved	Major
Largely achieved	Fully achieved	None
	Largely achieved	None
	Partially achieved	Major
	Not achieved	Major

Fig. 5. Process attribute gap (Adapted from ISO/IEC 33015)

Number of process attribute gaps and process capability level	Process capability level gap
No major or minor gaps	None
No gap for level 1, and only minor gaps within level 2	Slight
A minor gap for level 1, or a single major gap within level 2	Significant
A major gap at level 1, or more than one major gap within level 2	Substantial

Fig. 6. Process capability level gap (Adapted from ISO/IEC 33015)

	Extent of process capability level gap		
Process capability level where gap occurs	Slight	Significant	Substantial
2 - Managed process	Low risk	Medium Risk	**High Risk**
1 - Performed process	*Not Applicable*	**High risk**	**High Risk**

Fig. 7. Risk associated with each process capability level (Adapted from ISO/IEC 33015)

4.2 Applying the Adapted PRD Process to the DPIA Context

1. **Define PRD Process**

In the DPIA context, PRD inputs and type of risk are already defined (see Sect. 4.1). Moreover, the description of the envisaged processing activities is considered as an input to the establishment of the context. In particular it helps to select relevant processes to assess by reviewing lawfulness conditions. Indeed, regarding the legal basis of the personal data processing activities, some rights should not be effective. For instance, if the legal basis of a processing activity is compliance with a specific regulation, then the data subject cannot exercise his or her right to data portability. So, the *right to portability* process will be excluded from the scope.

Establishing the context also allows to identify internal and external actors to interview to establish the processes' capability level. Usually, actors to interview are the data controller, the processor(s) if any, the Data Protection Officer, and persons in charge of supporting the exercise of the rights of the data subject related to the processing activities.

2. **Assess Process**

Each selected process is assessed against the Data Control Process Assessment Model using the assessment process documented in the TIPA methodology; assessment results are displayed as process profiles.

3. **Analyze Process-related Risk**

Once process profiles are established, they are compared to target process profiles. Process attributes gaps are identified and consequences of the risk are indicated by process capability level where gap occurs. As mentioned previously, the target level set for DPIA is the capability level 2. Accordingly, consequences of risk could only be interpreted in terms of process performance and process management.

Process risk level is then tabulated by combining the extent of process capability level gap (measured on a scale from "none" to "substantial") with the capability level where the gap is observed. Establishing level of risk to data processing entails to combine the risk levels of each data control process required to enable data subject to exercise his or her rights. To this end, it was decided that the level of risk to data processing is the highest risk level of data control processes risk levels.

Figure 8 illustrates how the steps described previously and illustrated in Figs. 4, 5, 6 and 7 were applied to determine the process risk level for one particular data control process ('i.e. 'Right of portability'), and the consequence on the global data subject's rights level of risk for data processing activities.

Results of the application of the PRD explained before provide valuable inputs to the data controller and contribute to the overall DPIA. It helps identifying processes subject to a high-risk level, which require the data controller to taking quick correcting measures. If the processing of personal data results in a high risk and the controller does not take any measure to mitigate the risk, then "the supervisory authority shall be consulted prior to processing" (as required by article 36(1) of GDPR [6]).

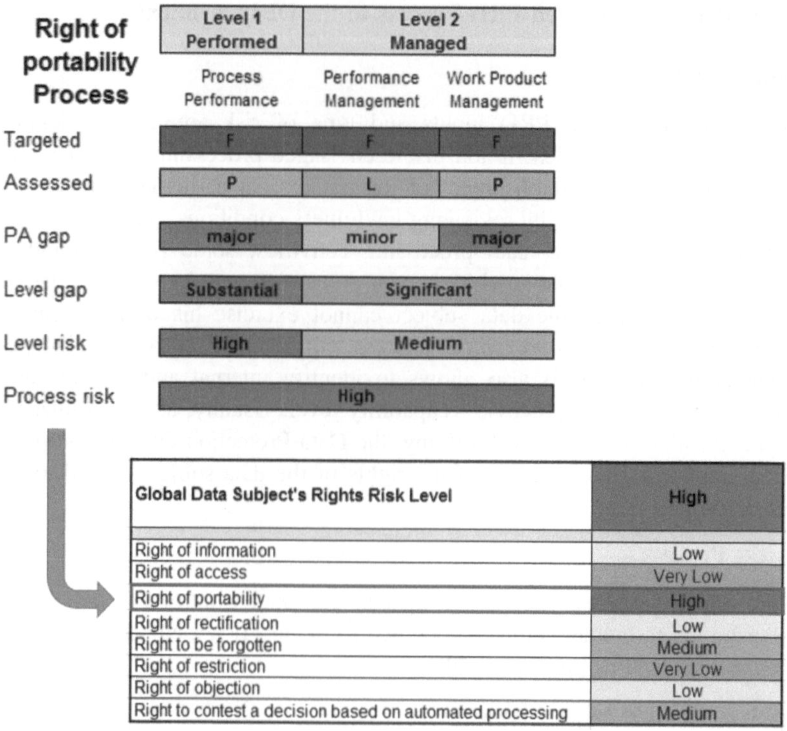

Right of portability Process
Level 1 Performed
Level 2 Managed
Process Performance
Performance Management
Work Product Management
Targeted
F
F
F
Assessed
P
L
P
PA gap
major
minor
major
Level gap
Substantial
Significant
Level risk
High
Medium
Process risk
High
Global Data Subject's Rights Risk Level
High
Right of information
Low
Right of access
Very Low
Right of portability
High
Right of rectification
Low
Right to be forgotten
Medium
Right of restriction
Very Low
Right of objection
Low
Right to contest a decision based on automated processing
Medium

Fig. 8. Right of portability process risk and impact on Global data subject's rights risk level

5 Conclusion

The paper explores how PRD described in the new (draft) standardization project ISO/IEC 33015, can help carrying out an assessment of the impact of personal data processing activities on the protection of personal data in the context of GDPR. This new regulation requires a DPIA to be performed in case "*a type of processing [...] is likely to result in a high risk to the rights and freedoms of natural persons*".

ISO/IEC 33015 is currently an early working draft under development within ISO/JTC1/SC7. The intent of this paper is not to promote the content of the document as is, but rather to try to understand the applicability of the approach, and particularly to which extent PRD as described in that draft standard might help carrying out an assessment of the impact of personal data processing activities on the protection of personal data.

This paper describes how the PRD approach can be adapted and used to support DPIA activities. It highlighted the complexity of the different steps and the possible instability of assumptions made for that purpose. Among these assumptions are the content of the target profile (limited to capability level 2 with all process attributes fully achieved). Experiments planed in a near future will definitely help evaluating the robustness of these assumptions. This will also probably provide valuable inputs for the next round of comments on the draft ISO document.

Other future works will also consist in exploring another approach where GDPR would provide requirements to define alternative process attributes for the process quality characteristic above level 1, and so propose a new measurement framework.

References

1. Picard, M., Renault, A., Barafort, B., Cortina, S.: Measuring readiness for compliance: a gap analysis tool to complete the TIPA process assessment framework. In: Kreiner, C., O'Connor, R.V., Poth, A., Messnarz, R. (eds.) EuroSPI 2016. CCIS, vol. 633, pp. 106–116. Springer, Cham (2016). https://doi.org/10.1007/978-3-319-44817-6_9
2. Cass, A., Völcker, C., Ouared, R., Dorling, A., Winzer, L., Carranza, J.M.: SPICE for SPACE trials, risk analysis, and process improvement. Softw. Process Improv. Pract. **9**(1), 13–21 (2004)
3. Garcia, M.A., Viale, E., Bellotti, M., Alchieri, J.C.: A process-oriented approach for functional safety implementation in the automotive industry. In: Mas, A., Mesquida, A., Rout, T., O'Connor, R.V., Dorling, A. (eds.) SPICE 2012. CCIS, vol. 290, pp. 118–128. Springer, Heidelberg (2012). https://doi.org/10.1007/978-3-642-30439-2_11
4. Ivanyos, J., Roóz, J., Messnarz, R.: Governance capability assessment: using ISO/IEC 15504 for internal financial controls and IT management. In: Internal Financial Control Assessment Applying Multilingual Ontology Framework - The MONTIFIC. Memolux Kft., FelelHos szerkesztHo és kiadó, Ivanyos János ügyvezetHo (2010)
5. ISO/IEC PDTR 33015.3: Information technology – Process assessment – Guide to process risk determination (2018)
6. Regulation (EU) 2016/679 of the European Parliament and of the Council of 27 April 2016 on the protection of natural persons with regard to the processing of personal data and on the free movement of such data, and repealing Directive 95/46/EC (General Data Protection Regulation) (2016)
7. CNIL – Guidelines on GDPA. https://www.cnil.fr/en/guidelines-dpia. Accessed 12 July 2018
8. AEPD – Guía práctica para las evaluaciones de impacto en la protección de los datos sujetas al RGPD. https://www.aepd.es/media/guias/guia-evaluaciones-de-impacto-rgpd.pdf. Accessed 12 July 2018
9. ISO/IEC 15504-4: Information technology – Process assessment – Part 4: Guidance on use for process improvement and process capability determination (2004)
10. ISO/IEC 330xx Information Technology - Process Assessment (2013, 2017)
11. ISO/IEC 33002: Information technology – Process assessment – Requirements for performing process assessment (2014)
12. Article 29 Data Protection Working Party. Statement 14/EN WP 218 on the role of a risk-based approach to data protection legal frameworks adopted on 30 May 2014. http://ec.europa.eu/justice/data-protection/article-29/documentation/opinion-recommendation/files/2014/wp218_en.pdf?wb48617274=72C54532
13. Article 29 Data Protection Working Party. Guidelines on Data Protection Impact Assessment (DPIA) and determining whether processing is "likely to result in a high risk" for the purposes of Regulation 2016/679. WP 248 rev.01 (2017)

14. Blume, P.: Data protection and privacy - basic concepts in a changing world. In: Scandinavian Studies in Law. ICT Legal Issues, vol. 56, pp. 151–164. Jure Law Books, Stockholm (2010)
15. McDermott, Y.: Conceptualizing the right to data protection in an era of big data. Big Data Soc. **4**(1), 1–7 (2017)
16. ISO Guide 73: Risk management – Vocabulary (2009)
17. Barafort, B., et al.: ITSM Process Assessment Supporting ITIL: Using TIPA to Assess and Improve your Processes with ISO 15504 and Prepare for ISO 20000 Certification, vol. 217. Van Haren, Zaltbommel (2009)
18. ISO/IEC 33020: Information technology – Process assessment – Process measurement framework for assessment of process capability (2015)
19. Barafort, B., Renault, A., Picard, M., Cortina, S.: A Transformation process for building PRMs and PAMs based on a collection of requirements – example with ISO/IEC 20000. In: 8th International SPICE 2008 Conference, Nuremberg (2008)

A Novel Model for Development Project Assessment in Automotive

Fabio Falcini and Giuseppe Lami(✉)

Consiglio Nazionale delle Ricerche, Istituto di Scienza e Tecnologie dell'Informazione, via Moruzzi 1, 56124 Pisa, Italy
{fabio.falcini,giuseppe.lami}@isti.cnr.it

Abstract. In the last two decades, automotive witnessed a continuous and unstoppable trend to innovation. Vehicles innovation is principally driven by electronics components and software that play today a predominant role for the vehicle's functions. Because the quality of on-board automotive electronic systems is strongly dependent on the quality of their development practices, car-makers and suppliers proactively focused on improvement of technical and organizational processes. In this setting, Automotive SPICE became a reference standard for the assessment and improvement of automotive electronics processes and projects. The effects of the application of Automotive SPICE in automotive industry have been substantially positive in terms of process awareness, possibility of benchmarking, development discipline, and incitement to improvement. Nevertheless, getting compliant in the short period to Automotive SPICE requirements may represent, in some contexts, a target hardly achievable, or even a chimera. In this paper we present a novel automotive-specific scheme for process evaluation and improvement. This scheme has been conceived taking into account the authors experience in automotive as Automotive SPICE principal assessors and it aims at setting up basic objectives in terms of process performance in terms of discipline, technical soundness and completeness in project deployment. The scheme is going to be validated by performing trials with real projects.

Keywords: Project evaluation · Process assessment and process improvement Adequacy

1 Introduction

Car OEMs (Original Equipment Manufacturer) are reshaping their vehicles from mechanical devices into elaborated digitally controlled systems. As a result, the software (with increasing demand in terms of size and complexity) is a crucial component since it is part of embedded systems called Electronic Control Units (ECU) that control electronically a large number of the vehicle functions. The number of ECUs, from economic to luxury vehicle models, is remarkably increased during the last fifteen/twenty years. Electronics is so pervasive in today's cars that almost all the main features and functionalities are controlled by software; not to mention the innovation driven by the deep-learning-based systems that are becoming pervasive in automobiles [8]. In this setting, the quality of on-board automotive electronic systems is strongly

I. Stamelos et al. (Eds.): SPICE 2018, CCIS 918, pp. 73–85, 2018.
https://doi.org/10.1007/978-3-030-00623-5_6

dependent on the quality of their development practices. Accordingly, car-makers and suppliers are proactively focusing on the improvement of technical and organizational processes.

To face and support such a tremendous trend towards innovation, several models and standards addressing both automotive system and software development are available for the automotive market. These models and standards have typically a strong focus on processes; among them the most relevant and influencing are Automotive SPICE [1] and ISO 26262 [4].

The application of such standards, in particular Automotive SPICE, produced undoubted positive effects on the automotive industry in the last years. Advancements have been achieved in terms process awareness, possibility of benchmarking, development discipline, and incitement to improvement [7].

Nevertheless, the specifics and the complexities reached by today's automotive software-intensive systems have shown that current models and standards have some limitations in responding to the needs of the automotive industry [5, 6]. In particular, the automotive players are in need of the following aspects: more focus on projects rather than a pure process-centered approach, improved technical guidance, and explicit links to already established automotive quality frameworks. Several initiatives and studies have been conducted with the aim of finding out solutions to such problems [9–11].

In this context, the authors have developed a novel scheme addressing both project evaluation and process improvement and targeting a hand-on approach for the practitioners. This scheme in called Process Improvement Scheme for Automotive (PISA Model).

The PISA Model is going to be applied in practice by means of trials on real projects with the aim of getting feedbacks and identifying improvement indications for the next releases.

In this paper we provide a description of the structure and the contents of the PISA Model and we provide a comparative analysis between Automotive SPICE and the PISA Model as well. This paper is structured as follows: in Sect. 2 the PISA Model purpose, structure, and contents are introduced. In Sect. 3 a comparison between the PISA Model and Automotive SPICE is provided. Finally, in Sect. 4 conclusions are provided.

2 Process Improvement Scheme for Automotive (PISA Model)

The purpose of the PISA (Process Improvement Scheme for Automotive) Model is to provide the automotive community with a quality model with innovative features that targets the specific needs of the automotive industry in the context of the development of electronic systems.

Explicitly, the peculiar needs for an effective quality model in the context of automotive electronics developments are:

- Ability to evaluate the project performance in the context of automotive in order to provide usable feedbacks on the project risk level;

– Ability to evaluate process capability in the context of automotive, as a means to identify risks associated to development processes.

The PISA model addresses both project evaluation and process improvement in a balanced fashion and targets a hand-on approach for the practitioners.

The PISA model, in the context of electronic automotive systems, addresses:

1. System-level development
2. Electronic and mechanics hardware-level development
3. Software level development.

The PISA Model fits the characteristics of automotive developments by incorporating automotive technical and procedural requirements as well as a more project-centered perspective into a standard process framework.

2.1 From Process Model to Process Improvement Scheme

Conceptually, the PISA Model can be defined as an automotive-specific "augmentation" of a process model, conceived to better serve the needs of automotive electronics developments.

Although it is generally accepted that the quality of a product depends on the quality of the underlying development process, more than a decade of field experience has definitely outlined some specific weaknesses in the existing process models applied in automotive to assess processes. These weaknesses can be summarized as:

1. schemes to evaluate automotive projects in automotive lack in comprehensiveness and pragmatism;
2. some process elements to be addressed to achieve compliance are indeed marginal and not worthwhile.

The PISA Model has been conceived with the aim of overtaking the previous weaknesses. Therefore processes belonging to the PISA Model have been defined to be synthetic and to embrace the whole product development lifecycle including development processes at system, hardware, software level.

The PISA Model allows the assessment of development projects with respect to a new quality characteristic: Adequacy.

A project is said being Adequate (i.e. fulfill the quality characteristic of Adequacy) when the project performance includes the deployment of a core set of technical and managerial practices and when state-of-the-art technology is used.

Adequacy has been defined in order to integrate the concepts of: process capability, organizational maturity and technological readiness. In the following, the way these concepts have been addressed in the definition of the quality characteristics of Adequacy is described:

1. Process capability: the achievement of project adequacy is based on the performance of a precise set of technical and managerial practices. Performing a predefined set of practices is the basis of the achievement of process capability (as, for instance, in the case of Automotive SPICE). The combination of the PISA Model-provided practices allows to define the processes and addresses their capability as well.

2. Organizational maturity is defined as "the extent to which an organizational unit consistently implements processes within a defined scope that contributes to the achievement of its business needs". It's about the derivation of a unique rating valid for the whole organization calculated starting from ratings of single processes. The approach of the PISA Model is the same. As it will be described later in this section, the adequacy characteristic is derived by combination of the ratings of single processes.
3. Technological readiness is a novel element in automotive process models. Technology is a key element to achieve high quality process and to improve them as well. The PISA Model address this element by including among the adequacy indicators a set of requirements addressing the use of state-of-the-art technology.

Figure 1 the adequacy project quality characteristic is represented as integration of Process Capability, Organizational Maturity, and Technological Readiness.

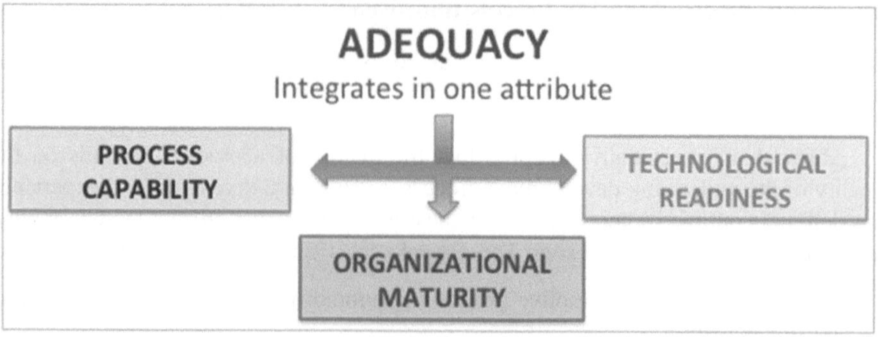

Fig. 1. Adequacy as an integration of process capability, organizational maturity and technological readiness.

In the following sub-sections the PISA Model is described by the three pillars it is composed of:

- Process Scope and Augmented Framework
- Process Structure and Requirements
- Evaluation and Rating System

2.2 Processes Scope and Augmented Framework

The PISA Model encompasses processes at technical and managerial levels that incorporate the backbone of a typical automotive project structure. The processes belonging to the PISA Model are twenty-two (22) in total (as shown in Fig. 2).

They are divided into five (5) Process Segments:

- Three (3) Technical Segments: System Engineering, Hardware Engineering, and Software Engineering
- Two (2) Coordination Segments: Management, and Sustenance.

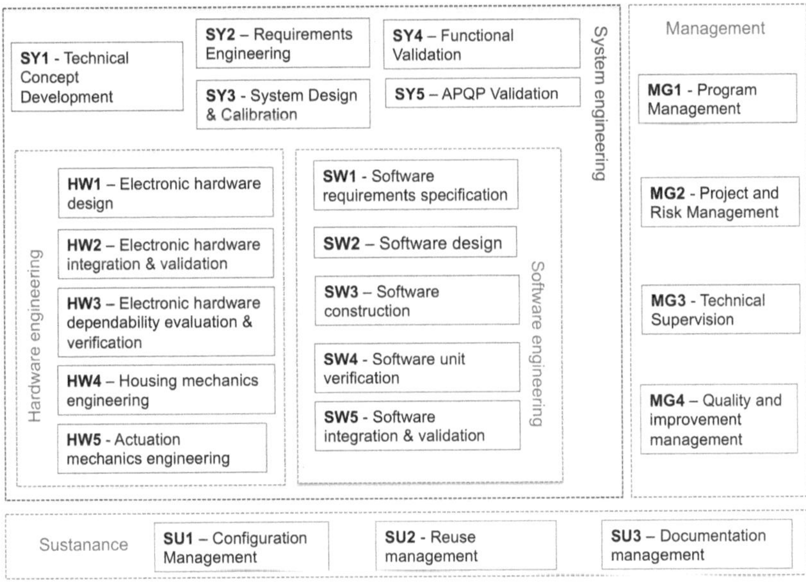

Fig. 2. PISA model processes.

In the following, the PISA Model processes are grouped by segment and shortly described.

System Engineering Segment processes address the product view – the processes belonging to this segment are described in Table 1:

Table 1. System engineering segment processes

Process Id. and Name	Pertinence
SY1 - Technical Concept Development	Early setup of the overall system architecture; this process acknowledges the fact that in the automotive market crucial design decisions are often taken during the commercial phases of the project
SY2 – Requirements Engineering	Definition, documentation and maintenance of requirements for development at system level
SY3 – System Design and Calibration	Definition of a detailed system design with strong focus on hardware-software interfaces and system calibration aspects. Such a level of design takes into account typical automotive design drivers such as “design for manufacturing”
SY4 – Functional Validation	Verification of the conformance of the developed system to its functional specification
SY5 – Advanced Product Quality Planning (APQP) Validation	Confirmation that the organization can produce products that meet customer requirements in a cost-effective and repeatable way

Hardware Engineering Segment processes address the product view – the processes belonging to this segment are described in Table 2:

Table 2. Hardware engineering segment processes

Process Id. and Name	Pertinence
HW1 – Electronic Hardware Design	Definition of electronics design, including the preparation of the physical layout
HW2 – Electronic Hardware Integration and Validation	Validation of electronic sub-system(s) from a functional and electrical point of views
HW3 – Electronic Hardware Verification and Dependability Evaluation	Performance of in-depth design verification as well as the performance of dependability analysis
HW4 – Housing Mechanics Engineering	Deployment of both the design and the verification of mechanical housing
HW5 – Actuation Mechanics Engineering	Deployment of both the design and the verification of actuation mechanical hardware

Software Engineering Segment processes address the product view – the processes belonging to this segment are described in Table 3:

Table 3. System engineering segment processes

Process Id. and Name	Pertinence
SW1 – Software Requirements Specification	Definition, documentation and maintenance of requirements for software development
SW2 – Software Design	Definition of the software architectural design following a multi-level and multi-perspective approach
SW3 – Software Construction	Deployment of consolidated best practices for the implementation of the software design
SW4- Software Units Verification	Deployment of verification activities to ensure correctness of software units. The robustness verification of software units is pivotal for this process
SW5 – Software Integration and Validation	Verification and validation of software sub-system(s) from a functional and performance point of views

Management Segment processes address the product view – the processes belonging to this segment are described in Table 4:

Table 4. Management segment processes

Process Id. and Name	Pertinence
MG1 – Program Management	High-level management of projects within the program umbrella and related customer interfacing
MG2 – Project and risk management	Management of projects according to automotive industry best practices
MG3 – Technical Supervision	Management of technical operative aspects of project activities
MG4 – Quality and Improvement Management	Assurance of the deployment of an adequate quality management. It also pertains the management of improvement initiatives

Sustenance Segment processes address the product view – the processes belonging to this segment are described in Table 5:

Table 5. Sustanance segment processes

Process Id. and Name	Pertinence
SU1 – Configuration Management	Deployment of configuration management at system, hardware and software levels
SU2 – Reuse Management	Management of the reuse of hardware and software elements
SU3 – Documentation Management	Deployment of a rigorous and lean documentation management

2.3 Process Structure and Requirements

The PISA Model process definition structure is composed of the following fields:

1. Process Name
2. Context of the Process: general information on the process and on its context of use.
3. Entry Criteria: pre-conditions that are expected to be satisfied when the process starts.
4. Input Work products
5. Requirements: definition of practices to be performed by the process. Each Process requirements is classified as High Priority or Low Priority.
6. Output Work Products and related content outline
7. Exit Criteria: conditions that are expected to be satisfied when the process ends.

The PISA model requirements are divided into three (3) categories:

a. Process Requirements
b. Governance Requirements
c. Technological Requirements

PISA Model requirements are prioritized in terms of impact on Adequacy evaluation. With this aim, requirements are classified as high-priority or low-priority.

2.4 Evaluation and Rating System

Evaluation and rating within the PISA Model is governed by the PISA Rating System (PISA-RS). The PISA-RS works according to a bottom-up approach. The following picture shows the conceptual path towards the project evaluation in terms of Adequacy.

As the Fig. 3. shows, the PISA-RS provides a step-wise, bottom-up mechanism to project evaluation that is based on process-specific sets of requirements belonging to three categories (process, governance, and technological).

Step 1: Compliance to process requirements. Compliance to all the requirements (Process, Governance, Technology) is verified starting from the analysis of related work products. Compliance is a binary property.

Step 2: Process rating. On the basis of the requirements compliance and their priority, the rating of each process in terms of Adequacy is determined.

Step 3: Segment rating. The weighted aggregation of process ratings determines the relevant process segment rating (segment rating level).

Step 4: Project rating. The combination of the process segments ratings determines the project rating in terms of Adequacy attribute.

In addition, a set of argumentations are provided in the PISA-RS on how to use the project-level Adequacy characteristic in the context of organizations benchmarking. These argumentations support the exploitation of the PISA Model to give a risk-based evaluation that is specifically referred to the involved organization (e.g. an ECU supplier).

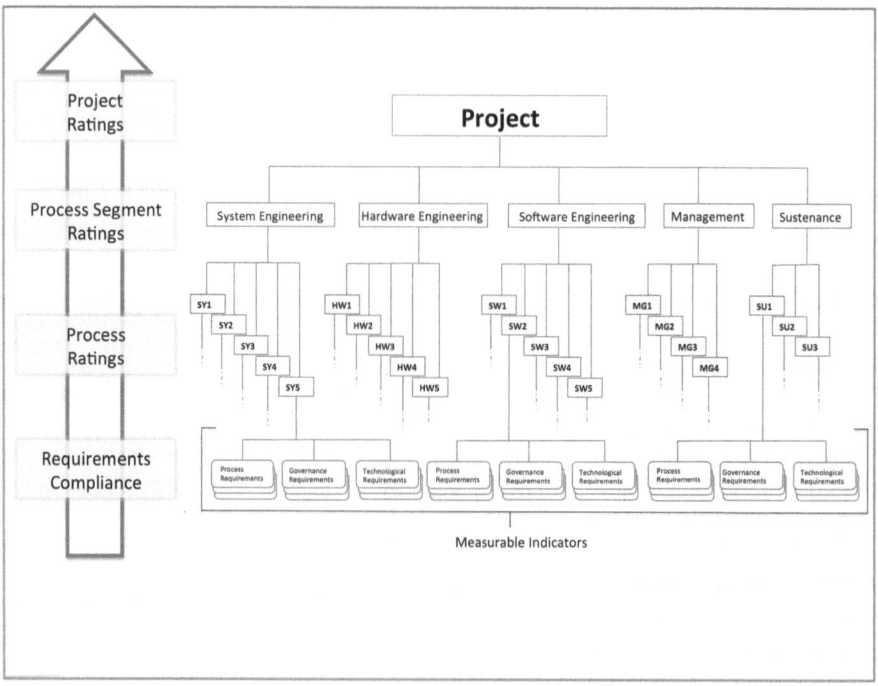

Fig. 3. PISA-RS Adequacy Rating Mechanism

Table 6 summarizes the rating attribute related to each element under evaluation at each step of the PISA-RS

Table 6. Hierarchy of PISA-RS attribute.

PISA Model Rating Level	Attribute
Project	Adequacy
Process Segment	
Process	
Requirement	Compliance

Table 7 describes the rating scale of the Adequacy attribute and associated semantics.

Table 7. Adequacy rating scale.

Adequacy attribute Rating Value	Meaning
Adequate	Project is run in a sound fashion and project objectives are not at risk Process improvement opportunities are limited in scope and criticality
Sufficient	Project is deployed satisfactorily and project objectives are largely not at risk Process improvement opportunities are present
Incomplete	Project is deployed nearly satisfactorily and project objectives are exposed to some noteworthy risk Significant Process improvement opportunities are present
Inadequate	Project objectives are at risk Process improvement opportunities are important and require immediate improvement action items

3 Comparison Between the PISA Model and Automotive SPICE

3.1 Introduction to Automotive SPICE

The Automotive SPICE standard - SPICE stands for Software Process Improvement and Capability dEtermination - provides a process framework that disciplines, at high level of abstraction, the software development activities and allows their capability assessment in matching pre-defined sets of numerous process requirements.

The focus on software capability determination by means of software process assessment has determined a common trend among the European Car Makers in using Automotive SPICE as a mean for determining a supplier's qualification mechanism.

Nowadays Automotive SPICE, as a *de-facto* process assessment and improvement standard, is used by OEMs to push software process improvement among their ECU (Electronic Control Unit) and software suppliers [2, 3]. Many of the OEMs are using also this standard to assess supplier capabilities and are requiring the achievement of specific rating. Thus it provides both a scheme for evaluating the capability of software processes and a path for their improvement. In extreme synthesis the four basic pillars of Automotive SPICE are: Process Reference Model (PRM) [1], Process Assessment Model (PAM) [1], Measurement Framework and Assessment Scope. For the first three concepts we refer to the bibliography. The Assessment Scope is a subset of the processes contained in Automotive SPICE PRM, where each process is associated with a target process capability level. The result of an Automotive SPICE assessment consists of the assignment of a rating to each single process in the assessment scope. In particular, the Hersteller Initiative Software (HIS) Scope is a subset of the processes contained in Automotive SPICE, which will be assessed by each manufacturer at least at Capability Level 2 [2]. The HIS Scope of the Automotive SPICE is the reference scope used by automotive OEMs for the qualification of suppliers of software-intensive car components. In Table 8 the whole Automotive SPICE PRM is presented, the processes in bold are those belonging to the HIS assessment scope. The HIS scope requires to assess those processes at least at capability level 2.

From Table 8 it results that processes in Automotive SPICE are conveniently grouped and large in number. The rational behind the HIS scope is to limit the impact on the practitioners by selecting the core of the engineering processes and only few additional fundamental processes.

Table 8. Automotive SPICE process reference model

Id.	Process Name	Id.	Process Name
ACQ.3	Contract agreement	**SUP.8**	**Configuration management**
ACQ.4	**Supplier monitoring**	**SUP.9**	**Problem resolution management**
ACQ.11	Technical requirements	**SUP.10**	**Change request management**
ACQ.12	Legal and administrative requirements	PIM.3	Process improvement
ACQ.13	Project requirements	SYS.1	Requirement elicitation
ACQ.14	Request for proposals	**SYS.2**	**System requirements analysis**
ACQ.15	Supplier qualification	**SYS.3**	**System architectural design**
MAN.3	**Project management**	**SYS.4**	**System integration & integration test**
MAN.5	Risk management	**SYS.5**	**System qualification testing**
MAN.6	Measurement	**SWE.1**	**SW requirements analysis**
SPL.1	Supplier tendering	**SWE.2**	**SW architectural design**
SPL.2	**Product Release**	**SWE.3**	**SW detailed design & unit construction**
SUP.1	**Quality Assurance**	**SWE.4**	**SW unit verification**
SUP.2	Verification	**SWE.5**	**SW integration & integration test**
SUP.4	Joint Review	**SWE.6**	**Software qualification test**
SUP.7	Documentation	REU.2	Reuse program management

3.2 PISA Model vs. Automotive SPICE

In this section a high-level comparison between the PISA Model and Automotive SPICE is provided. The comparison is focused on the following aspects of the two models:

- Scope
- Object of evaluation
- Amount of process indicators to address

Scope: The Scope of PISA Model is definite by 22 processes grouped into 5 process segments as shown in Sect. 2.2. The PISA Model application requires to take into account the whole set of processes. The only admitted derogations are those related to the scope of the project the PISA Model is applied to. In practice, some process segments or single processes can be avoided in the case the project doesn't include the related activities (e.g. if a project aims just at developing software, Hardware Engineering Segment shall be avoided).

In practice, the scope of Automotive SPICE is basically focused on a subset of the PRM processes (i.e. the processes belonging to the HIS scope). These processes don't address hardware engineering and part of the system engineering activities.

Object of evaluation: The PISA Model has been developed according to a flat approach. The compliance to the PISA Model is determined on the basis of the fulfillment of its requirements (that are classified as Process, Governance, and Technological requirements). The PISA Model rating mechanism guarantees the determination of the rating, in terms of Adequacy, for the project under evaluation (as described in Sect. 2.4). So, the PISA model provide the all the means to assign a quantitative rating to a project.

Originally, Automotive SPICE has been conceived as a model for the determination of the capability of processes. Consequently, several process instances (i.e. projects) were necessary to determine the capability rating of a process. Only after a long debate in the Automotive SPICE community, Automotive SPICE has been accepted as a mechanism to determine the capability of a single project as well. Anyway the Automotive SPICE capability rating is still affected by its original orientation to single process capability assessment. This is the reason why the HIS scope has been defined and it is used in practice: the HIS scope is an attempt to provide a unique rating for qualify an organizational process or a single project.

Amount of indicators/requirements to address: The PISA Model contains a definite set of requirements: the requirements of the PISA Model are in total 156. This includes 115 high priority requirements and 41 low-priority requirements. Each PISA Model requirements is process-specific, and a detailed description and explanation are included in the model itself. In particular, for each requirement the following information is provided:

- Requirement Id.
- Requirement name
- Clause (the requirement specification)

- Elaborations (information and data useful to understand, contextualize, and verify the requirements)
- Tips (practical suggestions for an effective and practical implementation of the requirement)
- Tailoring criteria (information and indication on how to face and interpret the requirements in specific contexts)
- Notes (any other relevant information)

In Automotive SPICE the amount of process indicators to be rated depends on the scope (i.e. the set of processes to assess and the target capability level). In addition, the process indicators for the determination of Capability Level 2 or higher, are expressed in a generic way (in fact, they are called Generic Practices) and consequently they need to be instantiated for any specific process they are applied to. Such an instantiation may not be easy because the difficulty to apply the same generic practice to engineering, management and support activities. If we limit to the processes belonging to the HIS scope, with Capability Level 2 as target, the amount of indicators to rate are: 303. This includes 127 Base Practices for Capability Level 1, and 11 Generic Practices for each process in the scope.

4 Conclusions and On-going Activities

In this paper we presented the PISA (Process Improvement Schema for Automotive) Model, a novel model aimed at providing the automotive community with a quality model with innovative features that targets the specific needs of the automotive industry in the context of the development of electronic systems.

The authors, on the basis of their wide experience in automotive, recognized that the existing and schemes used in automotive to assess and improve the development of electronic components for automobiles present some weaknesses and their application is not always respondent to players demands. The PISA Model has been conceived with the aim of overtaking such lacks. Therefore, processes belonging to the PISA Model have been defined to be synthetic and to embrace the whole product development lifecycle including development processes at system, hardware, software level.

The PISA Model allows the assessment of development projects with respect to a new quality characteristic: Adequacy.

A project is said being adequate (i.e. fulfill the quality characteristic of adequacy) when the project performance includes the deployment of a core set of technical and managerial practices and when state-of-the-art technology is used.

A preliminary comparison between the PISA Model and Automotive SPICE shows that the first is more simple and more comprehensive because it includes also processes addressing hardware design, implementation, and validation. Moreover the assessment of projects according to the PISA Model is more objective because it requires to verify only process-specific requirements, each of them is described in detail.

The PISA Model is going to be applied on real projects in order to get feedbacks on its suitability for the intended use. With this aim, we planned and we are performing a trials campaign with the following purposes:

- Evaluate the ease of use, the completeness and the correctness of the PISA Model;
- Assess the capability of the PISA Model to serve as a driver for improvement;
- Assure its alignment with the State of the Art and Practice
- Spreading the knowledge of the PISA Model in the automotive community;
- Study possible relationships and dependencies with other automotive-relevant standards.

The trials we are carrying out on real projects will provide feedbacks to evaluate the responsiveness of the PISA Model and, possibly, undertaking some changes.

To do that we are cooperating with leading organizations and companies located in Asia. Results and analysis of the trials will be published as they will be available.

References

1. VDA QMC Working Group 13/Automotive SIG: Automotive SPICE Process Assessment/Reference Model, ver. 3.1, Verband der Automobil industrie (2017). http://www.automotivespice.com/fileadmin/software-download/AutomotiveSPICE_PAM_31.pdf
2. Hoermann, K., Mueller, M., Dittman, L., Zimmer, J.: Automotive SPICE in Practice: Surviving Implementation and Assessment. Rocky Nook, San Rafael (2008). ISBN 978-1933952291
3. Fabbrini, F., Fusani, M., Lami, G., Sivera, E.: A SPICE-based supplier qualification mechanism in automotive industry. Soft. Process Improv. Pract. J. **12**, 523–528 (2007)
4. ISO 26262: - Road Vehicles - Functional Safety, International Organization for Standardization (2011)
5. Niazi, M., Wilson, D., Zowghi, D.: Critical success factors for software improvement implementation: an empirical study. Softw. Process Improv. Pract. **11**, 193–211 (2006)
6. Niazi, M., Ali Babar, M., Verner, J.M.: Software process improvement barriers: a cross-cultural comparison. Inf. Softw. Technol. **52**(2010), 1204–1216 (2010)
7. Fabbrini, F., Fusani, M., Lami, G., Sivera, E.: Software engineering in the European automotive industry: achievements and challenges. In: COMPSAC, pp. 1039–1044. IEEE Computer Society (2008)
8. Falcini, F., Lami, G., Costanza, A.M.: Deep learning in automotive software. IEEE Softw. **34**(3), 56–63 (2017)
9. Kreiner, C., et al.: Automotive knowledge alliance AQUA – integrating automotive SPICE, Six Sigma, and functional safety. In: McCaffery, F., O'Connor, Rory V., Messnarz, R. (eds.) EuroSPI 2013. CCIS, vol. 364, pp. 333–344. Springer, Heidelberg (2013). https://doi.org/10.1007/978-3-642-39179-8_30
10. Lami, G., Falcini, F.: Is ISO/IEC 15504 applicable to agile methods? In: Abrahamsson, P., Marchesi, M., Maurer, F. (eds.) XP 2009. LNBIP, vol. 31, pp. 130–135. Springer, Heidelberg (2009). https://doi.org/10.1007/978-3-642-01853-4_16
11. Johannessen, P., Halonen, Ö., Örsmark, O.: Functional safety extensions to automotive SPICE according to ISO 26262. In: O'Connor, R.V., Rout, T., McCaffery, F., Dorling, A. (eds.) SPICE 2011. CCIS, vol. 155, pp. 52–63. Springer, Heidelberg (2011). https://doi.org/10.1007/978-3-642-21233-8_5

SPI Methods and Reference Models

Evolving PRO2PI Methodology Considering Recent Challenges and Changes in the SPI Context

Clenio F. Salviano(✉)

CTI: Centro de Tecnologia da Informação Renato Archer,
Rodovia D. Pedro I, km 143.6, Campinas, SP 13069-90, Brazil
Clenio.Salviano@cti.gov.br, Clenio.Salviano@gmail.com

Abstract. The requirements for process measurement frameworks defined in ISO/IEC 33003 introduced relevance challenges and changes in Software Process Improvement (SPI) research and practical context. In addition, other five challenges and changes are identified. They are having specific practices for capability evolution, doing SPI with agility and more, having reference models for innovation, doing SPI education, and the need of a theory of SPI. Hence, comprehensive methodologies for SPI should be analyzed and evolved to consider this new SPI context. PRO2PI Methodology (Process Capability/Modeling Profile for Process Improvement), as an example of a methodology for SPI, is analyzed in face of its current utilization and how it stands in terms of these identified recent challenges and changes in SPI context. Then the design of PRO2PI evolution to consider this new SPI context is commented.

Keywords: Software Process Improvement · ISO/IEC 330xx
Process measurement framework · PRO2PI Methodology

1 Introduction

Software Process Improvement (SPI) has contributed significantly to the improvement of development and other activities related to software. Consequently, new concepts and technologies are eventually consolidated to challenge and expand SPI and impact its practical and research context. The publication of the ISO/IEC 15504 standard set in the early 2000s, for example, caused this impact and expanded SPI by consolidating concepts, requirements and examples of reference models and process assessments methods.

Recently, the requirements for process measurement frameworks defined in ISO/IEC 33003 [3] introduced relevance challenges and changes in SPI research and practical context. ISO/IEC 33003 states that a "process measurement framework shall identify and address a single process quality characteristic, which shall be defined on the basis of a multidimensional construct and as a set of process attributes" [3]. Before the publication of the first set of ISO/IEC 330xx family of standards [1–5], SPI was strongly tied with process capability. Therefore reference models, assessment methods, and improvements methods for SPI are tied with process capability concept. Process

I. Stamelos et al. (Eds.): SPICE 2018, CCIS 918, pp. 89–103, 2018.
https://doi.org/10.1007/978-3-030-00623-5_7

measurement frameworks, based on process quality characteristics other than process capability, such as, for example, safety, agility, and systems thinking, expand SPI to broaden its application.

In addition, distinct process practices of generic profile group for Very Small Entities (VSE) from ISO/IEC 29110 [6, 7] and distinct specific practices for each capability level of each practice area in the recent version of CMMI (CMMI Development V2.0) [8], to characterize process evolution towards capability, instead of generic capability practices, also caused challenges and changes in SPI context. There are additional challenges and changes in the SPI context that are identified later in this article.

Hence, comprehensive methodologies for SPI, such as, for example, PRO2PI Methodology (Process Capability/Modeling Profile for Process Improvement) [9–12], should be analyzed and evolved to consider this challenging new SPI context. Such analyses and evolution are relevant SPI research and practical theme.

Therefore, the main objective of the research presented in this article is to analyze PRO2PI Methodology in face of these recent challenges and changes in SPI context and then design PRO2PI evolution to guide better process improvement in this context. To guide the achievement of this objective, it is decomposed into four guided-oriented sub-objectives:

(a) Identify recent challenges and changes in SPI research and practical context;
(b) Describe current utilization of PRO2PI;
(c) Analyze PRO2PI in face of its current utilization and identified recent challenges and changes in SPI context; and
(d) Design PRO2PI evolutions to consider those recent challenges and changes in SPI context.

The meaning of SPI needs some considerations. First, the term software in SPI is used here for historical reasons. It actually means a broader scope, including systems, services and others. Actually, SPI should be knowledge working process improvement, including software, systems, services and other processes. There is a shift to knowledge working intense organizations, as identified by Peter Drucker [13]. What has been done for software process, including SPI, can be used for knowledge working processes. Second, although ISO/IEC 330xx Family of Standards, and its previous versions as ISO/IEC 15504 Set of Standards [14, 15] are international standards of process assessment, they have been causing an impact in SPI as well. Therefore they should be considered as reference for SPI. ISO/IEC TR 33014:2013 [16], for example, provides a guide for process improvement. Therefore SPI is considered here as knowledge working process improvement, which includes assessment based process improvement on software process.

Following the four guided-oriented sub-objectives defined, this article is structured into six sections. This first section is an introduction. Second section presents the history and current version of PRO2PI Methodology. Third section introduces two recent utilization of PRO2PI. Fourth section presents six identified recent challenges and changes in SPI research and practical context, and comments on their impact on PRO2PI Methodology evolution. Finally, fifth section presents some conclusions.

2 PRO2PI Methodology

PRO2PI is an innovative process improvement methodology. It evolves current model based SPI towards a modeling driven SPI. PRO2PI development began in 2002 based on my experience in process improvement with ISO/IEC 15504-5 Process Assessment Model [9, 10]. The motivation for improvement was the techniques to choose the processes to be used in each improvement cycle in each company. The processes chosen for improvement and their respective current and intended capability levels formed the Process Capability Profile for Process Improvement. A profile was chosen in each company based on the analysis of its characteristics, problems and objectives. A profile is validated in terms of the degrees of attendance to eight properties (quality characteristics): relevant, feasible, opportunistic, systemic, representative, traceable, specific, and dynamic.

The PRO2PI Methodology has been conceived in many cycles of exploration, application and consolidation following the industry-as-laboratory approach proposed by Potts [17]. Potts argues that the traditional research-then-transfer approach has problems because it treats research and its application by industry as separate, sequential activities. In the proposed research approach, there is stronger connection at start because knowledge of problem is acquired from practitioners in industry.

During these cycles, we identified two other types of profiles that, in addition to Process Capability Profile, also drive a process improvement cycle. We named them Process Enactment Description and Process Performance Indicator. A Process Enactment Description is structured with life cycle, roles, activities and artifacts. A Process Performance Indicator model is structured with information needs, information product, indicator and measures.

These three types of profiles were identified using a modeling view of SPI [18]. They are actually different models of the process. During a cycle of SPI, these three types of process models should drive the process improvement (Fig. 1).

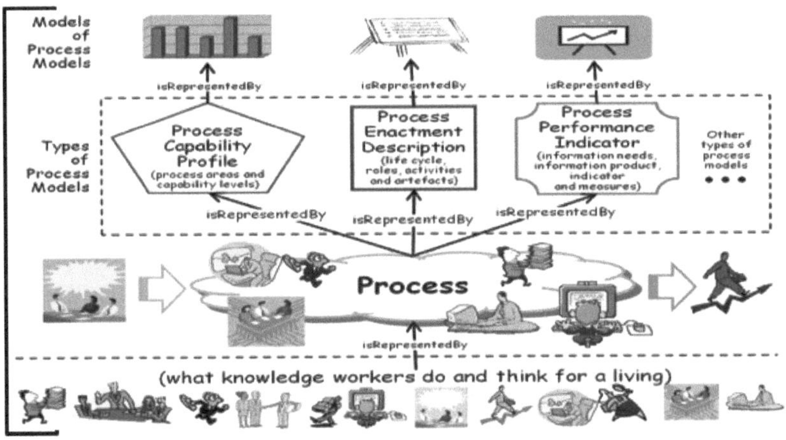

Fig. 1. Process as a model and types of process models for SPI [18]

In a previous article [18], I presented a modeling view of SPI. First I presented a set of related concepts from Bézivin [29], Favre [28] and other authors [30], including concepts of model, its three elements (system, intended goal and aspects), how it follows the Limited Substitutability Principle, metamodel (as a model of a language of models, rather than a model of a model), how a model is used as a specification model or as a descriptive model and theirs co-evolution, modeling and chain of models. Then I concluded "modeling is essential to software process improvement, because every human action is preceded by the construct (implicit or explicit) of chains of specification and descriptive models".

Then I proposed chains of models to represent process and three most relevant types of process models for SPI: Process Capability Profile, Process Enactment Description and Process Performance Indicator. The relationship between a model and a system is "isRepresentedBy". After this modeling view, the methodology evolved from "Process Capability Profile" to "Process Modeling Profile".

PRO2PI is named as a methodology in the meaning of methodology used by Schreiber and Akkermans [19] in Knowledge Engineering. A methodology is a sequence of feedbacks cycles (as a pyramid) with a worldview based on a set of principles that form the baseline of a methodology. This worldview is grounded in theories that provide the essential concepts for establishing the methodology. The methods and tools provide the key to enable the practical application of the methodology. The use of this methodology produces feedback that feeds the other "layers" of the pyramid and enables the evolution of the methodology.

PRO2PI Methodology has been developed with five major methodological components (Fig. 2). A definition phrase, initials and "label name" identify each methodological component of PRO2PI. The "label name" is a name of a Brazilian music album with a cover that resembles in a specific manner the component. The methodology diagram in Fig. 2 also has a "label name", in this case, "*Maritmo*".

The five methodological components are:

(a) Process Modeling Profile Metamodel (PRO2PI-MMOD, MMOD or *Geraes*): A metamodel of different architectures of good practices reference models to allow that elements from them could be used in a Process Modeling Profile to guide an SPI Cycle. Currently, there is a metamodel for Process Capability Profile. This metamodel defines a consensual agreement on how elements of a process should be selected to produce a given PRO2PI as a model of a process.

(b) Process Modeling Profile Quality Model (PRO2PI-QMOD, QMOD or *Passarin*): A quality model of a Process Modeling Profile. This model is used to verify the quality of PRO2PI to guide an improvement cycle. Currently there is a quality model for Process Capability Profile.

(c) Method Framework for Engineering Models (PRO2PI-MFMOD, MFMOD or *Livro*): A method framework to develop a reference model based on context and characteristics of a segment or domain.

(d) Method for Process Improvement Cycle (PRO2PI-CYCLE, CYCLE or *Uakti*): A method to guide a process improvement cycle driven by a dynamic PRO2PI. This method includes a function to define, update and use a PRO2PI. It also defines six phases. The first phase Prepare for improvement cycle starts after a decision and

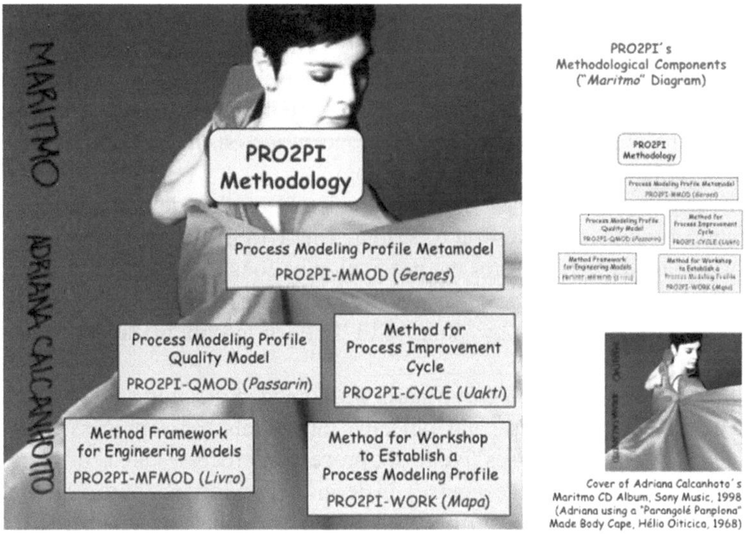

Fig. 2. Methodological Components of PRO2PI Methodology [18]

commitment for improvement. The second phase is Establish improvement references. The third phase is Prepare for improvement actions. The fourth phase is Implement improvement actions. The fifth phase is Prepare improvement institutionalization. The sixth phase is Institutionalize improvements.

(e) Method for Workshop to establish a Process Modeling Profile (PRO2PI-WORK, WORK or *Mapa*): A method to guide the implementation of the first four phases of PRO2PI-CYCLE in a VSE. This method has been developed to be used in the first phases of traditional process improvement cycle or PRO2PI-CYCLE cycle.

Recently, a new methodological component has been added. With the increase in its use and the importance of education of SPI, PRO2PI-WORK4E (and its evaluation model) consolidated as the sixth element. PRO2PI-WORK4E ("for (*four* **4**) **E**ducation") (or simply WORK4E) is a customized version of PRO2PI-WORK method to teach SPI. Both WORK and WORK4E guide the first phases of an SPI cycle and the learning process of SPI. While WORK focuses on starting an SPI cycle with learning SPI ("doing SPI with learning SPI"), WORK4E focuses on learning SPI by starting an SPI cycle ("learning SPI by doing SPI") [20].

3 Recent Use of PRO2PI: WORK4E and CERTICS

In the last four years, from April 2014 to May 2018, I have been working with PRO2PI methodology in two components. First, I am reviewing, using and evaluate WORK4E. Second, I am using MFMOD for the development and evolution of CERTICS Reference Model as a model for innovation in software.

Recently, in 2016, 2017 and 2018, WORK4E has been used in three editions of a course to introduce SPI. An evaluation of 2017 edition was performed with a specific evaluation model [20]. Here, I presented an analysis of the results from last three editions [2016–2018] in terms of the PRO2PI Methodology. Such analyses are not described in the previous article. Here we concentrate on the SPI cycle developed by the students in terms of PRO2PI Methodology.

The courses are for professionals, working in IT, with a degree in IT related area. The duration is short, around 40 h, distributed in 1 to 2 months. The method guides courses where the possibilities for the production or construction of SPI knowledge are created with the development of a proposal for an SPI cycle in the professional's work environment ("learning SPI by doing SPI"). Each group of students develops a proposal.

The key activity from each group starts with the identification and description of an Organizational Unit, problems and objective and goals for a process improvement cycle. Then each group analyses five to six processes, processes areas or practice areas (named as process area in the course) in terms of importance and risk. Then they estimate process capability level of each one. Finally, each group selects two process areas to be the PRO2PI.

Figure 3 presents a representation of each process area presented, with its identification, name and source reference model, and a version of the choices of two of them by each group to be a PRO2PI. These choices were in 2016, 2017 and 2018 editions of an introduction to SPI course with PRO2PI-WORK4E. Each line connecting two process areas indicates them as process areas chosen to be a PRO2PI.

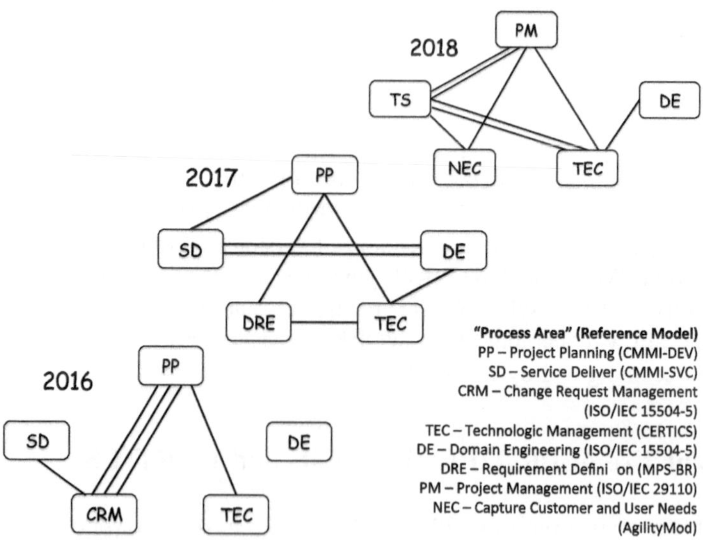

Fig. 3. Twenty PRO2PI with two process areas each

In 2016 edition, five processes area were presented: PP, SD, CRM, TEC and DE. There were five groups. Three groups chose PP and CRM as the process area and process to be a PRO2PI. Other group chose SD and CRM. Another group chose PP and TEC. In 2017 edition, five processes area were presented: PP, SD, DRE, TEC and DE. So, for this edition, DRE process area replaced CRM. There were seven groups. Two of them chose SD and DE. The other five groups chose PP and SD; PP and DRE; PP and TEC; and DRE and TEC. In 2018 edition, five processes area were presented: PM, TS, NEC, TEC and DE. So, for this edition, PM, TS and NEC replaced PP, SD and DRE. There were eight groups. Two groups chose PM and TS. Other two groups chose PM and TEC. The other four groups chose PM and NEC; PM and TEC; TS and NEC; and TEC and DE.

As there were a diversity of characteristics of the twenty Organizational Units and also a diversity of their problems and improvement objectives and goals, a diversity of selected pairs of process areas were expected. This diversity was achieved. In general, the argument, expressed in each one of the twenty proposals for improvement, for choosing the pair of areas was considered satisfactory and consistent with the Organizational Unit, its problems and its improvement objective and goals.

The other recent utilization of PRO2PI is related with the CERTICS Model. The Brazilian Government established a public policy instrument to identify and stimulate software production resulting from technology development and innovation carried out in Brazil. In order to accomplish this effort, CERTICS software process assessment methodology was created and established in Brazil. CERTICS was developed using PRO2PI-MFMOD. Its construction has been based on the reality of local software development organizations, in effort to achieve consensus within the community of interest, and guided by methodological references including the ISO/IEC 15504 (SPICE) Standard. CERTICS Methodology includes an Assessment Reference Model and an Assessment Method [21].

CERTICS Assessment Reference Model is a model for innovation and defines four competence areas (following the concept of process of a Process Assessment Model – PAM) named as Technological Development (DES), Technological Management (TEC), Business Management (GNE) and Continuous Improvement (MEC). Each Competence Area involves, with different emphases, aspects of both technological and correlated competencies. Each Competence Area is characterized by a key question, followed by a brief description and a set of Outcomes. Each Competence Area is achieved if their outcomes are achieved.

CERTICS Assessment Reference Model defines only capability level 1 for each competence area, and maturity level 1 with the four competence areas as the Basic Process Set with no additional elements. CERTICS Assessment Reference Model is compliant with ISO/IEC 15504 Requirements for Process Reference Models, Process Assessment Models and Organizational Maturity Models [21].

CERTICS was developed to be used for certification. Therefore it defines only maturity level 1. In order to be used as improvement model and to facilitate its usage with other models, three evolutions are performed, using parts of PRO2PI-MFMOD. First, we knew that the granularity was too high, compared with other models. So, instead of relate an area as a process, we relate each area as a group and then an outcome of an area as a process. Each relevant element of a CERTICS outcome became an outcome. Second, we rewrote sentences from passive to active voice. Finally we included the capability dimensions, for levels 2 and 3, following ISO/IEC 33020. A prototype version has been developed and used in two editions of a CERTICS Process Assessment course. This prototype version is named CERTICS-SAE Process Assessment Model. SAE stands for Simplified, Adapted and Extended. It is simplified because it is composed of only five of sixteen processes (identified by DES.1, TEC.1, TEC.3, GNE.3 and MEC.1) of the Model (PRM), which are detailed with Basic Practices, and four Capability Levels (0, 1, 2 and 3), of which three are detailed with Process Attributes (Table 1).

Table 1. Summary of the CERTICS-SAE process assessment model

Processes and Basic Practices [BP]	Capability Levels and Process Attributes
DES.1 Architecture Competence	Level 0 - Incomplete
DES.1 [BP1] Maintain Architecture Information	Level 1 - Performed
DES.1 [BP2] Design or Upgrade the Architecture	PA1.1: Process Execution
DES.1 [BP3] Link to Architecture Professionals	Level 2 - Managed
DES.1 [BP4] Residency of Architecture Professionals	PA2.1: Management of Execution
TEC.1 Use of Technological R & D Results	PA2.2: Product Management
TEC.1 [BP1] Technological Motivation or Uncertainty	Level 3 - Established
TEC.1 [BP2] R&D Results	PA3.1: Process Definition
TEC.1 [BP3] Use of R&D Results	PA3.2: Process Usage
TEC.3. Introduction of Technological Innovations	
TEC.3 [BP1] Innovative Culture	
TEC.3 [BP2] Technological Innovations	
TEC.3 [BP3] Confirmation of Technological Innovation	
GNE.3 Evolution of the Software Related Business	
GNE.3 [BP1] Strategy for Technological Evolution	
GNE.3 [BP2] Strategy for Business Evolution	
GNE.3 [BP3] Breakdowns and Results	
MEC.1 Management of Qualified Professionals	
MEC.1 [BP1] Management of Professionals	
MEC.1 [BP2] Professional Training	
MEC.1 [BP3] Incentive to Professionals	

CERTICS-SAE was used in two editions of two classes on process assessment model and process assessment, in 2016 and 2017. In those classes, the original CERTICS and the CERTICS-SAE models were presented. CERTICS-SAE was presented as an example of model which a typical structure. Process assessment was presented and exercised in practical cases with CERTICS-SAE.

4 Recent Changes in the SPI Context and PRO2PI Methodology

In my view, there are six recent challenges and changes in SPI research and practical context more relevant for a process improvement methodology such as PRO2PI. As recent, I mean the last four years, from May 2014 to June 2018. Two of them are more related with structure based on new concepts. They are already mentioned in the introduction of this article. We can name them as Other Process Quality Characteristic and as Specific Practices for Capability Evolution. Other three of them are more related to the practical side. We can name them as SPI with Agility, Models for Innovation and SPI Education. Finally, there is one of them more related with the need of a theory. We can name it as Theory of SPI.

Other Process Quality Characteristic comes from the recent revision of ISO/IEC 15504 as the ISO/IEC 330xx family of Standards. It defines the requirements for process measurement frameworks other than capability. ISO/IEC 33003 [3] defines requirements for process measurement frameworks. Up to that, SPI was strongly related with only process capability.

SPI has been based on the underlying process management premise, "the quality of a system or product is highly influenced by the quality of the process used to develop and maintain it" [9, 10]. A second premise is based on process capability and organizational capability maturity. Process capability is "a characterization of the ability of a process to meet current or projected business goals" [12]. Organizational capability maturity is "the extent to which an organization has explicitly and consistently deployed processes that are documented, managed, measured, controlled, and continually improved" [10]. This is the definition of organizational maturity. As the model is capability maturity and the concept of capability is already assumed, I understand that the word capability is implicit in that definition. It is well recognized that those premises are based on the principles of statistical quality control by Shewhart, refined by Deming, Crosby and Juran, and applied to software by Humphrey, Radice and others.

With Process Measurement Framework, SPI is no longer necessarily related with process capability. Process capability is now a possible Process Measurement Framework. ISO/IEC 33003 mentions process capability, process security, process agility and process safety, as examples of Process Measurement Framework. ISO/IEC 33020 defines a process measurement framework for the assessment of process capability, conformant with the requirements of ISO/IEC 33003. Within this process measurement framework, the measure of capability is based upon a set of process attributes. Each process attribute defines a measurable property of process capability.

In order to consider Other Process Quality Characteristic, PRO2PI Methodology has already a starting direction: The modeling view of SPI with three types of profiles. Using this starting direction, there is a need to review two components: MMOD and MFMOD. Currently, MFMOD has only a version of a metamodel for Process Capability Profile. This metamodel needs to model the definition and utilization of different process measurement framework instead of having only the process capability metamodel, as it is now. The MFMOD needs to include orientation do define or choose a process measurement frameworks to be used in a reference model, instead of using only process capability framework, as it is now.

Specific Practices for Capability Evolution means the way two most recent versions of relevant reference models define the evolution of processes. As already mentions, they are the distinct process practices of generic profile group for Very Small Entities (VSE) from ISO/IEC 29110 [6, 7] and distinct practices for each capability level of each practice area in the recent version of CMMI (CMMI Development V2.0) [8], to characterize process evolution towards capability, instead of generic capability practices, as in previous versions of CMMI and in ISO/IEC 15504. ISO/IEC 330xx expects generic practice for a measurement framework.

In order to consider Specific Practices for Capability Evolution, PRO2PI Methodology needs to review two components: MMOD and MFMOD. Currently, MMOD model specific practices for each process and the utilization of generic practices for measurement levels [25]. MMOD needs to be changed to combine both possibilities: specific or generic practices for measurement levels. The MFMOD needs to include orientation do define or choose a combination of specific or generic practices for measurement framework for a reference model.

SPI with Agility is about integrating agility, lean and other in SPI. Agility has been around since the launching of the manifesto for agile software development in 2001. So the term agility is used here as expressed in this manifesto. The manifesto proposed four agile values (individuals and interactions, working software, customer collaboration and responding to change) over traditional correspondent ones, considered more associated with SPI (processes and tools, comprehensive documentation, contract negotiation and following a plan). The signatories of the manifesto declared that while there is value in these traditional items, they value more the agile items. At that time, agile manifesto was an alternative to SPI.

Since then, we have seen practical success and broad dissemination of agility, continuity of practical success and even broader dissemination of SPI and many practical applications of integrated agile and SPI. Then, there have been efforts to understand this integration. In a CMU/SEI technical report [33], the authors claim that although agile development methods and CMMI best practices are often perceived to be at odds with each other, there are benefits from using both. They propose that CMMI and Agile champions work together. The recent version of CMMI (CMMI Development V2.0) declares a further integration with agile

There is no need to a significant additional revision of PRO2PI Methodology in order to consider SPI with Agility. A recent article by Kuhrmann et al. [22] supports SPI with Agility. They present the results of a combined Systematic Literature Review and Systematic Mapping Study (SLR/SMS) on SPI. The objectives were to capture the domain of SPI, to provide a snapshot of the available publication pool, and to investigate research trends. 18,686 publications were identified from 1989 to 2015. They selected and analyzed 769 publications.

Among the results, they classified the 769 publications in terms of categories of research type, contribution type and main focus. They identified four research trends in SPI. These research trends and the number and percentage of articles, based on the main focus of each one, are: New or customized SPI models (295) (38%), SPI success factors (126) (16.4%), SPI for SMEs (116) (15.1%) and SPI and agility (73) (9.5%).

In a recent analysis, sixteen maturity models related to Research, Development and Innovation were identified over a period of sixteen years [2002–2017] [23]. There are two models in the first four-year period [2002–2005], three models in the period [2006–2009], four in [2010–2013] and finally seven models in the last period [2014–2017]. This significant increase of number of models in the last period, and the fact that most of them are for innovation, indicates the increasing relevance of this theme (Models for Innovation).

There is no need to significant additional revision of PRO2PI Methodology in order to consider Models for Innovation, as demonstrated with how it was used to develop CERTICS and CERTICS-SAE models.

SPI Education means the challenging effort of education of Software Process Improvement. A recent international workshop, for example, focused on the new challenges for and best practices in software process education, training and professionalism [32]. In this workshop, all articles mention this challenging effort. One of them, for example, a systematic mapping study on SPI education concludes: "in spite of its [SPI] importance, increasing its coverage in educational settings is still challenging" [32, pp. 7–17]. Another article introduces a research to understand SPI education oriented to software industry needs [32, pp. 70–74].

As described in the recent utilization of PRO2PI Methodology, the PRO2PI WORK4E already covers SPI Education. There is no need to significant additional revision of PRO2PI Methodology in order to consider SPI Education. Of course, it does not solve SPI Education, but only provide one way to deal to teach SPI.

SPI with Agility, Models for Innovation and SPI Education may need different Process Measurement Frameworks. They should progress towards maturity following different specific process quality characteristics. These will be supported by PRO2PI Methodology with its evolution for Other Process Quality Character.

Finally, there is the challenge of providing a Theory of SPI. Kuhrmann et al. [22] supports this challenge. They concluded their SLR/SMS on SPI stating "there is a lack of discussions and critical comparisons of the approaches in practice and few on theories and models of SPI". "Although SPI is around for decades, we still miss a sound theory about SPI" [22, p. 26].

David Card already identified the reasons for this missing sound theory of SPI in 2004: "SPI has become a driving force in the global software industry. However, it has not become a popular topic of rigorous research, especially at universities. [...] [SPI] approaches have evolved or been adapted to software engineering largely without the participation of the academic research community. [...] One issue that inhibits the deployment of these approaches today is that these approaches are considered competitors. In reality they are all based on very similar concepts and techniques. The packaging obscures the underlying principles. Eliciting and refining underlying principles is the role of science." [24]

PRO2PI Methodology needs a theory of SPI. In order to pursue a theory of a modeling driven SPI, there is a need to understand the concept of theory itself. Shirley Gregor, for example, examines the structural nature of theory in Information Systems [26]. She addresses issues of causality, explanation, prediction, and generalization that underlie an understanding of theory. Then she proposes a taxonomy to classify information systems theories with respect to the manner in which four central goals are addressed: analysis, explanation, prediction, and prescription. Finally, she identifies five interrelated types of theory: (1) theory for analyzing, (2) theory for explaining, (3) theory for predicting, (4) theory for explaining and predicting, and (5) theory for design and action.

Even though I generalize SPI from software to knowledge workers processes, it still has strong connections with Software Engineering. Therefore concerns about a theory of software engineering should be considered. Johnson et al., for example, proposes an effort towards a theory of software engineering [34]. Jacobson and Meyer [35] presented steps towards a theory of software engineering and its validation: model de nature of methods (for software engineering), find the kernel (the mother of all methods) and describe each interesting method using the kernel. These steps had been used to produce the SEMAT (Software Engineering Methods and Theory) Kernel, as the essence of Software Engineering [36].

PRO2PI is a methodology for modeling driven SPI in the meaning of Model Driven Engineering (MDE). Ty, for example, explains the relationship between "model-based" and "model-driven" [27], in this case on a clearer target, a function. He suggested defining model-based in terms of "a function is model-based if it is based on the model (s) of the functional target, i.e. the thing that will be influenced by the function; thus, say a system is model-based if its major functions are model-based". Then, he suggested defining model-driven in terms of "a model-based function/system is model-driven, if the model is changeable in the system at runtime, e.g., allows to change it when the function is executing or before each execution". Therefore "model-based" is a special case of "model-driven".

There are efforts to a better understanding of MDE with research towards a model theory of MDE. Favre [28], Bézivin [29], Seidwitz [30] and Muller et al. [31], for example, provide insights for a model theory of MDE. These results should be used for a model theory of modeling driven SPI.

5 Conclusion

Among the six identified recent challenges and changes in SPI context, Other Process Quality Characteristic is certainly the one that has the most impact in the practical and research context, causing the most significant expansion of SPI.

Analysis of the PRO2PI methodology, as an example of a methodology for SPI, in relation to these six identified recent challenges and changes in SPI context, especially Other Process Quality Characteristic, indicates two directions. First, it corroborates PRO2PI as a promising methodology. Even without being developed with the Other Process Quality Characteristic prediction, PRO2PI already has a concept to be evolved based on the multiple types of profiles from the SPI modeling view. For Specific Practices for Capability Evolution, and Other Process Quality Characteristic there is a need to update basically two PRO2PI components: MMOD and MFMOD. The most recent utilization and the fact of already supporting some of the identified challenges and changes, in this case, Models for Innovation and SPI Education, also helps in this corroboration. For SPI with Agility, together with Models for Innovation and SPI

Education, there is no need to update PRO2PI. The need for a Theory of SPI was already identified for PRO2PI.

Second direction is that, even though PRO2PI already has a basis, it needs to be revised to incorporate evolutions to fully support three of the six challenges and changes: Other Process Quality Characteristic, Specific Practices for Capability Evolution and Theory of SPI. The fact that Other Process Quality Characteristic has been defined in ISO/IEC 33003 based on a solid theory of measurement, backed by the practice of SPI, indicates that there is sufficient practice for a theory of SPI. The search for model theory for MDE and theory for software engineering indicate a path to a model theory of modeling driven SPI.

A limitation of this research is that the identification of these six challenges and changes did not follow a systematic approach. They are identified using subjective experience and observation. They are also influenced by the needs and characteristics of PRO2PI Methodology, as an example of SPI Methodology. Each one of them, however, is supported by independent objective results. Other Process Quality Characteristic is introduced by ISO/IEC 33003 [3], a major player in SPI context. Two major reference models introduce specific Practices for Capability Evolution: CMMI V2.0 [8] and ISO/IEC 29110 [6]. Models for Innovation is supported by the increase in the number of reference models for that [23]. SPI Education is supported by a workshop on that subject [32]. SPI with Agility, and a Theory of SPI are supported by a recent comprehensive SLR/SMS on SPI [22].

This article is more a critical reflection on relevance recent challenges and changes in SPI research and practical context. The presented impact of these recent challenges and changes in PRO2PI Methodology is an example. Each SPI methodology should be reviewed and evolved considering these six and possibly other challenges and changes in the context of SPI to provide better support for SPI.

References

1. ISO/IEC: ISO/IEC 33001:2015 – Information technology – Process assessment – Concepts and terminology, 19 p. (2015). www.iso.org
2. ISO/IEC: ISO/IEC 33002:2015 – Information technology – Process assessment – Requirements for performing process assessment, 16 p. (2015). www.iso.org
3. ISO/IEC: ISO/IEC 33003:2015 – Information technology – Process assessment – Requirements for process measurement frameworks, 22 p. (2015). www.iso.org
4. ISO/IEC: ISO/IEC 33004:2015 – Information technology – Process assessment – Requirements for process reference, process assessment and maturity models, 9 p. (2015). www.iso.org
5. ISO/IEC: ISO/IEC 33020:2015 – Information technology – Process assessment – Process measurement framework for assessment of process capability, 18 p. (2015). www.iso.org
6. ISO/IEC: ISO/IEC 29110-4-1:2018 – Systems and software engineering – Lifecycle profiles for Very Small Entities (VSEs) – Part 4-1: Software engineering - Profile specifications: Generic profile group 18 p. (2018). www.iso.org
7. O'Connor, R., Laporte, C.: The Evolution of the ISO/IEC 29110 set of standards and guides. Int. J. Inf. Technol. Syst. Approach **10**(1), 1–21 (2017). ISSN 1935-570X

8. CMMI Institute: CMMI V2.0 Driving Performance Through Capability – Help Center (2018). https://cmmiinstitute.zendesk.com/hc/en-us/categories/115002163747-CMMI-V2-0. Accessed 06 Jun 2018
9. Salviano, C.F., Jino, M., Mendes, M.J.: Towards an ISO/IEC 15504-based process capability profile methodology for process improvement (PRO2PI). In: International SPICE Conference Proceedings, Lisbon, Portugal, pp. 77–84, April 2004
10. Salviano, C.F.: A Proposal Oriented by Process Capability Profiles for the Evolution of Software Process Improvement (original in Portuguese as Uma proposta orientada a perfis de capacidade de processo para evolução da Melhoria de Processo de Software), Ph.D. thesis, FEEC Unicamp (2006)
11. Salviano, C.F.: Model-driven process capability engineering for knowledge working intensive organization. In: SPICE 2008, Nuremberg, Germany, pp. 1–9 (2008)
12. Salviano, C.F.: A Multi-model process improvement methodology driven by capability profiles. In: Proceedings of IEEE COMPSAC, Seattle, USA, pp. 636–637 (2009). https://doi.org/10.1109/compsac.2009.94
13. Drucker, P.: Landmarks of Tomorrow - A Report on the New 'Post-Modern' World. Harper & Row, New York (1959)
14. ISO/IEC: ISO/IEC 15504-1 – Information Technology – Process Assessment – Part 1: Concepts and Vocabulary (2004)
15. ISO/IEC: ISO/IEC 15504-2 – Information Technology – Process Assessment – Part 2 - Performing An Assessment (2003)
16. ISO/IEC: ISO/IEC TR 33014:2013 – Information technology – Process assessment – Guide for process improvement, 41 p. (2015). www.iso.org
17. Potts, C.: Software-engineering research revised. IEEE Softw. **10**(5), 19–28 (1998)
18. Salviano, C.F.: A modeling view of process improvement. In: O'Connor, R.V., Rout, T., McCaffery, F., Dorling, A. (eds.) SPICE 2011. CCIS, vol. 155, pp. 16–27. Springer, Heidelberg (2011). https://doi.org/10.1007/978-3-642-21233-8_2
19. Schreiber, G.T., Akkermans, H.: Knowledge Engineering and Management: The CommonKADS Methodology. MIT Press, Cambridge (2000)
20. Salviano, C.F.: Teaching software process improvement: the PRO2PI-WORK4E method and its evaluation model. Softw. Qual. Prof. **20**(2), 16–26 (2018)
21. Salviano, C.F., Alves, A.M., Stefanuto, G.N., Maintinguer, S.T., Mattos, C.V., Zeitoum, C.: CERTICS - an ISO/IEC 15504 conformance model for software technological development and innovation. In: Mitasiunas, A., Rout, T., O'Connor, R.V., Dorling, A. (eds.) SPICE 2014. CCIS, vol. 477, pp. 48–59. Springer, Cham (2014). https://doi.org/10.1007/978-3-319-13036-1_5
22. Kuhrmann, M., Diebold, P., Munch, J.: Software process improvement: a systematic mapping study on the state of the art (2016). https://doi.org/10.7717/peerj-cs.62
23. Salviano, C.F., Machado, C.F.: Research, Development and Innovation Management based in Software Process Improvement (Original in Portuguese as Gestão de Pesquisa, Desenvolvimento e Inovação baseada em Melhoria de processo de Software), CTI Renato Archer Technical report, 10 p. (2018)
24. Card, D.N.: Research directions in software process improvement. In: Proceedings of 28th International Computer Software and Applications Conference (COMPSAC 2004), p. 238. IEEE Computer Society, 27–30 September 2004
25. Banhesse, E.L., Salviano, C.F., Jino, M.: Towards a metamodel for integrating multiple models for process improvement. In: IEEE 38th Euromicro Conference on Software Engineering and Advanced Applications SEAA, pp. 315–318 (2012)
26. Gregor, S.: Nature of theory in Information Systems. MIS Q. **30**(3), 611–642 (2006)

27. Ty: Distinguishing Model-Driven from Model-Based, in Think in models blog (2013). https://thinkinmodels.wordpress.com/2013/08/01/distinguishing-model-driven-from-model-based/. Accessed 1 June 2017
28. Favre, J.M.: Towards a basic theory to model driven engineering. In: Proceedings of the UML International Workshop on Software Model Engineering (WISME), Lisbon, Portugal (2004)
29. Bézevin, J.: On the unification power of models. Softw. Syst. Model. **4**, 171–188 (2005)
30. Seidewitz, E.: What models mean. IEEE Softw. **20**(5), 26–32 (2003)
31. Muller, P.-A., Fondement, F., Baudry, B., Combemale, B.: Modeling modeling modeling. SOSYM **11**(3), 347–359 (2012)
32. O'Connor, R.V., Mitasiunas, A., Ross, M. (eds.): Proceedings of 1st International Workshop on Software Process Education, Training and Professionalism. Gothenburg, Sweden, 85 p. (2015). http://ceur-ws.org
33. Glazer, H., Dalton, J., Anderson, D., Konrad, M., Shrum, S.: CMMI® or Agile: Why Not Embrace Both!, Technical Note, CMU/SEI-2008-TN-003 (2008)
34. Johnson, P., Ekstedt, M., Jacobson, I.: Where's the Theory for Software Engineering? IEEE Softw. **25**(5), 94–96 (2012)
35. Jacobson, I., Meyer, B.: Methods Need Theory. Dr. Dobb's Journal, 06 August 2009
36. Jacobson, I., Seidewitz, E.: A New Software Engineering. Commun. ACM **57**(12), 49–54 (2014)

An Ontology-Based Model for ITIL Process Assessment Using TIPA for ITIL

Rafael Almeida[1(✉)], Inês Percheiro[1], César Pardo[2], and Miguel Mira da Silva[1]

[1] Instituto Superior Técnico, Universidade de Lisboa, Lisboa, Portugal
{rafael.d.almeida,ines.percheiro,mms}@tecnico.ulisboa.pt
[2] Electronic and Telecommunications Engineering Faculty, Universidad del Cauca, Popayán, Colombia
cpardo@unicauca.edu.co

Abstract. Researchers agree that ITIL is among the most valuable and popular frameworks currently being adopted and adapted by organizations. For ITIL, as a Process Reference Model (PRM), process management requires each process to be controlled to remain compliant with the objectives of both IT and business. PRMs are always related to a process assessment model (PAM) which holds all details to assess a specified process quality characteristic based on one or more PRM. In the literature, it is possible to find different ontology-based models for the ITIL PRM but, as far as the authors are aware, no ontology was proposed to represent an ITIL related PAM. This research intends to shed some light in this area by proposing an ontological approach using the METHONTOLOGY methodology for describing TIPA® for ITIL. This ontology provides a common vocabulary that solves some issues of consistency, conciseness, and completeness.

Keywords: ITIL · TIPA for ITIL · Ontologies · Methontology

1 Introduction

The awareness that business involvement is crucial has initiated a shift in the definition of IT Governance toward Enterprise Governance of Information Technology (EGIT) [36]. EGIT can be defined as "an integral part of corporate governance and addresses the definition and implementation of processes, structures and relational mechanisms in the organization that enable both business and Information Technology (IT) people to execute their responsibilities in support of business/IT alignment and the creation of business value from IT-enabled business investments" [36].

EGIT can be deployed using a mixture of structure, process, and relational mechanisms [11] that encourage behaviors consistent with the organization's mission, strategy, values, norms, and culture [39]. Some examples of process mechanisms are EGIT Frameworks, ISO Standards and Best Practices (hereafter all called practices) such as COBIT 5, ITIL, and ISO 27000 family. Researchers agree that these are the

I. Stamelos et al. (Eds.): SPICE 2018, CCIS 918, pp. 104–118, 2018.
https://doi.org/10.1007/978-3-030-00623-5_8

most valuable and popular practices currently being adopted and adapted by organizations [9, 12, 29, 31].

ITIL is a widely accepted best practices framework for implementing IT service management (ITSM) that provides descriptive guidance on the management of IT processes, functions, roles, and responsibilities related to ITSM [26], providing a wide range of prescriptive information, indicating what should be done instead of how it should be done [20]. For ITIL, as a Process Reference Model (PRM), process management requires each process to be controlled to remain compliant with the objectives of both IT and business [33]. Therefore, PRMs are always related to a process assessment model (PAM) which holds all details to assess a specified process quality characteristic based on one or more PRM. TIPA® for ITIL[1] is a well-known PAM for ITIL process assessment. TIPA is the result of more than ten years of research work, including experimentation on how to combine ITIL with the ISO/IEC 15504 [6]. TIPA uses the generic approach for process assessment published by the ISO in ISO/IEC 15504-2 – Process Assessment (now ISO/IEC 330xx series) (ISO/IEC 15504-1/2, ISO/IEC 330xx series). TIPA is a standards-based approach to ITIL (v2, v3 and v3 2011) assessment that can address challenges (posed by improving the quality IT processes) in several important ways by providing a repeatable, consistent method for conducting process assessment [5].

In the literature it is possible to find different ontology-based models for the ITIL PRM [20, 35], but, as far as the authors are aware, no ontology was proposed to represent an ITIL related PAM. Therefore, there is a gap in the literature both regarding the development and deployment of semantic systems that support ITIL assessments. This research intends to shed some light in this area by proposing an ontological approach to describing TIPA for ITIL. An ontology is an explicit specification of a conceptualization [16] that can represent knowledge formally, in a practical, unambiguous away.

To develop a TIPA for ITIL ontology, the authors used the METHONTOLOGY. This methodology enables the construction of ontologies at the knowledge level, i.e., the conceptual level, as opposed to the implementation level. In that way, in this paper, the authors intend to demonstrate that ontologies are a useful technique to incorporate a theoretical foundation on the subject of EGIT.

2 Theoretical Background

In this section, the authors present an extract of the main concepts related to this proposal. Likewise, we have also identified some efforts to define formal ontologies for ITIL, which are also analyzed in this section.

[1] http://tipaonline.org/tipa/tipa-for-itil/.

2.1 ITIL and TIPA for ITL

ITIL is a set of comprehensive publications providing detailed guidance on the management of IT processes, functions, roles, and responsibilities related to IT service management [26].

ITIL has evolved since its first version based on the recommendations from experienced IT professionals and academic researchers who are always thriving to improve and standardize the IT processes worldwide [1]. Now, instead of focusing on the service itself, the focus lay on this cycle of life, renewal and decommissioning of services, with a higher business-focused perspective [37].

ITIL benefits have been addressed from a few relevant academic researchers, that frequently evidenced the following benefits: improvement of Service Quality, improvement of Customer Satisfaction, improvement of Return on Investment [14, 27].

However, according to Strahonja [32], ITIL has also some weaknesses such as the lack of holistic visibility and traceability from the theory (specifications, glossary, guidelines, manuals, amongst others) to its implementations and software applications; its focus on the logical level of processes, instructing what should be done but not how; and its poorly definition of the information models corresponding to process description.

TIPA is the result of more than ten years of research work, including experimentation on how to combine ITIL with the ISO/IEC 15504 [6]. TIPA uses the generic approach for process assessment published by the ISO in ISO/IEC 15504-2 [21] – Process Assessment (now ISO/IEC 330xx series) (ISO/IEC 15504-1/2, ISO/IEC 330xx [22]). TIPA is a standards-based approach to ITIL (v2, v3 and v3 2011) assessment that can address challenges (posed by improving the quality of product manufacture or IT processes) in several important ways by providing a repeatable, consistent method for conducting process assessment [5].

TIPA for ITIL PAM is based on ISO/IEC 15504 (ISO/IEC 15504-1, 2004; ISO/IEC 15504-2, 2003). It means that it relies on ISO/IEC 15504, which is a global reference for conducting process capability assessments. From an assessment perspective, TIPA for ITIL breaks down each process into base practices specific to each process and take into account generic practices, which are not restricted to any particular process [5]. To be more explicit, TIPA has the same structure as the original ISO/IEC 15504 PAM with Base practices and Generic Practices, and there are no additional components introduced.

2.2 Ontologies

Ontologies are disseminating in Computer Science [10, 18], and their importance is being recognized specifically in information modeling [3, 38] and information integration [7, 28, 40].

An ontology denotes a system of categories accounted for a particular vision of the world if it is perceived in a philosophical sense [18], and so, it defines a common vocabulary for researchers who need to share information in a domain [30]. It includes machine-interpretable definitions of basic concepts in a specific domain and the relations among them [30]. Additionally, they can provide semantic context by adding semantic information to models [35].

In that way, Gruber [17] defines an ontology as a "specification of a conceptualization", in which vocabulary can only be created to represent knowledge if ontologies or conceptualizations provide a formal representation [19].

According to Textor et al. [34], ontology-based models satisfy the requirements on the need for formal meta-models flexible and expressive enough to allow both technical and non-technical domains to be modeled separately and connect the concepts of different models. In short, it is possible to say that an ontology describes a hierarchy of concepts related by subsumption relationships [18] and ontologies are meant to clarify the structure of knowledge of a domain [8], and formally represent all the knowledge of that domain [19].

An ontology has the following main components [10]:

- **Classes:** Represent concepts organized in taxonomies.
- **Relations:** Association between concepts of the domain, defined as any subset of a product of n subsets. Ontologies frequently contain binary relations to express concept attributes where the first argument is the domain and the second is the range.
- **Formal Axioms:** Used to infer new knowledge, to model sentences that are always true and to represent knowledge that cannot be formally defined by other components and to verify the consistency of the ontology.
- **Instances:** Represent elements or individuals in an ontology.

Ontologies are evaluated through verification and validation, in which the correct process of ontology building and the representation of the domain of disclosure are assessed [2, 15].

2.3 ITIL Ontologies

In the literature, several ontologies were proposed for describing ITIL. An ontology-based model for ITIL has been proposed by Henrique et al. [20] with the goal of describing Configuration Items (CI) (software modules, hardware components, or staff members) and the processes dependent on them by creating a Knowledge Base describing processes, CIs, and their relationship.

Valiente et al. [35] proposed Onto-ITIL, an ontology based on the ITIL V3 Service Management Model that aims to achieve formalization of ITSM domain. Onto-ITIL provides a mechanism for managing interoperability, consistency checking and decision making, and can be used as a knowledge base for ITIL based process implementations, allowing IT service providers to add semantics and constraints to the data associated with the different ITIL-based processes that underpin a business, so that they can share and reuse information in a homogeneous way [35]. This ontology is defined in OWL DL, and its architecture is based on the ITIL service lifecycle.

However, as far as the authors are aware, no ontology was proposed to represent an ITIL related PAM.

2.4 Methontology

This methodology, developed by [13], aspires to produce ontologies at the knowledge level. The ontology building process respects an ontology life cycle based on evolving prototypes. For each ontology's prototype developed, the first activity executed is the schedule activity where all the tasks to be performed are identified, arranged and a survey of the needed resources is done.

During the ontology's life cycle three different types of activities are performed in parallel carrying an intra-dependency relationship, as portrayed in Fig. 1: the *management* activities, the *development* activities, and the *support* activities.

In the *management* activities, the control activity guarantees that the tasks to be performed meet the performance requirements and the quality assurance activity ensures the quality of every output of the ontology development process.

The support activities fluctuate during the ontology's lifecycle and include knowledge acquisition, integration, evaluation, documentation and configuration management.

Regarding the *development* activities, in the first activity, namely Specification, one should establish a prototype and state the ontology significance by defining its intended uses and the presumed end users. The *Conceptualization* activity is crucial for the ontology development. During the Conceptualization activity, all the knowledge gathered will be structured and organized. METHONTOLOGY highlights that a conceptual model should be developed and then formalized to be later implemented in an ontology implementation language.

In this methodology, the Conceptualization activity includes a set of tasks that aim to structure knowledge.

In Task 1, a glossary of terms is built, and the terms to be included in the ontology are identified, as well as their natural language definition. Task 2 is where the concept taxonomies are built to define the concept hierarchy. Task 3 proposes to build ad-hoc binary relation diagrams to establish ad hoc relationships. In Task 4 a concept dictionary is built to specify the properties and relations that describe each concept of the taxonomy, containing all the domain concepts, relations, their instances, their class and the instance attributes. Task 5 takes the previous ad-hoc binary relations and details them in a relation table. Task 6 complements Task 5 by describing in detail each instance attribute on a concept dictionary. Task 7 is about describing the class attributes, and Task 8 is about describing each constant value used as values in data properties producing a constant table.

After describing the concepts, ad-hoc binary relationships, instance attributes, classes and constants, first-order logic is used to define the formal axioms in Task 9 and in Task 10 the rules of the ontology are described in a rule table. Lastly, in Task 11, the instances of the conceptual model of the ontology are defined and presented in an instance table.

Following the Conceptualization, we have the *Formalization* activity where the conceptual model is transformed into a semi-computable or formal model to be implemented in the next activity, the *Implementation* activity. The last activity from development stage is the *Maintenance* activity, in which the ontology should be corrected and updated to be later reused by other ontologies or applications.

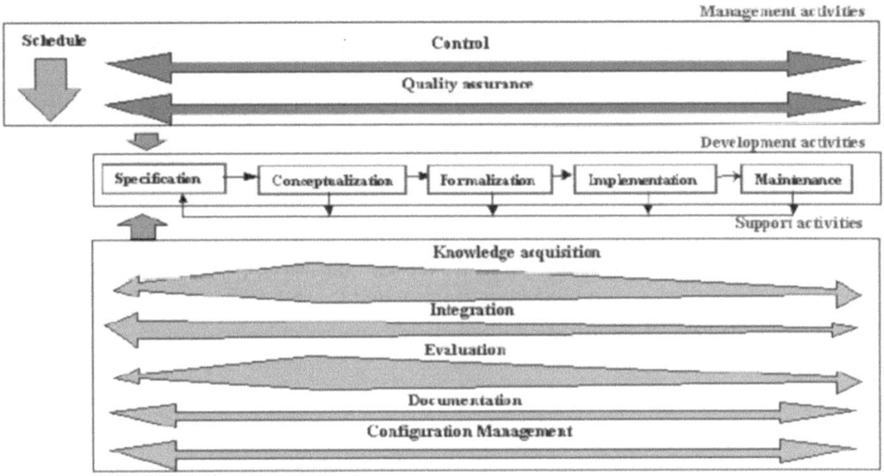

Fig. 1. METHONTOLOGY Lifecycle.

3 Proposal

In this section, the authors present and explain how the METHONTOLOGY was used to develop a TIPA for ITIL Ontology. In the scope of this research, a methodology with a life cycle is beneficial because it can give a scheduled structure to the ontology development, specifying in this way a chronology for the ontology development activities and the stages coupled to them.

Starting with the specification activity, the authors defined the scope of this proposal as an ITIL "Process Assessment" that is translated into the use of TIPA for ITIL PAM. As it was stated before, TIPA for ITIL is based on ISO/IEC 15504-330xx series and is a method for conducting process assessments. Therefore, this ontology intends to be used by ITIL and ITSM assessors and experts to perform process assessment using TIPA for ITIL, and therefore improve the management of their IT services, infrastructures, and resources [5].

The first step of the conceptualization activity is to propose a model that aims to represent the structure of the ontology. ArchiMate[2]® is typically used for high-level processes and their relations to the enterprise context, but it is not intended for detailed workflow modeling [25]. ArchiMate provides a uniform representation for diagrams that describe Enterprise Architectures (EA). Since the motivational layer is essential to model the PAMs, ArchiMate seemed to be a suitable language for this activity. In this paper, the authors used the latest version of the language - ArchiMate 3.0.

Figure 2 illustrates the conceptual model that serves as a draft to the rest of the ontology construction and that later is formalized into the ontology. This model represents the knowledge acquired that will be translated into an ontology development language and become machine-readable. Unfortunately, due to space limitations, it is

[2] http://pubs.opengroup.org/architecture/archimate3-doc/.

not possible to present the descriptions of the ArchiMate processes and the relationships that are used to represent the TIPA for ITIL Ontology conceptual model. However, we advise readers to consult them on [24].

The concepts presented in Fig. 2 were extracted from the TIPA from ITIL book [5] that designed the structure of the PAM according to the ISO/IEC 15504-2:2003 requirements.

Regarding Fig. 2, there is a term that deserves a particular discussion: the option for the term "Expected Result" instead of the term "Outcome" from ISO/IEC 15504 standard was purposely done by the TIPA for ITIL developers [5] to diminish the terminology disparities in the ITSM community and to ensure the understanding of this concept with no loss of significance.

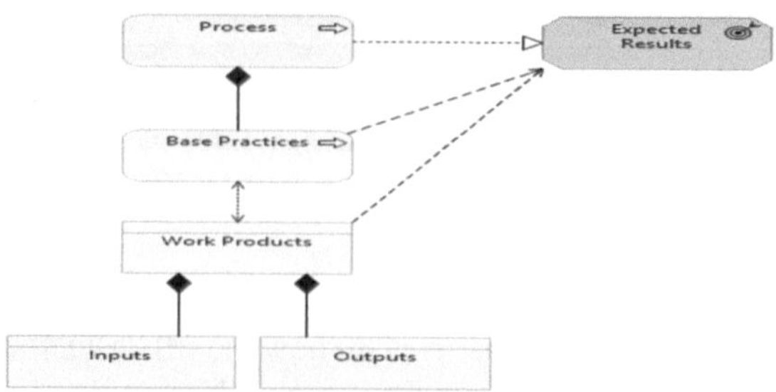

Fig. 2. A conceptual model for the TIPA for ITIL Ontology using ArchiMate.

The authors would like to clarify that (a) the measurement framework used is ISO/IEC 33020; (b) the PAM indicators for PA1.1 for capability level 1 are base practices and work products; and (c) the ontology only focuses on the indicators of PA1.1 for capability level 1.

As defined in the TIPA for ITIL publication, a PAM is related to one or more PRMs, and it forms the basis for the collection of evidence and rating of process capability. Both base practices and work products are indicators to address the expected results of the processes on the PAM scope and determine the process capability level [5].

After a model for the implementation of the Ontology is created, the conceptualization tasks, proposed in METHONTOLOGY, can take place. Due to space limitations, the authors present the outputs of the conceptualization tasks collectively. The output of Task 1 is the development of a glossary that identifies the concepts presented in the ontology together with their descriptions (Table 1).

Once the ontology's terms were defined, we set the concept hierarchies by building a concept taxonomy, as Task 2 proposes, defining the disjoint relations between them. In the TIPA for ITIL Ontology, all concepts share a disjoint-decomposition relation because they do not share instances.

The output from Task 3 is presented in Fig. 3. Figure 3 represents a diagram that establishes the ad-hoc relationships between concepts of the same concept taxonomy and was obtained by using the VOWL plugin in Protégé.

Table 1. A Glossary of terms and a concept dictionary.

Class Name	Description [4]	Class attributes	Relations
Process	A structured set of activities designed to accomplish a specific objective. A process takes one or more defined inputs and turns them into defined outputs. It may include any of the roles, responsibilities, tools and management controls required to deliver the outputs reliably. A process may define policies, standards, guidelines, activities, and work instructions if they are needed	process-name purpose lifecycle stage	hasObjective isComposedBy Uses Produces
Work Product	Structured sets of data that make the process work and that are expected to be produced by the process. Inputs are gradually converted into outputs	workproduct-name workproduct-description characteristics	isRelatedToAsOutp isRelatedToAsInput supportsAsInput supportsAsOutput isUsed isProduced
Base Practice	A set of actions designed to achieve a particular result. Base practices are usually defined as part of processes or plans and are documented in procedures	basepractice-name basepractice-description	hasOutput hasInput helpAchieve composes
Expected Result	The expected results required from a process, activity or organization to ensure that its purpose will be fulfilled. Expected results are usually expressed as measurable targets	expectedresult-description	isSupportedByInput isSupportedByOutp achievedBy

In Task 4, the properties and relations that describe each concept of the taxonomy are specified on a concept dictionary. Table 1 presents not only this dictionary but also a glossary of terms. Following the establishment of the concept dictionary, the subsequent tasks (5, 6 and 7) detail respectively the ad hoc binary relations, the class attributes, and the instances.

Table 2 presents the ad-hoc Binary Relations of our ontology for Task 5. We can sum up Tasks 6 and 7 by detailing all the attributes as being Strings, as Fig. 3 evidence (the String boxes are automatically generated), with (0, 1) cardinalities, whether they exist or not.

Due to space limitations, it is not possible to present the constant table, the formal axioms and the rule table from Tasks 8, 9 and 10 respectively. Finally, in Task 11, we defined the instances in an instance table. Since our ontology has 107 instances, it would be inefficient to illustrate all these instances in this paper, and so, we present in the Demonstration Section a practical example of the implementation through the instantiation of the TIPA for ITIL ontology.

Table 2. Ad hoc Binary Relation Table of TIPA for ITIL Ontology

Relation Name	Source concept	Source card. (Max)	Target concept	Mathematical properties	Inverse relation
hasObjective	Process	1	ExpectedResult	Asymmetric Irreflexive	–
hasOutput	BasePractice	N	WorkProduct	Asymmetric Irreflexive	isRelatedToAsOutput
hasInput	BasePractice	N	WorkProduct	Asymmetric Irreflexive	isRelatedToAsInput
isComposedBy	Process	1	BasePractice	Asymmetric Irreflexive	Composes
IsSupported byInput	Expected Result	N	WorkProduct	Asymmetric Irreflexive	supportsAsInput
IsSupported byOutput	Expected Result	N	WorkProduct	Asymmetric Irreflexive	supportsAsOutput
helpAchieve	BasePractice	N	ExpectedResult	Asymmetric Irreflexive	achievedBy
Uses	Process	N	WorkProduct	Asymmetric Irreflexive	isUsed
Produces	Process	N	WorkProduct	Asymmetric Irreflexive	isProduced

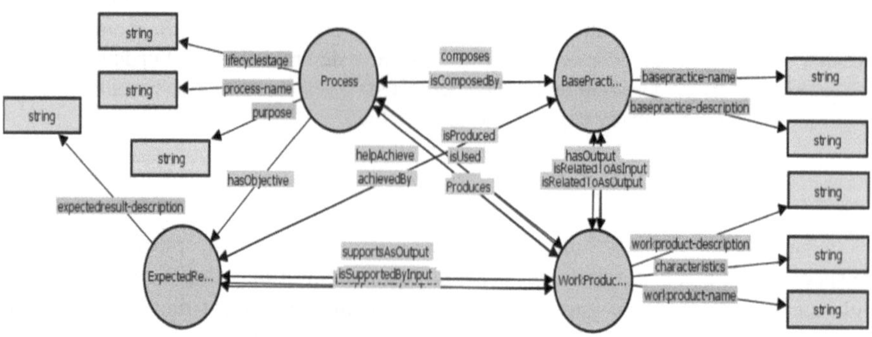

Fig. 3. Ad Hoc Binary relations diagram for TIPA for ITIL Ontology.

4 Demonstration

A demonstration was carried out in a Portuguese hospital. The authors assessed the ITIL Incident Management process to demonstrate the suitability of this proposal.

To understand the capability level of the ITIL Incident Management process, the authors performed semi-structured interviews. Interviews were conducted with two hospitals' IT decision-makers at the top and medium management levels usually responsible for all decisions concerning IT [23]. In this demonstration, the focus of the assessment was the process capability level 1. In this level, the process performance attribute is a measure of the extent to which the process purpose is achieved. The primary goal in this level is to analyze if the process achieves its objectives, expected results, and whether it shows some tangible evidence of process activities. A process is assessed through evidence indicators of the way it performs [5].

Two different approaches were used to demonstrate the TIPA for ITIL Ontology. Firstly, we demonstrate how the ontology can support the process assessment carried out in a Portuguese hospital by instantiating the ontology with examples of the hospital EA. In Fig. 4, a detailed example of the instantiated ontology is presented, allowing us to better structure, design and formalize the TIPA for ITIL assessment.

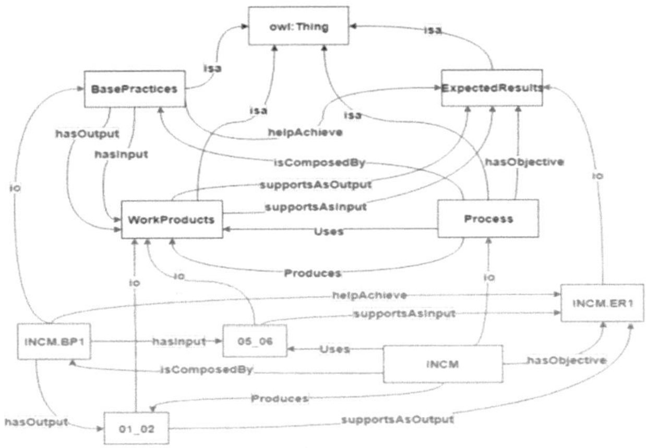

Fig. 4. Instantiated TIPA for ITIL Ontology.

Secondly, the ontology was used to answer some questions that are crucial when assessing the enterprise's process capability. Process performance indicators are specific to each process and are used to determine whether a process has achieved the process capability level 1.

Due to space limitations, the authors just selected the following expected result INCM.ER3 - "Incidents are resolved within agreed service levels to restore the normal service operation" to demonstrate the suitability of this proposal. To determine if this expected result is achieved we firstly inquired our ontology about which are the base practices that support this expected result. One can conclude through the relation achievedBy that the following base practices directly influence the achievement of INCM.ER3: INCM-BP2, INCM-BP3, INCM-BP4, INCM-BP5, INCM-BP6, INCM-BP7, INCM-BP9 (Fig. 5).

After that, one should use the TIPA for ITIL questionnaire to determine if these base practices are being correctly performed. Some questions that were used are: "Are there time limits to diagnose (and resolve) the incident in each specialized support line?"; "Is there a link to the SLAs?"; "When is an incident escalated to your manager or a higher authority level?".

Then, one should resort again to the ontology to examine which are the work products related to this specific expected result, by checking the isSupportedByInput and isSupportedByOutput relations. Regarding the process outputs, only the following

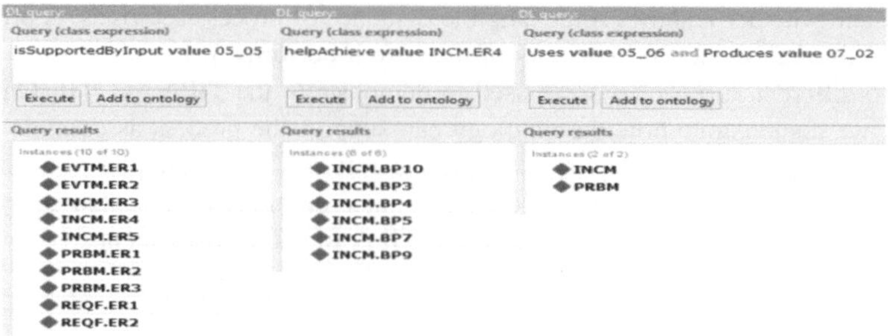

Fig. 5. DL Query answers for the defined competency questions.

outputs 05-04, 05-07, 02-07 and 07-02 influence the INCM.ER3. Regarding the inputs, only the 05-04, 05-05, 05-06, 02-07, 08-01, 02-06, 01-02, 05-02, 05-03 influence the INCM.ER3.

By using this information, one can assess the process capability of the chosen process. In this particular case, we examined the Portuguese hospital work products and base practices and concluded that the hospital achieved the process capability level 1. However, the hospital cannot achieve a process capability level 2 since the following expected result "Incidents are resolved within agreed service levels to restore the normal service operation" is largely (and not fully) achieved.

5 Evaluation

The ontologies' evaluation comprises two different kinds of judgments, a technical judgment, and a user judgment, from now on referred to as an ontology assessment [13]. The technical evaluation of the taxonomy presented in the ontology developed is processed with judgement of the content of the ontology with respect to a frame of reference, in this case we resort to competency questions, a set of questions in natural language to determine the scope of the ontology and to extract the main concepts of the ontology, their properties, relations and formal axioms.

The competency questions are firstly identified informally in natural language as requirement specifications for the ontology to answer once it is expressed in a formal language. These questions are not merely queries; they must be stratified so that they can be composed or decomposed into other competency questions.

For the evaluation of the TIPA for ITIL Ontology the following competency questions were defined: (a) If there is a problem with the Configuration Management System (CMS) what are the expected results that are not achieved? (b) Which Base Practices influence the Expected Result INCM.ER4 – "The incident impact on the business is minimized"? and (c) Which Process uses Known Error Databases (KEDB) and produces a Request for Change (RFC)?

During the various stages of the development lifecycle, the ontology was subjected to a technical verification to ensure that the ontology was being built correctly and to a technical validation, to ensure that it represented a reliable model of the real world to be formally defined. The previously defined competency questions were implemented in OWL DL and Fig. 5 presents the ontology answers to these questions.

The ontology assessment is focused on the user evaluation of the ontology's correct definition and performance based on consistency, completeness, and conciseness. The consistency assesses if contradictory knowledge can be inferred from the ontology. Completeness can only be assessed by proving the nonexistence of incompleteness, by determining if the individual definitions are well established and if all that is supposed to be stated in the ontology is present or can be inferred. If the ontology does not present redundancies and useless definitions, then the ontology can be assessed as concise.

For the assessment of the TIPA for ITIL Ontology 10 interviews with ITIL and TIPA for ITIL practitioners and specialists from Portugal, Brazil, and Luxembourg were performed. The ontology was, regarding the present definitions, consensually assessed as complete, consistent and concise for the scope of process assessment. It is important to emphasize that during the evaluation some important statements emerged. The practitioners stated that "having a TIPA for ITIL Ontology can be valuable to identify inconsistencies on ITIL" and that an ontology is "a useful resource to give a better vision and identification of the process architecture". Through an incremental process, it was possible to homogenize the concepts, the concept attributes and the relations established that are presented in our ontology.

Also, it is possible to conclude that one of the main benefits of using ontologies is that, by having the essential relationships between concepts built into them, one can enable automated reasoning about data, making assessments faster.

6 Conclusion

A consistent terminology for assessment processes based on ITIL model can provide an important instrument for understanding and support the right implementation of the ITIL model in an organization, as well as for strengthening this research domain. In this paper, the authors presented a summary of a formal Ontology based on TIPA for ITIL assessment process. This ontology provides a common vocabulary with the aim of resolving some issues of consistency, conciseness, and completeness that had been previously identified. Our primary objective was to provide a basis for discussion of the terms, concepts, and relations identified and related to this research domain.

As a support to our assertions, we have also provided a first application of the ontology through the instantiation of the TIPA for ITIL ontology in a Portuguese Hospital, more precisely to assess the ITIL Incident Management process.

The information obtained from this work will be used to tackle three streams as follow: the first stream focuses on updating and extend the ontology, although the ontology proposed here has been applied in a real case of implementation, in the quest to cover a broader range of needs, we hope to extend it and include more terms and relationships of practices that can be related to ITIL and TIPA. In the second stream, it should also be said that our ontology has been used to instance the terms related to TIPA for ITIL ontology. Therefore, it has shown that it can also be used as a basis for supporting the design and improvement of the organization's processes.

That being the case, we hope to develop a tool to support the definition of organizations' processes through our ontology. The information stored will be able to be used as a benchmark of processes for other organizations, as well as to help them while defining their processes. Finally, the third stream will focus on the automation, since the assessment process is currently a manual task, in this sense, as future work, the next step in this project will involve the automation of the assessment stage. This could be done through the development of algorithms which let us automatize some steps and extend the capability of the assessment process. There is already some research on this area, but we want to focus on multi-frameworks environments.

References

1. Ali, S.M.: Integration of information security essential controls into information technology infrastructure library-A proposed framework. Int. J. Appl. **4**(1) (2014)
2. Antunes, G., Bakhshandeh, M., Mayer, R., Borbinha, J.L., Caetano, A.: Using ontologies for enterprise architecture integration and analysis. CSIMQ **1**, 1–23 (2014)
3. Ashenhurst, R.L.: Ontological aspects of information modeling. Mind. Mach. **6**(3), 287–394 (1996)
4. Axelos: Glossary of Terms. ITIL® glossary and abbreviations. https://axelos.com/glossaries-of-terms. Accessed 18 July 2018
5. Barafort, B., Betry, V., Cortina, S., Picard, M., Renault, A., St-Jean, M., Valdés, O.: ITSM Process Assessment Supporting ITIL (TIPA). Van Haren (2009)
6. Barafort, Béatrix, Di Renzo, Bernard, Merlan, Olivier: Benefits resulting from the combined use of ISO/IEC 15504 with the Information Technology Infrastructure Library (ITIL). In: Oivo, Markku, Komi-Sirviö, Seija (eds.) PROFES 2002. LNCS, vol. 2559, pp. 314–325. Springer, Heidelberg (2002). https://doi.org/10.1007/3-540-36209-6_27
7. Bergamaschi, S., Castano, S., Di Vimercati, S.D.C., Montanari, S., Vincini, M.: An intelligent approach to information integration. In: Formal Ontology in Information Systems, pp. 253–267. IOS Press, Amsterdam (1998)
8. Chandrasekaran, B., Josephson, J.R., Benjamins, V.R.: What are ontologies, and why do we need them? IEEE Intell. Syst. **14**(1), 20–26 (1999)
9. Chatfield, A.T., Coleman, T.: Promises and successful practice in IT governance: a survey of Australian senior IT managers (2011)
10. Corcho, O., Fernández-López, M., Gómez-Pérez, A.: Ontological engineering: principles, methods, tools and languages. In: Calero, C., Ruiz, F., Piattini, M. (eds.) Ontologies for Software Engineering and Software Technology, pp. 1–48. Springer, Berlin (2006)
11. De Haes, S., Van Grembergen, W.: IT governance and its mechanisms. Inf. Syst. Control J. **1**, 27–33 (2004)
12. Debreceny, R.S., Gray, G.L.: IT governance and process maturity: a multinational field study. J. Inf. Syst. **27**(1), 157–188 (2013)
13. Fernández-López, M., Gómez-Pérez, A., Juristo, N.: Methontology: from ontological art towards ontological engineering (1997)
14. Gomes, C.F.S.: Gestão da cadeia de suprimentos integrada à tecnologia da informação. Cengage Learning Editores (2004)
15. Gómez-Pérez, A., Juristo, N., Pazos, J.: Evaluation and assessment of knowledge sharing technology. In: Towards Very Large Knowledge Bases, pp. 289–296 (1995)

16. Gruber, T.R.: A translation approach to portable ontologies. Knowl. Acquis. **5**(2), 199–220 (1993)
17. Gruber, T.R.: Toward principles for the design of ontologies used for knowledge sharing? Int. J. Hum. Comput. Stud. **43**(5–6), 907–928 (1995)
18. Guarino, N.: Formal ontology in information systems. In: Proceedings of the First International Conference (FOIS 98), 6–8 June, Trento, Italy. IOS Press (1998)
19. Guarino, N., Oberle, D., Staab, S.: What is an ontology? In: Staab, S., Studer, R. (eds.) Handbook on Ontologies, pp. 1–17. Springer, Heidelberg (2009). https://doi.org/10.1007/978-3-540-92673-3_0
20. Henrique, M., Hoppen, J., Todesco, J.L., Fileto, R.: ITIL Ontology Based Model for IT Governance: a Prototype Demonstration. UFSC, Florianópolis (2010)
21. ISO, I.: IEC 15504-2: 2003/Cor. 1: 2004 (E). Information technology-process assessment-part. 2 (2004)
22. ISO, I.: IEC 33000: Information Technology: Process Assessment. ISO (2015)
23. ITGI, I.: Board briefing on IT governance. Information Technology Governance Institute (2003). Disponível em http://www.itgi.org
24. Josey, A., Lankhorst, M., Band, I., Jonkers, H., Quartel, D.: An Introduction to the ArchiMate® 3.0 Specification. White Paper from The Open Group (2016)
25. Lankhorst, M.M., Aldea, A., Niehof, J.: Combining ArchiMate with other standards and approaches. In: Enterprise Architecture at Work, pp. 123–140. Springer, Heidelberg (2017). https://doi.org/10.1007/978-3-662-53933-0_6
26. Lema, L., Calvo-Manzano, J.-A., Colomo-Palacios, R., Arcilla, M.: ITIL in small to medium-sized enterprises software companies: towards an implementation sequence. J. Softw. Evol. Process **27**(8), 528–538 (2015)
27. Marrone, M., Kolbe, L.: ITIL and the creation of benefits: an empirical study on benefits, challenges and processes. In: ECIS, p. 66 (2010)
28. Mena, E., Kashyap, V., Illarramendi, A., Sheth, A.: Domain specific ontologies for semantic information brokering on the global information infrastructure. In: Formal Ontology in Information Systems, pp. 269–283. IOS Press, Amsterdam (1998)
29. Montenegro, C., de la Torre, A., Néjer, M., Zapata, M.: An experience to improving IT development into developing country public sector organizations. In: ECISM 2017 11th European Conference on Information Systems Management, p. 199. Academic Conferences and Publishing Limited (2017)
30. Noy, N.F., McGuinness, D.L.: Ontology development 101: a guide to creating your first ontology. Stanford knowledge systems laboratory technical report KSL-01-05 and Stanford medical informatics technical report SMI-2001-0880, Stanford, CA (2001)
31. Sahibudin, S., Sharifi, M., Ayat, M.: Combining ITIL, COBIT and ISO/IEC 27002 in Order to Design a Comprehensive IT Framework in Organizations, May 2008
32. Strahonja, V.: Definition Metamodel of ITIL. In: Barry, C., Lang, M., Wojtkowski, W., Conboy, K., Wojtkowski, G. (eds.) Information Systems Development, pp. 1081–1092. Springer, Boston (2009)
33. Taylor, S., Case, G., Spalding, G.: Continual service improvement. Stationery Office (2007)
34. Textor, A., Geihs, K.: Calculation of COBIT metrics using a formal ontology, May 2015
35. Valiente, M.-C., Garcia-Barriocanal, E., Sicilia, M.-A.: Applying an ontology approach to IT service management for business-IT integration. Knowl. Based Syst. **28**, 76–87 (2012)
36. Van Grembergen, W., De Haes, S.: Enterprise governance of information technology: achieving strategic alignment and value. Springer Science & Business Media (2009)

37. Van Sante, T., Ermersj, J.: Togaf 9 and itil v3. White Paper (2009)
38. Weber, R.: Ontological foundations of information systems. Coopers & Lybrand and the Accounting Association of Australia and New Zealand Melbourne (1997)
39. Weill, P., Ross, J.W.: IT governance: How top performers manage IT decision rights for superior results. Harvard Business Press (2004)
40. Wiederhold, G.: Intelligent integration of information. In: ACM SIGMOD Record, pp. 434–437. ACM (1993)

Adapting SPICE for Development of a Reference Model for Building Information Modeling - BIM-CAREM

Gokcen Yilmaz[1(✉)], Asli Akcamete[2], and Onur Demirors[3]

[1] Pamukkale University, 20020 Denizli, Turkey
gokcenyilmaz@gmail.com
[2] Middle East Technical University, 06800 Ankara, Turkey
akcamete@metu.edu.tr
[3] Izmir Institute of Technology, 35430 Izmir, Turkey

Abstract. Building Information Modelling (BIM) is highly adopted by Architecture, Engineering, Construction and Facilities Management (AEC/FM) companies around the world due to its benefits such as improving collaboration of stakeholders in projects. Effective implementation of BIM in organizations requires assessment of existing BIM performances of AEC/FM processes. We developed a reference model for BIM capability assessments based on the meta-model of the ISO/IEC 330xx (the most recent version of SPICE) family of standards. BIM-CAREM can be used for identifying the BIM capabilities of the AEC/FM processes. The model was updated iteratively based on the expert reviews and an exploratory case study, and was evaluated via four explanatory case studies. The assessment results showed that the BIM-CAREM is capable of identifying BIM capabilities of specific processes. In this paper, we present how we utilized ISO/IEC 330xx for developing BIM-CAREM as well as the iterations of the model and one of the explanatory case studies as an example.

Keywords: Building Information Modeling · ISO/IEC 330xx
BIM capability · SPICE

1 Introduction

Building Information Modeling (BIM) is a business process for generating and leveraging building data to design, construct and operate the building during its life-cycle [1]. Usage of BIM brings significant benefits in the facility life cycle. For example, it allows earlier collaboration of multiple design disciplines and use of the design model as basis for fabricated components [2]. Due to such benefits, many initiatives have been undertaken for adopting BIM as an emerging technology in various countries such as the US, the UK, Finland, Norway and Hong Kong [3].

Even after the adoption of BIM, Architecture, Engineering, Construction and Facilities Management (AEC/FM) organizations need to evaluate the performances of their BIM usages. Hence, various BIM capability and maturity models have been developed for meeting the different assessment purposes [4]. We identified six prevalent BIM capability and maturity models in the literature and each model was

I. Stamelos et al. (Eds.): SPICE 2018, CCIS 918, pp. 119–135, 2018.
https://doi.org/10.1007/978-3-030-00623-5_9

explained in detail in the review paper of Yilmaz et al. [5]. Later, we extended this literature review by adding two recently created models and these models were evaluated based on the identified criteria [6]. Users need to analyze these models in detail to choose the most appropriate model for their purposes. According to Wu et al. [4], most of these models share common metrics which are clustered into several categories; i.e. process, technology, organization, human and standard. This shows that models in the literature were not developed based on established standards.

As a response to these limitations, a reference model for BIM capability assessments namely BIM-CAREM was developed [6, 7]. BIM-CAREM was developed based on the meta-model of the ISO/IEC 330xx family of standards [8] which includes definitions and requirements for developing process reference models and measurement frameworks. This standard has been widely adapted into different domains such as software testing [9] and information security [10]. During the development, BIM-CAREM was updated iteratively through conducting expert reviews and an exploratory case study [6]. Finally, it was evaluated via explanatory case studies in four different AEC/FM companies [7].

The aim of this paper is to discuss how we used the principles and requirements explained in the ISO/IEC 330xx family of standards for creating the BIM-CAREM. We also present which parts of the standard were adapted and which parts were used without any change. We explained the benefits of using principles explained in ISO/IEC 330xx family of standards as well as the challenges that were faced during creation of BIM-CAREM. Moreover, iterations of the model via expert reviews and evaluation of the model via explanatory case studies are explained.

The literature review and research methodology for development of BIM-CAREM are presented in Sects. 2 and 3, respectively. Structure of BIM-CAREM is described in Sect. 4. While an explanatory case study is explained in Sect. 5 as an example, conclusions are discussed in Sect. 6.

2 Literature Review

Eight models, which were identified via systematic literature review and explained in detail in the review paper of Yilmaz et al. [5], were included in the development process of BIM-CAREM. These eight models were; Capability Maturity Model of the National Institute of Building Sciences [11], BIM Proficiency Matrix [12], BIM QuickScan [13], Virtual Design and Construction Scorecard [14], Organizational BIM Assessment Profile [15], VICO BIM Scorecard [16], BIM Maturity Matrix [17], and Multifunctional BIM Maturity Matrix [18]. These eight models were analyzed based on the five criteria and explained in the paper of Yilmaz et al. [6]. According to these findings, the limitations of these models are summarized as below.

Each model has been developed to meet specific assessment purposes. Similarly, according to the literature review of Giel et al. [19], models were developed to assess one of the three capabilities; organizational, project, and individual. Hence, selecting appropriate models for specific assessment purposes is time-consuming. Models were developed by inspiring from each other, since they share many common metrics. Metrics of these models can be clustered into four groups which are; process, organization (standard and personnel), technical (hardware and software) and data. There is not a broadly accepted and commonly used model in the literature, since most of these approaches were not developed based on established standards. Most of these models do not cover all BIM uses performed by BIM practitioners existing in the AEC/FM industry. Hence, while some of the models are more suitable to assess BIM performance of designer firms, some can be used for measuring BIM performance of facility owners. The models do not support BIM performance assessments of specific processes, such as those of construction. Moreover, metrics belong to process category are not comprehensive to cover all AEC/FM facility life cycle stages. These limitations are explained in the PhD dissertation of Yilmaz [7] in more detail.

Due to its adaptable structure, meta-model of ISO/IEC 330xx family of standards [8] was used to develop a reference model for BIM capability assessment called BIM-CAREM to eliminate the limitations given above. The recent ISO/IEC 330xx family of standards, which is one of the well-known capability and maturity models in the software engineering, replaced the ISO/IEC 15504 Software Process Improvement and Capability dEtermination (SPICE) standard which provides guidance on how to utilize process assessment for conducting process improvement. Two of the parts belonging to ISO/IEC 330xx family of standards, which are ISO/IEC 33003 and ISO/IEC 33004, are important for users who want to develop process reference models and process measurement frameworks. While ISO/IEC 33003 [20] provides requirements for developing process measurement frameworks, ISO/IEC 33004 [21] gives requirements for development of process reference, process assessment and maturity models.

The ISO/IEC 15504 and ISO/IEC 330xx have been taken as a basis for creating new capability and maturity models required in different domains and sectors. ISO/IEC 33063 [9] is a process assessment model for software testing and contains a set of process quality characteristics to be used for assessing capabilities of software testing processes. Automotive SPICE [22] is developed conformant with the requirements of a process assessment model defined in the ISO/IEC 15504-2 [23]. It is used to assess the software development in automotive industry [22]. MDevSPICE [24] is developed to meet the specific safety-critical and regulatory requirements of the medical device domain. It consists of process reference model and process assessment model. Process reference model includes 24 processes from system level and supporting processes described in ISO/IEC 12207 [25]. Process assessment model consists measurement framework with six levels of capability which is based on the ISO/IEC 15504-2 [26]. SPICE4Space [27] is based on the ISO/IEC 15504-5 [28], and it includes assessment model for space software practices.

The AgilityMod [29] is developed based on the ISO/IEC 15504-2 [26] for assessing the agility levels of software development projects. In this study, the core of the agile projects, which are called aspects, are determined and defined as well as the agility levels and their related aspect attributes [29]. Aspects are sets of interrelated and interacting activities. A web-based agility assessment tool is created based on the AgilityMod to facilitate automatic agility assessment and the tool is tested though multiple case studies [30]. In relation with AgilityMod a measurement capability assessment method is also developed [31]. This model enables assessing the measurement capability of aspects (sets of interrelated and interacting activities) defined by

AgilityMod. The measurement capability levels and their associated generic practices are created based on the ISO/IEC 330xx too [31].

ISO/IEC 15504 or ISOIEC/330xx is adapted to other non-software domains as well. For example, ISO/IEC 33052 [32] is a process reference model for information security management and describes the processes related to information security management system. ISO/IEC 33072 [10] introduces an information security management process assessment model which is composed of both a process reference model and a process measurement framework. ISO/IEC 33071 [33] introduces an integrated process assessment model for enterprise processes which integrates selected process models and standards into a single model. A SPICE based Government Process Capability Determination Model namely Gov-PCDM is developed for assessing the capabilities of the processes of public organizations [34]. Definitions of the Financial and Physical Resource Management (PFPRM) processes are exemplified based on the requirements defined in the ISO/IEC 15504-2 [26]. The model has been evaluated in three different organizations. The results showed that the measurement framework defined is capable of identifying the capability levels and of the proposed PFPRM process definitions and creating roadmaps for process improvements [34].

3 Research Methodology for Development of the BIM-CAREM

We developed the BIM-CAREM based on the meta-model of ISO/IEC 330xx family of standards [8]. Later, we updated the model in terms of the feedbacks gathered via expert reviews and an exploratory case study. Finally, the model was evaluated through four explanatory case studies. The research tasks followed for developing the BIM-CAREM are depicted briefly in Fig. 1.

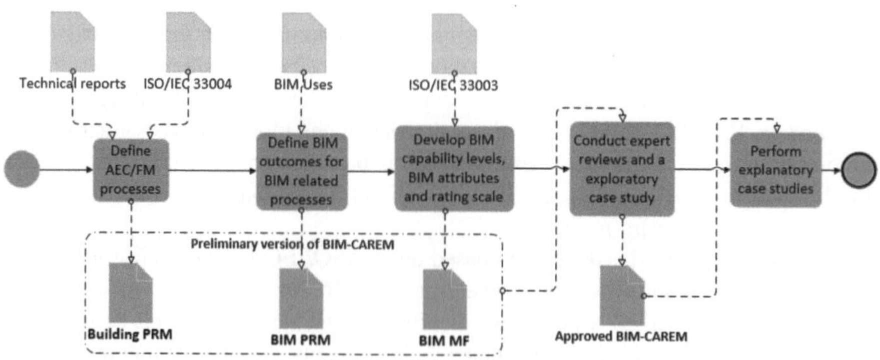

Fig. 1. The research tasks and the parts of the standard used in these tasks

The Building PRM and the BIM PRM were developed based on the principles explained in the ISO/IEC 33004-Requirements for Process Reference, Process Assessment and Maturity [21]. We have also used ISO/IEC 24774- Systems and software engineering – Life cycle management – Guidelines for Process Description [35] as an exemplar model. The BIM MF was created in conformance to the ISO/IEC 33003 - Requirements for Process Measurement Frameworks [20] as depicted in the Fig. 1. We also used, the ISO/IEC 15504-5 An Exemplar Process Assessment Model [28] and the ISO/IEC 33020- Process Measurement Framework for Assessment of Process Capability [36] for analyzing the example process descriptions and process capability levels. Table 1 presents the terminology which is used in MF of the BIM-CAREM in relation with the terminology of SPICE.

Table 1. Terminology used in the BIM MF

Terminology in ISO/IEC 33003 and ISO/IEC 33004	Terminology in BIM-CAREM
PRM	**Building/BIM PRM**
Process Purpose	Process Purpose
Process Outcome	Process/BIM Outcome
Base Practice	Base Practice
Work Product	Work Product
Process MF	**BIM MF**
Process Capability Levels	BIM Capability Levels
Process Attribute	BIM Attribute
Process Attribute Outcome	BIM Attribute Outcome
Generic Practice	Generic Practice
Generic Work Product	Generic BIM Work Product
Generic Resource	Generic Resource
Rating Scale	Rating Scale

3.1 Creating the Building/BIM PRMs and the BIM MF

According to the requirements defined in the ISO/IEC 33004 [21], the domain of the process reference models is the AEC/FM industry. Building PRM was developed before the BIM PRM. In order to decide which facility life cycle stages were included in the Building PRM, RIBA Plan of Work [37] was used. Conceptual Planning (P), Architectural Design (ARCH D), Structural Design (STR D), Building Services Design (BS D), Geotechnical Design (GEO D), Construction (C) and the Facility Management (FM) were included in the Building PRM. Key AEC/FM processes of each phase included in Building PRM were determined by taking two important technical reports [38, 39] as basis. Building PRM consists of 37 key AEC/FM processes. In order to define all AEC/FM processes systematically, a definition template was created based on the requirements stated in ISO/IEC 33004 [21] and ISO/IEC 24774 [35]. This template is composed of process purpose, process outcomes, base practices and work products. Each of the 37 AEC/FM processes in Building PRM was defined by using this template. An example process definition of Building PRM can be seen in Fig. 3.

BIM aspect was not included in the AEC/FM process definitions, since the reports, which were taken as basis for creating process definitions, have definitions of traditional AEC/FM processes and do not include BIM. Therefore, BIM related AEC/FM processes were marked and included in the BIM PRM. BIM PRM has 28 processes of Building PRM in total. In other words, BIM PRM was a subset of Building PRM. Each process in BIM PRM was defined based on the process purpose and BIM outcomes instead of process outcomes. BIM outcomes were defined based on the BIM uses identified by analyzing various resources such as surveys, reports and articles identified in the literature. Details about creation of BIM outcomes can be found in the PhD dissertation of Yilmaz [7]. Process purpose and base practices of the processes included in the BIM PRM remained the same as that of the processes included in Building PRM. An example process description belonging to BIM PRM can be seen in Fig. 4.

After BIM capability levels and their BIM attributes were created based on the principles given in ISO/IEC 33003 [20], rating scale given in ISO/IEC 33020 [36] was used without any modification. Four BIM capability levels were defined since they were sufficient without omitting any significant type of BIM utilization in AEC/FM industry. Two BIM attributes for each BIM capability levels were defined based on the recurring key words identified in the BIM uses. These BIM uses were selected from various resources such as surveys, guidelines and articles, and then collected in an Excel workbook. Recurring nouns and verbs were identified via Natural Language Analysis (NLA) method [40], and frequent words were used to create BIM attributes. Details about creation of BIM capability levels and their BIM attributes can be found in the dissertation [7]. Generic BIM work products and generic resources were developed based on the recurring keywords identified [7], BIM handbook [2] and various BIM guidelines. Rating scale of BIM-CAREM was same as the one defined in the ISO/IEC 33020 [36]. Validity and reliability of the BIM capability levels and their associated BIM attributes were established based on the expert reviews and the exploratory case study which are explained in Sect. 3.2.

3.2 Updating the BIM-CAREM

BIM-CAREM was updated based on the reviews of four experts who are working in the AEC/FM industry either as BIM managers or as BIM consultants. Three versions of BIM-CAREM were created. The first version of BIM-CAREM was reviewed by Expert 1 and second version of BIM-CAREM was then created. BIM A1.2 BIM Skills was added as BIM attribute for Level 1-Performed BIM. Although, this is not a requirement of performed level stated in the ISO/IEC 33003 [20], BIM skilled employees are necessary for performance of each process. BIM A3.1 Corporate-wide BIM Deployment was also added as a BIM attribute for Level 3-Optimized BIM.

Third version of BIM-CAREM was developed after expert reviews with Expert 2, Expert 3 and the exploratory case study. According to feedback of Expert 2, the terminology used in defining design processes of BIM PRM was corrected. Additionally, each BIM outcome was tagged with one of the two values namely "essential BIM use" and "enhanced BIM use" as defined in National BIM Guide for Owners [41]. According to reviews of Expert 3, one BIM attribute outcome of BIM A3.1 Corporate-wide BIM Deployment was updated. The previous version of this BIM attribute outcome could have been used for assessing processes belong to a specific type of organization. The latest version of the attribute became more generic to be used for measuring processes belong to various types of organizations such as designers and general contractors. An exploratory case study was performed to identify whether further updates were required or not. Architectural, structural and building services processes of an engineering and design firm located in Istanbul were assessed by using BIM-CAREM. According to the findings, identified BIM capability levels were the same as the levels expected by the interviewees. Details about the exploratory case study can be found in Yilmaz et al. [6]. We have not added or removed any BIM attributes within this iteration.

Finally, third version of BIM-CAREM was approved by Expert 1 and Expert 4, since most of their comments were covered before. In other words, the third version of BIM-CAREM is the final and approved version of BIM-CAREM. We have not added or removed any BIM capability levels. Four levels of BIM capability were approved by all of the experts. It has been stated that the model has a systematic approach for conducting assessments.

4 BIM-CAREM

The BIM-CAREM is composed of two dimensions which are BIM process dimension and the BIM capability dimension. As presented in Fig. 2, while BIM process dimension consists of the Building PRM and BIM PRM, the BIM capability dimension contains BIM MF. Details about the BIM-CAREM such as definitions of BIM capability levels can be found in the PhD dissertation of Yilmaz [7].

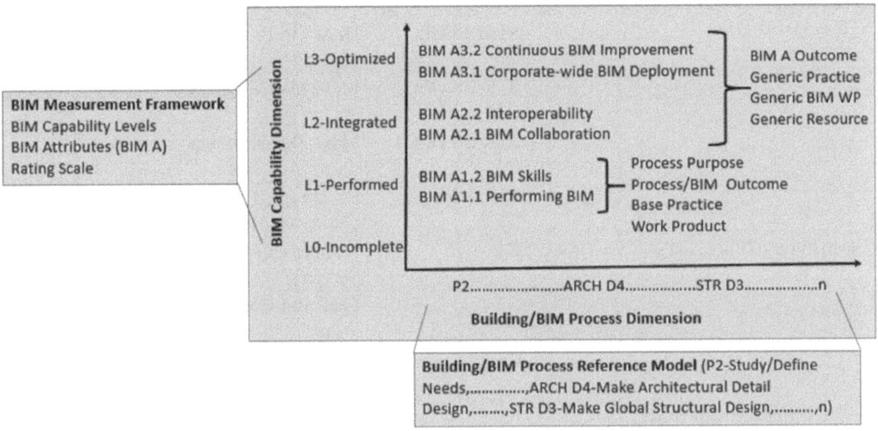

Fig. 2. The BIM-CAREM and its components

BIM-CAREM was developed to be used for assessing BIM capabilities of AEC/FM processes of facility life cycle. BIM-CAREM allows users to make formal assessments of AEC/FM processes by using BIM MF. AEC/FM processes to be measured can be selected from BIM PRM which is a subset of Building PRM. The BIM MF consists of four BIM capability levels and the BIM attributes which are used to characterize BIM capability of an implemented process.

While Building PRM consists of 37 key AEC/FM processes, BIM RPM contains 28 of these processes. In other words, only BIM related processes of Building PRM were included in the BIM PRM. The list of AEC/FM processes included in Building PRM are given in Table 2. Processes which are related to BIM was marked with "Y" and included in BIM PRM as well.

Table 2. Key AEC/FM processes included in Building PRM/BIM PRM

Phase ID	Process ID	Process name	Rel. to BIM? (Y/N)
Conceptual Planning (P)	P1	Assign Planning Team	N
	P2	Study/Define Needs	Y
	P3	Study Feasibility	Y
	P4	Develop Program	N
	P5	Develop Project Execution Plan	Y
	P6	Select And Acquire Site	Y
Architectural Design (ARCH D)	ARCH D1	Draw Up Brief	N
	ARCH D2	Draw Up Program	Y
	ARCH D3	Make Global Design	Y
	ARCH D4	Make Detail Design	Y
	ARCH D5	Do Design Tasks During Construction	Y
Structural/Building Services/Geotechnical Design (STR/BS/GEO D)	STR/BS/GEO D1	Draw Up Brief	N
	STR/BS/GEO D2	Draw Up Program	N
	STR/BS/GEO D3	Make Global Design	Y
	STR/BS/GEO D4	Make Detail Design	Y
	STR/BS/GEO D5	Do Design Tasks During Construction	Y
Construction (C)	C1	Acquire Construction Services	Y
	C2	Plan And Control The Work	Y
	C3	Provide Resources	Y
	C4	Build Facility	Y
Facilities Management (FM)	FM1	Plan/Control Facility	Y
	FM2	Manage Operations	Y
	FM3	Monitor Facility Conditions And Systems	Y
	FM4	Evaluate Conditions And Detect Problems	Y
	FM5	Develop Solutions	Y
	FM6	Select Plan Of Action	Y
	FM7	Implement Plan	Y

Each process in Building PRM was defined in terms of the process purpose, process outcomes, base practices and work products. Process purpose indicates the high level objective of performing the process [8]. Process outcome is an observable and assessable result of the successful achievement of the process purpose [8]. Base practice is an activity or a set of activities which contributes to process purpose achievement [8]. Work product is an artefact associated with the execution of the processes in Building PRM. Figure 3 presents 'Build Facility' belonging to Building PRM as an example process description.

Process ID	C4
Process name	Build Facility
Process purpose	The purpose of the Build Facility is to construct the facility according to the design using available resources.
Process outcomes	As a result of successful implementation of Build Facility: 1. Daily distribution plan is created based on the construction execution plan. 2. Resources are distributed to the appropriate work areas. 3. Facility elements are constructed by consuming resources. 4. Completed work is checked regarding to quantity, quality, and location of the product and constructed facility is approved. 5. Constructed building systems are tested, permits are obtained, facility is started up and facility is handed over to the owner.
Base practices	1. Plan the daily work: Utilize instructions for conducting the daily work based on the construction execution plan. (Outcome 1) 2. Distribute the resources: Transport the needed resources to the appropriate work areas based on the daily distribution plan. (Outcome 2) 3. Do the physical work: Construct the facility elements. (Outcome 3) (BIMout 1,2,3) 4. Inspect and approve the work: Check the completed work to assure that the quantity, quality, and location of the product is sufficient and that the contract requirements were fulfilled and approve the constructed facility. (Outcome 4) (BIMout 4) 5. Turn over the completed work: Test and adjust the building systems, obtain the occupancy permit, start up the facility and submit operation information to the owner. (Outcome 5) (BIMout 5)

Work Products	
1. Progress information (Outcome 1)	12. Environment
2. Construction execution plan	13. Partially consumed resources (Outcome 3)
3. Daily plan (Outcome 1)	14. Completed facility elements (Outcome 3)
4. Environment and governmental requirements	15. Inspection records information (Outcome 4)
5. Field experience	16. Daily approval plan
6. Available resources and mobilized site	17. Approved work (Outcome 4)
7. Distribution progress information (Outcome 2)	18. Inspections
8. Distributed resources (Outcome 2)	19. Handover information (Outcome 5)
9. Distribution priorities	20. Startup plan
10. Work progress information (Outcome 3)	21. Post construction information (Outcome 5)
11. Daily work plan	22. Facility (Outcome 5)

Base Practice	Inputs	Outputs
BP1	2,4,5	1,3
BP2	3,6,9	7,8
BP3	8,11,12	10,13,14
BP4	14,16,18	15,17
BP5	17,20	19,21,22

Fig. 3. Process description of Build Facility in Building PRM

BIM PRM was derived from Building PRM and created to define BIM related AEC/FM processes in terms of BIM. Each process in BIM PRM was defined in terms of the process purpose, BIM outcomes, base practices, and work products. Figure 4 presents the same process, which is Build Facility, included in the BIM PRM. While process purpose and base practices of Build Facility remained the same, BIM outcomes

Process ID	C4
Process name	Build Facility
Process purpose	The purpose of the Build Facility is to construct the facility according to the design using available resources.
BIM outcomes	As a result of successful implementation of Build Facility: 1. Daily work is executed based on 4D plan. 2. 3D location identification: Physical locations of elements on site are pinpointed for construction layout. (Enhanced BIM Use) 3. Facility is constructed by using BIM. 4. Quality assurance is conducted via BIM and site data such as pictures and point clouds. 5. Operation data is handed over to the owner with BIM.

BIM Work Products	
1. Facility (BIMout 3)	4. Locations points (BIMout 2)
2. Progress information (BIMout 1)	5. Daily work (BIMout 1)
3. Quality assurance (BIMout 4)	6. Handover information (BIMout 5)

Fig. 4. Process description of Build Facility in BIM PRM

and BIM work products were defined for each process included in the BIM PRM. BIM outcome is an observable and assessable result of the successful achievement of the process purpose in terms of BIM. BIM work product is a BIM artefact associated with the execution of the BIM related processes included in the BIM PRM.

BIM MF has four BIM capability levels which are Level 0- Incomplete, Level 1-Performed, Level 2-Integrated, and Level 3-Optimized. The BIM capability levels, and their BIM attributes are presented in Fig. 2 and Table 3.

Table 3. No of BIM attributes and associated BIM attribute outcomes

BIM Cap. Lev.	BIM A	BIM attribute outcomes
Level 1-Performed	BIM A1.1 Performing BIM	(a) The process achieves its defined BIM outcomes
	BIM A1.2 BIM Skills	(a) Staff with BIM skills and/or BIM experience are employed
		(b) Employees are supported in taking BIM trainings
		(c) BIM related processes are assigned to the BIM trained and/or BIM experienced employees or peer learning is encouraged
Level 2-Integrated	BIM A2.1 BIM Collaboration	(a) Requirements and strategies are defined for supporting BIM collaboration between internal and external parties
		(b) Requirements and strategies are defined for exchanging the model and the facility information between phases and processes
		(c) Defined BIM collaboration strategies are implemented
		(d) Defined exchange strategies of the model and the facility information are implemented
	BIM A2.2 Interoperability	(a) Interoperable formats are made available and used to support data exchange between BIM software and other construction software applications
Level 3-Optimized	BIM A3.1 Corporate-wide BIM Deployment	(a) Model is used for all processes and embraced by all team members
		(b) Required facility information for different processes are extracted from the model and provided for the use of all team members

(continued)

Table 3. (*continued*)

BIM Cap. Lev.	BIM A	BIM attribute outcomes
		(c) Change management and synchronization of the model are established and the model updates are tracked
		(d) BIM objects and facility information are collected in a library for reusing this information in future projects
	BIM A3.2 Continuous BIM Improvement	(a) A feedback mechanism is created to identify common causes of variations in BIM usage
		(b) Improvement opportunities, which are derived from feedback mechanism and from new BIM technology trends and best practices, are identified
		(c) An implementation strategy is established to achieve BIM improvement objectives

BIM capability level indicates an organization's BIM leverage capability in their building processes and is characterized by BIM attributes. BIM capability levels except from Level 0, related BIM attributes and their BIM attribute outcomes are presented in Table 3. BIM attribute is an observable phenomenon to be measured for identifying BIM capability level of a construction organization's process in formal BIM capability assessments. BIM attribute outcome (AO) is the observable result of a BIM attribute achievement.

Example generic BIM work products and generic resources with respect to the number of the BIM attribute outcomes are given in Table 4. The names of the BIM attribute outcome are presented in the table. Generic BIM work product (WP) is a BIM artefact associated with the execution of a process. Generic resource (GR) is resources which are required for executing a process.

Rating scale of the BIM-CAREM is the same as the one given in the ISO/IEC 33020 [36]. Rating scale is a rating schema to be used in BIM capability assessments for identifying the degree of achievement of BIM attributes. The BIM attributes are rated based on the below rating scale:

- N Not Achieved 0 to $\leq$ 15% achievement,
- P Partially Achieved $>$ 15% to $\leq$ 50% achievement,
- L Largely Achieved $>$ 50% to $\leq$ 85% achievement, and
- F Fully Achieved $>$ 85% to $\leq$ 100% achievement.

In order to calculate the composite ratings of the BIM attributes, we followed the procedures of aggregation using medians as explained in ISO/IEC 33020 [36].

Table 4. Example generic BIM WPs and example GRs defined for each of the BIM attribute outcome

No of BIM AO	Example generic BIM WP	Example GR
1.1a)	BIM work products	BIM authoring tools for model generation, analysis Tools
1.2a)	Job advertisement descriptions	BIM expert
1.2b)	BIM training records	BIM training budget
1.2c)	A strategy for assigning the BIM roles and responsibilities	Employees with BIM skills
2.1a)	Documents, reports and etc. which defines BIM collaboration strategies and/or procedures	Construction information and documentation standards and guidelines
2.1b)	BIM Execution Plan	Common data environments
2.1c)	Shared models for coordination	Collaboration tools
2.1d)	Existence of defined standard data formats for exchanging the model and the facility information	Process owners and stakeholders
2.2a)	Models and facility information represented with interoperable formats	Interoperable formats
3.1a)	Company-wide BIM execution plan	Virtual Reality Services
3.1b)	Model views	Model View Definitions
3.1c)	Version control of the model according to change requests	BIM server
3.1d)	Custom libraries such as 3D object libraries	Databases to store, gather and integrate the model and facility information
3.2a)	Mechanism for identifying and documenting BIM variations	Software for identification of problems in BIM utilization
3.2b)	Innovation meetings within the organization	Technical reports about new BIM technologies
3.2c)	Strategy to implement BIM improvement objectives	Employees such as BIM experts

5 A Case Study

Final version of the BIM-CAREM was evaluated via four explanatory case studies. The goal of these case studies was to determine the applicability of the BIM-CAREM for identifying the BIM capabilities of AEC/FM organizations. Case study conducted with Company B is presented as an example in this section. Company B is a structural design and engineering firm located in Ankara. Structural design of steel and concrete frames were evaluated within the context of the case study. A semi-structure interview was performed with manager of the company, three civil engineers and two technicians. Pre-defined interview questions were asked for primary data collection, and notes were taken. Secondary data was collected via direct observations of assessment indicators such as 3D models created by using BIM and structural analysis of the models. Additionally, whole interview was audio recorded. Case report of Company B was written based on the audio record, notes taken during the interview, and the secondary data collected. Rating of each BIM attribute was given based on this report. We used the rating scale explained in Sect. 3. It is four points ordinal scale which includes Not achieved (N-red), Partially achieved (P-yellow), Largely achieved (L-blue) and Fully achieved (F-green) and Not Applicable (NA-grey). In Table 5, the colored schema of the assessment ratings for Case Study 1 are provided.

Table 5. BIM attribute ratings of structural design of steel and reinforced concrete frames in Company B

	Level 1-Performed BIM		Level 2-Integrated BIM		Level 3-Optimized BIM	
Phase / BIM Attribute	BIM A1.1	BIM A1.2	BIM A2.1	BIM A2.2	BIM A3.1	BIM A3.2
STR D-Structural Design of Steel Frames	F	F	L	F	L	P
STR D-Structural Design of Reinforced Concrete Frames	F	F	L	F	P	P

Figure 5 shows the achieved BIM capability levels of the assessed two processes which are structural design of steel and concrete frames. For a BIM capability level to be reached, all BIM attributes should be largely or fully achieved.

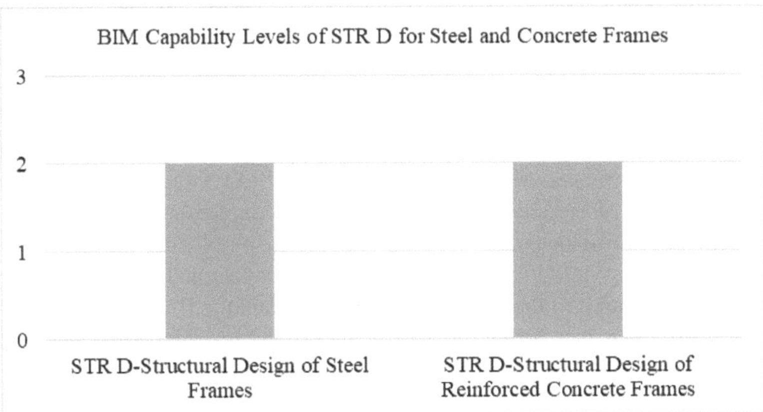

Fig. 5. Achieved BIM capability levels of structural design of steel and concrete frames

After the assessment, a questionnaire was applied to the interviewees to validate the findings of the case study. We asked them four questions which are given in Table 6 and requested them to rate each question from 1 to 5.

According to their answers and the ratings given, we concluded that BIM-CAREM can be used for identifying BIM capabilities of AEC/FM processes. Details of the rest of the four case studies can be found in the PhD dissertation of Yilmaz [7].

Table 6. Ratings given by interviewees for assessment results found via BIM-CAREM

Question	Rating
BIM-CAREM is capable of identifying BIM capabilities of AEC/FM processes	4
BIM-CAREM can be utilized for identifying BIM capabilities of AEC/FM processes	5
BIM-CAREM is helpful to understand BIM related gaps of AEC/FM processes by identifying their BIM capabilities	5
To what extent do the assessment results match with the existing BIM capabilities of your processes?	5

6 Conclusions

We followed the principles explained in the ISO/IEC 330xx family of standards to develop the BIM-CAREM. The model was updated iteratively through expert review and the exploratory case study, and later it was evaluated via explanatory case studies. It would have taken more time to develop such a holistic model, if we have not used the structure of the ISO/IEC 330xx which has significant amount of information for the users who will adapt it into different domains.

The ISO/IEC 33004 [21] was used for creating the Building/BIM PRM, since the important points and requirements of developing a process reference model are explained in this part. We did not face any significant difficulty in applying the procedures given in both of these standards. However, we put most of our effort in describing the process outcomes/BIM outcomes and the base practices. The Building/BIM PRM contains process definitions in terms of process purpose and process/BIM outcomes, as well as base practices and work products.

We followed the procedures explained in the ISO/IEC 33003 [20] for creating the BIM MF. This part of the standard contains sections explaining how to define capability levels and their associated attributes. We also inspired from the ISO/IEC 33020 [36] while generating definitions of BIM capability levels and their associated BIM attributes. Determination of the BIM capability levels and the BIM attributes took time, since they were updated in terms of expert reviews and an exploratory case study, as explained in Sect. 3.2. The BIM MF includes BIM capability levels, BIM attributes, and outcomes of these BIM attributes resultant of performing generic practices. The generic BIM work products and the generic resources were also defined within the context of the BIM MF. The elements given in ISO/IEC 33020 [36] are the examples for us while creating the generic BIM work products and generic resources.

We used the same procedures explained in the ISO/IEC 33003 [20] without any change for creating the rating scale and choosing the aggregation method. Thus, using the structure of the ISO/IEC 330xx saved significant amount of time. Nevertheless, a paper [42], which is about aggregation methods of constructs such as BIM attributes in qualitative research, was helpful to understand the aggregation methods of higher order constructs.

Various statistical methods are suggested for testing the validity and the reliability of the constructs, but further reading is required to understand and apply the right statistical test. The BIM capability levels and BIM attributes were validated by BIM experts who rated the BIM capability levels and their associated BIM attributes via an online questionnaire. The results of the online questionnaire can be found in the Yilmaz et al. [6]. Considering the results of the multiple case studies, we conclude that BIM-CAREM can be used to identify the BIM capability levels of the AEC/FM processes.

Acknowledgement. Attendance to SPICE 2018 is funded by Pamukkale University with project number 2018KKP219.

References

1. NBIMS: National BIM Standard - United States ® Version 3 - Scope (2015). https://www.nationalbimstandard.org/. Accessed 01 Jul 2018
2. Eastman, C., Teicholz, P., Sacks, R., Liston, K.: BIM Handbook. Wiley, Hoboken (2008)
3. Edirisinghe, R.: Comparative analysis of international and national level BIM standardization efforts and BIM adoption. In: 32nd CIB W78 Conference (2015)
4. Wu, C., et al.: Overview of BIM maturity measurement tools. J. Inf. Technol. Constr. **22**, 34–62 (2016)
5. Yilmaz, G., Akcamete, A., Demirors, O.: A review on capability and maturity models of building information modelling. In: Lean and Computing in Construction (2017)
6. Yilmaz, G., Akcamete, A., Demirors, O.: BIM-CAREM: a reference model for BIM capability assessments. Autom. Constr., Under Review, July 2018
7. Yilmaz, G.: BIM-CAREM: a reference model for building information modelling capability assessment (2017). http://library.metu.edu.tr/search/?searchtype=X&searcharg=BIM-CAREM&searchscope=15. Accessed 30 Jul 2018
8. ISO/IEC: ISO/IEC 33001 Information technology – Process assessment – Concepts and terminology (2015). https://www.iso.org/obp/ui/#iso:std:iso-iec:33001:ed-1:v1:en. Accessed 01 Jul 2018
9. ISO/IEC: ISO/IEC 33063 Information technology – Process assessment – Process assessment model for software testing (2015). https://www.iso.org/obp/ui/#iso:std:iso-iec:33063:ed-1:v1:en. Accessed 01 Jul 2018
10. ISO/IEC: ISO/IEC 33072 Information technology – Process assessment – Process capability assessment model for information security management (2016). https://www.iso.org/obp/ui/#iso:std:iso-iec:ts:33072:ed-1:v2:en. Accessed 01 Jul 2018
11. NBIMS: National BIM Standard United States ® Version 3 - Minimum BIM (2015). https://www.nationalbimstandard.org. Accessed 01 Jul 2018
12. IU Arhictect's Office: BIM Proficiency Matrix (2009). http://www.iu.edu/~vpcpf/consultant-contractor/standards/bim-standards.shtml
13. BIM Supporters B.V.: BIM QuickScan Tool (2010). https://app.bimsupporters.com/quickscan/. Accessed 04 Apr 2018
14. Kam, C., Senaratna, D., Xiao, Y., McKinney, B.: The VDC Scorecard: Evaluation of AEC Projects and Industry Trends. CIFE Working Paper #WP136 (2013). https://stacks.stanford.edu/file/druid:st437wr3978/WP136.pdf. Accessed 03 Jul 2018
15. PennState CIC: Organizational BIM Assessment Profile (2012). http://bim.psu.edu/resources/owner/bim_planning_guide_for_facility_owners-version_2.0.pdf. Accessed 27 Jun 2018
16. VICO Software: VICO BIM Scorecard Survey. https://www.surveymonkey.com/r/9YCHVXC. Accessed 25 Aug 2017

17. Succar, B.: Building information modelling maturity matrix. In: Handbook of Research on Building Information Modeling and Construction Informatics: Concepts and Technologies, pp. 65–103 (2010)
18. Liang, C., Lu, W., Rowlinson, S., Zhang, X.: Development of a multifunctional BIM maturity model. J. Constr. Eng. Manag. **142**(11), 06016003 (2016)
19. Giel, B., McCuen, T.: MINIMUM BIM - 2nd Edn. Proposed Revision. Building Innovation, pp. 1–35 (2014)
20. ISO/IEC: ISO/IEC 33003 Information technology – Process assessment – Requirements for process measurement frameworks (2015). https://www.iso.org/obp/ui/#iso:std:iso-iec:33003:ed-1:v1:en. Accessed 01 Jul 2018
21. ISO/IEC: ISO/IEC 33004 Information technology – Process assessment – Requirements for process reference, process assessment and maturity models (2015). https://www.iso.org/obp/ui/#iso:std:iso-iec:33004:ed-1:v2:en. Accessed 01 Jul 2018
22. Automative Sig: Automotive SPICE Process Assessment Model (2007). http://www.automotivespice.com/fileadmin/software-download/Automotive_SPICE_PAM_30.pdf. Accessed 01 Jul 2018
23. ISO/IEC: The ISO/IEC 15504 – 3 Information technology - Process assessment - Part 3: Guidance of performing an assessment (2012)
24. Zanoni, M., Perin, F., Fontana, F.A., Viscusi, G.: Development of MDevSPICE – the medical device software process assessment framework Marion. J. Softw. Evol. Process **26** (12), 1172–1192 (2014)
25. ISO/IEC: The ISO/IEC 12207 Systems and software engineering–Software life cycle processes (2008)
26. ISO/IEC: The ISO/IEC 15504 – 2 Information technology - Process assessment - Part 2: Performing an assessment (2012)
27. Cass, A., Völcker, C., Ouared, R., Dorling, A., Winzer, L., Carranza, J.M.: SPICE for SPACE trials, risk analysis, and process improvement. Softw. Process Improv. Pract. **9**(1), 13–21 (2004)
28. ISO/IEC: The ISO/IEC 15504 – 5 Information technology - Process assessment - Part 5: An Exemplar Process Assessment Model (2006). https://www.iso.org/standard/60555.html. Accessed 03 Jul 2018
29. Top, O.O., Demirors, O.: A reference model for software agility assessment: AgilityMod. In: SPICE, pp. 145–158 (2015)
30. Adali, O.E., Top, O.O., Demirors, O.: Assessment of agility in software organizations with a web-based agility assessment tool. In: Proceedings of the 43rd Euromicro Conference on Software Engineering and Advanced Applications SEAA 2017, pp. 88–95 (2017)
31. Salmanoğlu, M., Coşkunçay, A., Yıldız, A., Demirörs, O.: An exploratory case study for assessing the measurement capability of an agile organization. Softw. Qual. Prof. **20**(2), 36–47 (2018)
32. ISO/IEC: ISO/IEC 33052 Information technology – Process reference model (PRM) for information security management (2016). https://www.iso.org/obp/ui/#iso:std:iso-iec:ts:33052:ed-1:v1:en. Accessed 01 Jul 2018
33. ISO/IEC: ISO/IEC 33071 Information technology – Process assessment – An integrated process capability assessment model for Enterprise processes (2016). https://www.iso.org/obp/ui/#iso:std:iso-iec:33071:ed-1:v1:en. Accessed 01 Jul 2018
34. Gökalp, E., Demirörs, O.: Model based process assessment for public financial and physical resource management processes. Comput. Stand. Interfaces **54**, 186–193 (2017)
35. IEEE: ISO/IEC TR 24774 - Systems and Software Engineering Life Cycle Management: Guidelines for Process Description (2012). https://www.iso.org/obp/ui/#iso:std:iso-iec:tr:24774:ed-2:v1:en. Accessed 01 Jul 2018

36. ISO/IEC: ISO/IEC 33020 Information technology – Process assessment – Process measurement framework for assessment of process capability (2015). https://www.iso.org/obp/ui/#iso:std:iso-iec:33020:ed-1:v1:en. Accessed 01 Jul 2018
37. RIBA: RIBA Plan of Work (2013). https://www.ribaplanofwork.com/. Accessed 09 Nov 2017
38. Technical Research Center of Finland: Construction Process Model (1997). https://www.vtt.fi/inf/pdf/tiedotteet/1997/T1845.pdf. Accessed 01 Jul 2018
39. The Pennsylvania State University CIC: An Integrated Building Process Model (1990). https://www.pennstatecic.org/uploads/5/1/2/1/51219339/tr_001_sanvido_1990_ibpm.pdf. Accessed 01 Jul 2018
40. Abbott, R.J.: Program design by informal English descriptions. Commun. ACM **26**(11), 882–894 (1983)
41. NBIMS: National BIM Guide for Owners (2017). https://www.nibs.org/?nbgo. Accessed 01 Jul 2018
42. Johnson, R.E., Rosen, C.C., Chang, C.-H.: To aggregate or not to aggregate: steps for developing and validating higher-order multidimensional constructs. J. Bus. Psychol. **26**(3), 241–248 (2011)

ISO/IEC 15504 [illegible] information technology — Process assessment [illegible] Process [illegible] Accessed 01 Jul 2018 [illegible]

[illegible] Accessed 01 Jul 2018

[illegible]

[illegible]

[illegible] (2017) [illegible] Accessed 01 [illegible]

[illegible]

SPI Education and Management Issues

REFES Model for Leadership as Practice in Software Process Improvement Initiatives

Alessandra C. Zoucas[1], Cristiano J. de A. Cunha[1], and Clenio F. Salviano[2(✉)]

[1] Programa de Pos-Grad. em Eng. e Gestao do Conhecimento - PPGEGC, Univ. Fed. de Santa Catarina - UFSC, Florianopolis, Brazil
alessandrazoucas@gmail.com, 01cunha@gmail.com

[2] CTI: Centro de Tecnologia da Informação Renato Archer, Rodovia D. Pedro I, km 143.6, Campinas, SP 13069-901, Brazil
Clenio.Salviano@gmail.com

Abstract. Leadership is a relevant aspect for the success of Software Process Improvement (SPI) initiatives. Leadership as Practice is an approach characterized by perspectives of practices and understands leadership as a social process contextually situated. A multi-case qualitative research was conducted, with three initiatives of SPI. Data was collected by means of fifteen semi-structured interviews, in depth, with involved subjects in the studied cases, besides the documentation available by companies that participated in the study. The analyses technique employed for the investigation of leadership practices was the thematic analyses. In each of the SPI initiatives researched, the same five distinct practices were found: Responsiveness, Empowering, Facilitation, Engagement and Structuring. These five practices are defined as the REFES Model. The present investigation demonstrated that the context of practices is not limited to their social context, but instead is increased for the own practice, by participating at the context of other practices. Therefore, it was concluded that leadership in SPI initiatives usually involve complex network of relationships, practices and structures and that it mostly occurs vertically, formally and collaboratively.

Keywords: Leadership · Leadership as Practice
Software Process Improvement

1 Introduction

Understanding the phenomenon of leadership in the context of Software Process Improvement (SPI) initiatives is relevant of both practice and research. Leadership is one of the main critical success factors in SPI initiatives [1]. This article presents the REFES Model as a thematic map with five leadership practices identified in practical SPI initiatives: Responsiveness, Empowerment, Facilitation, Engagement, and Structuring (REFES). This model is a result from a research conducted under Leadership as Practice paradigm [2–4] in the SPI practice.

Understand leadership practices in SPI initiatives contributes to a more effective management of these initiatives. Previously, we conducted studies as a preparation for

I. Stamelos et al. (Eds.): SPICE 2018, CCIS 918, pp. 139–153, 2018.
https://doi.org/10.1007/978-3-030-00623-5_10

this research [5, 6]. Their results confirmed the interest of the academy, reinforcing the viability and the opportunity of continuity of this research.

The objective of a research described in this article is to understand leadership in SPI initiatives from the perspective of Leadership as Practice. This objective is detailed into four more specific objectives:

(a) Identify leadership activities in the context of the SPI initiatives studied.
(b) To identify the relationships established among the leadership practices in the SPI initiatives studied.
(c) Analyze Leadership as Practice in the context of the SPI initiatives studied.
(d) Define a model as a thematic map with leadership practices.

The original research and its results are fully described in a Ph.D. Thesis [7]. The original research and its fully description are an expanded version of the contents of this article and includes the description of the leadership practices, their analyzes in light of sociological theory, their classification as horizontal, vertical, formal, informal, individual and collaborative, and points of convergence and divergence among the activities that constitute the leadership practices. Two other articles describe specific results of this thesis. One describes a bibliometrics study on Leadership as Practice [8] and another describes the approach used to identify key competencies of leaders in SPI [9]. This article concentrates in the REFES Model. REFES Model is a name given in this article for the original thematic map produced as a major result of the research.

2 Leadership in SPI and Leadership-as-Practice

Organizational success is influenced by the satisfaction of those involved in their processes, whether they are employees or clients and one way to increase satisfaction is the actions and initiatives quality improvement. SPI has been used by organizations to quality improvement. Leadership has been an essential aspect of SPI Initiatives. In the context of quality management, the leader must establish the purpose and direction of the organization [10].

An integrative review of the literature was conducted to examine scientific work dealing with this phenomenon in SPI initiatives is at the heart of other areas related to the study. During the analysis of the articles selected in the integrative review of the literature, it was verified that there are no investigations that seek to understand the leadership during SPI initiatives [5, 6]. This confirmed that there was an unprecedented and relevant research opportunity for both academia and organizations interested in SPI and leadership.

In the literature studied, it was observed that, despite the large volume of publications with different definitions of the term leader, most leadership research attributes to an individual, a leader, the responsibility to exert influence over a group of people [11]. Northouse proposes the definition of leadership as a process involving a group of people, acting in a coordinated way, to achieve common goals [12].

From the published works on Leadership as Practice, some authors understand that leadership is a social phenomenon, composed of processes, practices and interactions between groups that share a direction focused on the achievement of objectives of common interest [3]. Leadership in organizations often involves a complex web of relationships, practices, and structures [13]. In this sense, those involved in organizations need to articulate to define strategies that support the achievement of business objectives [14].

The main researchers of this subject are Carroll et al. [2], Crevani et al. [3] and Raelin [4]. Their works are most cited in the scientific bases studied. These researchers argue about the need to understand empirically practices and daily leadership interactions. These three publications are responsible for disseminating the term Leadership as Practice and define its main terms. The essence of Leadership as Practice is the conception that leadership occurs as a practice, rather than residing in the traits or behaviors of specific individuals. Leadership as Practice is not concerned with revealing what a person thinks or does, but on identifying "how" leadership emerges and unfolds [4]. In Leadership as Practice, leadership is a social phenomenon, composed of processes, practices and interactions between groups that share a direction with a focus on the achievement of objectives of common interest.

3 Research Methodology

This research uses a qualitative, empirical-descriptive approach through multiple case study strategy, which aims to understand the processes that cooperate to carry out an event or phenomenon [15]. It was adopted as a worldview the perspective located in Morgan's interpretive quadrant [16], which defines reality as a product of subjective and inter-subjective experience of individuals. Thus, we explored in depth the Leadership as Practice in SPI initiatives, and adopted the interpretive perspective for the analysis of data collected in in-depth interviews with those involved in these initiatives [17].

The case study is a research strategy that aims to show and characterize the occurrence and possible evolution of a given phenomenon. By means of the detailed analysis of an individual case, it is assumed that it is possible to acquire knowledge about the phenomenon investigated based on an in-depth study of the case. In this sense, "through a deep and exhaustive dive into a delimited object, the case study allows penetration into a social reality, not fully achieved by a sample survey and exclusively quantitative evaluation" [18].

4 Research Process

This research was carried out in three SPI initiatives in which the first author of this article carried out consultancies to implement the improvements. The first author carried out research on the companies and the production of its results. The second and third authors oriented the work and wrote this article, respectively, besides participating in specific aspects of the research.

These three different SPI initiatives were selected, as three distinct cases, to investigate the phenomenon of leadership. According to Merriam [25] guidelines, we used a small non-probabilistic sample of SPI initiatives. Thus, we consider SPI initiatives in companies that have been successful in official evaluation at the initial maturity levels of CMMI-DEV or MR-MPS-SW reference models. For the sample, we selected three SPI initiatives. Each SPI initiative studied was carried out between December 2014 and March 2015 in a company from Santa Catarina state, independent of the branch of business, and established in Florianópolis city. We decided to study SPI initiatives in Florianópolis because it is highlighted in Brazil in the technology sector and for easy access to selected companies. All companies accepted the invitation to participate in the research.

Considering that the cases selected for this study are compatible with each other, we chose to study multiple cases in order to obtain more convincing data and generate a more robust result. The cases were selected based on objective criteria. The study included data collection, documentation identification, interviews and data analyses.

The data collected in documentation and interviews transcription were examined through thematic analysis. Thematic analysis is a systematized method in six phases, to identify, analyze and report patterns in the data collected, as follows [19]:

(a) Phase 1: Familiarization with the data;
(b) Phase 2: Initial generation of codes;
(c) Phase 3: Search of topics;
(d) Phase 4: Review of potential issues;
(e) Phase 5: Definition and denomination of themes;
(f) Phase 6: Report production.

We interviewed fifteen participants from SPI initiatives with different profiles. The interviews took place between July–September 2016, totaling 10 h and 35 min of audio. After the interview, we would forward the audio for transcription.

In the cases studied, we identified five leadership practices. During the analysis of the data collected, we verified that each identified practice included from one to eleven activities that constituted it. For the purposes of this study, we named these activities with a verb in the infinitive, to show that they are actions motivated by different situations. Thus, we also present the practices with a definition and activities that constitute the practices of leadership, aiming to express what was considered to identify each leadership practice in the SPI initiatives studied:

(a) Responsiveness: actions that aim to respond quickly and appropriately to a given situation, including the activities of identifying opportunity for improvement; identify knowledge (culture); and verify improved process;
(b) Empowerment: actions aimed at creating the necessary conditions and responsible autonomy for those involved to carry out activities related to the SPI initiative, including the activity of empowering those involved in the SPI initiative;
(c) Facilitation: actions to support a group of people to understand their common objectives, helping them to identify how to achieve these objectives, and to check for discrepancies between what was planned and what was done, including activities to identify diversion or impairment; determine corrective action, and manage conflict;
(d) Engagement: actions that aim to awaken in the involved feelings in favor of the SPI initiative, including activities of: establishing a relationship of trust; to explain the

desire of high management to perform improvement meetings; publish improved process; reporting the status of the SPI initiative and recognizing achievements;

(e) Structuring: actions that aim to organize activities to be carried out so that the SPI initiative can be successfully completed, including activities to: analyze the feasibility of the SPI initiative; hire consulting; select involved in the SPI initiative; select and recruit resource to act on the SPI initiative; engaging those involved in the SPI initiative; plan improvement activities; select improvement to be implemented; to charge those involved to carry out the improvement activities with which they have committed themselves; select pilot project; and determine the training of those involved.

In order to identify leadership practices and activities that constitute these practices, we read twice each document collected and each interview transcribed. We also listened the audio from the interviews and verified the correspondent transcribed content to confirm the understanding, since the voice intonation of the interviewee could provided useful information for the interpretation of the data collected. We carry out this process until we were familiar with the data and thus we were able to identify initial codes in documents and in interview excerpts where some leadership action was mentioned during the SPI initiative. In this way, we identified different meanings and patterns in the data collected. Initially we marked more than 85 codes for each organizational unit.

In revising the codes, we realized that some of them were redundant and could be put together in just one code. At this stage of the research, we usually identified new codes with each new interview analyzed. This fact made we return a few times to the content already analyzed, to verify if the new code would apply to them as well. In some cases, the new code was unique to a particular interview or document. In other cases, the new code could actually be applied to excerpts from interviews or documents previously analyzed.

It should be noted that, during this phase of the research, we also group the codes into sets that, by the Thematic Analysis method, are called themes. On October 2016, the research resulted in more than 40 codes and more than 270 quotations in each organizational unit studied, distributed in eight themes. At this point in the research, there were 1,008 coded excerpts from the 15 interviews.

We presented the identified codes and themes to a research group at a meeting held on October 17, 2016. At that meeting, it was proposed that each topic should be considered as a leadership practice, and each code as an activity carried out within the practice of leadership. So, we revised, once again, the initial themes, to ensure its adherence to the research question and to the definition of practice.

In the sequence, we continued to analyze the interviews conducted and, although there were no other stakeholders willing to be interviewed, theoretical saturation was identified at the moment when the interviewees reaffirmed the information reported by previous interviewees from the same organizational unit. Thus, they no longer contribute with new information to the research.

After reviewing and coding all the data collected, as well as grouping them into themes, we performed a detailed analysis of each identified topic, aiming to reduce them to about twenty codes and five to seven themes per organizational unit studied, as indicated by Creswel and Plano Clark [17]. Another question that accompanied us during this phase was the scope of the theme, related to what each theme should and should not contain. In answering this question, we made the themes identified increasingly atomic, that is, without a shadow area in relation to the other themes identified in the research.

At the end of this phase, as a result, we identified 22 codes in the case of company 1. In company 2, we identified 23 codes, and in company 3 we identified 25. In this way, we interpreted codes as the activities performed within the leadership practices in the initiatives SPI studied. In all the cases studied, we identified five themes (leadership practices), as can be seen in Table 1.

Table 1. Number of activities within each leadership practice

Subject (leadership practice)	Company 1	Company 2	Company 3
Responsiveness	3	3	5
Empowerment	1	1	1
Facilitation	9	9	11
Engagement	6	7	5
Structuring	3	3	3
Total	22	23	25

Each subject (leadership practice) identified is related to one or more codes (activities that constitute the practice of leadership). From that point, we replaced the terms themes and codes that were used in the thematic analysis, and we began to adopt the terms "practice of leadership" and "activity that constitutes the practice" because they are the terms used in the field of study of Leadership as Practice.

5 Leadership Practices: The REFES Model as Thematic Map

There are five leadership practices: Responsiveness, Empowerment, Facilitation, Engagement, and Structuring. In each case studied, leadership practices were impacted by other leadership practices. This relationship between practices can be observed through a thematic map. This is an expected element in the execution of phase 5 of thematic analysis [19]. Therefore, the thematic map of Leadership as Practice in the SPI initiatives studied was developed from the analysis and interpretation of the data collected in this research.

In this sense, by generating a satisfactory mapping of Leadership as Practice of each SPI initiative, the impact of one practice on another was repeated in them. As a result, very close thematic maps in the three cases were identified. So, relationships among the leadership practices found in the SPI initiatives were analyze together. To support the construction of the thematic map, we initially constructed Table 2 to record data on the key relationships between impacting and impacted leadership practices (themes).

Table 2. Mapping of leadership practices in SPI initiatives studied

Impacting practice	Activity	R	Activity	Impacted practice
Responsiveness	Identify improvement opportunities	A	Analyze the feasibility of the SPI initiative	Structuring
Responsiveness	Identify improvement opportunities	B	Contract consulting	Structuring
Responsiveness	Identify improvement opportunities	J	Select improvement to implement	Structuring
Responsiveness	Verify improved process	M	Select improvement to implement	Structuring
Empowerment	Empower those involved in the SPI initiative	F	Identify deviation or impairment	Facilitation
			Determining corrective action	Facilitation
			Manage conflict	Facilitation
Structuring	Select involved in the SPI initiative	C	Establish trust relationship	Engagement
Structuring	Select and recruit resource to act on the SPI initiative			Engagement
Structuring	Select involved in the SPI initiative	E	Empower those involved in the SPI initiative	Empowerment
Structuring	Select and recruit resource to act on the SPI initiative			Empowerment
Structuring	Obtain commitment of those involved in the SPI	D	Explicit the desire of top management	Engagement
Structuring	Contract consulting	=	Plan the improvement activities	Structuring
Engagement	Make improvement meetings	G	Select improvement to be implemented	Structuring
Engagement	Make improvement meetings	H	Establish trust relationship	Engagement
Engagement	Hold improvement meetings	I	Identify knowledge (culture)	Responsiveness

(*continued*)

Table 2. (*continued*)

Impacting practice	Activity	R	Activity	Impacted practice
Engagement	Hold improvement meetings	L	Check improved process	Responsiveness
Engagement	Make improvement meetings	Q	Determining empowerment of stakeholders	Structuring
Engagement	Publish Improved Process	K	Select pilot project	Structuring
Engagement	Report SPI initiative status	O	To charge those involved in the execution of committed improvement activities	Structuring
Engagement	Report status of the SPI initiative	P	Determine Corrective Action	Facilitation
Facilitation	Identify deviation or impairment	=	Determine Corrective Action	Structuring
Facilitation	Determine Corrective Action	N	Select involved in the SPI initiative	Facilitation
Facilitation	Manage conflict	=	Determine Corrective Action	Facilitation

The granularity of this analysis considered the impact found among the activities that constitute each of the five practices identified and the impact relationships of one over the others, which are identified from the letters presented in R (for Relationship) column. These letters were inserted in the text that follows Table 1, in which we analyze its content, to support its interpretation. Equality sign (=) represents the cases that we have identified as the relation between activities of the same practice.

The Responsiveness practice was the first to be identified in this research, since the SPI initiatives were materialized based on the response given to the improvement opportunities found in these organizational units.

Responsiveness impacted on the Structuring practice (A) when the sponsors of the SPI initiatives analyzed the technical, resource and financial viability, i.e. if there was knowledge and experience of the team members, if there was a collaborator available to carry out the improvement activities and resources the SPI initiative. This analysis culminated in the hiring of the consultancy specialized in software process improvement for the organizational units targeted for improvements (B). Therefore, the same team of consultants was responsible for guiding all SPI initiatives studied, supporting them in the planning of improvement activities. Since these two activities constitute the same practice, although one has impacted the other, this does not show any influence between practices.

During the implementation of the Structuring practice, employees were selected or recruited to be involved in the improvement activities. These employees had their roles and responsibilities explicitly assigned, so they received the trustworthy investment from the sponsor, who gained their commitment to the SPI initiative. This shows the impact of Structuring practice in Engagement practice (C). The commitment of other levels of the organization was also observed when the members of the High Management explained their interest in the SPI initiative and their desire for it to succeed. In this way, the impact of practice Structuring in Engagement (D) practice was evidenced.

The sponsors provided adequate conditions for these employees to carry out the work and also gave them responsible autonomy to act and make decisions. Therefore, practice Structuring directly impacted on Empowerment practice (E). With the Empowerment of those involved in the SPI initiative, they were better able to both carry out the planned improvement activities and perform the activities of the Facilitation practice when it was motivated by some situation. This shows the impact of Empowerment practice in Facilitation practice (F).

The practice Structuring is constituted of greater number of activities than the other practices of the leadership. Thus, still in the domain of this practice, improvement activities were planned and formalized in the tools that the organizational units used to manage their projects. Among these activities was the need to "select improvements" that were typically carried out in a group, during the activity "to make improvements", which is in the scope of the Engagement practice. This again shows that the practice Structuring has impacted on the Engagement practice (G).

It was also during the "make improvement meetings" activity that, in discussing options that could be selected to improve the process, consultants found room to "establish a relationship of trust" with the selected members to be involved in the SPI initiative, Structuring and Engagement (H). Also during the improvement meetings, Project Manager 2 and Project Improvement Team Leader 3 sought to gain the trust of the other members of their respective teams, again showing the relationship between the Structuring and Engagement practices (H).

The "improvement meetings" favored options for improving the process to be suggested by both the consultant and those involved in the improvement activities. These suggestions originated in the experience and culture of the organizational unit or the knowledge of the participants themselves, again presenting the impact of the practice. When the suggestion for improvement was considered as a quick and appropriate response to improve the process, it was selected, approaching the practice of Practicing Structuring (J).

When the processes were modeled and incorporating the selected improvements, they were published in the organizational and collaborative knowledge bases of the respective SPI initiatives. This was intended to engage the team in the use of the improved process in pilot projects, which again characterizes the relationship between Structuring and Engagement practices (K).

However, after the pilot project started, improvement meetings were held to discuss and verify the improved process. This shows the impact of Engagement in Responsiveness practice (L). In response to adaptation requests, other improvements were selected to fit some of the processes. This reality again shows how Responsiveness practice has impacted on Structuring practice (M).

We would like to emphasize that it was especially after the start of pilot projects that most of the conflicts identified and reported in this research occurred. To resolve these conflicts, corrective actions were planned and assigned to those involved with the improvements. This shows the impact of practice Facilitation in Structuring practice (N).

In the field of Engagement practice, there have been periodic reports on the status of improvement activities for the sponsor and other stakeholders in the SPI initiative. This activity helped those involved to understand the situation of improvement activities and, where appropriate, the sponsors were charged with carrying out their activities, engaging them in the SPI initiative. This exemplifies once again how the practice Structuring has impacted on the Engagement practice (O). In addition, when the status reports of the SPI initiatives identified some significant deviation, corrective actions were taken to maintain commitments to the SPI initiative, showing how Engagement practice impacted on Facilitation practice (P).

The training of those involved in the improved processes took place during the meetings of improvement in companies 1 and 2. These actions characterize the impact of the practice Engagement in the Structuring practice (Q). In company 3, this training was carried out in the classroom, in the form of training.

Finally, the recognition of the work, which was manifested by the directors of the company 1 and 2, constitutes the practice Engagement. When it was done, this practice was not impacted or impacted by another practice. Therefore, it is not represented in Table 1. Figure 1 shows the thematic map, as the REFES Model, resulting from the analysis of the relationship between impacting and impacted practices in the SPI initiatives studied.

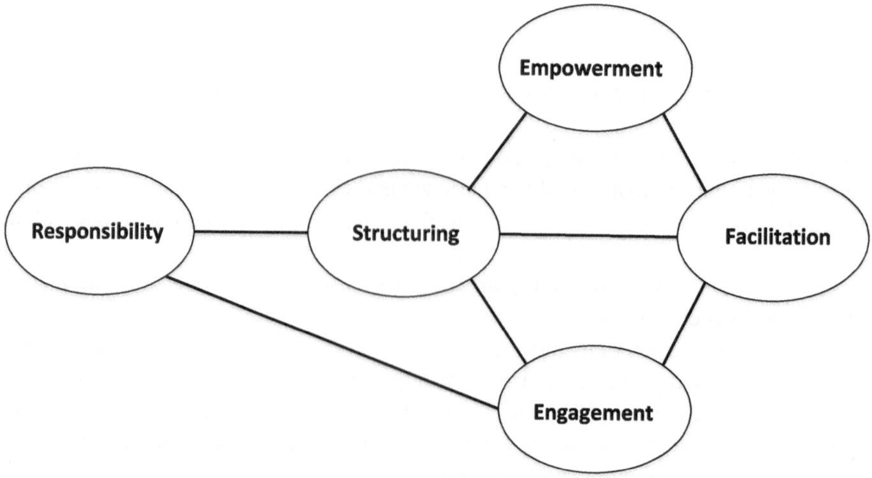

Fig. 1. REFES Model

In the REFES Model presented, each line represents a link between the leadership practices encountered, this means that the implementation of one leadership practice directly impacted on the implementation of the other leadership practice.

To support the analysis of the generated model and to obtain a contribution of synthesis and visual representation of the relations between the practices, we applied the concepts of the Theory of Graphs.

In this research, we identified edges (relations) between the vertices (leadership practices), composed of the following set of vertices V = {Responsiveness, Empowerment, Structuring, Engagement and Facilitation} and the respective set of edges E = {(Responsiveness, Structuring), (Structuring, Empowerment), (Empowerment, Facilitation), (Engagement, Engagement), (Engagement, Facilitation) and (Facilitation, Structuring). Therefore, the graph found has five vertices and seven edges, as shown in Fig. 2. Figure 2 presents the REFES Model as a thematic map resulting from the analysis of the relationship between impacting and impacted leaderships practices in the SPI initiatives studied.

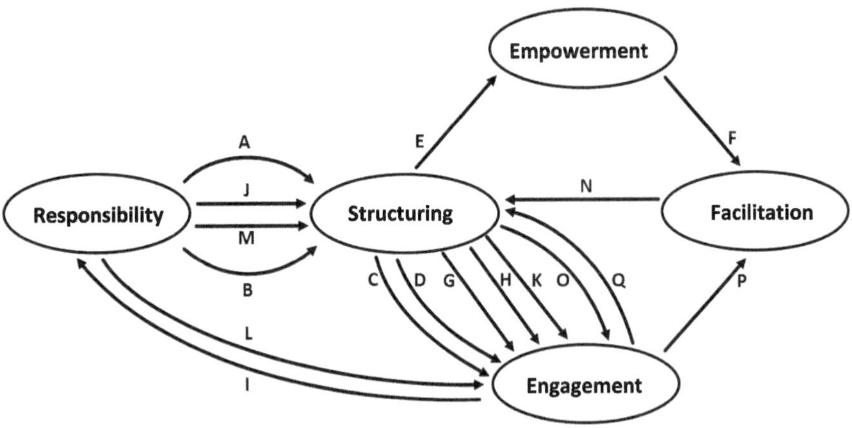

Fig. 2. REFES Model with impacting and impacted leaderships practices

The degree of emission of a vertex V corresponds to the number of edges that start from V. The higher the degree (leadership practices), the greater is the number of times this practice has impacted the practice at the opposite end of the edge. Therefore, among the five leadership practices found, the practice that most impacted the others is Structuring, with a degree of emission equal to seven. It is in the implementation of the Structuring practice that there are more leadership interferences, especially in Engagement practice.

Then, the Responsiveness practice was the one that most impacted the others, with a degree of emission equal to five. Empowerment and Facilitation are the practices with less impact on other practices, but are not less important for the success of the SPI initiatives. Both practices had a degree of emission equal to one.

The degree of reception of a vertex V corresponds to the number of edges that arrive in V. The higher the degree of vertex reception (leadership practices), the greater is the number of times this practice has been impacted by the practice at the opposite end of the edge. Therefore, among the five leadership practices found in the SPI initiatives studied, the practice that was most impacted by the others was Engagement, with a degree of reception equal to seven. This shows that the Engagement practice was the one that received the most interference from the leadership practices in the SPI initiatives studied.

However, the practices less impacted by other practices, but not less important than the others for the success of the SPI initiatives studied, are Facilitation, with an emission degree equal to two, in addition to the practices of Responsiveness and Empowerment, both with a degree of issue equal to one.

Thus, this study presented the leadership practices found in the SPI initiatives studied, the relationship between them, and the practices that have more and less impact on the others. However, it was not possible to measure which of these practices is the most significant or least significant for the execution of the SPI initiatives studied, since the objective of this study was to understand how practices occur and thus also found relationships between them. Therefore, we did not carry out a more in-depth study on the degree of influence that one practice had on another.

6 Discussion

The results presented in this work were extracted from an investigation carried out with the objective of understanding how leadership occurs in the SPI initiatives from the perspective of Leadership as Practice.

This study identified leadership practices, activities within these practices (specific objective “a”), and situations that motivated such activities in three different cases. This contribution is in line with the view of Endrissat and von Arx [24, p. 295], when the authors state that “practices are situated because leadership is found in micro activities that are embedded in a specific situation.”

Another contribution is understanding of how leadership occurred in the cases studied and supported the construction of the thematic map that represent the causal relationships of certain practices over others (specific objectives “b”, “c” and “d”). This is probably an unprecedented finding in the studies on Leadership as Practice, since in the studies researched we did not identify studies that discussed or presented how causal relationships are established between leadership practices.

To perform the research, we used an approach of qualitative interview in depth, using a semi-structured interview script. Data were collected from a total of three sponsors (including one managing director, one administrative manager and one development manager), five project managers, three requirements analysts, one development coordinator, two system analysts and developers, and one project leader SPI) distributed in three distinct organizational units, which were successful in the official evaluation of software process reference model.

The results of the interviews were complemented, where possible, by documentary evidence such as meetings minutes, planning of the SPI initiative, the modeling process, report and plan of the official evaluation of software processes, among other documents provided by the participating organizational units.

Although it has not found other research on Leadership as Practice in SPI initiatives, the results of this study are similar to the findings of Bolden [20], which examined leadership practices in higher education; of Collinson and Collinson [21] in the education sector; and Gronn [22], in which the authors observed the practice of vertical leadership, as well as the horizontal influence of informal or inter-institutional leaders. The results of this research also resemble Meier's report [23], which, when analyzing Leadership as Practice in hospital units, identified that labor relations and collaborative sharing coexisted with the formal medical liability that the pulmonary medicine consultant and his fellow consultants performed.

During the analysis of the leadership practices found in the three cases studied, we identified that all organizational units received advice from the same process implementing institution and obtained the same level of process maturity. Therefore, the three organizational units have implemented Project Management and Requirements Management processes. Therefore, we identified that there was also a procedural aspect, common to all three cases, which is related to the process improvement implementation approach used by the team of consultants. As the SPI implementation process followed the same steps in all three cases and pursued the same goal in terms of maturity level, this may be the motivating factor for similar leadership practices and similar activities to be found in all the cases studied.

7 Conclusion

In this study we presented the practices of leadership in three SPI initiatives, the relation between the practices found in this context, as well as the practices that have more and less impact on one another.

Regarding the limitations of this research, it was not possible to measure which of these practices was the most significant or least significant for the success of the SPI initiatives, because our objective was to understand how leadership practices occur, and thus we also found relationships between them. Therefore, we did not carry out a more in-depth study of the degree of influence of one practice over another. Another limitation is that the model was abstracted only from those three organizations. The model does not necessarily is valid for other organizations.

In the research we aimed to analyze the leadership in SPI initiatives, investigated by the perspective of Leadership as Practice. Therefore, the account of how leadership has occurred and the results of analysis are centered on agency and structure. Thus, we did not seek to deepen the understanding of the different theories of leadership in organizations, such as distributed leadership and shared leadership, even though they were evidenced in the SPI initiatives studied.

Due to the access to the stakeholders and the documents generated in the SPI initiatives studied, the research allowed us a description of the leadership as it occurred in the daily work of the SPI initiatives and an analysis that evidenced facts that contributed to the studies from the perspective of Leadership as Practice.

The analyses technique employed for the investigation of leadership practices was the thematic analyses. In each of the SPI initiatives researched, five distinct practices were found: Responsiveness, Empowering, Facilitation, Engagement and Structuring.

Before or during an SPI initiative, we need to consider these practices and their activities to improve the benefits to the organization through Leadership as Practice. The present investigation demonstrated that the context of practices is not limited to their social context, but instead is increased for the own practice, by participating at the context of other practices. Therefore, it was concluded that leadership in SPI initiatives usually involve complex network of relationships, practices and structures and that it mostly occurs vertically, formally and collaboratively.

References

1. Montoni, M., Rocha, A.R.C.: Using grounded theory to acquire knowledge about critical success factors for conducting software process improvement implementation initiatives. Int. J. Knowl. Manag. **7**(3), 43–60 (2011)
2. Carroll, B., Levy, L., Richmond, D.: Leadership as practice: challenging the competency paradigm. Leadersh. Q. **4**(4), 363–379 (2007)
3. Crevani, L., Lindgren, M., Packendorff, J.: Leadership, not leaders: on the study of leadership as practices and interactions. Scand. J. Manag. **26**, 77–86 (2010)
4. Raelin, J.: From leadership-as-practice to leaderful practice. Leadersh. Q. **7**(2), 195–211 (2011)
5. Zoucas, A., Cunha, C., Salviano, C.F., Thiry, M.: Revealing the influence of leadership on software process improvement initiatives. In: Proceedings of Eighth International Conference on the Quality of Information and Communications Technology, pp. 149–152, September 2012
6. Zoucas, A., Thiry, M., Cunha, C.: Understanding the influence of leadership as practice in software process improvement initiatives (original in Portuguese as Compreendendo a influência da Liderança nas Iniciativas de Melhoria de Processo de Software). In: Proceedings of SBQS – Simpósio Brasileiro de Qualidade de Software. Fortaleza (2012)
7. Zoucas, A.: Leadership as practice in software process improvement initiatives (original in Portuguese as Liderança como Prática em Iniciativas de Melhoria de Processo de Software), Ph.D. Thesis in Engineering and Knowledge Management at Federal University of Santa Catarina - UFSC, Brazil (2017)
8. Zoucas, C.A., Cunha, C.J.C.A.: Leadership as practice: a bibliometric study. Bus. Manag. Rev. **5**(11), 01–12 (2016)
9. Zoucas, C.A., Cunha, C.J.C.A.: Knowledge acquisition approach to identify key competencies of leaders in software process improvement initiative (original in Portuguese as Abordagem de aquisição de conhecimento para identificar competências-chave de líderes em iniciativa de Melhoria de Processo de Software). In: Proceedings of VI Congresso Internacional de Conhecimento e Inovação (CIKI), Bogotá, Colômbia, 31 October–1 November 2016
10. ISO – International Organization for Standardization: ISO 9000-2015. Quality management systems — Fundamentals and vocabulary (2015)
11. Burns, J.M.: Leadership. Harpercollins Publishers, New York (2010)
12. Northouse, P.G.: Leadership: Theory and Practice, 5th edn. Sage Publications, Thousand Oaks (2010)
13. Chreim, S.: The (non) distribution of leadership roles: considering leadership practices and configurations. Hum. Relat. **68**(4), 517–543 (2015)
14. Heifetz, R.A.: Leadership Without Easy Answers. The Belknap Press of Harvard, Cambridge (2009)

15. Bogdan, R.C., Biklen, S.K.: Qualitative Research for Education: an Introduction to Theory and Methods. Allyn & Bacon, Boston (1992)
16. Morgan, G.: Paradigmas, metáforas e resolução de quebra-cabeças na teoria das organizações. In: Caldas, M.P., Bertero, O. (eds.) teoria das organizações, pp. 12–33. Atlas, São Paulo (2007)
17. Creswell, J.W., Plano Clark, V.L.: Designing and Conducting Mixed Methods Research. Sage Publications, Thousand Oaks (2007)
18. Martins, G.A.: Estudo de caso: Uma reflexão sobre a aplicabilidade em pesquisas no Brasil. RCO – Revista de Contabilidade e Organizações – FEARP/USP **2**, 8–18 (2008)
19. Braun, V., Clarke, V.: Using thematic analysis in psychology. Qual. Res. Psychol. **3**(2), 77–101 (2006)
20. Bolden, R.I., Petrov, G., Gosling, J.: Tensions in higher education leadership: towards a multi-level model of leadership practice. High. Educ. Q. **62**(4), 358–376 (2008)
21. Collinson, M., Collinson, D.: 'Blended leadership': employee perspectives on effective leadership in the UK FE Sector. Centre for Excellence in Leadership, Lancaster (2006)
22. Gronn, P.: Hybrid leadership. In: Leithwood, K., Mascall, B., Strauss, T. (eds.) Distributed Leadership According to the Evidence. Routledge, NewYork (2008)
23. Meier, N.: Configurations of leadership practices in hospital units. J. Health Organ. Manag. **29**(7), 1115–1130 (2015)
24. Endrissat, N., von Arx, W.: Leadership practices and context: two sides of the same coin. Leadersh. Q. **9**(2), 278–304 (2013)
25. Merriam, S.B.: Qualitative Research in Practice: Examples for Discussion and Analysis, 439 p. Jossey-Bass, San Francisco (2002)

Teaching Software Processes and Standards: A Review of Serious Games Approaches

Alejandro Calderón[1(✉)], Manuel Trinidad[1], Mercedes Ruiz[1], and Rory V. O'Connor[2]

[1] University of Cádiz, Cádiz, Spain
{alejandro.calderon,manuel.trinidad, mercedes.ruiz}@uca.es
[2] Dublin City University, Dublin, Ireland
rory.oconnor@dcu.ie

Abstract. Software process education is an important field within software engineering that requires a more practical and realistic, learning and teaching approach. In the context of education, serious games is a field that is growing rapidly as a way to provide alternative approaches to the traditional pedagogical learning/teaching process. The main objective of this work is to analyze the state of the art in relation to serious games for software process education with the aim to identify the current studies and existing serious games that deal with this field. A systematic literature review was performed following a predefined procedure that involves automatically searching in scientific digital databases. 152 papers were found by the automatic searches in the digital databases and 24 papers were selected as primary studies. Results show that researchers are more interested in addressing the design and use of serious games for software process education than the design of simulation models to support the design of serious games for software process education. Consequently, 21 serious games for software process education were identified and categorized.

Keywords: Systematic literature review · Software process · Serious games Education · Gamification

1 Introduction

Game-based learning has the potential to move trainers and students into a new learning/teaching approach where the game guides students to discover and experiment their knowledge acquisition. In this context, the game turns into the main element of this teaching approach, using game stories, mechanics, components, dynamics and features, as the main elements within the learning/teaching process. The games applied in this context for educating or training users are called Serious Games (SGs) [1, 2].

Recently, SGs have emerged as a field of opportunity that is growing rapidly and have attracted attention from both practitioners and researchers as a way to provide an alternative approach to the traditional pedagogical ones [3]. In this context, SGs can be a possible solution to overcoming the necessity of a more practical and realistic

I. Stamelos et al. (Eds.): SPICE 2018, CCIS 918, pp. 154–166, 2018.
https://doi.org/10.1007/978-3-030-00623-5_11

learning/teaching process that allows students to acquire real-life experience and involve in a social, fun and effective software process education [3, 4].

Although several studies have been conducted on different fields related to SGs and software engineering such as education in software engineering [5], education in software process standards [6] and quality assessment [7], no study has yet characterized the state of the art of software process education. There to discover the current state of the art of SGs for software process education and identify their features, we conducted a systematic literature review (SLR) based on the guidelines proposed by Kitchenham and Charters [8] and Calderon et al. [6]. The main objective of this paper is to identify the research topics of the studies related to SGs for software process education and to characterize the current SGs available for software process education.

The remainder of this paper is organized as follows: Sect. 2 analyzes the works related to our proposal. Section 3 provides the methodology used for conducting our SLR. Section 4 shows and discusses the outcomes of this review. Finally, in Sect. 5 conclusions are presented and future works are briefly provided.

2 Related Works

An initial study that involves automatic searches in several academic databases was performed in order to observe if there exists any previous secondary study that aims to characterize the state of the art of SGs for software process education.

As a result, we found several literature reviews such as the mapping review of Heredia et al. [9] that characterizes the state of the art of the practice on software process education, the SLR of Kosa et al. [3] that classified the different uses of games in the field of software engineering education or the review of Petri et al. [7] that identifies the methods for evaluating SGs for software engineering education. In addition, in a previous work, we conducted a multivocal literature review to identify the SGs for software process standards education [6]. However, the majority of them are focused on the general scope of software engineering education without identifying the particularities of the software process education field.

Two works were directly related to the field of software process education [6, 9]. In [6], the authors focused on the specific area of software process standards education. Concretely, they identified three SGs for teaching the ISO/IEC 12207 [10], the ISO/IEC 29110 [11] and the ISO/IEC 15504 [12] and concluded that SGs have potential as supporting tools for software process standards education, although, more research and experimental outcomes are needed in order to observe the full potential of SGs as learning resources for teaching in this field. On the other hand, in [9], the authors analyzed the literature to clarify the general characteristics of the software process education and the training initiatives in the field, but SGs was not the main topic under study.

Hence, no secondary study that characterized the state of the art of software process education has been found. For that reason, in this work, we have conducted a review to characterize the state of the art of the scope of SGs for software process education and, thus, to identify the current SGs of this field.

3 Method

This work aims to analyze the current studies related to the field of SGs for software process education. To elicit the state of the art of this scope was conducted a SLR based on the best practices and guidelines for conducting SLRs in software engineering proposed by Kitchenham et al. [8, 13] and the scientific selection process described by Calderon et al. [6]. According to Kitchenham and Charters [8], SLR is an effective and recommended methodology for investigating empirical studies in order to analyze a topic or research question, once the most reliable evidence comes from adding all empirical studies on a particular topic. Figure 1 illustrates the systematic process followed to conduct this SLR.

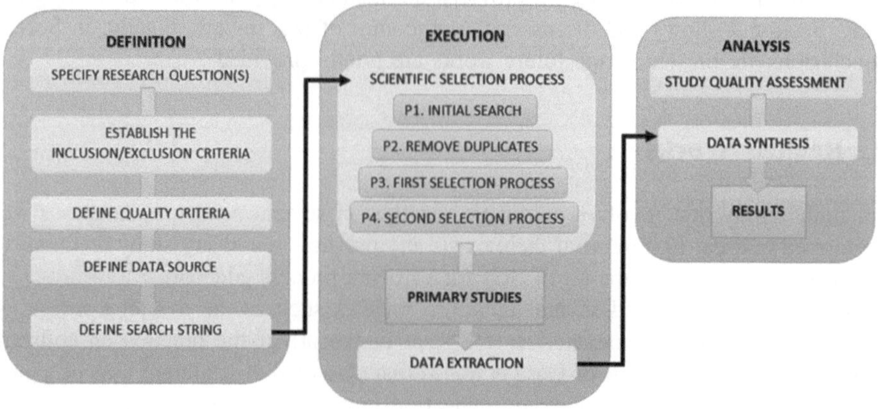

Fig. 1. Systematic process.

3.1 Definition

Our investigation aims to characterize the state of the art of SGs for software process education. In accordance with this purpose, we conducted an SLR that addresses the following research questions:

- RQ1: Which studies deal with the scope of SGs for software process education?
- RQ2: Which SGs are focused on software process education?

Taking into consideration our research objective and questions, we established the inclusion and exclusion criteria to select only relevant studies, as below:

Inclusion Criteria. The analyzed study deals with the scope of SGs for software process education. The analyzed study introduces a SG for software process education. The analyzed study described the educational features of a SG for software process education. The analyzed study evaluates a SG for software process education. The analyzed study adds value to the field of SGs for software process education. The study was written in English.

Exclusion Criteria. The analyzed study presents the results of evaluating a SG for software process education but it does not show any information about the educational features of the SG. The analyzed study is focused only on theoretical and philosophical aspects without introducing any learning resource related to the field of SGs for software process education. The analyzed study only has its abstract available and it is not possible to find its full-text. The analyzed study does not provide the required information clearly. The analyzed study was written in a language other than English.

Quality Criteria. The quality factors were identified and analyzed according to the main topic of our review and the information that analyzed studies were able to provide us. A questionnaire consisted of four quality assessment questions (QA) was defined as the quality instrument. The five questions used were the following:

- QA1. Does the study introduce a SG for software process education?
- QA2. Does the study allow retrieving the information related to the main features of the SG for software process education?
- QA3. Does the study allow knowing the type of SG?
- QA4. Does the study allow identifying the learning objectives of the SG?

Each question was answered YES (Y) or NO (N). The scoring procedure was Y = 1 an N = 0. Thus, the total number of Ys defined the quality assessment score of each study.

Data Sources. The digital databases were chosen regarding their relevance in the domain of our study, including IEEE Xplore, ISI Web of Science, SpringerLink, ACM Digital Library, SCOPUS and Wiley Online Library.

Search String. To construct the search string, we first need to identify the search terms of this work. For that reason, we performed some initial searches to test and calibrate the search string. Finally, we defined the search string as the following Boolean expression: *game **AND** "software process" **AND** (education **OR** training **OR** teaching).* Based on the search string, it was customized in conformance with the search engine of each digital database involved in the study.

3.2 Execution

The SLR was executed during spring of 2018 with Table 1 showing the evolution of the list of papers during the ***scientific selection process*** regarding each digital database.

During the first phase of the scientific selection process (***P1. Initial search***), the search string was applied to the selected digital databases and as a result, we found a total of 152 papers. The second phase of the scientific selection process consisted of analyzing the papers found in the first phase in order to remove duplicates (***P2. Remove duplicates***) and consequently, we excluded 77 papers. In the third phase of the scientific selection process (***P3. First selection process***), we analyzed the title and abstract of the 77 papers that passed the previous phase considering the inclusion and exclusion criteria and as a result, 40 papers were included and 27 papers were excluded. Finally, in the fourth phase of the scientific selection process (***P4. Second selection process***), a complete reading of the 40 papers selected in the previous phase was performed, and

Table 1. Evolution of the studies retrieved in each digital database.

Digital database	Studies retrieved	Distinct studies retrieved	Studies that passed the first selection process	Primary studies
IEEE Xplore	24	3	2	1
ISI Web of Science	23	2	1	1
SpringerLink	19	16	6	1
ACM Digital Library	25	24	13	9
SCOPUS	50	21	16	11
Wiley Online Library	11	9	2	1
Total	152	75	40	24

the inclusion and exclusion criteria were again applied. As a result, in the final phase, 16 papers were excluded, and 24 papers were considered for data extraction, with these 24 papers defining the primary studies of our SLR.

Data Extraction. During the extraction process, the primary studies were read completely to collect all the needed information and ensure that the data were accurate. All the collected data were stored in a spreadsheet. This allowed placing all the information of the study in the same location, at the same time that made the analysis and comparison of the collected data during the synthesis process easier. The data of the selected papers was classified according to the following criteria:

- The main topic of the study (addressing RQ1).
- Name of the SG/tool (addressing RQ2).
- Description of the SG/tool (addressing RQ2).
- Type of SG/tool (addressing RQ2).
- The learning objectives of the SG (addressing RQ2).

3.3 Analysis

Once we have extracted the data from the primary studies, we conducted the analysis phase in where the primary studies were evaluated for quality and the data synthesis took place to answer the research questions defined.

Study Quality Assessment. We evaluated the primary studies for quality using the quality criteria defined in Sect. 3.1. Figure 2 shows the coverage of every QA in the quality questionnaire. We can observe how the four QA were covered at a rate higher than 90% by Yes answer. Concretely, QA1 was covered 100% by Yes answer, while QA2, QA3, and QA4 were covered 96% by Yes answer. Hence, the majority of the primary studies provided all the required information to answer the research questions.

Data Synthesis & Discussion. In this section, we discuss our findings and answers to the research questions that were addressed in this SLR, as a result of the data synthesis process.

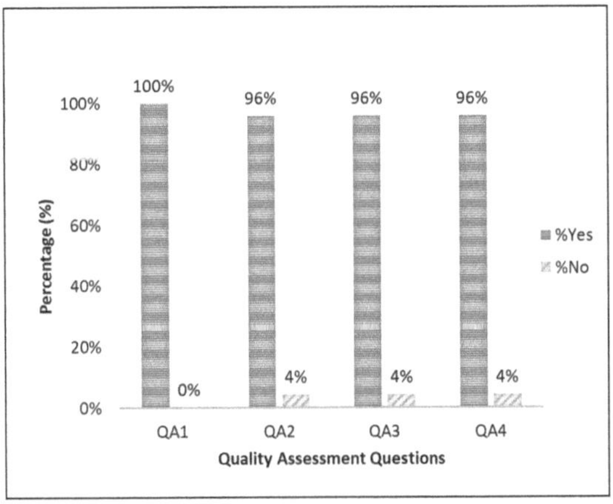

Fig. 2. Quality assessment results.

RQ1: Which studies deal with the scope of SGs for software process education?

The aim of this question was to identify the current studies that deal with the scope of SGs for software process education with the goal to state the main research topics of this field. We analyzed the information about the main objectives of our primary studies. As a result, we observed that the analyzed studies are focused on two main topics: games for software process education (*Games*) and software process simulation models for educational games (*Models*). As Table 2 shows, 17 of the primary studies deal with the topic *Games*, a primary study deal with the topic *Models* and 6 primary studies deal with both topics: *Games* and *Models*.

Table 2. Studies per topic addressed.

Topic	Description	Primary studies
Games	The study deals with SGs for software process education	[6, 14–29]
Models	The study deals with tools to define simulation models for designing SGs to teach in software process	[30]
Games/Models	The study deals with the both topic described above	[31–36]

Regarding the year of publication of the different retrieved studies, Fig. 3 shows the evolution of publications considering the two main topics. In this figure, a study that deals with the two identified topics, at the same time, appears reflected in both data series. As we can observe, all the studies were published between 2003 and 2018. In 2005, 2012 and 2016 were the years when more studies were published regarding the topic *Games*. On the other hand, 2005 was the year when more studies were published regarding the topic *Models*. This allows us to observe that there are more interest and effort applied to the research topic of *Games* than in the topic of *Models*.

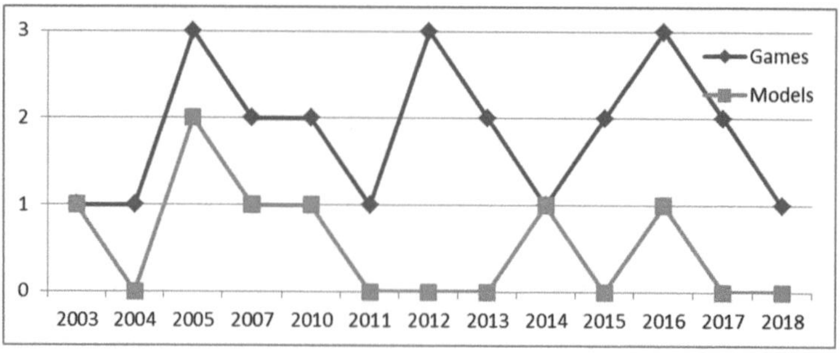

Fig. 3. Number of studies regarding the year of publication per topic.

RQ2: Which SGs are focused on software process education?

The aim of this question was to identify the existing SGs for software process education and categorize them regarding their features. To answer this question, we collected the information related to the name, description, type of game and learning objectives of each retrieved SG. A total of 21 different SGs were retrieved from the studies found through this review. These SGs are the following:

- **SimSE** is an educational, graphical, interactive, simulation environment based SG that allows instructors to model software engineering processes and allows their students to practice, and learn these processes in an engaging and effective manner, without the time and scope constraints of the academic environment [6, 14, 17, 31, 33–35].
- **SimjavaSP** is a simulation game whose aim is that student's acts as the project manager to develop a software project within the required time and budget, and of acceptable quality [14].
- **SESAM**, Software Engineering Simulation by Animated Models, is a simulation game to teach software engineering principles and practices. SESAM presents students with a kind of software engineering adventure game, where they have to assume the role of a project manager, aiming to complete a project within given time and budget by a team of simulated, virtual software engineers [14].
- **AMEISE**, A Media Education Initiative for Software Engineering, is a project management adventure game based on the core ideas behind SESAM. AMEISE extends the spectrum of educational situations that SESAM is able to offer [14].
- **The Incredible Manager** is a simulation-based game that allows students to act as a project manager, being responsible for planning, executing, and controlling a software project. The aim of the game is to complete a project whose cost and schedule are established during a planning phase and approved by stakeholders [14].
- **Open Software Solutions (OSS)** is a simulation environment to provide students with interactive software engineering case studies. The OSS simulates an office building, with each project having one floor; the student 'joins' the company as a member of one of these project teams [14].

- **MO-SEProcess** is a Multiplayer Online Software Engineering Process game based on SimSE. It allows students to participate in a realistic software engineering process that involves real-world components not present in class projects [14, 17].
- **SimVBSE** is a game for students to better understand value-based software engineering and its underlying theory [14].
- **The Software Process Simulation Game** is a simulation game for understanding software processes by creating an environment in which students can discover the strengths and weaknesses of each of the process models [19].
- **Problems and Programmers (PnP)** is an educational software engineering card game that simulates the software process. As a game-based simulation, PnP provides students with an experience that is similar to a class project, but requires no deliverables to be built. It can therefore be played quickly and through repeated use illustrate many different aspects of the software process [6, 18, 25].
- **SiMPS** is a simulation game that focus on software process improvement training [32].
- **EnactMe** is a simulation game that aims to provide a complementary training to the process' role users through simulation [32].
- **NoName1** is a role-playing game aiming to teach some educational objectives concerning specific software development process such as the organizational process [16].
- **NoName2** is a serious computer game that allows students to manage virtual software projects using agile software engineering practices. Students will be able to experiment with various agile process improvement practices while managing a virtual development team [15].
- **ProDec** is a simulation-based SG to teach, assess and motivate students in software project management that allows them to acquire experience in a risk-free environment and improve their skills as project leaders in their professional life [6, 20, 28, 29].
- **Go for it!** is an educational game for contributing to teach in the ISO/IEC 29110 standard elements where students are encouraged to understand the project management process of Basic profile [6, 21].
- **DesignMPS** is a computer game designed to support the teaching of software process modeling by reinforcing relevant concepts and providing software process modeling exercises [6, 22].
- **Competitive Bidding Game** is designed to help students understand process concepts and be able to apply knowledge of software process in near-realistic software projects [23, 24].
- **SPIAL** is a graphical and interactive game-based simulation environment for teaching or reinforcing software process improvement and software engineering concepts [36].
- **NoName3** is a board game for understanding the V-Model [26].
- **Floors** is a SG that proposes an interactive learning experience to introduce ISO/IEC 12207 by creating different floors of a virtual environment where various processes of the standard are discussed and implemented [6, 27].

Table 3. SGs for software process education.

Serious game	Type	Learning objectives	Primary studies
SimSE	Computational-Simulation	Software engineering processes	[6, 14, 17, 31, 33–35]
SimjavaSP	Computational-Simulation	Software engineering processes	[14]
SESAM	Computational-Simulation	Software engineering processes	[14]
AMEISE	Computational-Simulation	Software engineering processes	[14]
The incredible manager	Computational-Simulation	Software engineering processes	[14]
OSS	Computational-Simulation	Software engineering processes	[14]
MO-SEProcess	Computational-Simulation	Software engineering processes	[14, 17]
SimVBSE	Computational-Simulation	Software engineering processes	[14]
The software process simulation game	Computational-Simulation	Software process models	[19]
PnP	Card game	Software process concepts and practices	[6, 18, 25]
SiMPS	Computational-Simulation	Software process improvement	[32]
EnactMe	Computational-Simulation	Software process concepts and practices (Process' role users)	[32]
NoName1	Role-Playing game	Software process concepts and practices (Organizational process)	[16]
NoName2	Computer game	Software process improvement	[15]
ProDec	Computational-Simulation	Software process standards (ISO/IEC 29110; ISO/IEC 12207) and software management processes (ISO 21500)	[6, 20, 28, 29]
Go for it!	Card game	Software process standards (ISO/IEC 29110)	[6, 21]
DesignMPS	Computer game	Software process models	[6, 22]
Competitive bidding game	Role-Playing game	Software process concepts and practices	[23, 24]
SPIAL	Computational-Simulation	Software process improvement	[36]
NoName3	Board game	Software process models	[26]
Floors	Computational-Simulation	Software process standards (ISO/IEC 12207)	[6, 27]

In Table 3, we summarized the information collected from the identified SGs for software process education. Specifically, Table 3 shows the type of game, the learning objectives of the game and the primary studies that deal with each SG.

Five categories were defined to categorize the SGs retrieved from the primary studies: Computer game, Computational-Simulation, Board game, Card game, and Role-Playing game. The category Computer game refers to SGs developed as computer software. The category Computational-Simulation refers to SGs developed as computer software that use computational simulation techniques such as agent-based modeling, system dynamics or discrete-event simulation. The category Board game refers to SGs developed as a board game. The category Card game refers to SGs developed as a card game and the category Role-Playing game refers to SGs developed as role-play simulation. Figure 4 provides the percentages of SGs regarding their type of game. We can see that the category most frequent is Computational-Simulation game with more than 65% of the retrieved SGs.

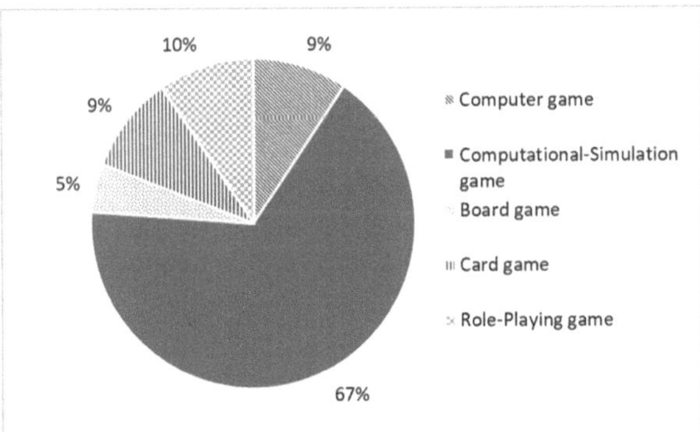

Fig. 4. Type of game.

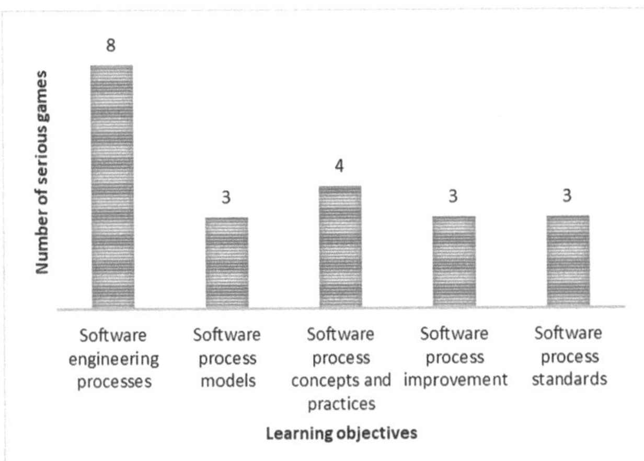

Fig. 5. Number of serious games regarding their learning objectives.

On the other hand, considering the learning objectives of these SGs, we can identify 5 main knowledge areas related to software process. As Fig. 5 shows, eight SGs aim to teach general and specific lessons about the software engineering processes. Four SGs aim to train in specific or general concepts and practices of software process such as organizational processes or process' role users. Three SGs focus on software process models education, others three on teaching software process improvement and the last three SGs retrieved have as learning objectives to support software process of well-known standards such as the ISO/IEC 29110, ISO/IEC 12207 or ISO 21500 standards.

4 Conclusions

In this paper we have presented an SLR related to SGs for software process education, where we selected 24 papers from 152 found in 6 digital databases until May of 2018. We organized and categorized the information obtained to provide an answer to each of the two research questions set which aim to provide an overview of the main research topics addressed in the field under review, as well as to identify the current SGs for software process education. The selected studies and the retrieved SGs have been classified. These classifications offer an initial baseline for further research within the field of SGs for software process education.

Results show that researchers are more interested in addressing the design and use of SGs for software process education than the design of simulation models to support the design of SGs for software process education. Consequently, 21 SGs for software process education were identified. The majority of these SGs were designed as computer games that use computational simulation techniques in order to offer students a risk-free learning environment where they can learn the concepts and practices of several software process knowledge areas such as software engineering processes, software standards processes or software process improvement.

Compared to other related research areas such as SGs for software project management or computing education, we can observe that by comparison not that many works have been published in the field of SGs for software process education. For that reason, it will be helpful to complement this review searching for the current studies of the grey literature – the diverse and heterogeneous body of material available outside, and not subject to, traditional academic peer-review processes –, as well as, to deeper analyze the identified SGs in order to explore the full potential of SGs for software process education.

Acknowledgments. This work has been carried out during a post-doctoral contract, funded by the Program of Promotion and Impulse of Research and Transfer at University of Cádiz 2018-2019, and a pre-doctoral contract for the training of research personnel, funded by the University of Cádiz through the University Research and Transfer Plan (UCA/REC01VI/2017).

This work was funded by the Spanish National Research Agency (AEI) with ERDF funds under projects Badge People (TIN2016-76956-C3-3-R) and the Andalusian Plan for Research, Development, and Innovation (grant TIC-195).

References

1. Abt, C.: Serious Games. University Press of America, Lanhan (2002)
2. Zyda, M.: From visual simulation to virtual reality to games. Computer **38**, 25–32 (2005)
3. Kosa, M., Yilmaz, M., O'Connor, R., Clarke, P.: Software engineering education and games: a systematic literature review. J. Univers. Comput. Sci. **22**(12), 1558–1574 (2016)
4. Dorling, A., McCaffery, F.: The gamification of SPICE. In: Mas, A., Mesquida, A., Rout, T., O'Connor, Rory V., Dorling, A. (eds.) SPICE 2012. CCIS, vol. 290, pp. 295–301. Springer, Heidelberg (2012). https://doi.org/10.1007/978-3-642-30439-2_35
5. Caulfield, C., Xia, J., Veal, D., Maj, S.P.: A systematic survey of games used for software engineering education. Mod. Appl. Sci. **5**(6), 28–43 (2011)
6. Calderón, A., Ruiz, M., O'Connor, R.V.: A multivocal literature review on serious games for software process standards education. Comput. Stand. Interfaces **57**, 36–48 (2018)
7. Petri, G., von Wangenheim, C.G.: How games for computing education are evaluated? A systematic literature review. Comput. Educ. **107**, 68–90 (2017)
8. Kitchenham, B., Charters, S.: Guidelines for Performing Systematic Literature Reviews in Software Engineering. Keele University and Durham University Joint Report (2007)
9. Heredia, A., Colomo-Palacios, R., Amescua-Seco, A.: A sytematic mapping study on software process education. In: Proceedings of the International Workshop on Software Process Education, Training and Professionalism, Gothenburg, Sweden (2015)
10. ISO/IEC: ISO/IEC 12207:2008 - Systems and software engineering — Software life cycle processes (2008)
11. ISO/IEC: ISO/IEC TR 29110-1:2016 - Systems and software engineering – Lifecycle profiles for Very Small Entities (VSEs) – Part 1: Overview (2016)
12. ISO/IEC: ISO/IEC 15504-1:2004 Information Technology – Process Assessment – Part 1: Concepts and Vocabulary (2004)
13. MacDonell, S., Shepperd, M., Kitchenham, B., Mendes, E.: How reliable are systematic reviews in empirical software engineering? IEEE Trans. Softw. Eng. **36**(5), 676–687 (2010)
14. Pieper, J.: Learning software engineering processes through playing games: suggestions for next generation of simulations and digital learning games. In: The Second International Workshop on Games and Software Engineering: Realizing User Engagement with Game Engineering Techniques (2012)
15. Maxim, B.R., Kaur, R., Apzynski, C., Edwards, D., Evans, E.: An agile software engineering process improvement game. In: Frontiers in Education Conference (FIE) (2016)
16. Zuppiroli, S., Ciancarini, P., Gabbrielli, M.: A role-playing game for a software engineering lab: developing a product line. In: 25th Conference on Software Engineering Education and Training (CSEE&T) (2012)
17. Zhu, Q., Wang, T., Tan, S.: Adapting game technology to support software engineering process teaching: from SimSE to MO-SEProcess. In: The Third International Conference on Natural Computation (ICNC) (2007)
18. Baker, A., Navarro, E.O., Van Der Hoek, A.: Problems and programmers: an educational software engineering card game. In: 25th International Conference on Software Engineering (2003)
19. Srinivasan, J., Lundqvist, K.: A constructivist approach to teaching software processes. In: 29th International Conference on Software Engineering (ICSE) (2007)
20. Calderón, A., Ruiz, M.: Coverage of ISO/IEC 12207 software lifecycle process by a simulation-based serious game. In: Proceedings of SPICE, Dublin, Ireland (2016)

21. Sanchez-Gordón, M.-L., O'Connor, R.V., Colomo-Palacios, R., Herranz, E.: Bridging the gap between SPI and SMEs in educational settings: a learning tool supporting ISO/IEC 29110. In: Kreiner, C., O'Connor, R.V., Poth, A., Messnarz, R. (eds.) EuroSPI 2016. CCIS, vol. 633, pp. 3–14. Springer, Cham (2016). https://doi.org/10.1007/978-3-319-44817-6_1
22. Chaves, R., Von Wangenheim, C., Furtado, J., Oliveira, S., Santos, A., Favero, E.: Experimental evaluation of a serious game for teaching software process modeling. IEEE Trans. Educ. **58**(4), 289–296 (2015)
23. Rong, G., Zhang, H., Shao, D.: Where does experience matter in software process education? An experience report. In: 27th Conference on Software Engineering Education and Training, CSEE and T (2014)
24. Rong, G., Zhang, H., Shao, D.: Applying competitive bidding games in software process education. In: Software Engineering Education and Training (CSEE&T) (2013)
25. Carrington, D., Baker, A., Van Der Hoek, A.: It's all in the game: Teaching software process concepts. In: Frontiers in Education Conference, FIE (2005)
26. Landes, D., Sedelmaier, Y., Pfeiffer, V., Mottok, J., Hagel, G.: Learning and teaching software process models. In: Global Engineering Education Conference (EDUCON) (2012)
27. Aydan, U., Yilmaz, M., O'Connor, R.V.: Towards a serious game to teach ISO/IEC 12207 software lifecycle process: an interactive learning approach. In: Rout, T., O'Connor, R.V., Dorling, A. (eds.) SPICE 2015. CCIS, vol. 526, pp. 217–229. Springer, Cham (2015). https://doi.org/10.1007/978-3-319-19860-6_17
28. Calderón, A., Ruiz, M., O'Connor, R.V.: Coverage of the ISO 21500 standard in the context of software project management by a simulation-based serious game. In: Mas, A., Mesquida, A., O'Connor, R.V., Rout, T., Dorling, A. (eds.) SPICE 2017. CCIS, vol. 770, pp. 399–412. Springer, Cham (2017). https://doi.org/10.1007/978-3-319-67383-7_29
29. Calderón, A., Ruiz, M., O'Connor, R.V.: Coverage of ISO/IEC 29110 project management process of basic profile by a serious game. In: Stolfa, J., Stolfa, S., O'Connor, R.V., Messnarz, R. (eds.) EuroSPI 2017. CCIS, vol. 748, pp. 111–122. Springer, Cham (2017). https://doi.org/10.1007/978-3-319-64218-5_9
30. Chaves, R.O., Lobato, W.A.D.L., Tavares, E.M.D.C., Oliveira, S.R., Miranda, T.C., Favero, E.L.: Intelligent behavior simulation module for software process elements. In: Brazilian Symposium on Games and Digital Entertainment (SBGAMES) (2011)
31. Navarro, E.O., Van Der Hoek, A.: Software process modeling for an educational software engineering simulation game. Softw. Process: Improv. Pract. **10**(3), 311–325 (2005)
32. Chaves, R.O., Favero, E.L., Tavares, E.M.D.C., Oliveira, S.R.: A software process simulator machine for software engineering simulation games. In: Brazilian Symposium on Games and Digital Entertainment (SBGAMES) (2010)
33. Navarro, E.O., Van Der Hoek, A.: Design and evaluation of an educational software process simulation environment and associated model. In: 18th Conference on Software Engineering Education & Training (2005)
34. Navarro, E.: SimSE: a software engineering simulation environment for software process education. Doctoral Dissertation (2005)
35. Navarro, E., Van Der Hoek, A.: SimSE: an interactive simulation game for software engineering education. In: The 7 th IASTED International Conference on Computers and Advanced Technology in Education, Kauai, Hawaii (2004)
36. Peixoto, D., Resende, R., Pádua, C.: An educational simulation model derived from academic and industrial experiences. In: Frontiers in Education Conference, FIE (2013)

Interpretation and Reporting of Process Capability Results: Focus on Improvement

Suren Behari(✉), Aileen Cater-Steel, Anup Shrestha, and Jeffrey Soar

School of Management and Enterprise, University of Southern Queensland, Toowoomba, Australia
{Suren.Behari,Aileen.Cater-Steel,Anup.Shrestha, Jeffrey.Soar}@usq.edu.au

Abstract. A global financial services company followed a software-mediated process assessment (SMPA) approach based on ISO/IEC 15504, ISO/IEC 20000 and the IT Infrastructure Library (ITIL®). Using an action research approach, the Incident Management, Problem Management, and Change Management processes were assessed at two points in time during an ITSM process improvement project. This paper analyzes the results of the process assessments, highlights issues with the interpretation of the results, and offers an alternative method to report process capability results to motivate process improvement. The study found that by using the proportion of SMPA recommendations as a proxy measure for process improvement, the processes did improve yielding fewer recommendations in cycle 2 when compared to cycle 1 of the action research.

Keywords: ITSM process assessment · ISO/IEC 15504 · ISO/IEC 20000-4 IT service management · Process improvement

1 Introduction

Rapid advanced development in IT technologies has created new opportunities for the strategic use of technology for business benefits [1]. Organizations need efficient Information Technology Service Management (ITSM) processes to cut costs, but ironically, in order to implement highly capable processes, there are significant costs involved, both in terms of time and resources. A way to achieve better performing and higher capable processes is to employ methods to compare an organization's processes against best-practice standards to identify performance gaps and receive guidance to improve the processes. Many of the existing process improvement methods require large investments [2].

A number of best practice frameworks have been created with the foundational goals of creating measures/processes to control, monitor and evaluate activity in the organization. The prevailing view of IT governance is that the outcomes or focus of these measures is to create strategic alignment, risk management, performance management, delivery of business value through IT, as well as capability management [3].

The research was based on a single case study of a global financial services firm *Company X* that had implemented the ITIL framework to improve the quality of its IT

I. Stamelos et al. (Eds.): SPICE 2018, CCIS 918, pp. 167–181, 2018.
https://doi.org/10.1007/978-3-030-00623-5_12

services. Company X is a global services company with over 200 employees, headquartered in Silicon Valley, California USA, with offices in New York, London, Singapore, Tokyo and Bangalore. Company X has about 70 in IT staff fielding incidents, problems and changes in the system. The Assessment team was led by the Director of Engineering at Company X, an experienced scholar-practitioner who was supervised by an accredited SPICE Assessor.

Company X began to scrutinize its IT group's performance to ensure that it was in line with the overall business performance and contributed to the business' bottom line. Company X embarked on implementing three ITSM processes: Incident Management, Problem Management and Change Management, and are now looking at improving these processes to lower costs, improve efficiency and offer higher service levels. The business drivers for process improvement are service availability and reliability and for continual improvement.

2 ITSM Process Assessments

Process assessment is described in the literature as a series of steps targeted to compare an organization's everyday processes with reference processes that comprise typical activities for the process at different capability levels [4]. Process assessments are primarily conducted by organizations to benchmark results against an international standard [5]. The international standard for process assessment ISO/IEC 33002 suggests that process assessments can be used for process improvement or to determine process capability [6]. One of the primary goals of process assessment is to provide guidance to improve processes as suggested in ISO/IEC 33014 that provides a guide for process improvement [7].

Practitioner resources suggest that organizations prefer an easy, cost-effective and timely process assessment mechanism that unveils a realistic indication of process capability [8]. This is particularly true for smaller organizations that are undertaking their first experience with assessments [5].

The *Software-Mediated Process Assessment (SMPA)* approach to process assessment was chosen to assess the capability of IT service management processes, for its alignment with international standards, its transparency and efficiency, and its ability to objectively measure feedback from stakeholders [9]. The SMPA approach uses online surveys for data collection and a decision support system for analysis and reporting. The detailed design of the SMPA approach is described in [9]. The SMPA approach allocates assessment questions to the survey participants, via an online interface, based on their role within each process: process performers; process managers; and external process stakeholders. Questions are based on the process assessment model (PAM) and sourced from an exemplar PAM for ITSM (ISO/IEC 15504 part 8). The PAM for ITSM [10] consists of a set of base practices to achieve the process outcomes and a set of generic practices for process management (CL2), standardization (CL3), quantitative measurement (CL4) and innovation (CL5) of process capability [9].

Process attribute achievement ratings are calculated from the online survey respondents by the software tool using the measurement framework of the ISO/IEC 15504 standard. This standard is currently being revised and transformed into a new standard family of ISO/IEC 33000 series [11]. The references made to ISO/IEC 15504 standards as applied in this research can be viewed as a specific and valid instance of the ISO/IEC 33000 standard series in terms of the process assessment model and the measurement framework [12]. While the new standard series presents a generic and more abstract view of process assessment, it still corresponds to related ISO/IEC 15504 content. The measurement framework defined in ISO/IEC 15504-2 that was used in the SMPA method has been revised but it can be treated as a simpler instance of the new ISO/IEC 33020 standard [13].

The process capability score is calculated from the average rating of all responses and uses the process attribute achievement scale as shown in Table 1. The process capability level can then be derived from the attribute ratings.

Table 1. Process attribute achievement scale

Rating score	Description	Score percentage	Mean value of response (x)
Fully	There is certainty that process activities are usually performed	>85%–100%	92.5
Largely	Process activities are performed in the majority of cases	>50%–85%	67.5
Partially	Process activities are performed but not frequently	>15%–50%	32.5
Not	Process activities are not or rarely performed	0%–15%	7.5

Table 2. Process attribute assessment questions and knowledge items

Process attribute	No. of questions	No. of knowledge items	% Knowledge items/No. of questions
PA1.1 Incident Management	8	8	100.0
PA1.1 Problem Management	11	11	100.0
PA1.1 Change Management	14	14	100.0
PA2.1 Performance Management	24	21	87.5
PA2.2 Work Product Management	14	13	92.9
PA3.1 Process Definition	14	11	78.6
PA3.2 Process Deployment	13	9	69.2
Total	98	87	88.8

The SMPA tool generates recommendations for every question for PA1.1, and from PA2.1 onwards recommendation items are only generated when the process rating score is *Partially* (P) or *Not* (N). For PA1.1 questions are specific to the process, while from PA2.1 onwards the same questions are used for all processes. The detailed design and architecture of the SMPA approach has been previously published [2]. Table 2 shows the number of questions and recommendations (knowledge items) per process attribute.

3 Methodology

This research followed the cyclical process of action research to systematically measure ITSM process capability at two points in time. Company X decided to assess three ITSM processes: Incident Management, Problem Management and Change Management. Employees who were actively involved in each process at Company X were purposively selected for the study. The participants were drawn from five business units: Business Support, Operations, Trading Solutions, Execution Services, and Program Management. The research involved the measurement of three components: process capability, process performance and financial performance.

For this study, two rounds of data were collected from multiple primary and secondary sources [14] for the six month period 1 May 2015 to 31 October 2015, and 1 May 2016 to 31 October 2016. Qualitative methods were applied in the form of interviews, focus groups and observation [15]. In addition, quantitative methods used data from online surveys and the case company's internal systems to measure process performance and calculate costs.

The process capability measurement was facilitated by the use of the SMPA method. Although ISO/IEC 15504 provides for capability levels from zero (incomplete) to five (optimizing), only questions relating to level 1 (performed), level 2 (managed) and level 3 (established) of the SMPA tool were used, as it was anticipated from observation that the case organization was not performing higher than level 3.

The questionnaire data collection used the SMPA approach to enable the researcher and case study organization to assess ITSM process capability. The SMPA tool was hosted by an industry partner Assessment Portal Pty Ltd that specializes in online assessment services. Details of the case and the SMPA method have been presented in a previous paper [16].

4 Findings – Assessment Results

4.1 Assessment 1 – 2015

All three processes achieved process capability level 1. Process activities are performed. The process achieves its purpose but in a non-repeatable way and with few controls. During each instance, the process is not implemented in a managed fashion (planned, monitored, and adjusted). Work Products are not appropriately established, controlled, and maintained. Moreover, the way the process is managed is not uniform throughout the organization.

Incident Management

In order to generate the assessment profile for Incident Management, 77% of assessment survey responses were considered as valid answers. Invalid responses comprised 22% *Do not know* and 1% selected *Do not understand*. Out of the 28 invited participants, 2 participants did not attempt the survey. All process attributes scored *Largely*. The summary of the assessment results for the Incident Management process is shown in Table 3.

Table 3. Incident Management process assessment results

	Level 1	**Level 2**		**Level 3**	
Profile	PA1.1 Process Performance	PA2.1 Performance Management	PA2.2 Work Product Management	PA3.1 Process Definition	PA3.2 Process Deployment
Rating Score	L	L	L	L	L
% of responses	93%	93%	93%	93%	93%

Problem Management

Problem management had 84% valid assessment survey responses. Less than 1% of participants did not understand the questions and 16% did not know the answer to questions. All 21 invited survey participants completed the Problem Management assessment. The Process Performance attribute (PA1.1) scored *Largely*, while all other process attributes scored *Poorly*. The summary of the assessment results for the Problem Management process is shown in Table 4.

Table 4. Problem Management Process Assessment Results

	Level 1	**Level 2**		**Level 3**	
Profile	PA1.1 Process Performance	PA2.1 Performance Management	PA2.2 Work Product Management	PA3.1 Process Definition	PA3.2 Process Deployment
Rating Score	L	P	P	P	P
% of responses	100%	100%	100%	100%	100%

Change Management

In order to generate the assessment profile for Change Management, 80% of assessment survey responses were considered. 29% of participants chose the *Do not know* option while less than 1% did not understand the questions. Out of the 46 invited participants, 1 participant did not attempt the survey. The summary of the assessment results for the Change Management process is shown in Table 5.

Table 5. Change Management Process Assessment Results

	Level 1	**Level 2**		**Level 3**	
Profile	PA1.1 Process Performance	PA2.1 Performance Management	PA2.2 Work Product Management	PA3.1 Process Definition	PA3.2 Process Deployment
Rating Score	L	L	L	L	L
% of responses	98%	98%	98%	98%	98%

Improvement Plan

After the first assessment, the researcher facilitated a focus group workshop with a cross-section of survey participants at Company X, to enable group level discussion on the results of the process capability assessment report.

The recommendations for all three processes were discussed in detail, and a draft process improvement plan was developed at the workshop. Examples of some of the action items for process improvement are presented in Table 6.

Table 6. Examples of action items for process improvement

ITSM process	Action Plan
Incident Management	• Review Zendesk® (a cloud-based customer service platform used by Company X) for the incident logging workflow and communicate policy to field • Train Business Support staff on how to prioritize incidents
Problem Management	• Establish an Operating Level Agreement (OLA) between Engineering and Support, to set expected turnaround times for problem resolution • Ensure that all problem resolutions go through Quality Assurance (QA) and Change Management
Change Management	• Change the organization structure to relocate the Trading Solutions business unit from Sales to Engineering at Company X, so that all involved with Change Management follow the same procedure • Add a mandatory field to Zendesk to force one to enter the classification of proposed changes

4.2 Assessment 2 – 2016

In cycle 2 of the action research, process managers were more comfortable with identifying areas of process improvement and more enthusiastic about discussing challenges and implementing the process improvement plans. Less time was spent on planning meetings when compared to cycle 1. Process managers appeared to be complacent about the results of cycle 2, as they were aware of the effort put in to improve processes. Despite these efforts, the second assessment reported that all three processes were still rated at capability level 1.

Incident Management

The generated assessment profile for Incident Management considered 81% of assessment survey responses as valid answers as 19% of respondents selected the *Do not know* option. All process attributes scored *Largely*. The summary of the assessment results for the Incident Management process is shown in Table 7.

Table 7. Incident Management process assessment results

	Level 1	**Level 2**		**Level 3**	
Profile	PA1.1 Process Performance	PA2.1 Performance Management	PA2.2 Work Product Management	PA3.1 Process Definition	PA3.2 Process Deployment
Rating Score	L	L	L	L	L
% of responses	100%	100%	100%	100%	100%

Problem Management

Problem management had 90% valid assessment survey responses. All participants understood the questions with 10% choosing the *Do not know* option. All process attributes scored *Largely*. The summary of the assessment results for the Problem Management process is shown in Table 8.

Table 8. Problem Management process assessment results

	Level 1	**Level 2**		**Level 3**	
Profile	PA1.1 Process Performance	PA2.1 Performance Management	PA2.2 Work Product Management	PA3.1 Process Definition	PA3.2 Process Deployment
Rating Score	L	L	L	L	L
% of responses	100%	100%	100%	100%	100%

Change Management

Eighty percent of assessment survey responses were considered in generating the assessment profile for Change Management. The *Do not know* option was selected by 20% of participants while less than 1% did not understand the question. All process attributes scored *Largely*. The summary of the assessment results for the Change Management process is shown in Table 9.

Table 9. Change Management process assessment results

	Level 1	Level 2		Level 3	
Profile	PA1.1 Process Performance	PA2.1 Performance Management	PA2.2 Work Product Management	PA3.1 Process Definition	PA3.2 Process Deployment
Rating Score	L	L	L	L	L
% of responses	100%	100%	100%	100%	100%

5 Discussion

Management at Company X was interested in the results of the 2nd assessment to see if the actions taken had resulted in improvements to the capability of processes. Although the process attributes of Problem Management improved significantly, there was no change to the capability levels of any of the processes or the attribute ratings for Incident Management and Change Management.

5.1 Comparison of Assessment Results

Incident Management and Change Management scored *Largely* for all process attributes in both assessments, while Problem Management scored *Largely* for Performance Management (PA2.1) in both assessments, and *Partially* for all other process attributes in assessment 1 with *Largely* in assessment 2. The focus group discussion on these results revealed that although Incidents and Changes are directly related to Problems at Company X, there was a lack of knowledge of the Problem Management process by employees. Table 10 shows the comparison of process attribute ratings for assessment 1 and assessment 2.

Based solely on the process attributes, it is not evident whether there was a process capability improvement or not.

In discussion with Senior Management at Company X, an alternative approach was found to explore and report on the extent of process improvement in the 12 months between the initial and second assessment. A comparative analysis of the number of recommendations from the ITIL guidelines was conducted to determine if process capability improved year-over-year. These recommendations generated by the SMPA tool are closely aligned with the ISO/IEC 20000-4 [17] process reference model (PRM).

Table 10. Comparison of process attribute ratings for assessment 1 and assessment 2

Assessment	Level 1	Level 2		Level 3	
	PA1.1 Process Performance	PA2.1 Performance Management	PA2.2 Work Product Management	PA3.1 Process Definition	PA3.2 Process Deployment
Incident Management					
1	L	L	L	L	L
2	L	L	L	L	L
Problem Management					
1	L	P	P	P	P
2	L	L	L	L	L
Change Management					
1	L	L	L	L	L
2	L	L	L	L	L

Incident Management

Figure 1 shows a comparison of the number of recommendations for assessment 1 and 2 for Incident Management. In assessment 1 and assessment 2 there were no recommendations for Process Performance (PA1.1).

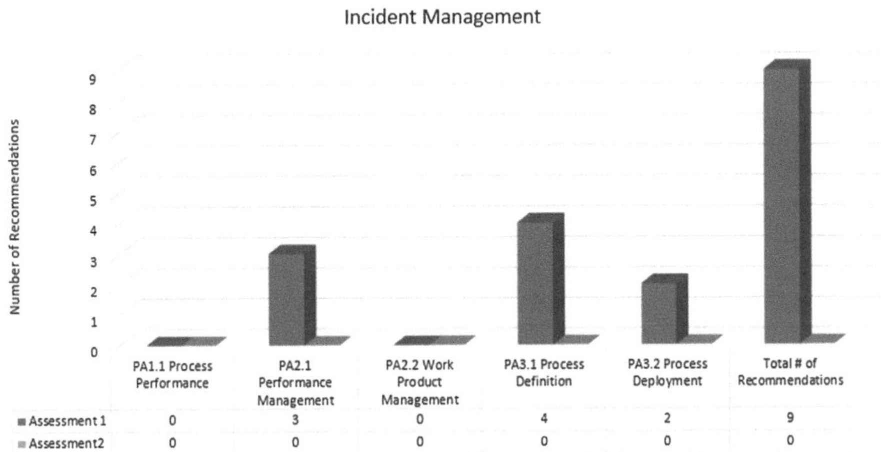

Fig. 1. A comparison of the number of recommendations between assessment 1 and 2 for Incident Management

There were three recommendations for Performance Management (PA2.1) for assessment 1 compared to none for assessment 2. For example, one of the recommendations for PA2.1 was: "The assumptions and constraints should be considered while identifying Incident Management KPIs so that the resultant KPIs are specific, measurable, achievable, relevant and timely (S.M.A.R.T.)". Work Product Management (PA2.2) had no recommendations for both assessments, while there were four recommendations for Process Definition (PA3.1) for assessment 1 with none for assessment 2. Process Deployment (PA3.2) in assessment 1 reported two recommendations, with none for assessment 2. This indicates that the incident management process improved from assessment 1 to assessment 2.

Problem Management

Figure 2 shows a comparison of the number of recommendations between assessment 1 and 2 for Problem Management. In both assessments there were no recommendations for Process Performance (PA1.1) while there were 11 recommendations for Performance Management (PA2.1) for assessment 1 with none for assessment 2. For example, one of the recommendations for PA2.1 was: "Problem Management process inputs and outputs should be regularly reviewed according to plan to ensure that the process activities are executed properly". Eight recommendations were reported for assessment 1 for Work Product Management (PA2.2), and none for assessment 2. Process Definition (PA3.1) had ten recommendations for assessment 1 with four for assessment 2, while Process Deployment (PA3.2) had five recommendations for assessment 1 versus 3 for assessment 2. The decrease in recommendations indicates that the Problem Management process had improved.

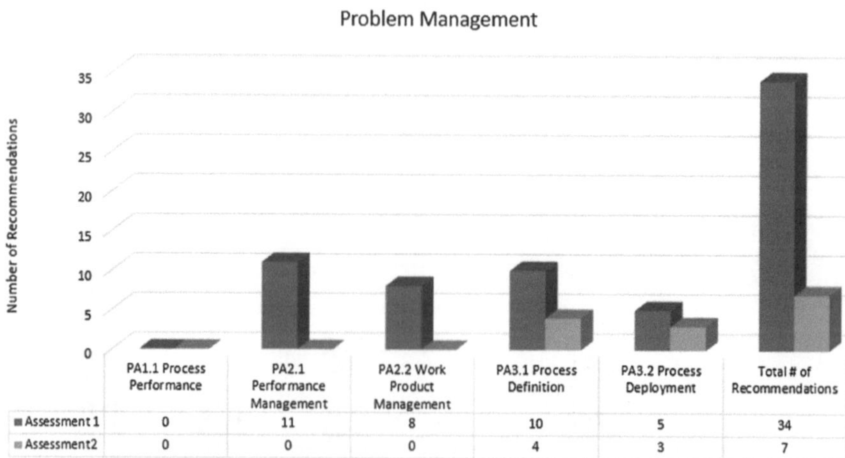

Fig. 2. A comparison of the number of recommendations between assessment 1 and 2 for Problem Management

Change Management
The Attribute Rating Scores for Change Management were identical for assessment 1 and assessment 2. However, a breakdown of the number of recommendations year-over-year revealed that the process improved in cycle 2. Figure 3 shows a comparison of the number of SMPA recommendations for assessment 1 and 2 for Change Management.

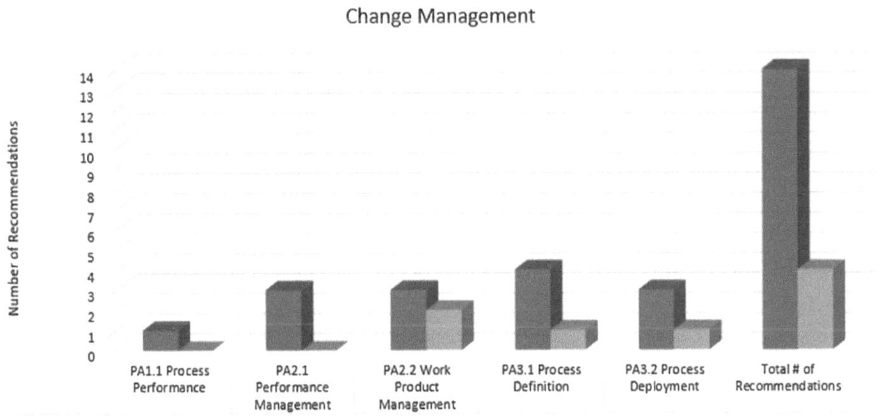

	PA1.1 Process Performance	PA2.1 Performance Management	PA2.2 Work Product Management	PA3.1 Process Definition	PA3.2 Process Deployment	Total # of Recommendations
Assessment 1	1	3	3	4	3	14
Assessment2	0	0	2	1	1	4

Fig. 3. A comparison of the number of recommendations between assessment 1 and 2 for Change Management

In assessment 1 there was one recommendation that was reported for Process Performance (PA1.1) with none for assessment 2. The recommendation reported for PA1.1 was: "Change management process overall must be reviewed and improved in order to fulfil its current and expected outcomes". There were three recommendations for Performance Management (PA2.1) in assessment 1 and none for assessment 2. Work Product Management (PA2.2) had three recommendations for assessment 1 with two for assessment 2. Process Definition (PA3.1) had four recommendations for assessment 1 with one for assessment 2, and Process Deployment (PA3.2) had three recommendations in assessment 1 with one for assessment 2.

Summary of Process Improvement
At the Process Performance (PA1.1) level every survey question had a corresponding one-to-one knowledge item. However at higher process attributes the same knowledge item was used for multiple questions in a number of instances since some of the questions were closely related and could be addressed by a single knowledge item. At Process Performance (PA1.1) level the recommendations are specific to the process in question. From Performance Management (PA2.1) onwards, the recommendations are developed as general guidelines that may apply to any process.

The average of the number of recommendations as a percentage of the total number of knowledge items for each process was used as the Key Performance Indicator

Table 11. Average recommendation ratio for all processes

Process attributes	Incident Management			Problem Management			Change Management		
	# of Knowledge items	Assessment 1	Assessment 2	# of Knowledge items	Assessment 1	Assessment 2	# of Knowledge items	Assessment 1	Assessment 2
PA1.1 Process Performance	8	0	0	11	0	0	14	1	0
PA2.1 Performance Management	21	3	0	21	11	0	21	3	0
PA2.2 Work Product Management	13	0	0	13	8	0	13	3	2
PA3.1 Process Definition	11	4	0	11	10	4	11	4	1
PA3.2 Process Deployment	9	2	0	9	5	3	9	3	1
Total # of knowledge items	62			65			68		
Total # of recommendations		9	0		34	7		14	4
Average recommendation ratio		15%	0%		52%	11%		21%	6%

(KPI) and incorporated into a model to link Process Capability, Process Performance and Financial Performance.

Table 11 shows the average percentage of recommendations over both assessments for the Incident Management, Problem Management, and Change Management processes, respectively. The average recommendation ratio decreased considerably from cycle 1 to cycle 2 demonstrating process improvement.

Although there was no change in the capability levels, process capability improved for all three processes as measured by the comparison of the number of recommendations in the process capability assessment reports in cycle 1 and 2. In particular, of the 62 potential recommendations for the Incident Management process, no recommendations were present in the assessment report in cycle 2 compared to nine recommendations in cycle 1. The Problem Management process was presented with 34 of the 65 potential recommendations in cycle 1, while only seven recommendations were presented in cycle 2. The Change Management process decreased from 14 recommendations in cycle 1 to four in cycle 2 out of a potential of 68 recommendations.

Combining the recommendations for improvement across the three processes showed an improvement in the total recommendations for improvement from 57 in cycle 1 to 11 in cycle 2.

Therefore, consistent with previous studies [18, 19], this study found that improving processes results in higher process capability attainment, as evident by a reduction in the number of recommendations for improvement.

6 Conclusion

In the context of the process improvement program at Company X, where only three processes were assessed, the Process Managers at Company X held the view that the process attribute ratings generated by the SMPA tool based on the four-point NPLF scale, were not sufficiently informative and representative of the process improvement gained for the three processes examined. The NPLF scale provided a good foundation, but the recommendations offered more granularity for process improvement for Company X. The decrease in the number of recommendations (assessment indictors) as a proxy measure of process improvement was more meaningful, and representative of the improvement achieved at a more granular level. It is interesting to note that the revised version of the process assessment standard (ISO/IEC 33020) provides finer granularity (than ISO/IEC 15504) with an option to report process attribute achievement on a six-point scale: N, P−, P+, L−, L+, F [13]. Future research will map the SMPA results to the new six point scale to explore its utility.

The inability to access the raw scores for the assessment was a limitation, as the SMPA tool normalized the arithmetic mean of survey responses to the NPLF rating scale. The assessment results may have been more accurate if the actual raw data were used to determine the capability level. This may have led to a different process improvement plan at Company X. To overcome this limitation, the novel approach of using the average number of knowledge items reported was undertaken for this study. Future research can use the actual data to determine process capability. The approach of using the recommendation ratio may be applied to tradition or manual process assessments as well.

To determine if there was an improvement at PA1.1, only the questions that scored P and N were considered using the recommendation ratio approach to determine process capability. Furthermore, only providing recommendations for questions that scored either a P or N for PA2.1 onwards may be viewed as a limitation of the SMPA tool, since no guidance is provided to reach F (Fully) from L (Largely).

A unique contribution of this research is the use of the number of recommendations as a proxy measure of process improvement rather than capability level or attribute achievement.

6.1 Implications to Researchers and Practitioners

The research contributes to the body of knowledge on ITSM process capability, by using a standards-based maturity model, ISO/IEC 15504 for the measurement of process capability, and adapting it to provide a fit-for-purpose measurement model. The adaption was to use the variation in the number of recommendations (generated by the SMPA report) based on process attributes to determine improvement in process capability rather than the process capability level. The account of the use of a transparent, efficient tool (SMPA) for process assessment contributes to the literature on process assessments.

The practical contribution of the research is that it offers an example from which other organizations can learn to measure their ITSM Process Capability for ITSM Process improvement.

Note. ITIL® is a Registered Trade Mark of AXELOS Limited and Zendesk® is a registered trademark of Zendesk Inc.

References

1. Galliers, R.D., Leidner, D.E.: Strategic Information Management: Challenges and Strategies in Managing Information Systems. Routledge, New York (2014)
2. Shrestha, A.: Development and evaluation of a software-mediated process assessment approach in IT service management. In: Faculty of Business, Education, Law and Arts. University of Southern Queensland (2015)
3. De Haes, S., Van Grembergen, W.: IT governance and its mechanisms. Inf. Syst. Control J. **1**, 27–33 (2004)
4. Barafort, B., Rousseau, A.: Sustainable service innovation model: a standardized IT service management process assessment framework. In: O'Connor, R.V., Baddoo, N., Cuadrago Gallego, J., Rejas Muslera, R., Smolander, K., Messnarz, R. (eds.) EuroSPI 2009. CCIS, vol. 42, pp. 69–80. Springer, Heidelberg (2009). https://doi.org/10.1007/978-3-642-04133-4_6
5. Juran, J., Godfrey, A.: Juran's Quality Handbook. McGraw-Hill, New York (1999)
6. ISO/IEC: ISO/IEC 33002:2015 Information technology – Process assessment – Requirements for performing process assessment. International Organization for Standardization, Geneva (2015)
7. ISO/IEC: ISO/IEC 33014:2013 Information technology – Process assessment – Guide for process improvement. International Organization for Standardization, Geneva (2013)

8. Mainville, D.: 2014 ITSM Industry Survey Results (2014). http://i.navvia.com/2014-itsm-survey-results
9. Shrestha, A., et al.: Software-mediated process assessment for IT service capability management. In: 22nd European Conference on Information Systems. ECIS, Tel Aviv, Israel (2014)
10. ISO/IEC: ISO/IEC TS 15504-8 Information Technology - Process Assessment - Part 8: An Exemplar Process Assessment Model for IT Service Management. International Organization for Standardization, Geneva, Switzerland (2012)
11. ISO/IEC: ISO/IEC JTC1/SC7 WG10 Transition from ISO/IEC 15504 to ISO/IEC 330xx, in Standing Document. International Organisation for Standardisation (2017)
12. Shrestha, A., et al.: Benefits and relevance of international standards in a design science research project for process assessments. Comput. Stand. Inter. **60**, 48–56 (2018)
13. ISO/IEC: ISO/IEC 33020:2015 Information technology – Process assessment – Process measurement framework for assessment of process capability. International Organization for Standardization, Geneva (2015)
14. Myers, M.: Qualitative Research in Business & Management. SAGE Publications Limited, Thousand Oaks (2008)
15. Oates, B.J.: Researching Information Systems and Computing. SAGE, London (2006)
16. Shrestha, A., Cater-Steel, A., Toleman, M., Rout, T.: Evaluation of software mediated process assessments for IT service management. In: Rout, T., O'Connor, R.V., Dorling, A. (eds.) SPICE 2015. CCIS, vol. 526, pp. 72–84. Springer, Cham (2015). https://doi.org/10.1007/978-3-319-19860-6_7
17. ISO/IEC: ISO/IEC TR 20000-4:2010 – Information Technology – Service Management – Part 4: Process Reference Model. International Organisation for Standardisation, Geneva, Switzerland (2010)
18. Cater-Steel, A., Toleman, M., Rout, T.: Process improvement for small firms: an evaluation of the RAPID assessment-based method. Inf. Softw. Technol. **48**(5), 323–334 (2006)
19. Jäntti, M., Rout, T., Wen, L., Heikkinen, S., Cater-Steel, A.: Exploring the impact of IT service management process improvement initiatives: a case study approach. In: Woronowicz, T., Rout, T., O'Connor, R.V., Dorling, A. (eds.) SPICE 2013. CCIS, vol. 349, pp. 176–187. Springer, Heidelberg (2013). https://doi.org/10.1007/978-3-642-38833-0_16

[illegible] Interpretation and Reporting of Process Capability Results [illegible]

Madhavan, D.: 2014 ITSM Industry Survey Results (2014). http://[illegible]

[illegible] et al.: Software-mediated process assessment for IT service [illegible] 22nd European conference on Information Systems (ECIS) [illegible]

[illegible]

[illegible] for Standardization [illegible]

ISO/IEC 15504-[illegible] ISO/IEC JTC1/SC7 [illegible] ISO/IEC 15504 [illegible] Development [illegible] (2015)

[illegible] Research project for process assessment [illegible] (2016)

ISO/IEC TS [illegible]: Information technology — Process assessment — [illegible] framework for assessment of process capability [illegible]

[illegible] (2015)

[illegible] Research [illegible] Management [illegible] Volume [illegible]

[illegible] Press (2003)

[illegible]

[illegible]

[illegible] Process improvement [illegible] (2017)

[illegible] Process improvement [illegible] 2nd [illegible]

[illegible]

[illegible]

[illegible]

SPI Knowledge and Change Processes

Introducing Requirements Change Management Process into ISO/IEC 12207

Sajid Anwer[2(✉)], Lian Wen[1,2], Terry Rout[1], and Zhe Wang[1,2]

[1] Institute for Integrated and Intelligent Systems, Griffith University, Brisbane, Australia
{l.wen, t.rout, zhe.wang}@griffith.edu.au

[2] School of Information and Communication Technology, Griffith University, Brisbane, Australia
Sajid.anwer@griffithuni.edu.au

Abstract. Requirements Engineering (RE) is one of the critical phases of any software development life cycle. Business and technology evolution increasingly poses many challenges and becomes a source of continuous change in RE. Changes to software are inevitable in the development process and are a source of project risk. During the last decade many Requirements Change Management (RCM) models have been proposed, but this area appears to remain rudimentary in software process standards. Configuration management process has been introduced in ISO/IEC 12207:2017; however, it does not fully address RCM problems. This paper proposes an RCM Process (RCMP) to address this issue. The process is extended to a theoretical model based on seven core essentials that were identified in the literature. Furthermore, the process is modeled in a Composition Tree (CT), a semi-formal graphic notation, and then we have compared the new process with existing Configuration Management (CM) process to highlight the differences. Our proposed process significantly addresses the deficiencies of existing change management process.

Keywords: Requirements engineering · Requirements change
Process standards · Change management · Behavior engineering
Composition tree

1 Introduction

During the last decade, significant attention has been paid by the researchers in the field of requirements engineering [1]. Requirements development and requirements management are the two main aspects of this field [2]. Requirements development mainly addresses the requirements elicitation and specification, while requirements management deals with the management of current requirements and the change of requirements.

Software development is a dynamic process, and requirements change or evolution is inevitable and driven by a number of factors such as change in market trends, software and system requirements, business goals, and customer needs [1]. The continuous change and management of software requirements is still an open challenge in

I. Stamelos et al. (Eds.): SPICE 2018, CCIS 918, pp. 185–199, 2018.
https://doi.org/10.1007/978-3-030-00623-5_13

the field of software engineering [2]. Bano et al. [3] and Kobayashi and Maekawa [4] specified that effective change management is one of the main factors that determines software failure or success.

In recent years, a number of Requirements Change Management (RCM) models have been proposed in the literature; however, effective RCM is still an open challenge. Industry professionals proposed and practiced some of the ISO/IEC standards, but those standards have not fully addressed the problems of this area. ISO/IEC 12207: 2008 [5] discusses some aspects of RCM among the outcomes of the requirements analysis process. ISO/IEC 12207: 2017 [6] and ISO/IEC 15288: 2015 [7] outline the configuration management process and discuss the change management in the context of configuration management as an activity. The goal of Configuration Management (CM) is to set and maintain consistency among project products and product versioning. In fact, CM is critical in maintaining control in the development and maintenance of systems not just for system execution. In contrast, change management addresses the requested changes to individual products, e.g. project requirements, design, and scope etc. [8]. Configuration Management is considered as a supporting process in software requirement change and mainly addresses the challenges of evolution and maintenance areas [9–11].

In this study, we propose a Requirements Change Management Process (RCMP) and theoretical model that addresses the deficiencies identified in existing research and industry practices. The proposed RCMP is defined in terms of process purpose and process outcomes. A certain set of activities has been identified and presented as theoretical model to support and explain the process outcomes. Our proposed model is based on seven core essentials: identification, analysis, negotiation and approval, implementation, verification, update deliverables, and communication.

Process outcomes are usually defined in natural languages and may have different interpretations for different users, which could cause ambiguity. A Composition Tree (CT), as a semi-formal graphic notation [12], is used to model the proposed process, in order to reduce ambiguity among different users. A CT is also used to compare the proposed process with the existing configuration management process defined in ISO/IEC 12207:2017. A comparison of results shows the similarities and highlights the significant differences between the two processes. Our proposed process significantly addresses the deficiencies of existing Configuration Management Processes (CMP) and also existing change management models.

Thus, this paper addresses the following question: **What are the deficiencies of existing requirements change management processes currently followed by industry?**

The rest of this paper is organized as follows: Sect. 2 briefly discusses the background of requirements engineering, RCM, and existing RCM models presented in the literature. Previous research related to software process standards and composition tree is also discussed in this section. The proposed RCMP and theoretical model is elaborated in Sect. 3. Section 4 discusses the CT modeling of our process and compares it with the existing process, and Sect. 5 presents the conclusion and possible future recommendations.

2 Literature Review

This section discusses the existing researches in the field of requirements change, software process and composition tree. Requirement change is generally undesirable but is an inevitable element in software engineering. Accordingly, RCM is one of the critical parts of the software development life cycle. In contrast, previous research around software engineering paid scant attention towards RCM and overlooked this very basic component of the software development process.

2.1 Software Requirements Change

Bhatti et al. [13] proposed a formal RCM approach to manage the RC of both small and complex systems in a six-phase process. However, the proposed approach missed two major elements of this process. First, the management of change request in a well-defined database. Second, it did not state the approval process of implemented change from concerned stakeholders, which is very important and is an integral part of any RCMP. This process also missed the change schedule part in the already implemented schedule.

Saima et al. [14] proposed a well-documented process model in accordance with roles, activities, and artifacts involved in the RCMP. They also discussed the pre and post conditions of each model activity, which is a unique approach to check model completeness. However, the proposed approach lacked a change request repository to verify the status of already implemented changes. The proposed approach is also dependent on Unified Modeling Language (UML) as an artifact used in RCM process and hence cannot be generalized.

Nurmuliani et al. [15] mainly addressed a few components of RCM process, including change impact analysis and possible causes of change. They proposed a complete model, but it lacked integral elements of RCM process, such as formal change request initiation, schedule adjustment according to the new change, and the updating of affected artifacts. Jessada and Amnart [16] conducted a pilot study to address the RC problem using UML. This study covered very limited scope of complete RCM process and missed the change impact on cost and schedule, change implementation, and change verification and validation.

Niazi et al. [17] recommended a RCM model that implements CMMI level 2 practices [18] and empirically validates their approach. The proposed model implements the RCM model in five steps starting from request initiation followed by request validation and implementation step. The last step of this model is to update the required artifacts, which is preceded by the verification step after implementing the request. The proposed model covers most of the important elements of RCM model. However, the requirement pool or database is not updated after the implementation and verification step, which is very critical part of any RCM model. Another model presented by Khan et al. [19] overcomes the deficiencies of the above-mentioned approach and introduces the concept of batch processing. However, this approach did not cover the change impact analysis element of RCM process.

Jayatilleke and Lie [20] conducted a systematic literature review of RCM models based on causes of change, already developed process, and techniques to handle RC.

Formal and semi-formal processes of RCM are being critically evaluated and found number of short comings in already developed processes. Leffingwell and Widrig [21] recommended a process model that elaborates this problem in good detail, but verification of proposed model is missing that limits the stability of system. Similar deficiencies have been reported in another study conducted by Ince [22].

Kobayashi and Maekawa [4] proposed a RCM model based on 4W (What, Where, Who, When) to address this problem. They use formal specification language GSL to define the process activities, which ensures the completeness of this model. However, all the activities are defined at very abstract level and it seems difficult to implement these activities and ultimately limits the applicability of this model. Another deficiency is that effected artifacts are not mentioned. Another study conducted by Ajila [23] depicts the similar deficiencies along with the cost and effort estimation problem.

In summary, significant work has been done in the RCM domain and a number of models have been proposed in the literature, some of which have been empirically validated. However, many critical factors related to RCM problems are still missing in the literature and need attention from researchers.

2.2 Software Process Standards

Software process models are abstract "representations of a process architecture, design or definition" [33]. Normally, software life cycle activities are formalized more precisely by using software process model's syntax, notations, and semantics [34]. Behavior Engineering provides a graphic notation CT, to represent software process models. Researchers have defined many software process standards with the help of industry professionals that formalize the software development life cycle activities. ISO/IEC 24774 outlines the standard format for software process as process title, purpose, outcomes, activities, and tasks [24].

RCM is critical in software life cycle processes; project success largely depends upon the effective management of this activity. In industry, many ISO standards are currently in practice, but RCM issues are still not fully addressed in these standards. ISO/IEC 12207: 2008 [7] discusses some part of RCM as the outcomes of requirements analysis process.

In recent years, industry has realized the importance of RCM in success and stability of software development. ISO/IEC 12207: 2017 [8] and ISO/IEC 15288: 2015 [9] outline the configuration management process and discuss change management in the configuration management process. In software systems, configuration management and change management are two separate processes. Configuration management's goal is to set and maintain consistency among project products and product versioning. In fact, configuration management handles the overall execution of system. In contrast, change management addresses the requested changes to individual products, e.g. project requirements, design, and scope etc. [10]. Configuration management can be considered as a supporting process in software requirements change and mainly copes the challenges of evolution and maintenance areas [11–13]. Similarly, configuration management and change management processes are defined in Information Technology Infrastructure Library (ITIL). However, ITIL mainly focuses on delivering information technology services to the companies instead of developing projects.

In summary, despite of the importance of the requirements change management, ISO standards do not address this critical success factor. To address this specific research gap, we have proposed an RCMP in this paper. We have also designed a theoretical model in light of the proposed process.

2.3 Composition Trees

The guidelines or processes written in natural languages are always context dependent and ambiguous, due to the nature of the human languages. Similarly, the software processes written in natural language are difficult to translate into applicable form. The process of translating the user requirements into unambiguous and consistent form is another problem that has had to be faced in the software engineering discipline. Over the years, a number of modelling techniques have been used to overcome this problem. Behavior engineering effectively solved the problem through translating the user requirements into some intuitive and semi-formal graphic notations called behavior trees (BT) and CT [35].

Behavior trees is a formally defined graphical notation used to model system behaviors [36]. While CT is used to model the static information and it can model software processes more precisely and less ambiguously [37]. Originally, CT was used to model and describe the components composition of component based systems [14]. The states, attributes, and relationships provide the summary information about the system components [38].

Like BT, CTs can be constructed by translating the functional requirements one by one. This subsection explains the process of composition tree development with the help of a small case study. Detailed description about composition trees can be found at the Behavior Engineering Website [39].We take a microwave oven as an example to explain the composition tree building process.

System: Microwave Oven

- R1: When the light is off, door is closed, and the button is not pushed then the oven will be in idle state.
- R2: When the button is pushed, then the light will be turned on and oven starts cooking.
- R3: If the button is pushed while the oven is cooking, cooking time will be increased by one minute.
- R4: If the oven times-off and light turned off then the beeper emits a sound to indicate the cooking is finished.

The complete CT, expected states and components generated through integrating all the requirements is shown in Fig. 1. There are some obvious advantages of using CT over natural language description:

- Usually the information described in natural languages are context dependent and ambiguous. On the other hand, the information presented in CT is more precise and not ambiguous.

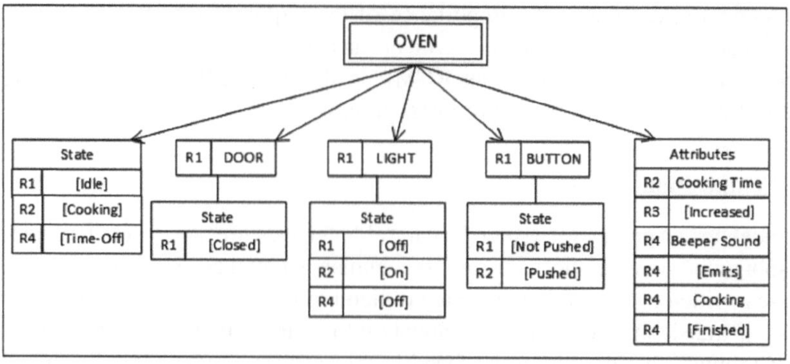

Fig. 1. The complete integrated tree for a microwave oven

- All the information's are integrated at one place, so it is easy to identify requirement defects.
- Because the complete information of one component is arranged at one place, so it is easy to design and implement specific component.

3 Proposed Requirements Change Management Process

This section introduces the proposed software requirements change management process through its purpose and outcomes, which is a typical way to define process in many standards [24]. In Sect. 2.1, we discuss the number of models proposed in literature and discuss the shortcomings, i.e. change impact analysis, impacted artifacts modification, and change communication etc. In Sect. 2.2., we discuss the ISO process standards and explores the potential research gap. Currently, change management is only highlighted as a part of configuration management.

The goal of CM is to maintain consistency between all components of the system and control the overall execution of the system, in contrast, change management process goal is to manage and control change in individual products of the project or system. Accordingly, we propose a requirement change management process to overcome this deficiency. Proposed process outcomes are further elaborated with the help of seven phase's theoretical model.

3.1 Definition

Purpose: The purpose of RCMP is to manage and control requirement changes of system elements or items and make them available to concerned parties.

Outcomes: As a result of the successful implementation of the software requirement change management process:

1. Items to be changed are identified and recorded.
2. Change Impacts are analyzed.

3. The cost and schedule of changing items are estimated.
4. Changes to the items under requirement change are approved.
5. Changes to the items under requirement change are implemented.
6. Changes to the items under requirement change are verified and validated.
7. Changed items deliverables are updated and communicated to concerned parties.

3.2 Requirements Change Management Process Model Description

This subsection explains the theoretical model defined based on the proposed RCMP. Figure 2 shows the theoretical model core elements with a set of activities and tasks. The source of change can be either internal or external serving the purpose of RCMP model input. The project management and maintenance team requests are considered as internal requests, while external requests come from customers or other stakeholders. The change description and reason of the change is also included in the change request. Based on the input request, the change request will be saved in change requirement pool for future reference in parallel with requirement identification. Ince model [25] highlights this point as a fundamental element of RCMP model. The use of appropriate documents is the most crucial element of this activity. Vision document, software requirement specification document, UML products [16], and behavior trees [26] are common documents used as input for this purpose.

The second stage of the RCMP model is change analysis. This activity comprises of many tasks including impact analysis, cost and schedule estimation. The consistency with business goals [27, 28], other system requirements and development and operational constraints are the major functions performed in impact analysis. Cost and schedule estimation and risk analysis [29] are also included in this stage.

The next stage is negotiation and approval of change request. A CCB is responsible for authorizing the negotiation and approval process [17]. In small teams, normally project managers act as CCB, but in large teams some other team members and system analysts are also included in CCB [30]. The CCB first discusses the impact analysis and cost & schedule estimation reports with both the development team and the external stakeholders. After discussion with all the stakeholders, the CCB will make a decision, either the change request would be accepted, rejected, or sent back to change identification stage for more information before the next iteration of change analysis. Rejected requests would be stored in change request pool for future reference and accepted requests would be forwarded to implementation stage.

The fourth stage is to implement the approved change. Change implementation was identified as a core activity in previous research. Change implementation mainly depends on the type of documents used to identify the requested change [13, 28]. In this phase, changes will be implemented in all the impacted documents.

After that, implemented changes will be verified and validated according to the change request [31] and it is also a critical part of a RCM process [32]. The changes that are failed due to implementation issues will be sent back to implementation stage. The changes that are successfully passed will move forward to the next stage and be stored in the change request pool for future reference. The third possible output of this stage would be that the implemented changes are sent back to change identification stage for reassessment.

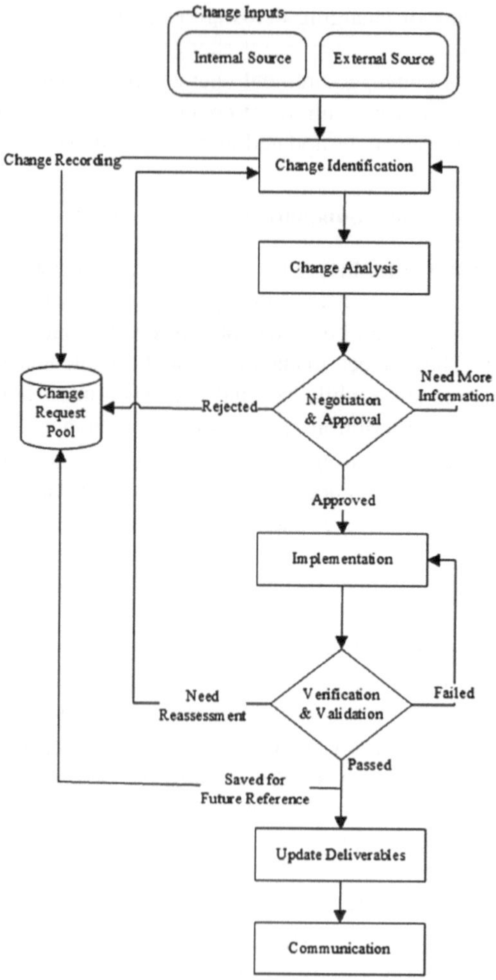

Fig. 2. The requirements change management process model

In the next stage, all deliverables including requirements, design, code, and testing products that have been impacted due to requested change will be updated. In last stage, the modified deliverables will be communicated to all the stakeholders so that everyone will use the updated version.

4 Comparison with Existing Models

This section compares the proposed RCMP with current configuration management process defined in standards. Initially, software processes are written in natural languages in a standard format. It is usually difficult to compare with its counterpart also defined in natural languages. Previous research reveals that Behavior Engineering

(BE) notations can be used to model and verify process standards [36]. Composition tree is a part of BE and it is used to model and compare the process standards. ISO/IEC 12207: 2017 [8] and ISO/IEC 15288: 2015 [9] outlines the configuration management process and discusses the change management in context of configuration management. In the next subsection, CT is used to model the configuration management process outcomes.

4.1 Composition Tree Modeling of Configuration Management Process

To model ISO/IEC 12207: 2017 configuration management process, first the list of nouns and acronyms are identified from process outcomes. The identified list includes components and attributes of components in CT. The process name is the root of the CT and then we go through each outcome one-by-one to identify the components, states, and their relationships and integrate these in the initial CT.

Process Name: Configuration Management Process

Process Purpose: The purpose of Configuration Management Process is to manage and control system elements and configurations over the life cycle. Configuration Management also manages consistency between a product and its associated configuration definition.

Process Outcomes:

1. Items requiring configuration management are identified and managed.
2. Configuration baselines are established.
3. Changes to the items under configuration management are controlled.
4. Configuration status information is available.
5. Required Configuration audits are completed.
6. System releases and deliveries are controlled and approved.

Configuration Management Process, item, configuration, and deliveries and releases (DRL) are the list of components identified based on process outcomes. Figure 3 illustrates the CT of ISO/IEC 12207: 2017 configuration management process. The component Item are the work products of individual phases, such as requirement specification document, design document, source code, testing document, etc. are defined as items. The "*" sign indicates that the component may have more than one instance.

4.2 Composition Tree Modeling of Configuration Management Process

This subsection presents the composition tree of the proposed RCMP. Similar technique is used to construct composition tree of RCMP.

Process Name: Requirement Change Management Process

Purpose: The purpose of RCMP is to manage and control a requirement change of systems elements or items and make them available to concerned parties.

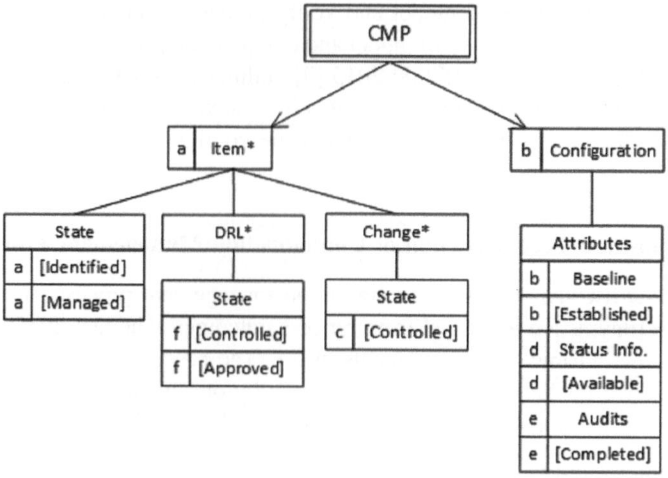

Fig. 3. Configuration management process composition tree

Process Outcomes:

1. Items to be changed are identified and recorded.
2. Impact analysis of changing items are performed.
3. The cost and schedule of changing items are estimated.
4. Changes to the items under requirement change are approved.
5. Changes to the items under requirement change are implemented.
6. Changes to the items under requirement change are verified.
7. Changed items deliverables are controlled and communicated to concerned parties.

Requirement Change Management Process, items, and Concerned Parties (CP) are the list of components identified based on process outcomes. Figure 4 illustrate the composition tree of proposed RCMP. The component items are the work products of individual phases, such as requirement specification document, design document, source code, testing document, etc. are defined as items. The "*" sign indicates that the component may have more than one instance.

4.3 Comparison Between Requirement Change Management Process and Configuration Management Process

This subsection applies the CT comparison algorithm to identify the differences and similarities between the CMP and the RCMP. This comparison is based on a label matching tree algorithm, which is used to compare different versions of behavior trees [26].

The fundamental task of the two-step merging algorithm is to find the matching node in CT node names, i.e. components, states etc. to form the basis of same nodes. First, the components or states are identified that serve the same purpose but may be called by different names, and then a mapping between these terms needs to be defined.

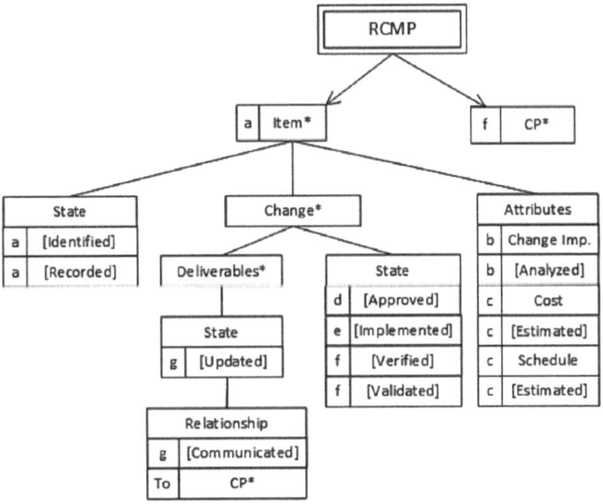

Fig. 4. Requirements change management process composition tree

In our paper no such term exists and therefore this step will be skipped. In the second step, different versions or different trees will be merged to form a Comparison Composition Tree (CCT). To simplify this step, one tree would be called the 'old tree' and the other the 'new tree'. In CCT, the root is a combination of root names of both trees. Complete information and the differences between both trees can be easily understood in a CCT.

For clear and precise understanding, a CCT follows a display convention. The nodes that are part of both the old and the new trees will be represented with single line boundary. Dotted boundary lines are used to represent the nodes that are only part of the old tree, while bold boundary lines are used to represent the information that only exists in the new tree. This is a brief description of tree merging algorithm, complete tree merging algorithm details are discussed in [38].

The CMP 12207:2017 and RCMP CCT is shown in Fig. 5, and the root is a combination of both tree roots. A number of similarities and differences are found in the CCT.

- There is one component called Configuration defined in the CMP ISO 12207: 2017, but no such component exists in the RCMP.
- There are no attributes defined for item or work products in the CMP ISO/IEC 12207:2017, whereas a number of attributes for item or work products are identified in the RCMP.
- Deliveries and Releases (DLR) are defined as a component in the CMP ISO/IEC 12207:2017, whereas no such component existing in the RCMP.
- One state of component item or work product called identified is a part of both trees, while managed state exists only in the CMP ISO/IEC 12207:2017, and recorded sate only exists in RCMP.

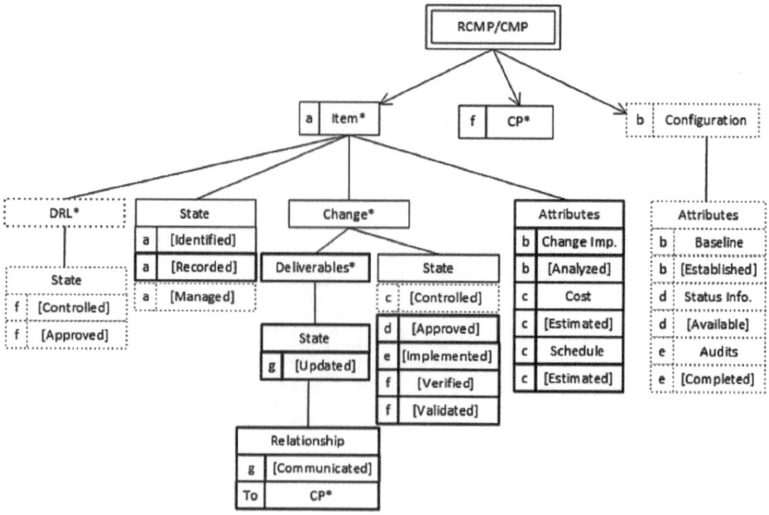

Fig. 5. The comparison composition tree between configuration management process of 12207 and proposed requirements change management process

- No attributes defined for component change which is a sub component of item in CMP ISO/IEC 12207:2017, while we have one attribute for this component in the RCMP.
- For the sub component "change", only one state called controlled is presented in the CMP ISO/IEC 12207:2017, contrary to the RCMP we have other four states, one sub component with an associated state called updated.
- Lastly, one relationship of the sub component Deliverables is also defined in RCMP, but no such component defined in the CMP ISO/IEC 12207:2017.

In summary, we can analyze that deficiencies in the CMP related to change management are thoroughly addressed in the RCMP. Configuration management mainly deals with version control and system configuration related activities, and the CMP addresses these activates in detail. In contrast, change management is discussed very little in the CMP. The complete change process of item or work products defined with only one state called controlled, whereas the RCMP addresses the change management issue in detail. The RCMP identified the attributes related to the item or work products that need to be changed. Different states, such as approved, implemented, verified, and validated, through which the item or work products need to pass through in the change process also mentioned in the RCMP. Another important element of the differences is to update the deliverables, such as requirements, design documents, source code, and test cases based on the required change is also included in the RCMP as a subcomponent. Lastly, it is also necessary to make sure that all the stakeholders will use the same updated version of all deliverables; therefore, relationship is defined as the updated state of component deliverables representing the communication among all stakeholders.

5 Conclusion and Future Work

This research has addressed several deficiencies of the existing RCM models in standards by proposing a software requirement change management process. A certain set of activities has been identified to support and explain the proposed process. To better understand this process, a seven-stage theoretical model is presented. The seven stages are: identification, analysis, negotiation and approval, implementation, verification and validation, update deliverables, and communication. To avoid ambiguity, a CT is used to model the proposed process. Composition Trees are also used to compare the proposed model with the existing CMP proposed in ISO/IEC 12207:2017. A CCT is constructed to highlight the differences and similarities between the two processes. The CCT reveals that the RCMP addresses several RCM problems in more detail than the existing CMP. In future, a questionnaire will be conducted with industry professionals to empirically validate the proposed model. The applicability of the proposed model in global software development paradigm is worthy of future investigation.

References

1. Barry, E.J., Mukhopadhyay, T., Slaughter, S.A.: Software project duration and effort: an empirical study. Inf. Technol. Manag. **3**(1–2), 113–136 (2002)
2. Kasser, J.E.: Object-oriented requirements engineering and management (2003)
3. Bano, M., Imtiaz, S., Ikram, N., Niazi, M., Usman, M.: Causes of requirement change-a systematic literature review (2012)
4. Kobayashi, A., Maekawa, M.: Need-based requirements change management. In: Proceedings of the Eighth Annual IEEE International Conference and Workshop on the Engineering of Computer Based Systems, ECBS 2001, pp. 171–178. IEEE (2001)
5. ISO/IEC 12207: 2008 - Information Technology - System engineering- System life cycle process
6. ISO/IEC 12207: 2017 - Information Technology - System engineering- Software life cycle process
7. ISO/IEC 15288: 2015 - Information Technology - System engineering- System life cycle process
8. P.M. Institute, Practice Standard for Project Configuration Management, Project Management Institute (2007)
9. Harker, S.D., Eason, K.D., Dobson, J.E.: The change and evolution of requirements as a challenge to the practice of software engineering. In: Proceedings of IEEE International Symposium on Requirements Engineering, pp. 266–272. IEEE (1993)
10. McGee, S., Greer, D.: Sources of software requirements change from the perspectives of development and maintenance. Int. J. Adv. Softw. **3**, 186–200 (2010)
11. Mohan, K., Xu, P., Cao, L., Ramesh, B.: Improving change management in software development: integrating traceability and software configuration management. Decis. Support Syst. **45**(4), 922–936 (2008)
12. Dromey, R.G.: System composition: constructive support for the analysis and design of large systems. In: Systems Engineering/Test and Evaluation Conference, SETE 2005, Brisbane, Australia (2005)

13. Bhatti, M.W., Hayat, F., Ehsan, N., Ishaque, A., Ahmed, S., Mirza, E.: A methodology to manage the changing requirements of a software project. In: 2010 International Conference on Computer Information Systems and Industrial Management Applications (CISIM), pp. 319–322. IEEE (2010)
14. Imtiaz, S., Ikram, N., Imtiaz, S.: A process model for managing requirement change. In: Proceedings of the Fourth IASTED International Conference on Advances in Computer Science and Technology. ACTA Press, Langkawi (2008)
15. Nurmuliani, N., Zowghi, D., Powell, S.: Analysis of requirements volatility during software development life cycle. In: Proceedings of the 2004 Australian Software Engineering Conference, pp. 28–37. IEEE (2004)
16. Tomyim, J., Pohthong, A.: Requirements change management based on object-oriented software engineering with unified modeling language. In: 2016 7th IEEE International Conference on Software Engineering and Service Science (ICSESS), pp. 7–10. IEEE (2016)
17. Niazi, M., Hickman, C., Ahmad, R., Ali Babar, M.: A model for requirements change management: implementation of CMMI level 2 specific practice. In: Jedlitschka, A., Salo, O. (eds.) PROFES 2008. LNCS, vol. 5089, pp. 143–157. Springer, Heidelberg (2008). https://doi.org/10.1007/978-3-540-69566-0_14
18. C.P. Team: CMMI for Development, version 2.0 (2018)
19. Khan, A.A., Basri, S., Dominic, P.: A process model for requirements change management in collocated software development. In: 2012 IEEE Symposium on E-Learning, E-Management and E-Services (IS3e), pp. 1–6. IEEE (2012)
20. Jayatilleke, S., Lai, R.: A systematic review of requirements change management. Inf. Softw. Technol. **93**, 163–185 (2017)
21. Leffingwell, D.: Managing Software Requirements: A Use Case Approach. Pearson Education India (2003)
22. Makarainen, M.: Software change management processes in the development of embedded software. VTT Publ. **4**(1), 6 (2000)
23. Ajila, S.A.: Change management: modeling software product lines evolution. In: Proceedings of the 6th World Multiconference on Systemics, Cybernetics and Informatics, Orlando, Florida, pp. 492–497 (2002)
24. ISO/IEC TR 24774 - Software and systems engineering – Life cycle management – Guidelines for process description (2007)
25. Ince, D.C.: Introduction to Software Quality Assurance and Its Implementation. McGraw-Hill, Inc., New York (1995)
26. Wen, L., Dromey, R.G.: From requirements change to design change: a formal path. In: Proceedings of the Second International Conference on Software Engineering and Formal Methods, SEFM 2004, pp. 104–113. IEEE (2004)
27. Lock, S., Kotonya, G.: An integrated framework for requirement change impact analysis. In: 4th Australian Conference on Requirements Engineering (1999)
28. Hussain, W., Zowghi, D., Clear, T., MacDonell, S., Blincoe, K.: Managing requirements change the informal way: when saying 'No' is not an option. In: 2016 IEEE 24th International Conference on Requirements Engineering (RE), pp. 126–135. IEEE (2016)
29. Bohner, S.A.: Impact analysis in the software change process: a year 2000 perspective. In: ICSM, vol. 96, pp. 42–51 (1996)
30. El Emam, K., Holtje, D., Madhavji, N.H.: Causal analysis of the requirements change process for a large system. In: Proceedings of the International Conference on Software Maintenance, pp. 214–221. IEEE (1997)
31. Zowghi, D., Offen, R., Nurmuliani, N.: Impact of requirements volatility on the software development lifecycle (2000)

32. Olsen, N.C.: The software rush hour (software engineering). IEEE Softw. **10**(5), 29–37 (1993)
33. Feiler, P.H., Humphrey, W.S.: Software process development and enactment: Concepts and definitions. In: Second International Conference on the Software Process, Continuous Software Process Improvement, pp. 28–40: (1993). IEEE
34. Scacchi, W.: Process models in software engineering. Encyclopedia of software engineering (2001)
35. Dromey, R.G.: Climbing over the "No Silver Bullet" brick wall. IEEE Softw. **23**(2), 120–119 (2006)
36. Tuffley, D., Rout, T.: Behavior engineering as process model verification tool. In: The Proceedings of the 10th International SPICE Conference (2010)
37. Dromey, R.G.: Formalizing the transition from requirements to design. In: Mathematical Frameworks for Component Software: Models for Analysis and Synthesis: World Scientific, pp. 173–205 (2006)
38. Wen, L., Tuffley, D., Rout, T.: Using composition trees to model and compare software process. In: International Conference on Software Process Improvement and Capability Determination, pp. 1–15. Springer (2011)
39. Behavior Engineering Website. www.beworld.org/BE/

Measuring Change in Software Projects Through an Earned Value Lens

Pinar Efe[1(✉)], Onur Demirors[2,3], and Boualem Benetallah[3]

[1] Bilgi Grubu Ltd., Ankara, Turkey
pinar.efe@gmail.com
[2] School of Computer Science and Engineering, University of New South Wales, Sydney, Australia
[3] Department of Computer Engineering, Izmir Institute of Technology, Izmir, Turkey

Abstract. Earned Value Management (EVM) is a common performance management tool for project management. EVM enables depicting the project progress in terms of scope, cost and schedule and provides future predictions based on trends and patterns. Even though EVM is widely used in various disciplines like manufacturing and construction, it is not common in software industry. One reason for this underutilization is the mismatch of an inherent nature of the software projects and the traditional EVM. Traditional EVM ignores change effort but it is predominant in software projects. We have developed cEVM as an extension to the traditional EVM to incorporate change and subsequent rework and evolution costs to measure earned value in software development projects more accurately. In this study, we focus on two applications of cEVM we performed to explore the usability of cEVM and to compare cEVM with traditional EVM. This paper discusses the results of the case studies as well as benefits and difficulties of cEVM.

Keywords: Earned Value Management · Software project management Performance Measurement · Reworking · Change management

1 Introduction

Earned Value Management (EVM) is a quantitative performance management tool that is in use for more than 50 years [1]. It objectively measures the project progress and performance in terms of scope, cost and schedule and estimates the future of the project. It basically compares the planned and actual work and calculates the value of the accomplished work. In spite of its wide spread use and success in many industries such as mining and construction, it is largely underutilized in the software industry. We believe it is related with an inherent property of software projects [2]

Software projects face a significant factor of change that is not frequently encountered in traditional fields of engineering [3–5]. In traditional fields such as manufacturing and construction, once the problem is defined, it can be assumed to be stable and change is neither very common nor physically possible. If a task is

I. Stamelos et al. (Eds.): SPICE 2018, CCIS 918, pp. 200–214, 2018.
https://doi.org/10.1007/978-3-030-00623-5_14

completed once, it is assumed that there will be no frequent changes on that but in software projects it is a common practice.

The earlier approach to deal with the problem in the software industry was to avoid changes by making better analysis and better plans. The objective was to stabilize products and processes but it did not produce desired effects [6] and has been never enough to prevent or avoid change [3, 4]. The studies show that software specialists spend about 30% to 50% of their time on rework [5, 7, 8]. In software development projects, a completed task might be redone after sometime during the project execution because of various reasons like defects and improvements.

Once it was clear that change cannot be avoided, various solutions have been proposed for its management. With the emergence of agile methods change is accepted as inevitable and the modern approach become embracing and managing the change instead of avoiding or preventing it. Today, agile approaches are used by a large amount of software organizations in the world [9, 10] but they do not have the variety of the tools that exists for traditional project management [10]. We believe traditional project management methods, tools and techniques need to be adapted or replaced by more effective ones considering the change factor to provide best of both worlds.

EVM is based on the traditional project management approach. It assumes that the plan established at the beginning will be stable during the execution of the project. The initial planning and baselines are very important for EVM, since it fundamentally describes how much the project align with the initial plan. EVM does not offer any special treatment for later changes and rework.

The main drawback of EVM for software projects is the influence of late effort spent for change of completed tasks [2]. The effort and cost spent later do not increase the value earned and the same is value for the change. The accomplished scope is still considered to be the same but costs more. As a result, EVM depicts an incorrect picture to project managers about the progress and the future of the project. The effort spent for change including unpredictable changes, requirement and design changes, software bugs, improvements, technical debts is ignored. If there were no changes and we did it absolutely right in every aspect for the first time, we would not have such a discussion and we would have had the same EV in every calculation.

The change oriented extension, cEVM, has been proposed [11] in order to overcome the change related drawbacks of EVM by introducing measures related with change. The model brings change aspect into the traditional EVM based on any kind of rework and evolution costs and incorporates them into scope, cost and schedule aspects to enable better visualization of software projects progress.

In this study, we conducted two case studies in two different companies to explore the usability of cEVM compared to the traditional EVM and an iterative project. We have explored if it helps to manage software development projects better comparing to traditional EVM. The first project is rather suitable to target of EVM since it applies traditional project management approach and waterfall life cycle model. The second project utilize an iterative development approach. We selected these projects to observe if/how cEVM could be used or extended for iterative and agile projects. We obtained promising results in both cases that we were able to calculate the progress as well as future estimates more precisely using cEVM. We have also faced some challenges that require further studies.

The paper is structured as follows. Section 2 summarizes the background on EVM. Section 3 presents cEVM with new measures briefly. Section 4 presents the application studies, with the background of the projects and results of the application and discusses the findings. Section 5 draws conclusion.

2 Background

This section presents the relevant background on EVM including the history and overview of the method.

The Earned Value concept in its most fundamental form has been used in industrial manufacturing in the early American factories since the late 1800s [1]. EVM formally introduced as a project management tool by the US Navy as part of the PERT/Cost methodology in 1962. Later in 1967, the US Department of Defense (DoD) formally issued Cost/Schedule Control Systems Criteria, which incorporates the EV concept with thirty-five criteria and mandated their use on systems developed for DoD. The private industry did not utilize EVM in the industrial projects except governmental contracts due to the complexity till the mid of the 90s.

After simplification of EVM in 1997, it has been evolved and was formally issued as a standard by American National Standards Institute (ANSI) [12]. The usage has been spread out to the other governmental agencies and private industry and the other nations e.g. Australia, Canada, and Sweden [13]. Project Management Institute (PMI) involved an overview of EVM in the first version of the PMBOK and broadened in subsequent versions [14, 15]. In 2007, PMI published a separate guideline "Practice Standard of Earned Value Management" to empower its role [16].

Furthermore, Agile EVM has been proposed as a light-weight adaption of EVM for agile project management [17–19]. Agile EVM does not aim to replace current agile metrics. Instead, it is just an additional one to existing others to increase the visibility of the project status and to support decision making. It particularly utilizes the terminology defined in Scrum and contains a simplified set of EV calculations adapted from traditional EVM.

EVM is all about planning, which results a Performance Measurement Baseline (PMB) and then controlling/measuring progress and performance according to this plan/baseline [20]. It has three key data elements:

- **Planned Value (PV)** is the sum of all the budgets for all planned work at any given time in the project schedule, corresponds to established PMB. The performance is measured against PV, typically plotted cost versus time with S-shaped curve.
- **Earned Value (EV)** is the value of the work progress at a given point in time, expressed in terms of PV.
- **Actual Cost (AC)** is the summation of the resources spent in accomplishing all work performed for the time period.

The key data elements are the basics of EVM (see Fig. 1). The other EVM metrics involving variances, indices, forecasts are originated from these elements (see Table 1).

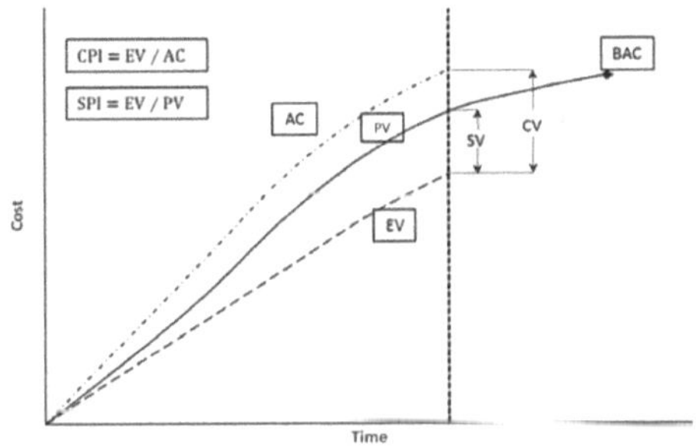

Fig. 1. EVM measures

Table 1. EVM metrics

Metric	Equation	Description
Schedule Variance (SV)	EV – PV	The difference between the planned value of the work scheduled and the value of the work accomplished
Schedule Performance Index (SPI)	EV – AC	Index showing the efficiency of the time utilized
Cost Variance (CV)	EV – AC	The difference between the values of the work accomplished and the actual cost incurred
Cost Performance Index (CPI)	EV/AC	Index showing the efficiency of the utilization of the resources allocated to the project
Budget at Completion (BAC)	Total PV	Cost of total estimated work in the plan
Estimate to Complete (ETC)	(BAC – EV)/CPI	Estimated cost required to finish all the remaining work
Estimate at Completion (EAC)	AC + ((BAC – EV)/CPI), AC + ETC, BAC/CPI	Projected final cost required to finish complete work and based on a statistical prediction using the performance indexes
Variance at Completion (VAC)	BAC – EAC	The difference between what the project was originally baselined to cost, versus what it is now estimated to cost

The variances reflect the project current status comparing the planned and actual data elements. The indices depict how efficiently cost and schedule used and also show the trends of the progress. They also enable predicting the future of the project based on the fundamental principle that trends and patterns in the past determine the future.

3 cEVM Overview

cEVM provides integrating the change aspect into traditional EVM by defining change related concepts, measures and metrics [11]. Change results in reworking and/or evolution costs and the distinguishing feature of cEVM is to incorporate rework and evolution costs into actual costs and to calibrate EV based on this total cost and its trends in time.

cEVM defines the following key measures in addition to PV, EV and AC: Reworking and Evolution Cost (REC), Total Cost (TC), Cost Factor (cf), First-time Completion Efficiency (ftce), Expected Reworking and Evolution Cost (RECexp), and Estimated EV (EVest) (see Table 2). Plus, cEVM improves the performance metrics of traditional EVM (see Table 3).

Table 2. cEVM measures

Metric	Equation	Description
Reworking and Evolution Cost (REC)	EV − PV	Rework and evolution cost occurring after once a task completed, including bugs, defects, improvements
Total Cost (TC)	REC + AC	Total cost of project summing up rework and evolution cost with actual cost
Change Factor (cf)	REC/ACt − 1	Index showing the change ratio of the task, phase or project
First-time Completion Efficiency (ftce)	1 − cf	Index showing what percentage of the task, phase or project done right at first time
Expected Reworking and Evolution Cost (RECexp)	AC * cf	Total expected rework and evolution cost for the completed tasks according to the change factor
Estimated Earned Value (EVest)	EV * TC/ (AC + RECexp)	Calibrated EV according to the change trends

4 cEVM Applications

Two applications of cEVM have been conducted to explore the usability of cEVM and to compare the benefits regarding the traditional EVM.

Two projects applying different software development approaches have been selected. The first project is the software development part of a large-scale integration project with waterfall approach and the second one is a maintenance project with iterative approach using Scrum.

We used written documents, which are mainly the project plans, progress reports, sprint backlogs, error reports, and semi-structured interview methods to collect data. Two interviews with project managers have been performed to get the brief project info, to gather data and to clarify the issues.

Table 3. cEVM performance metrics

Metric	Equation
Estimated Schedule Variance (SVest)	EVest – PV
Estimated Schedule Performance Index (SPIest)	EVest/PV
Estimated Cost Variance (CVest)	EVest – TC
Estimated Cost Performance Index (CPIest)	EVest/TC
Estimated Variance at Completion (VACest)	BAC – EACest
Estimate To Complete - Estimated (ETCest)	(BAC – EVest)/CPIest
Estimate at Completion - Estimated (EACest)	TC + ((BAC – EVest)/CPIest), TC + ETCest, BAC/CPIest
Estimated Total Reworking and Evolution Cost (ETREC)	cf * (BAC – EVest) + REC
Estimate To Complete Reworking and Evolution Cost (TCRECest)	cf *(BAC – EVest)

These two case applications initially performed around 2014–2015 in the scope of the PhD thesis of the author [21], which mainly focus on quality dimension for EVM. Afterwards, this study has been revised for cEVM in 2018.

4.1 Application I

The organization is the Turkish subsidiary of a global company serving consultancy and systems integration services on various business sectors including financial services, health, public sector, retail, telecommunications and transportation. It employs nearly seven hundred engineers and holds ISO 9001:2008 and ISO/IEC 27001 certifications.

The project is the development of command and control system that integrates emergency management solution with fifteen applications. The project started in March 2011 and planned completion date was September 2011. It was completed with two months delay. It is a sub-project of a large scaled integration project. We focus on the software development project since our aim is to apply cEVM on software projects.

The project follows waterfall development methodology which is tailored according to their project needs. The development phases, including detailed analysis, design and testing activities, follow initial analysis and design phase. At the end, deployment & training phase located.

The project team includes 15 full-time software developers and a project manager. There are no specific analyst, developer or test engineer roles in the team, all engineers are doing all the tasks depending on the needs.

Java technologies together with Oracle Fusion and TCL/TK scripting have been used during development. MSSQL was used for database management system. The requirements and test cases were stored on MS Excel. MS Project and MS Excel were project management tools while Bugzilla was for managing the errors and changes.

Applying EVM and cEVM

The case study first conducted in January 2015 and revised in March 2018. At the beginning, we contacted the project manager via e-mail. Then we explained the study and discuss the needs in a semi-structured interview. Afterwards, he delivered us the project data in MS Project and Excel sheets.

The documents include the released project plan and realization data of the plan as well as the error reports exported from Bugzilla to an excel sheet. All the necessary data for the EVM and cEVM application were gathered from these documents. We resolve the conflicts and get more project details by means of second semi-structure interview in a face-to-face meeting and resolve the problems.

We applied EVM and cEVM every four weeks, so the month is used as the time unit during applications. The effort, in person-hour, is used as cost unit.

First, EVM application has been conducted based on the project plan that the project manager provided. Table 4 shows EVM application results and Fig. 2 presents the EVM graph.

Table 4. Case I EVM application results

	Month	PV	AC	EV	SPI	SV	CPI	CV	EAC	VAC	ETC
1	Mar	2034	2340	1836	0,90	−198	0,78	−504	16369	−3526	14029
2	Apr	4284	5490	3726	0,87	−558	0,68	−1764	18923	−6080	13433
3	May	6174	7740	5436	0,88	−738	0,70	−2304	18286	−5443	10546
4	Jun	7974	10053	6984	0,88	−990	0,69	−3069	18487	−5644	8434
5	July	10134	12618	8829	0,87	−1305	0,70	−3789	18355	−5512	5737
6	Aug	12474	15210	10719	0,86	−1755	0,70	−4491	18224	−5381	3014
7	Sep	12843	15705	11088	0,86	−1755	0,71	−4617	18191	−5348	2486
8	Oct		17523	12843	1,00	0	0,73	−4680	17523	−4680	0

cEVM application has been started with collecting RECs from the error reports. We calculated TC and cf, ftce, RECexp and EVest sequentially based on that (see Table 5 and Fig. 3). Afterwards, the performance metrics have been calculated (see Table 6).

Results

Initial EVM application shows that the project has a cost overrun and a delay in the schedule from the beginning to the end of the project as both seen in EVM graph and performance metrics.

cEVM firstly underlines reworking and evolution costs. At the beginning of the project, there is rather low REC, 45 person-hours in the second period of cEVM after the analysis and design phase. It increases considerably starting from the third phase and keeps its rising trend around 4000 person-hours through the end of September, when the project is planned to be completed. The project has total 5535 person-hours costs spent for reworking and evolution when it is completed with almost two months delay.

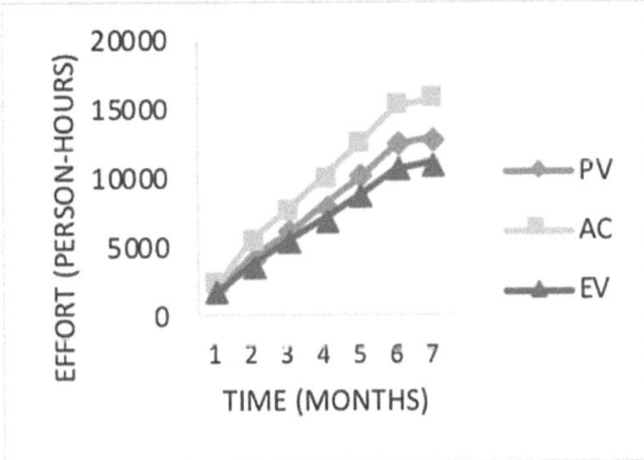

Fig. 2. Case I EVM graph

Table 5. Case I cEVM application results

	PV	AC	EV	REC	TC	cf	ftce	RECexp	EVest
1	2034	2340	1836	0	2340	0,00	1,00	0	1836
2	4284	5490	3726	45	5535	0,02	0,98	106	3686
3	6174	7740	5436	684	8424	0,12	0,88	964	5261
4	7974	10053	6984	1242	11295	0,16	0,84	1613	6762
5	10134	12618	8829	2196	14814	0,22	0,78	2756	8507
6	12474	15210	10719	3249	18459	0,26	0,74	3916	10345
7	12843	15705	11088	4077	19782	0,27	0,73	4210	11014
8		17523	12843	4698	22221	0,30	0,70	5242	12536
9				5535	23058	0,32	0,68		

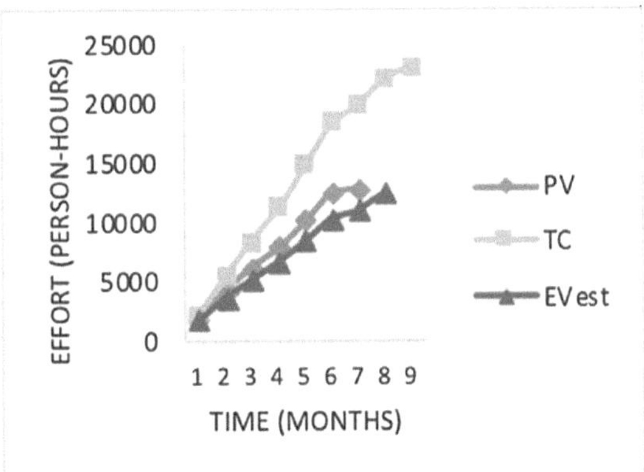

Fig. 3. Case I cEVM graph

Table 6. Case I cEVM performance metrics

	SPIest	SVest	CPIest	CVest	EACest	VACest	ETCest
1	0,90	−198	0,78	−504	16369	−3526	14029
2	0,86	−598	0,67	−1849	19287	−6444	13752
3	0,85	−913	0,62	−3163	20565	−7722	12141
4	0,85	−1212	0,60	−4533	21453	−8610	10158
5	0,84	−1627	0,57	−6307	22364	−9521	7550
6	0,83	−2129	0,56	−8114	22916	−10073	4457
7	0,86	−1829	0,56	−8768	23067	−10224	3285
8	0,98	−307	0,56	−9685	22765	−9922	544

RECs constitute the significant part of the total costs. cEVM presents the actual cost more accurately. TC of cEVM shows that the final cost is almost double of the planned one, 12843 vs 23058 person-hours.

Change factor, cf, highlights that there is an increasing change in the project, almost the percentage of 30%. Hence, ftce indicates that around 70% of the tasks completed right first time in the project.

RECexp, changing between 106 to 5242, gives a clue about how much total REC cost is expected for the completed part based on the past change trends. EVest of cEVM presents the current earned value more accurately considering expected RECs of implemented features.

By means of EVM, the cost overrun starts with 500 person-hour and increases later till 4680 person-hour with CPI changing between 0,78 to 0,69. This low-cost performance index gives an alarm about the cost problem of the project. Subsequently, the value of EAC is calculated around more than 18000 person-hours, which costs more than 5000 person-hours than planned value.

cEVM results spot serious cost problems considering TC and EVest and so expect more cost overrun than EVM. CPI is changing between and CV is 0.78 to 0.54. The cost variance exceeds 9000 person-hours. Based on the improved CPI, cEVM estimates completion budget more accurately. The project manager expects the final budget, EAC, around 22000 person hours during the project execution and variance nearby 10000 person hours.

According to EVM application, the delay in the schedule is also considerable starting from the second phase. SPI is changing between 0.90 to 0.86. The tasks are not implemented on time and the project is behind the schedule with the percentage of 86%. cEVM has relatively better SPI, from 0.90 to 0.83, and SV values, from −200 to −2000, than EVM.

Even though EVM reflects the latency and cost overrun in the project, cEVM presents significantly more accurate numbers and much better future estimates by revealing significant but hidden reworking and evolution costs.

4.2 Application II

The organization is a software development company, developing various e-government projects for a specific government organization. It employs approximately 60 software engineers and holds ISO/IEC 20000 and ISO/IEC 27001 certifications.

The project is the maintenance of a web-based procurement tool that provides managing complex tenders, bids and contracts for a large amount of audiences. The maintenance project was started in February 2013 and planned completion date was November 2013. It has been completed at the beginning of January 2014.

The project follows iterative development approach with Scrum practices. The team includes 7 staff, which are part-time project manager, scrum master also working as software engineer, two software engineers, a senior test engineer and a part-time quality manager. The project team was not fully dedicated to this project, a team member might have also some other responsibilities in another project in some sprints.

The project was developed using .NET Framework. The new features, changes, improvements and errors were stored in Microsoft Team Foundation Server (TFS). MS Project was utilized for project management and MS Word and MS Excel were used for documentation of requirements and testing.

Applying EVM and cEVM

The study initially conducted in May 2014 and revised in April 2018. Firstly, we sent the case study statement to the project manager via e-mail and then conducted an initial meeting with the project manager and quality manager to discuss the details of the study. Afterwards, we scheduled an additional meeting as a semi-structured interview with the quality manager and obtain the brief overview of the project as well as explain the needs of a case study in detail. Finally, the quality manager provided the project data, basically sprint plans, resource utilization reports, error reports and exported all to the excel sheets. We arranged another meeting to discuss the inconsistencies.

The document that they provide includes the bugs fixed and new features from the feature list as distributed into the monthly releases. We applied EVM and cEVM monthly according to these releases. The effort, in person-hour, was used as cost unit.

Table 7. Case II EVM application results

	Month	PV	AC	EV	SPI	SV	CPI	CV	EAC	VAC	ETC
1	Feb	101	96	86	0,85	−15	0,90	10	4646	−484	4550
2	Mar	750	831	752	1,00	2	0,90	79	4599	−437	3768
3	Apr	1619	1712	1560	0,96	−59	0,91	152	4568	−406	2856
4	May	2207	2392	2185	0,99	−22	0,91	207	4556	−394	2164
5	Jun	2558	2814	2537	0,99	−21	0,90	277	4616	−454	1802
6	Jul	2970	3179	2878	0,97	−92	0,91	301	4597	−435	1418
7	Aug	3203	3480	3160	0,99	−43	0,91	320	4583	−421	1103
8	Sep	3460	3716	3378	0,98	−82	0,91	338	4578	−416	862
9	Oct	3703	4036	3667	0,99	−36	0,91	369	4581	−419	545
10	Nov	4162	4553	4151	1,00	−11	0,91	402	4565	−403	12

We initially applied EVM on the project considering the high-level project plan including planned features and their realizations. Table 7 shows the EVM application results and Fig. 4 is the graphical representation of EVM.

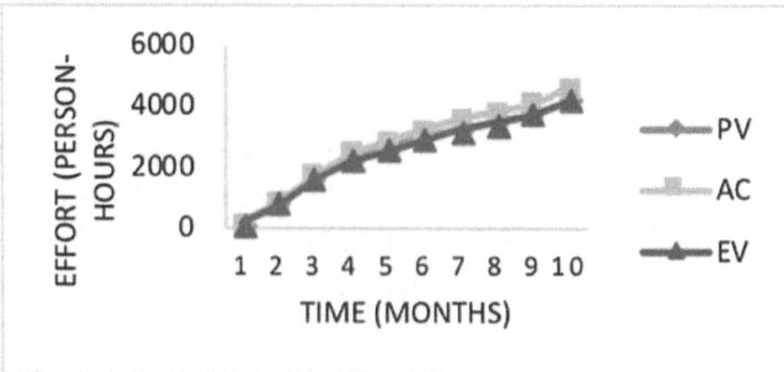

Fig. 4. Case II EVM graph

We applied cEVM just after EVM implementation. The application has been started with the collecting RECs. Next, the cf calculation is accomplished considering TC. Accordingly, RECexp, EVest, ftce are calculated. The application results are given in Table 8. Figure 5 shows the graphical representation of cEVM application. Additionally, Table 9 presents the performance analysis according to cEVM.

Table 8. Case II cEVM application results

	PV	AC	EV	REC	TC	cf	ftce	RECexp	EVest
1	101	96	86	0	96	0,00	1,00	0	86
2	750	831	752	25	856	0,26	0,74	216	615
3	1619	1712	1560	93	1805	0,11	0,89	192	1479
4	2207	2392	2185	341	2733	0,20	0,80	476	2082
5	2558	2814	2537	418	3232	0,17	0,83	492	2480
6	2970	3179	2878	491	3670	0,17	0,83	555	2829
7	3203	3480	3160	550	4030	0,17	0,83	602	3120
8	3460	3716	3378	579	4295	0,17	0,83	618	3347
9	3703	4036	3667	639	4675	0,17	0,83	694	3624
10	4162	4553	4151	758	5311	0,19	0,81	855	4076
				955	5508	0,21	0,79		

Results
The initial EVM application results show that the project has a cost overrun but almost on time.

cEVM makes reworking and evolution costs visible and adds them to the ACs as in the first case study. Initially, it starts with 25 person-hours then it increases till 955 person-hours at the end. The project is completed almost one month delay. cEVM represents all the costs more accurately including hidden RECs, which is around 5508 person-hours.

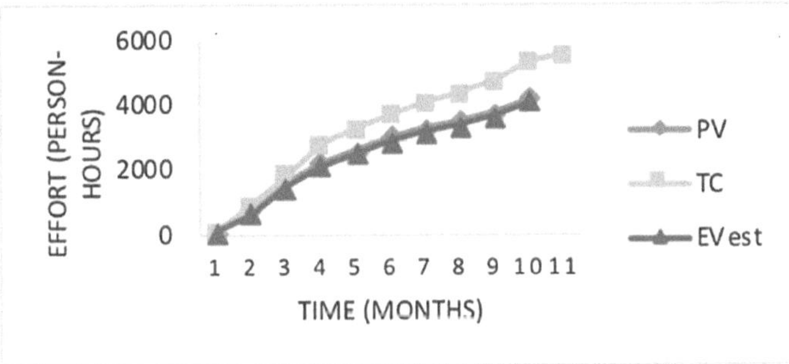

Fig. 5. Case II cEVM graph

Table 9. Case II cEVM performance metrics

	SPIest	SVest	CPIest	CVest	EACest	VACest	ETCest
1	0,85	−15	0,90	10	4646	−484	4550
2	0,82	−135	0,72	241	5797	−1635	4941
3	0,91	−140	0,82	326	5079	−917	3274
4	0,94	−125	0,76	651	5464	−1302	2731
5	0,97	−78	0,77	752	5423	−1261	2191
6	0,95	−141	0,77	841	5399	−1237	1729
7	0,97	−83	0,77	910	5376	−1214	1346
8	0,97	−113	0,78	948	5340	−1178	1045
9	0,98	−79	0,78	1051	5369	−1207	694
10	0,98	−86	0,77	1235	5422	−1260	111

Change factor shows that almost 20% of the tasks are under change. The ftce index, the ratio of the tasks completed right first time, is decreasing around 0,80.

RECexp, changing between 216 to 855 person-hours, shows how much cost is expected for reworking and evolution based on the trends. Using this value, cEVM presents adjusted EVest values, which are much better indication of the gained value comparing to EV.

Based on EVM calculations, the cost overrun starts with 10 person-hours and increases till 400 person-hours with the CPI index over 0,90. CPI already gives an alarm about minor cost problem. The metrics show that EAC will be around 4600 person-hours while variance at completion is nearby 1200 person-hours.

The CPI of cEVM is around 0,77, rather lower than EVM's CPI. cEVM presents more severe cost variance exceeding 1200 person-hours and so provides us to estimate more cost overrun than EVM. cEVM calculates that the project will be completed around 5400 person-hours, which is almost 800 person-hours more than EVM's estimate and much better estimation for 5508 person-hours total cost.

According to EVM application, the schedule seems on track with SPI index between 0.97 to 1 after the initial phase. Based on that, the tasks were mostly implemented on time and the deadlines almost met without any delay. The delay is relatively seen better by means of cEVM, with SPI changing between 0,82 to 0,98.

In summary, during execution of the project, the project manager understands the cost problems more clearly and expects more cost overruns utilizing cEVM. It also gives much better future estimates and allows the project manager to re-plan the activities or budget or scope based on this fact.

4.3 Discussion

We obtained promising results in both cases in regard to cEVM. Change is a critical challenge for software projects applying different life cycle models. In waterfall project the change factor measured around 30% while in iterative one it was around 20%. It is not surprising that waterfall project has more change than iterative one since we plan the project in detail at the beginning in waterfall but iterative project has continuous refinement of plan during execution of project.

Even though there is a huge amount of rework and evolution effort in software projects, these efforts frequently are not well managed. They are mostly perceived as troubles that need to be fixed immediately and fixed by the team members who supposed to perform other tasks. In both cases there were no change related task planned. The change 20%–30% has been realized in an unplanned way. This frequently results in low morale and burnout due to the endless evening and weekend overtime of the development team which in turn causes poor quality that results in more rework later on.

Highlighting these change efforts by making change costs visible by means of cf and REC will help project managers to expose the project's status clearly. The results of both case studies show that the software project's current status is more clearly depicted and project's future is more accurately estimated by cEVM in comparison to EVM.

The case studies show that incorporating change costs into actual costs, cEVM provides much better evaluation of the budget. CPI values are significantly better comparing to the ones that are calculated with traditional EVM. Schedule evaluations are also better due to better EV estimation but are not dramatically improved by cEVM. Additionally, the case study results spot that cEVM provides much better future estimates. Completion budgets of both cases are estimated fairly better by cEVM than EVM.

As observed in both applications, the forecasts of estimated completion budget, EAC, are very close to the actual ones by cEVM.

We also detected that cf as defined in cEVM by itself is a simple and an effective indicator of change. The project managers could track cf trends during project and make root cause analysis when required.

The most significant difficulty we encountered is the availability and the validity of the change related effort data. The effort data is not collected and tracked properly in many software organizations. Organizations to implement cEVM should make issue tracking more systematic and keep effort data. It might bring additional cost of change data collecting to organizations.

5 Conclusion

This study presents the results of applying change oriented EVM on two software projects. The results show that cEVM provides clearer progress information and more accurate future estimates in comparison to traditional EVM.

We explored the usability of cEVM and based on the case study results, we can summarize the main benefits of cEVM as follows:

- reveals hidden change related costs and integrating them into project and performance management
- measures the change status of a project in addition to schedule and cost
- estimates the project progress more precisely comparing to traditional EVM
- estimates project future more accurately in comparison to traditional EVM

cEVM helps to increase project visibility by means of revealing hidden but huge rework and evolution cost. Increased visibility brings more accuracy to the projects. It mainly affects the calculations of the total costs and the earned value and so the project is measured more accurately. Besides, cEVM provides better predictability, which is vital for a project manager to take action as soon as possible. More accurate progress metrics result in more accurate and realistic future estimates that increases the predictability. cEVM provides more accurate actual cost, more precise performance metrics and more accurate future estimates.

We plan to perform further case studies to better comprehend the applicability of cEVM for the different type of projects (e.g. micro services, embedded systems).

Briefly, EVM is a powerful technique to reflect project progress in terms of scope, time and cost. cEVM makes it more usable for software projects incorporating change. cEVM provides significant improvements with change both on measuring the progress clearly and on estimating the future correctly. Change is inevitable for software projects and cEVM is designed to embrace it.

References

1. Anbari, F.: Earned value project management method and extensions. Proj. Manag. J. **34**(4), 12–13 (2003)
2. Efe, P., Demirors, O.: Applying EVM in a software company: benefits and difficulties. In: Proceedings of the 39th EUROMICRO Conference on Software Engineering and Advanced Applications (SEAA), Santander, Spain (2013)
3. Cass, A.G., Sutton, S.M., Osterweil, L.J.: Formalizing rework in software processes. In: Oquendo, F. (ed.) EWSPT 2003. LNCS, vol. 2786, pp. 16–31. Springer, Heidelberg (2003). https://doi.org/10.1007/978-3-540-45189-1_3
4. Twentyman, J.: The crippling costs of IT project rework. Inside Knowledge, 15 June 2005
5. Charette, R.N.: Why software fails. IEEE Spectr. **42**(9), 42–49 (2005)
6. Uskarci, A., Demirors, O.: Do staged maturity models result in organization-wide continuous process improvement? Insight from employees. Comput. Stand. Interfaces **52**, 25–40 (2017)
7. Ebert, C., Dumke, R.: Software Measurement: Establish - Extract -Evaluate - Execute. Springer, Berlin (2010). https://doi.org/10.1007/978-3-540-71649-5

8. Laporte, C.Y., Berrhouma, N., Doucet, M., Palza-Vargas, E.: Measuring the cost of software quality of a large software project at bombardier transportation. Softw. Qual. Prof. J. **14**(3), 14–31 (2012)
9. Coskuncay, A., Demirors, O.: Software development in Turkey. IT Prof. **17**(3), 10–13 (2015)
10. VersionOne: 12th Annual State of Agile (2018). https://explore.versionone.com/state-of-agile/versionone-12th-annual-state-of-agile-report
11. Efe, P., Demirors, O.: A change oriented model for earned value management and its application in software development projects. IEEE Trans. Softw. Eng. in review
12. ANSI/EIA -748A: American National Standard Institute/Electronic Industries Alliance/Standard for Earned Value Management Systems (1998)
13. AS 4817-2006: Project performance measurement using Earned Value (2006)
14. Project Management Institute: A Guide to the Project Management Body of Knowledge (PMBOK® Guide), 1st edn. Newtown Square (2000)
15. Project Management Institute: A Guide to the Project Management Body of Knowledge (PMBOK® Guide), 6th edn. Newtown Square (2017)
16. Project Management Institute: Practice Standard for Earned Value Management. Project Management Institute, Newtown Square (2005)
17. Cockburn, A.: Crystal Clear: A Human-Powered Methodology for Small Teams. Pearson Education Inc., Upper Saddle River (2005)
18. Sulaiman, T., Barton, B., Blackburn, T.: AgileEVM – earned value management in scrum projects. In: Proceedings of AGILE 2006 Conference, Minnesota, USA (2006)
19. An Industry Practice Guide for Agile on Earned Value Management Programs, version 1.2, National Defense Industrial Association, 26 March 2018
20. Project Management Institute: Practice Standard for Earned Value Management. Newtown Square (2011)
21. Efe, P.: Quality Integrated Earned Value Management. Ph. D. dissertation, Middle East Technical University (2015). etd.lib.metu.edu.tr/upload/12619220/index.pdf

Semantic Model Based Approach for Knowledge Intensive Processes

Madhushi Bandara[1(✉)], Fethi A. Rabhi[1], and Rouzbeh Meymandpour[2]

[1] University of New South Wales, Sydney, Australia
{k.bandara,f.rabhi}@unsw.edu.au
[2] Capsifi, Sydney, Australia
rmeymandpour@capsifi.com

Abstract. Many business processes present in modern enterprises are loosely defined, highly interactive, involve frequent human interventions. They are coupled with a multitude of abstract entities defined within an enterprise architecture. Further, they demand agility and responsiveness to address the frequently changing business requirements. Traditional process modelling and knowledge management technologies are not adequate to represent and support those processes. In this paper, we discuss how a process management system based on semantic models can be used to address the needs of non-traditional and knowledge intensive processes. The modelling capabilities of the framework are demonstrated via a case study and evaluated using set requirements that KIP supporting process management system should have. Finally, we discuss how this semantic model based solution can be improved further to cater for the management and execution of knowledge-intensive business processes in a broader context.

Keywords: Knowledge intensive processes · Semantic modelling Ontology

1 Introduction

Knowledge-intensive Processes (KIPs) are processes whose conduct and execution are heavily dependent on knowledge workers performing various interconnected knowledge intensive decision making tasks. KIPs are knowledge, information and data centric in nature and require substantial flexibility at design- and run-time [18]. They have to be understood in the knowledge dimension of the processes and considering the role of human-centred knowledge [9]. To support KIPs the knowledge and collaboration dimensions need to be integrated with the traditional control flow/data dimensions and consider them as a whole by possibly reshaping the process life cycle [11]. The processes such as the diagnostic and treatment process in the medical domain, emergency management process, and artful processes conducted by engineers, researchers or managers can be identified as some examples of KIPs [9].

I. Stamelos et al. (Eds.): SPICE 2018, CCIS 918, pp. 215–229, 2018.
https://doi.org/10.1007/978-3-030-00623-5_15

To address the ad-hoc and frequently changing nature of KIPs, related techniques and tools should support process agility. One obstacle in supporting agile process re-engineering is the gap between organizational level process models and the models built for execution [8,10]. The models built for execution capture the current state of the organizational goals, strategies, and structures, but do not explicitly define them and create the associations between high-level concepts and the execution models. As a result, once the high-level concepts such as strategies and goals change the mapping exercise corresponding to the whole analysis process should be repeated.

In Bandara et al. [3], we proposed a construct to capture processes called "Digital Interaction" (DI), which is defined as part of an enterprise architecture model. It aims to support the dynamic composition of concrete services, a set of interactions and underlying knowledge and information concepts that deliver value to the customer. This composition can capture complex interactions involving humans, events or programming entities such as web services. The basis of the proposed framework is an ontology-based knowledge repository. Embedding DIs in an architectural framework facilitates organizations to manage associations between high level and execution concepts with less effort, as well as to re-engineer and deploy them rapidly in response to business changes.

In this paper, we demonstrate the capabilities of the DI framework for process modeling, and evaluate how such semantic model based process management system can support for KIPs with the aid of the detailed set of requirement defined by Ciccio et al. [9]. We will discuss the background of process modelling approaches followed by a brief introduction to KIP components and requirements in Sect. 2. Section 3 describes the DI framework. In Sect. 4 we demonstrate how DI can be used for KIP modelling, using a case study involving data analytic processes. Section 5 presents the evaluation of the framework and the paper concludes in Sect. 5.

2 Related Work

2.1 Semantic Modeling for KIP

There are two main approaches to process modelling [1] - graphical modes and rule specifications popular in workflow coordination. These modeling approaches limit their focus on specific features or capabilities of a process [13]. Yet the dynamic nature of unconventional business processes is not sufficiently addressed in these approaches [1]. Integrating service-oriented architecture provides a certain flexibility for process modelling and links the execution models to the business level process models. Yet research efforts that focus on the composition of business processes with services such as Cauvet et al. [5] are limited in their contribution to a static description of an executable process.

There are studies that address challenges related to non-traditional business processes such as SmartPM [14] which offers a certain flexibility via run-time adaptation of processes with BPMN 2.0 based modeling schema. ArtiFact-GSM [6] proposes an event-driven, declarative and data-centric approach for business process modelling and highlights the importance of information models as business artifacts to address change management.

Ontologies are proposed for business process management in multiple research works such as Hepp and Roman [12], and Weber et al. [19]. Approaches such as PROMPTUM [7] aim to integrate domain ontologies with business processes to provide semantic quality and traceability between domain knowledge and process models. Rao et al. [16] propose to use ontology-based knowledge maps for process re-engineering, demonstrating the level of traceability achieved by an ontology. Yet they provide limited support for KIP management and can be improved by formalizing knowledge representation around KIPs and linking that knowledge to execution-level process model to provide agility in KIP management and execution.

To address these limitations we employed our experience in studying data analytic process engineering [2,4,15] to design Digital Interaction framework [3] that supports flexible process modeling and management incorporating knowledge representation.

2.2 Components and Requirements for KIP Supporting Systems

Based on scientific literature and real-world application scenarios, Ciccio et al. [9] define a set of formal characteristics of KIPs and six fundamental components (Fig. 1). They define *Data and Knowledge Elements* and the *Knowledge Action* tightly coupled with each other. *Rules and Constraints* define intra- and inter-dependencies between Data and Knowledge Elements and the Knowledge Action. *Goals* are defined by *Knowledge Workers* and achieved via Knowledge Action. *Environment* is the context of process and impacts all aspects.

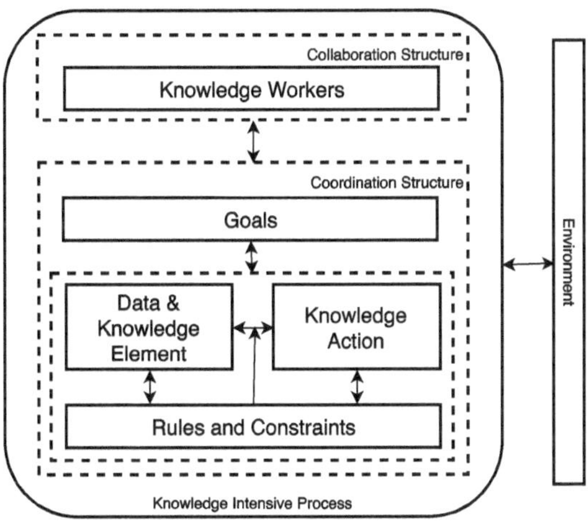

Fig. 1. Components of KIP [9]

Ciccio et al. [9] extend their work by presenting 25 requirements a system should fulfill to support KIPs. The list of requirements is listed in the Table 1. Each requirement is related to one component in the Fig. 1. We employ these components and requirements designed by Ciccio et al. to place the proposed DI framework among existing KIP supporting systems and evaluate its contribution.

3 Digital Interaction Framework

This section provides a brief introduction to the DI framework proposed in [3]. It is based on a construct called "Digital Interaction" defined as a dynamic composition of concrete services, set of interactions and underlying information concepts which can be easily converted into execution level code that deliver value to the stakeholders. This was developed as an extension to the CAPSICUM framework, which is an integrated semantic meta-model for representing different layers of business architecture such as strategies, value streams and high-level processes [17].

The digital interaction construct we propose consists of four parts: service, information, interaction and digital interaction. Main components of the meta-model are Information, Service, Interaction and Digital Interaction, as illustrated by four ovals in Fig. 2. Within each oval, we represent the ontological concepts related to each component and relationships among them. The prefixes "capsi" and "di" are used with concept names to differentiate concepts predefined in CAPSICUM framework and what is proposed in the DI meta-model respectively.

The objective of the information meta-models is facilitating organizations to represent their business objects. The main concept in the information meta-model is di:Information, which is an extension of capsi:Concept. Any information concept related to an organization can be modelled as a subclass of di:Information concept and extended with related properties of type rdf:Property.

The Interaction meta-model captures mechanisms in which inputs or outputs are exchanged between different entities. Some example interactions are messages or events passed within a computer system or human providing inputs through a user interface such as filling a form. Particularly human interactions are frequent and crucial to drive KIPs. By modelling these interactions, we make them flexible, malleable and interpretable. The Interaction meta-model circled in Fig. 2 models the di:Interaction concept as a subclass of capsi:Interaction. It is further extended to three subclasses: form-based, message-based and event-based interactions. Organizations can extend this further to incorporate other interaction types. di:InteractionField is used to represent parameters used or exchanged in an interaction.

Service meta-model is the main building block which links the user-defined interactions and information into actual execution. The service model has to be self-contained so we can create an executable workflow based on it. Our service model is captured by di:Service concept and have parameters named as di:ServiceField to capture concepts used or exchanged in a service.

The process composition is done via DI meta-model, which is an integration of Interaction and Service concepts, linked together via di:FlowLogic and di:ServiceInteractionFieldMapping as shown in Fig. 2. The concept di:ServiceInteractionFieldMapping is used to map inputs from interactions to the service parameters so that a service can be invoked automatically followed by interactions. This composition is created as an instance of the di:DigitalInteraction concept.

The concept di:FlowLogic defines the control flow between different components of the DI. di:FlowLogic is authorized by a service or an interaction which initiates a flow. It contains a set of rules which evaluate a set of InteractionFields or ServiceFields and if they match expected values defined through the information model, respective service, interaction or Digital Interaction is triggered. For example, we can define a Boolean interaction field and create a di:FlowLogic to trigger two services depending on whether the value of the interaction field is true or false.

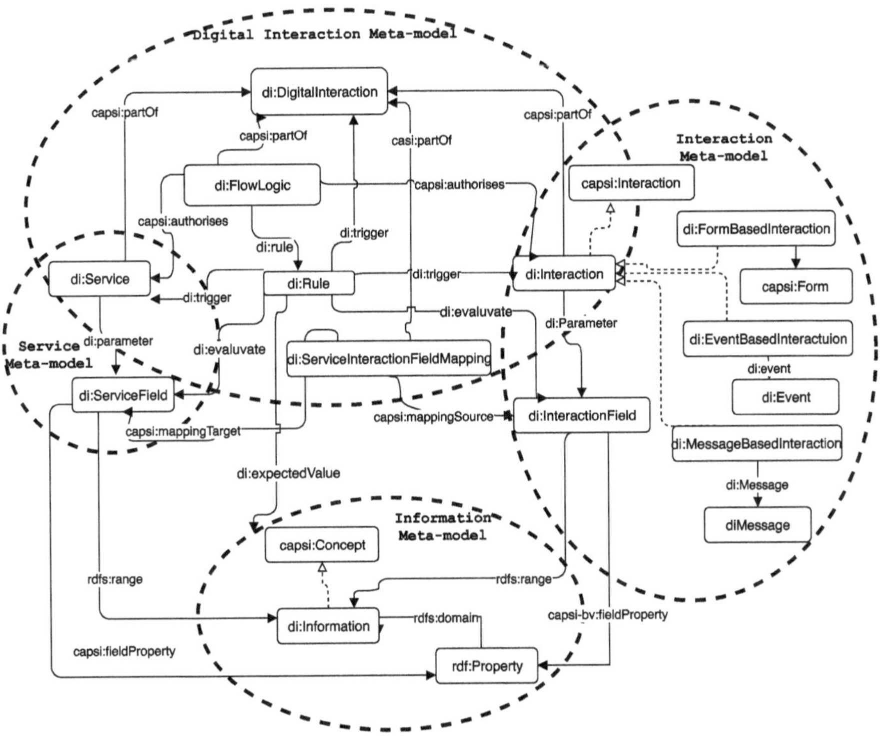

Fig. 2. Main components of the Digital Interaction meta-model with related Information, Service and Interaction model components

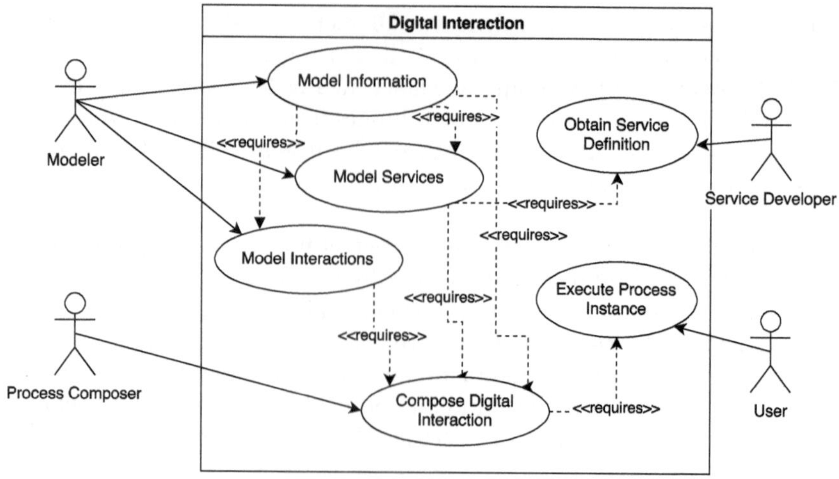

Fig. 3. Use case diagram for Jalapeno-DI extension

The CAPSICUM framework is supported by the Capsifi[1] Jalapeno platform, a cloud-based enterprise architecture modelling platform backed by a triple store for linked data and model management. It allows the definition, analysis, and management of CAPSICUM models as well as exporting the models in machine-readable form (RDF, XSD, JSON) via a GUI. We extended the Capsifi Jalapeno tool and developed Jalapeno-DI extension, a prototype of the DI Framework to demonstrate its capabilities.

Figure 3 shows the use cases that are supported in Jalapeno-DI extension. The first task is the modelling of information, services, and interactions by Modeler. Then the process composer can Compose DI using them. An end user will execute those digital interactions to conduct respective KIPs. Section 4 presents a case study which will elaborate on this further.

4 Case Study

4.1 Dynamic Modelling and Analytics

For our case study, we used a large organization that supports a wide range of data analytics business processes to support the day-to-day decision making. As Fig. 4 illustrates, the organization relies on multiple information repositories arranged into 3 categories: domain-specific knowledge, analytics models and data obtained from different sources. This information changes frequently in response to changes in the external environment and needs to be frequently updated. Within this case study, we select three example KIPs related to predictive analytics as examples to be implemented via the DI framework.

[1] https://www.capsifi.com/.

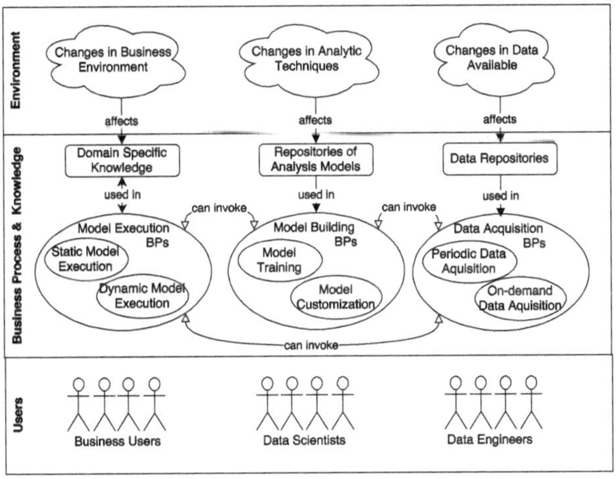

Fig. 4. Overview of case study

Example 1: The first example (DI-1) requires a capability where an analyst can import different datasets, apply predefined prediction models for a specific time period and generate a report. This is realized using three services (REST APIs) that import datasets from given data sources, execute a predictive model and export results. The process and related knowledge are presented in the top rectangle of Fig. 5. The figure illustrates the different stages of this Digital Interaction which uses a mix of form-based interactions and invocation of services.

Example 2: Example 2 (DI-2) is used by analysts to create new prediction models by selecting training and test data and feeding them to an algorithm. Generated prediction models can be included under Model Specification knowledge. The process is captured in the bottom rectangle of Fig. 5.

Example 3: This (DI-3) is an example where agility is needed to respond to changing business requirements. New requirement arises to extend DI-1 and allow users to create new prediction models if a suitable model is not found. This is done via linking Select Prediction Model interaction to DI-2 through two event-based interactions as shown in Fig. 5.

To demonstrate the capability of the proposed framework we modelled the three examples via Jalapeno-DI extension.

4.2 Modelling the Example 1

- **Model Information.** We identified four high-level information concepts related to DI-1: Data Source, Dataset Format, Dataset and Prediction Model and their associated properties. Together they can capture domain knowledge and information sufficient to conduct an analysis. We reused existing ontologies when available. For example, Dataset Format and Dataset concepts are

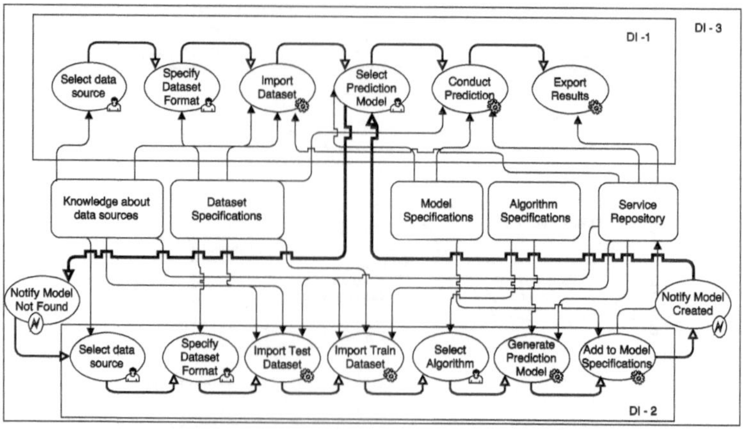

Fig. 5. Example Digital Interaction 3 as a combination of DI-1 and DI-2

adapted from RDF Cube vocabulary[2]. A prediction model was developed using PMML[3] (Predictive Modelling Markup Language) schema.

- **Model Services.** Our example DI-1 implementation leverages three services, modeled within Jalapeno-DI extension. They are 1. Import Dataset 2. Conduct Prediction 3. Export Result.
- **Model Interactions.** We defined 5 interactions: Select data source, Specify dataset format, Import Dataset, Select Prediction Model, Conduct Prediction. Import Dataset and Conduct Prediction interactions provide parameters necessary for respective service executions, while other three aid in the decision making. All interactions are backed by information models to provide suggestions for decision making and to identify parameters user should provide.
- **Compose Digital Interaction.** We model the Digital Interactions, for example, DI-1 that starts with Select data source interaction, followed by Specify dataset format and Import Dataset. Import Dataset interaction triggers the Import Dataset service. Then Select Prediction Model interaction and Conduct Prediction service are linked respectively. Dataset returned from the Import Dataset service is mapped to Execute Model service. Export Results service is triggered immediately after the completion of the Execute Model service to generate a report for the user.

Each link between two components of a DI is captured through di:FlowLogic. To link fields of Interactions with Services, di:ServiceInteraction-FieldMapping concept is used. For example, Data Source returned by Import Dataset service is mapped as the input for Conduct Prediction service.

[2] https://www.w3.org/TR/vocab-data-cube/.
[3] http://dmg.org/pmml/v4-3/GeneralStructure.html.

Once this DI is designed, an execution engine is necessary to create graphical user interfaces from interactions and handle different service calls. Different users can use this DI to conduct individual prediction tasks.

4.3 Modelling the Example 2

We need to define a new DI for the process that creates a new prediction model (DI-2). We reuse information model, Import Dataset service, Select data source, Specify dataset format and Import Dataset interactions. A new information model called Algorithm Specifications is created to capture analytics algorithms such as linear regression. New services were created to Generate Prediction Model and Add them to Model Specifications.

4.4 Modelling the Example Digital Interaction 3

To create DI-3 we extend DI-1. Select Prediction Model interface is updated with a checkbox field (Model Unavailable), which user can tick if a suitable model is not available. Two new event-based interactions are defined, one to capture whether a model is available or not, other to know when a new model is created.

DI-3 is formed by aligning interactions and services as shown in Fig. 6. We included a decision followed by Select Prediction Model interaction to represents a flow-logic for rule-based navigation. This di:FlowLogic instance is defined based on the Model Unavailable field and triggers Notify Model not Found Interaction or Conduct Prediction interaction accordingly. Notify Model Not Found interaction is followed by DI-2, which triggers Notify Model Created interaction at the completion and the DI-1 can continue. Further details of the DI modelling through Capsifi Jalapeno tool can be found at our website[4].

5 Evaluation of Digital Interaction for KIP Support

The proposed DI framework contains all components of a KIP supporting system illustrated in Fig. 1. Environment and Data and Knowledge Elements are captured in the information model. Knowledge Actions are captured in both Services and the interaction models. Rules and constraints are embedded in the di:FlowLogic, di:Rule and di:ServiceInteractionFieldMapping concepts. The process is captured in the Digital Interaction construct. Goals and Knowledge Workers components are not within the scope of the DI framework, but they are handled by CAPSICUM meta-model itself and inertly usable within the DI Framework.

To evaluate how DIs can contribute to uplift KIP management and execution, we selected the set of requirements proposed in literature [9]. Cicco et al. [9] had designed those requirements in order to benchmark the KIP supporting systems in different dimensions. They have published an evaluation of existing KIP

[4] http://adage.cse.unsw.edu.au/Resources/DigitalInteractionCaseStudy.

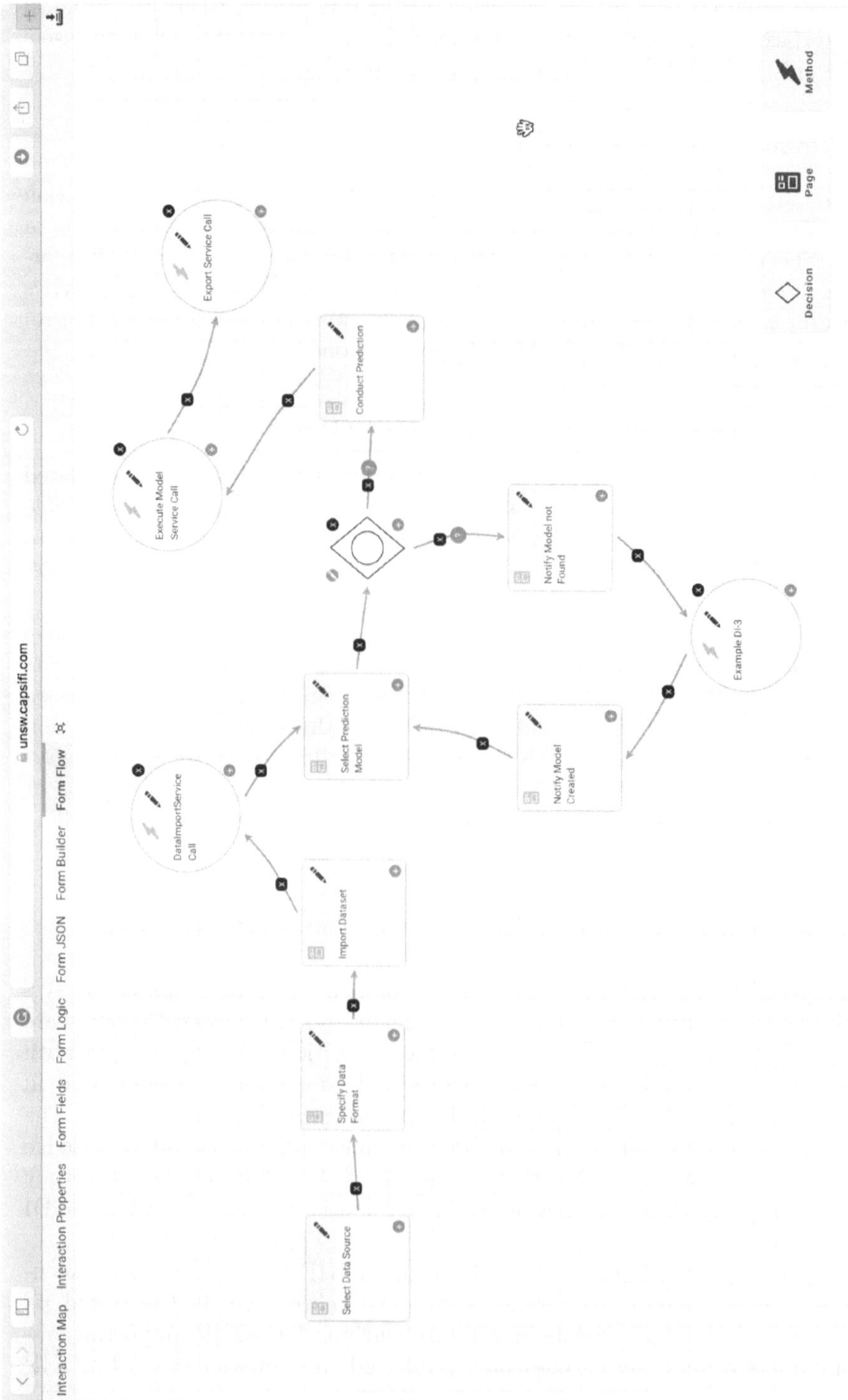

Fig. 6. DI-3 modelled in Jalapeno-DI Extension

Table 1. Compliance of DI to the requirements of KIP Supporting Systems

Component	Requirement	Jalapeno-DI Extension	SmartPM	ArtiFact-GSM
Data	R1 Data modeling	+	+	+
	R2 Late data modeling	+	–	–
	R3 Access to appropriate data	+	–	+
	R4 Synchronized access to shared data	–	–	–
Knowledge actions	R5 Represent data-driven actions	+	~	+
	R6 Late actions modeling	~	~	–
Rules and Constraints	R7 Formalize rules & constraints	+	+	+
	R8 Late constraints formalization	~	–	–
Goals	R9 Goals modeling	Inherent	–	–
	R10 Late goal modeling	~	~	–
Processes	R11 Support for different modeling styles	–	+	+
	R12 Visibility of the process knowledge	+	–	+
	R13 Flexible process execution	+	–	~
	R14 Deal with unanticipated exceptions	–	+	–
	R15 Migration of process instances	+	–	–
	R16 Learning from event logs	–	–	–
	R17 Learning from data sources	+	–	–
Knowledge Workers	R18 Knowledge workers modeling	Inherent	+	+
	R19 Formalize interaction between knowledge workers	Inherent	–	–
	R20 Define knowledge workers' privileges	Inherent	–	+
	R21 Late knowledge workers' model-ing	–	–	–
	R22 Late privileges modeling	–	–	–
	R23 Capture knowledge workers' decisions	+	+	+
Environment	R24 Capture and model external events	+	–	+
	R25 External events late-modeling	–	–	–

supporting systems such as SmartPM and ArtiFact-GSM alongside the requirements. Hence we adapted the same requirement based evaluation procedure to evaluate DI framework and compared the results with what is accomplished in SmartPM and ArtiFact-GSM. Table 1 presents our evaluation results. We use symbols (+), (−) and (∼) to indicate whether each system supports, not support or partially supports the respective requirement. There are some requirements (R9, R18, R19 and R20) marked as *Inherent*, that are not captured by the DI framework, but inherently supported by Capsicum framework.

When looking at the requirements satisfied by the Jalapeno-DI extension, we observed how all data, their properties as well as interrelationships (R1) relevant to a process can be captured through semantic models. Late data modeling (R2) is enabled by linking the information model to the interaction model and enabling new information creation via interactions. Query engine and form-based interaction are used to fetch and show appropriate data (R3). di:InteracionField concept maps the user actions with appropriate information models and enables to constraint actions based on information model (R5). di:Rule and di:FlowLogic closely follows the Event-Condition-Action pattern and enable users to define decision tables (R7). Users can access and visualize all the knowledge captured in the DI meta-model via GUI provided in the Jalapeno tool (R12). With DIs available on a canvas, users have the flexibility to edit and change the process execution (R13). The malleability of semantic models via Digital interaction framework naturally supports the migration of process instances from one information model or set of services to another (R15). The framework provides dynamic support for users based on the historical information and data stored in the information model (R17). All the processes defined via DIs have the capacity to capture knowledge workers' decisions via instantiating the di:FlowLogic (R23). Our information model is flexible and caters for external events coming from the environment and we can associate them with existing components of the information model (R23).

Goal modeling (R9), Knowledge workers and their privilege modeling (R18, R20) as well as defining the interaction between them such as which user/role is responsible for which part of the process is inherently supported by CAPSICUM framework and available for DI framework via capsi:Interaction concept.

We observe that by using a flexible semantic meta-model and supporting dynamic DI composition, the proposed framework fully or partially comply with most requirements supported by SmartPM and ArtiFactGMS with additional requirements such as late data modelling (R2), flexible process execution (R13), learning from data sources (R17) and formalize interaction between knowledge workers (R19). Detailed evaluation of SmartPM and ArtiFactGMS against these requirements can be found at [9].

In terms of limitations, our framework does not support fully for late actions, goal or event modelling, and constraint formalization of the process (R6, R8, R10) at its enactment. User actions at runtime are limited by what is pre-defined at the interaction model. Late knowledge worker modeling (R21) and privilege modeling (R22) are not supported in DI framework. Synchronized access to shared data (R4) and Deal with unanticipated exceptions (R14) are execution platform related requirements our prototype cannot comply with. Currently, we support only a single style of modelling based on actions and hence R11 is not achieved. Yet the semantic models have the capacity to expand and cater to different modelling styles such as data or event centric. Learning from event logs (R16) is another important requirement not supported. Finally, although we are able to capture execution instances of DIs, we do not provide an interface to explore and analyze them (R16).

6 Conclusion and Future Work

In the paper, we proposed a new ontology-based framework called DI to support knowledge-intensive processes management by providing agility and better knowledge representation. The framework is designed as an extension of the CAPSICUM framework [17]. We developed a prototype of the proposed framework on top of Capsifi Jalapeno platform and demonstrate its capabilities via a case study of designing predictive analytic process. The potential of our framework is evaluated through a set of requirements proposed in the literature for KIP support systems.

By implementing DI meta-model on top of CAPSICUM framework we enabled the linking of service concepts, interactions and DIs into the holistic enterprise architecture. We can define DI as a part of a high-level business process or model how different organizational value streams and strategies are linked to these processes. It provides context and traceability for the services, information, and interactions we define. Hence we get one step closer to better alignment between business and IT architecture of the organization.

One limitation of our study is the restriction imposed by extending the CAPSICUM framework. We lose a certain level of flexibility, especially when designing flow logic, as we are building on top of CAPSICUM ontologies. It is a trade-off we made as we believe the value of DI framework is enhanced by extending a framework that is already accepted and used by large-scale organizations.

According to the evaluation, late information modeling - actions, goals, constraints, privileges, actors is a major limitation of our framework. We plan to address in future by extending the architecture to support run-time modeling as well.

To learn from event logs, we plan to extend the information model to capture user insights and performance details for executed DI instances. For example, in the predictive analytics case study, we can extend the Prediction Model concept to record experiences from different users who used a particular model, its performance statistics for different datasets extracted from execution logs etc. Then a user can use that accumulated knowledge in future DI design and execution.

Further, to harness the full potential of DIs we need a good execution platform that can access semantic models and drive different interactions dynamically, fulfilling requirements such as synchronized access to shared data and dealing with unanticipated exceptions.

The main challenge in adapting DIs for an organization is designing a good information model that reflect business objects. This model is unique to an organization and developing it from scratch can be challenging. Our framework is designed to link existing information models (e.g.- RDF Cube to model Dataset used in the case study) easily. Hence designing a repository of abstract information models and guidelines for specific KIP domains such as data analytics, finance or marketing can lift the burden of information modelling and encourage many organizations to adapt DI framework.

We consider this work as a foundation for a new approach to solve challenges related to KIP management and execution using semantic models. As future goals to achieve that objective, we propose to extend DI to contain a knowledge layer that can enable knowledge workers to share their insights and experience, which can supports others in conducting similar KIPs and decision making.

Acknowledgments. We are grateful to Capsifi, especially Dr. Terry Roach, for providing Capsifi Jalapeno platform and sponsoring the research which led to this paper.

References

1. Baghdadi, Y.: Modelling business process with services: towards agile enterprises. Int. J. Bus. Inf. Syst. **15**(4), 410–433 (2014)
2. Bandara, M., Behnaz, A., Rabhi, F.A., Demirors, O.: From requirements to data analytics process: An ontology-based approach. In: Proceedings of the 5th International Workshop on the Interrelations between Requirements Engineering and Business Process Management at BPM 2018. Springer, Cham (2018). (in press)
3. Bandara, M., Rabhi, F.A., Meymandpour, R., Demirors, O.: A digital interaction framework for managing knowledge intensive business processes (manuscript submitted for publication) (2018)
4. Bandara, M., Rabhi, F.A.: Semantic modeling for engineering data analytic solutions. (manuscript submitted for publication) (2018)
5. Cauvet, C., Guzelian, G.: Business process modeling: A service-oriented approach. In: Proceedings of the 41st Annual Hawaii International Conference on System Sciences, pp. 98–98. IEEE (2008)
6. Cohn, D., Hull, R.: Business artifacts: a data-centric approach to modeling business operations and processes. IEEE Data Eng. Bull. **32**(3), 3–9 (2009)
7. Coşkunçay, A., Gürbüz, Ö., Demirörs, O., Ekinci, E.E.: PROMPTUM toolset: tool support for integrated ontologies and process models. In: Dumas, M., Fantinato, M. (eds.) BPM 2016. LNBIP, vol. 281, pp. 93–105. Springer, Cham (2017). https://doi.org/10.1007/978-3-319-58457-7_7
8. Demirors, O., Celik, F.: Process modeling methodologies for improvement and automation. In: IEEE International Conference on Quality and Reliability (ICQR), pp. 312–316. IEEE (2011)
9. Di Ciccio, C., Marrella, A., Russo, A.: Knowledge-intensive processes: characteristics, requirements and analysis of contemporary approaches. J. Data Semant. **4**(1), 29–57 (2015)
10. Filiz, C.Y., Demirors, O.: Utilizing process definitions for process automation: a comparative study. In: BPM and Workflow Handbook, Spotlight on Business Intelligence (2010)

11. Gronau, N., Weber, E.: Management of knowledge intensive business processes. In: 2nd International Conference on Business Process Management (2004)
12. Hepp, M., Roman, D.: An ontology framework for semantic business process management. Wirtschaftinformatik Proceedings **2007**, p. 27 (2007)
13. Kumaran, S., Liu, R., Wu, F.Y.: On the duality of information-centric and activity-centric models of business processes. In: Bellahsène, Z., Léonard, M. (eds.) CAiSE 2008. LNCS, vol. 5074, pp. 32–47. Springer, Heidelberg (2008). https://doi.org/10.1007/978-3-540-69534-9_3
14. Marrella, A., Mecella, M., Sardina, S.: SmartPM: an adaptive process management system through situation calculus, indigolog, and classical planning. In: KR (2014)
15. Rabhi, F., Bandara, M., Namvar, A., Demirors, O.: Big data analytics has little to do with analytics. In: Beheshti, A., Hashmi, M., Dong, H., Zhang, W.E. (eds.) ASSRI 2015/2017. LNBIP, vol. 234, pp. 3–17. Springer, Cham (2018). https://doi.org/10.1007/978-3-319-76587-7_1
16. Rao, L., Mansingh, G., Osei-Bryson, K.M.: Building ontology based knowledge maps to assist business process re-engineering. Decis. Support Syst. **52**(3), 577–589 (2012)
17. Roach, T.: CAPSICUM - A Semantic Framework for Strategically Aligned Business Architecture. Ph.D. thesis, University of New South Wales (2011)
18. Vaculin, R., Hull, R., Heath, T., Cochran, C., Nigam, A., Sukaviriya, P.: Declarative business artifact centric modeling of decision and knowledge intensive business processes. In: 15th IEEE International Conference on Enterprise Distributed Object Computing (2011)
19. Weber, I., Hoffmann, J., Mendling, J., Nitzsche, J.: Towards a methodology for semantic business process modeling and configuration. In: Di Nitto, E., Ripeanu, M. (eds.) ICSOC 2007. LNCS, vol. 4907, pp. 176–187. Springer, Heidelberg (2009). https://doi.org/10.1007/978-3-540-93851-4_18

SPI Compliance and Configuration

Transforming SPEM 2.0-Compatible Process Models into Models Checkable for Compliance

Julieth Patricia Castellanos Ardila(✉), Barbara Gallina, and Faiz Ul Muram

IDT, Mälardalen University, Box 883, 721 23 Västerås, Sweden
{julieth.castellanos,barbara.gallina,faiz.ul.muram}@mdh.se

Abstract. Manual compliance with process-based standards is time-consuming and prone-to-error. No ready-to-use solution is currently available for increasing efficiency and confidence. In our previous work, we have presented our automated compliance checking vision to support the process engineer's work. This vision includes the creation of a process model, given by using a SPEM 2.0 (Systems & Software Process Engineering Metamodel)-reference implementation, to be checked by Regorous, a compliance checker used in the business context. In this paper, we move a step further for the concretization of our vision by defining the transformation, necessary to automatically generate the models required by Regorous. Then, we apply our transformation to a small portion of the design phase recommended in the rail sector. Finally, we discuss our findings, and present conclusions and future work.

Keywords: Software process · Compliance checking · Regorous
SPEM 2.0

1 Introduction

Claiming compliance with process-based standards requires that companies show, via the provision of a justification which is expected to be scrutinized by an auditor, the fulfillment of its requirements [1]. The manual production of this justification is time-consuming and prone-to-error since it requires that the process engineer checks hundreds of requirements [2]. A process-based requirement is checkable for compliance if there is information in the process that corroborate that the requirement is fulfilled [3]. This checking can be facilitated by using FCL (Formal Contract Logic) [4], a rule-based language that can be used to generate automatic support to reason from requirements and the description of the process they regulate. In our previous work [5], we have presented our automatic compliance checking vision (See Fig. 1). It consists of the combination of process modeling capabilities via SPEM 2.0 [6]-reference implementation, specifically by using EPF (Eclipse Process Framework) Composer [7], and compliance checking capabilities via Regorous [8], an FCL-based reasoning methodology, and tool.

I. Stamelos et al. (Eds.): SPICE 2018, CCIS 918, pp. 233–247, 2018.
https://doi.org/10.1007/978-3-030-00623-5_16

In our vision, EPF Composer contributes with the appropriate (minimal set of) SPEM 2.0-compatible elements required by Regorous, which, in turn, produces a report that can be used to analyze and improve compliance.

In this paper, we define the transformation necessary (dotted line region shown in Fig. 1) to automatically generate the models required by Regorous, i.e., the FCL rule set, the structural representation of the process and the compliance effects annotations (cumulative interactions between process tasks that produce the desired global properties mandated by the standards [9]). Then, we apply our transformation to a small portion of the design phase recommended in the rail sector and discuss our findings.

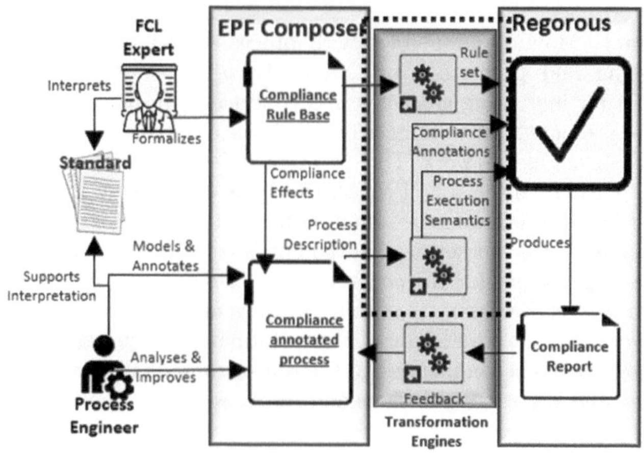

Fig. 1. Automated Compliance Checking Vision [5].

The rest of the paper is organized as follows. In Sect. 2, we recall essential background information. In Sect. 3, we present the transformations specification for generating Regorous inputs. In Sect. 4, we illustrate the transformation with a small example from the rail sector. In Sect. 5, we discuss our findings. In Sect. 6, we discuss related work. Finally, in Sect. 7, we derive conclusions and future work.

2 Background

In this section, we provide basic information on which we base our work.

2.1 EPF Composer

EPF Composer [7] is an open-source tool aiming at supporting the modeling of customizable software processes. We recall two open source standards used by

EPF Composer and also required in this paper. **UMA** (Unified Method Architecture) Metamodel [10], a subset of SPEM 2.0 [6], is used to model and manage reusable method content and processes. Method Content defines the core elements used in a process, i.e., *tasks*, *work products* and *roles*. Managed Content defines textual descriptions, such as *Concept* and *Reusable Asset*. *Custom Category* defines a hierarchical indexing to manage method content. A *delivery process* describes a complete and integrated approach for performing a specific project and it contains a *Breakdown Structure*, which allows nesting of tasks. **UML 2.0 Diagram Interchange Specification** [11] supports diagram interchange among modeling tools by providing an UML activity diagram representation. An *Activity* corresponds to a process, while a *Node* represents a point in the process, and an *Edge* is used to connects points. Nodes can be of different types. An *Activity Parameter Node* represents a task. *Initial and Final Nodes* represent the start and the end of the process. *Fork and Join Nodes* represent the parallel flows and *Decision and Merge Nodes* represent conditional behavior.

2.2 Regorous

Regorous [8] is a tool-supported methodology for compliance checking in which the compliance status of a process is provided with the causes of existing violations. To check compliance, Regorous requires a **rule set**, which is the formal representation of the standard's requirements in Formal Contract Logic (FCL) [4]. An FCL rule has the form $r : a_1, ..., a_n \Rightarrow c$, where r is the unique identifier, $a_1, ..., a_n$, are the conditions of the applicability of a norm and c is the normative effect. The different kind of normative effects can be found in [4]. A rule set is represented in the schema called *Combined Rule Set* from which we recall some elements. *Vocabulary* contains an element called *term*, which attribute *atom* is used to describe rule statements. The second element, called *Rule*, is used to define every rule of the logic. A rule is specified with the unique identifier called *label*, the description of the rule called *control objective*, and the actual rule called *formal representation*. Regorous current implemented tool uses the **Canonical Process Format (CPF)** [12], a modeling language agnostic representation that only describes the structural characteristics of the process. A *Canonical Process* is the container of a set of *Nets* which represent graphs made up of *Nodes* and *Edges*. Nodes types can be *(OR, XOR, AND) Splits/Joint*, which capture elements that have more than one incoming/outgoing edge. Nodes can also represent *Tasks* and *Events*, which are nodes that have at most one incoming/outgoing edge. The **compliance effect annotations**, which represents the fulfillment of a rule on a process element, are captured in Regorous by using a schema called *Compliance Check Annotations*. A *ruleSetList* contains the *ruleSets uri* which is the identification of the rule set. The *conditions* and the *taskEffects* represent the process sequence flow and the tasks respectively and have an associated *effects name* which corresponds to its actual compliance effects annotation.

2.3 Automatic Compliance Checking Vision: The Modeling Part

In this section, we recall the methodology used for modeling the SPEM 2.0-compatible models in EPF Composer required by Regorous. The methodology is explained with an example from ISO 26262 presented in [5]. The modeled requirement is obtained from part 6 clause 8, number 8.1, which states: *"Specify software units in accordance with the architectural design and the associated safety requirements"*. The formal representation of this requirement is presented in Eq. 1.

$$\begin{aligned} r2.1 &: addressSwUnitDesignProcess \Rightarrow [OANPNP] - performSpecifySwUnit \\ r2.2 &: performProvideSwArchitecturalDesign, performProvideSwSafetyRequirements \\ &\Rightarrow [P]performSpecifySwUnit \\ &r2.2 > r2.1 \end{aligned} \tag{1}$$

The modeling in EFP Composer required the creation of three plugins. Initially, we create a plugin for capturing standard's requirements (See Fig. 2), which contains not only their description in natural language e.g., *R2*, but also its atomization e.g., *r2.1* and *r2.2*. The requirement atomization is used to assign the rule representation (See Eq. 1). A second plugin is used to capture process elements, as depicted in Fig. 3.

Fig. 2. Requirements Plugin.

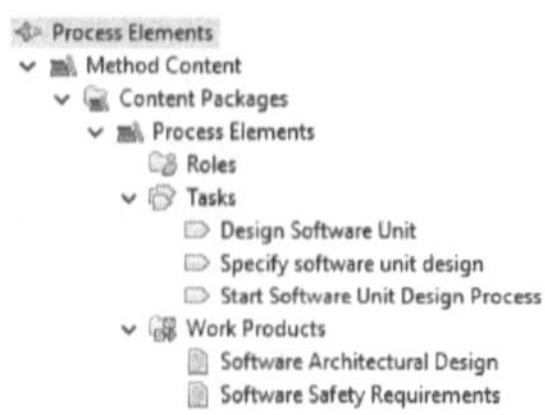

Fig. 3. Process Elements Plugin.

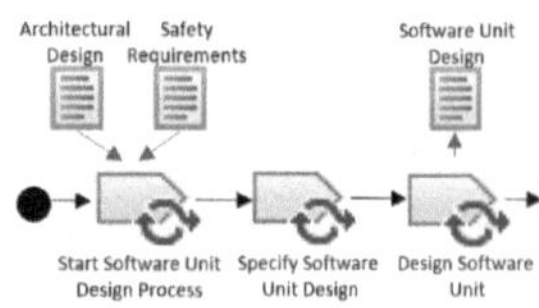

Fig. 4. Process Activity Diagram.

Finally, a third plugin is used to capture the compliance annotated tasks, in which we also create the delivery process and its corresponding activity diagram (See Fig. 4). To annotate the tasks, the concept that represents the compliance effects is added to the task. The reader can discover more details about the previous modeling in [5].

2.4 CENELEC EN 50128

CENELEC EN 50128 [13] is a standard that prescribes requirements for the development, deployment, and maintenance of safety-related software for railway control and protection application. The software component design phase is part of the lifecycle required by the software quality assurance, which states that the quality concerning the lifecycle shall address activities and tasks consistent with the plans (e.g., the safety plan). We recall some requirements corresponding to the software component design phase in Table 1.

Table 1. Requirements from the Rail Standard.

ID	Description
R1	Initiate component design phase
R2	Input documents: Software Design Specification
R3	A software component design shall be written under the responsibility of the designer

3 Generating Regorous Inputs

In this section, we present the two steps required to generate Regorous inputs, namely the **mapping** between the elements provided by EPF Composer and required by Regorous, and their **algorithmic solution**. We start with the mapping of the elements required for creating the **rule set**. As presented in Table 2, the information related to the rules is obtained from the *Delivery Process* provided by EPF Composer (described with UMA elements), and should conform to the Regorous schema called *Combined Rule Set*. Then, in Table 3, we present the mapping required for the process structure, which is provided in a UML activity diagram and required to be transformed to the canonical process (CPF). Finally, the *compliance effects annotations* require a structure that complies to the Regorous schema called *Compliance Check Annotations*. This information can be retrieved from EPF Composer taking into account that the process elements can be extracted from the process structure (described with UML elements) and the compliance effects annotations can be extracted from the delivery process (described with UMA elements). The mapping is presented in Table 4.

Table 2. Mapping elements from UMA to the rule set

UMA	Rule set	Mapping description
Reusable asset	Rule set	Reusable Asset is used in EPF composer to storage the information related to the rule set. Therefore, its information is transformed into the rule set required by Regorus. The attributes transferred are *name*, *presentationName* and *briefDescription*
Concept	Term	Concept is used in EPF Composer to storage the information related to the vocabulary used in the creation of the rules. Therefore its content is transformed into the vocabulary required in the rule set, specifically, each Concept is a Term. The attribute transferred is *name*
Content category	Rule	Content categories contain rules. Therefore, their content is transformed into the body of the rule. The attributes transferred are *name*, *presentationName*, and *briefDescription*

The algorithmic solution for obtaining the rule set, which mapping is described in Table 2, is presented in Algorithm 1. The algorithm initiates with

Table 3. Mapping elements from UML diagram to the canonical process

UML	CPF	Mapping description
Activity	Canonical process	The UML activity diagram is used in EPF Composer to describe the dynamics of the software process. Therefore, its information is transformed into a canonical process in CPF. The attribute transferred is *id*
Initial node	Start event	The initial node of the activity diagram becomes a node with type start event in CPF
Parameter node	Task type	Each parameter node in the activity diagram becomes a task type in the CPF. Attributes transferred are *id* and *name*
Control flow	Edge	Each control flow in the activity diagram becomes an edge in CPF. Attributes transferred are *id*, *name*, *source* and *target*
Final node	End event	The final node in the activity diagram becomes an end event type in CPF
Decision /Merge node	XOR Split /Join	The decision/merge nodes in the activity diagram becomes an XORSplit/XORJoin Type in CPF
Fork/Join node	AND split/Join	The fork/join nodes in the activity diagram becomes an ANDSplit/ANDJoin Type in CPF

Table 4. Mapping from UMA/UML metamodel to the compliance annotations

UML /UMA	Compliance annotations	Mapping description
Reusable asset	ruleSet	A reusable asset becomes a ruleSetList. The attribute transferred is the *name*
Edge	conditions	Each edge becomes a special element in the compliance annotations file called condition. The attribute transferred is the id
Node	Task effects	Each node becomes a Task Effect. The attribute transferred is the id. Then, the id is also used to search for the concepts that should be converted into the compliance Effects in the delivery process file
Concept	Effect	Every concepts associated to the task is transferred to the Effect. The attribute transferred is the name

the description of its required input (DeliveryProcess), and the expected output (RuleSet). Then, the input is parsed with the function *getElemementsByTagName*, which searches the elements to be mapped, with the function *Map* to the output. The first element searched is the *uma:ReusableAsset*, which attribute name is mapped to the rules URI. Then, the algorithm searches for the elements *uma:ContentCategory*, which provides the attributes *id*, *controlObjective* and *formalRepresentation* of each rule. Algorithm 2, which maps the elements described in Table 3, takes as input the UML Activity Diagram and provide the

Canonical Format. The function *getElementsByTagName* searches for every elements that describes process structure and maps it to their counterpart in CPF. The mapping of the process structural elements requires a unique identifier that is generated internally each time the function *Map* is used. Algorithm 3 describes the solution for mapping the elements presented in Table 4. The required inputs are the UML Activity Diagram and the DeliveryProcess. The expected output is the ComplianceEffectsAnnotations. The algorithm searches in the delivery process the element tagged as *uma:ReusableAsset* and mapped it to the rule

```
input  : DeliveryProcess
output: RulseSet
LoadFile (DeliveryProcess);
NodeReusableAsset←getElementsByTagName (uma:ReusableAsset);
Map (ruleSet←ReusableAsset);
conceptsList←getElementsByTagName (uma:Concept);
for i ← 0to getLength (ConceptsList) do
 | Map (Term.atom ←Concept.name)
end
contentCategoryList ← getElementsByTagName (uma:ContentCategory);
for j ← 0to getLength (contentCategoryList) do
    ruleControlObjective←getAttribute (briefDescription);
    if ruleControlObjective is not empty then
     | Map (rule←contentCategory)
    end
end
```

Algorithm 1: Algorithm for Obtaining the Rule Set.

```
input  : UMLActivityDiagram
output: CanonicalFormat
LoadFile (UMLActivityDiagram);
NodeActivity←getElementsByTagName (uml:Activity) ;
Map (CanonicalProcess← NodeActivity);
nodesList←getElementsByTagName (uml:node);
for i ← 0 to getLength (nodesList) do
    if nodeType=uml:ActivityParameterNode then
     | Map (TaskType←node)
    end
    if nodeType=uml:InitialNode then
     | Map (StatEvent←node)
    end
    if nodeType=uml:ActivityFinalNode then
     | Map (EndEvent←node)
    end
    if nodeType=uml:ForkNode then
     | Map (ANDSplitType←node)
    end
    if nodeType=uml:JoinNode then
     | Map (ANDJoinType←node)
    end
    if nodeType=uml:DecisionNode then
     | Map (XORSplitType←node)
    end
    if nodeType=uml:MergeNode then
     | Map (XORJoinType←node)
    end
end
edgesList←getElementsByTagName (uml:edge);
for j ← 0to getLength (edgeList) do
 | Map (Edge←edge)
end
```

Algorithm 2: Algorithm for Obtaining the Process Structure.

set. Similarly, the algorithm searches for the elements tagged as *uml:edge* and *uml:node* in the UML Activity Diagram and mapped them to the conditions and taskEffects respectively. The node id is used to search for the elements tagged as *uma:concept* in the DeliveryProcess, which is mapped to the effects.

```
input  : UMLActivityDiagram,DeliveryProcess
output: ComplianceEffectsAnnotations
LoadFile (UMLActivityDiagram, DeliveryProcess) ;
NodeReusableAsset (from DeliveryProcess)←getElementsByTagName (uma:ReusableAsset) ;
Map ((ruleSet←ReusableAsset) ;
edgesList(from UMLProcess)← getElementsByTagName (uml:edge);
for i ← 0 to getLength (edgeList) do
 | Map (conditions←edge)
end
nodeList(from UMLProcess)← getElementsByTagName (uml:node);
for j ← 0 to getLength (nodeList) do
    Map (taskEffects←node) TaskId←ObtainUMAValue(nodeList);
    ContentElementList(from DeliveryProcess)←
    getElementsByTagName(ContentElement);
    for k ← 0 to getLength (ContentElementList) do
        if ContentElementList.id = TaskId then
            ConceptsList(from DeliveryProcess)← getElementsByTagName(Concept);
            for l ← 0 to getLength (ConceptsList) do
             | Map (effects←Concept);
            end
        end
    end
end
```

Algorithm 3: Algorithm for Obtaining the Compliance Effects Annotations.

4 Models Checkable for Compliance from the Rail Sector

The purpose of this section is to provide evidence that the models provided by EPF Composer, and transformed with our algorithm, are checkable for compliance with Regorous. The software process model to be checked for compliance is the one modeled in Fig. 4 (originally created for compliance with an automotive standard). In this evaluation, three steps are required. Initially, we generate the compliance annotated software process in EPF Composer, following the methodology described in Sect. 2.3. Second, we apply the transformation described in Sect. 3. Finally, we verify that the models generated have enough information to be processed by Regorous. This verification is done manually, namely, we highlight the mapping of the elements required for checking compliance. We also check compliance with Regorous and describe the type of analysis that can be carried out after compliance checking.

We start by annotation a small portion of the design phase (modeled in Fig. 4) with the recommended requirements provided in the rail sector (see CENELEC requirements in Sect. 2.4). First, we formalize the standard's requirements applying the definitions for creating the rules presented in Sect. 2.2. As the formula 2) shows, the rule r1.1, which is the formalization of the requirement R1, defines an obligation of addressing the phase. Rules r.2.1 and r.2.2 are related to the requirement R2 in the following way: r.2.1 prohibits the specification of the design, but r.2.2 permits the specification of software units if the software design specification is obtained. Similarly to r.3.1 and r.3.2, which are related to requirement R3. Rule r.3.1 prohibits the production of software units, but r.3.2 permits them if not only the specification is performed but also is a designer has been assigned. In the previous rules, priority relations are defined to give higher priority to the permits over the obligations.

$$\begin{aligned}
&r1.1 : [OM]addressComponentDesignPhase\\
&r2.1 : addressComponentDesignPhase \Rightarrow [OANPNP] - performSpecifyComponentDesign\\
&r2.2 : obtainSoftwareDesignSpecification \Rightarrow [P]performSpecifyComponentDesign\\
&r3.1 : performSpecifyComponentDesign \Rightarrow [OANPNP] - produceSoftwareComponentDesign\\
&r3.2 : performSpecifyComponentDesign,\\
&assignDesigner \Rightarrow [P]produceSoftwareComponentDesign\\
&r2.2 > r2.1, r3.2 > r3.1
\end{aligned} \tag{2}$$

Standards requirements and the respective rules are modeled in EPF Composer in a plugin as depicted in Fig. 5.

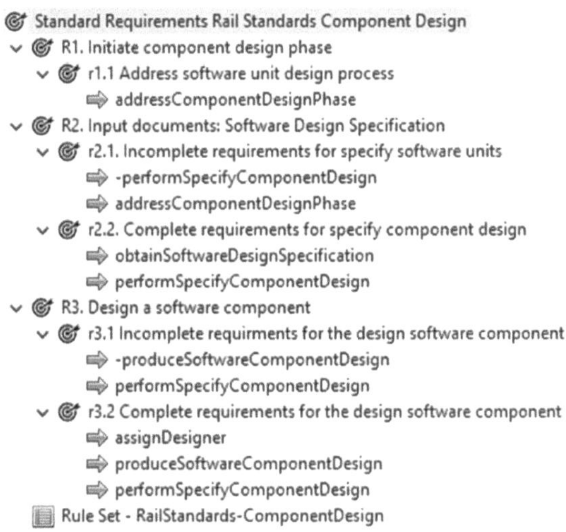

Fig. 5. Requirements Plugin.

Then, we import the plugin that contains the process elements (See Fig. 3). Finally, we create the plugin for annotating the process tasks. In this plugin, we copy the tasks from the plugin that contains the process elements and make them *contribute* to the original ones, which allows to extend them in an additional way. The tasks are annotated according to the compliance effects they represent. For this, we check the process model depicted in Fig. 4. As we see, the task *Start Software Unit Design Process* represents the initiation of the software component design and therefore it produces the compliance annotation *addressComponent-DesignPhase*. This task also responds to the compliance effect *obtainSoftware-DesignSpecification* since it has a work product with a similar name. Task *Specify*

Software Units responds to the compliance effect *performSpecifyComponentDesign*. Finally, the task *Design Software Unit* has a work product *Software Unit Design*, which makes the task respond to the compliance effect *produceSoftwareComponentDesign*. Once the tasks are annotated, we create the delivery process and the activity diagram, export the plugins and apply the transformations to obtain the Regorous inputs to check compliance.

In what follows, we provide essential code snippets, in which we highlight the mapping of the elements required for checking compliance. We start showing the generated *Rule Set*. As presented in Listing 1.1, the generated *Rule Set* has the elements *Vocabulary*, which contains the rules, described in EPF Composer with an *uma:concept*. It also contains the *rules*, which were described in the content category elements that correspond to the rules.

```
<?xml version="1.0" encoding="UTF-8" standalone="yes"?>
<RuleSet xmlns="http://www.nicta.com.au/bpc/CombinedRuleSetDefinition
    /0.1" uri="RuleSetRailStandards" >
  <Vocabulary>
    <Term atom="addressComponentDesignPhase"/>
    ...<!--other Term atoms -->
  </Vocabulary>
  <Rules>
    <Rule xmlns:xsi="http://www.w3.org/2001/XMLSchema-instance"
        xsi:type="DflRuleType" ruleLabel="r1.1">
      <ControlObjective>r1.1 Address software unit design process</
          ControlObjective>
      <FormalRepresentation>=&gt; [OANPP] addressComponentDesignPhase</
          FormalRepresentation>
    </Rule>
    ...<!--other rules -->
  <SuperiorityRelations>
    ...
  </SuperiorityRelations>
</RuleSet>
```

Listing 1.1. Rule set generated

In Listing 1.2, we present the generated process structure. We highlighted one *Node* that represents the start point of the process and one node that represents a task Type. An *Edge* represents a connection between the nodes.

```
<?xml version="1.0" encoding="UTF-8" standalone="true"?>
<ns4:CanonicalProcess name="Software Unit Design Process" ...>
  <Net id="1529072497607">
    <Node id="1529072497608" xsi:type="ns4:EventType" xmlns:xsi="http:
        //www.w3.org/2001/XMLSchema-instance">
      <name>Start</name>
      <attribute value="startevent1" typeRef="Id"/>
    </Node>
    <Node id="1529072497609" xsi:type="ns4:TaskType" xmlns:xsi="http:
        //www.w3.org/2001/XMLSchema-instance">
      <name>Start Software Design Process</name>
      <attribute value="StartSoftwareDesignProcessID" typeRef="Id"/>
    </Node>
    ...<!--other nodes -->
    <Edge id="1529072497612" targetId="1529072497609" sourceId="
        1529072497608" default="false">
    ...<!--other edges -->
  </Net>
</ns4:CanonicalProcess>
```

Listing 1.2. Process structure generated

In Listing 1.3, we present the compliance annotations. For example, the *rule set uri* is the rule set identification, *conditions element id* represent control flows identification, and the *taskEffects* represent the tasks, which *effects name* corresponds to the effects.

```
<?xml version="1.0" encoding="ASCII"?>
<cca:ComplianceAnnotations xmi:version="2.0" xmlns:xmi="http://www.omg.
    org/XMI" xmlns:cca="http://www.nicta.com.au/bpc/eclipse/
    ComplianceCheckAnnotations">
<ruleSetList>
   <ruleSets uri="RuleSetRailStandards"/>
</ruleSetList>
   <conditions elementId="_jNj1AExVEeiW4M4duzOA6Q"/>
   <conditions elementId="_jukQUExVEeiW4M4duzOA6Q"/>
   ...<!--other conditions-->
   <taskEffects elementId="_hCKUcExVEeiW4M4duzOA6Q">
      <effects name="addressComponentDesignPhase" negation="false">
      <effects name="obtainSoftwareDesignSpecification" negation="false">
   ...<!--other taskEffects -->
   <localVocabulary/>
</cca:ComplianceAnnotations>
```

Listing 1.3. Compliance annotations generated

Then, we checked compliance with Regorous. The report results (See Fig. 6) not only shows that the *process in non-compliant*, but also the description of the uncompliant situation, the element that may be the source of the violation, the rule that has been violated and the possible resolution. With this information, it may be easier for the process engineer to make a focused analysis to improve the compliance status. In the example, the rule 3.1 (highlighted in Fig. 5), refers to *Incomplete requirements for the design of software Components*, which means that we do not have the requirements in place to address the task called *Specify Software Unit Design*. To solve the uncompliant situation, we refer to the counterpart rule, which is the one marked as *r.3.2*, in which the compliance effects *assign designer* and *produceSoftwareComponentDesign* and *performSpecifyComponentDesign* are included. To be able to complete the assignment of these effects, we need to include a role called *designer* to the task *Specify Software Unit Design* as presented in Fig. 7. The improved process is again checked, resulting in a report with no violations of the rules.

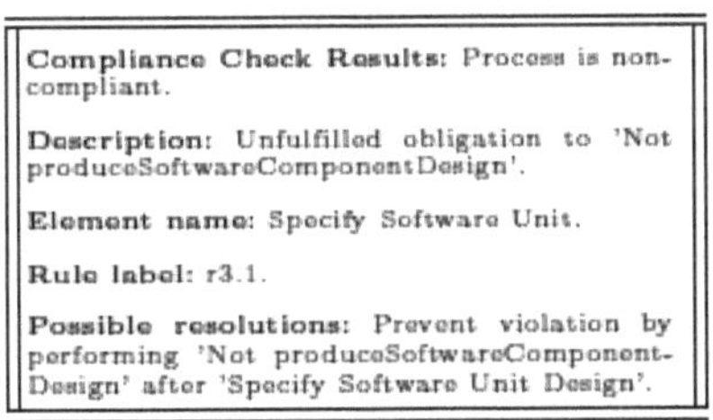

Compliance Check Results: Process is non-compliant.
Description: Unfulfilled obligation to 'Not produceSoftwareComponentDesign'.
Element name: Specify Software Unit.
Rule label: r3.1.
Possible resolutions: Prevent violation by performing 'Not produceSoftwareComponent-Design' after 'Specify Software Unit Design'.

Fig. 6. Compliance Report.

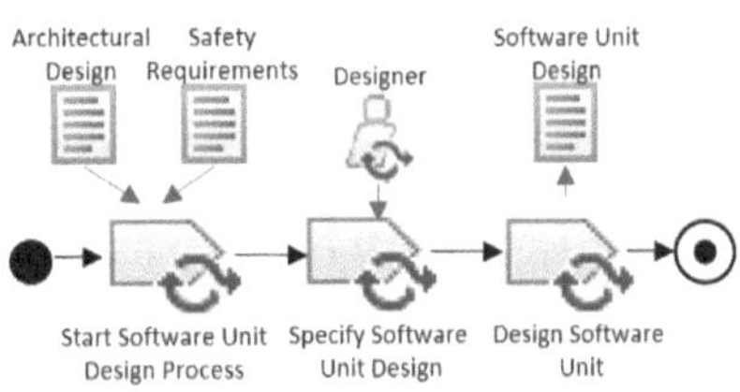

Fig. 7. Activity Diagram.

5 Discussion

Automated compliance checking of software processes with Regorous generates a compliance report that not only communicate the compliance status of the software process, i.e., whether the process is compliant or not, but also the sources of violations, i.e., the rules that have being violated and the target of the uncompliant situations (specific tasks), and possible resolutions. This information may increase **efficiency** in the process compliance since it permits the process engineer to focus on specific process elements and the reparation policies they may require. In the example presented in Sect. 6, it was clear, from the compliance report, that the task affected was *Specify Software Unit* and we focus on it to understand the missing process elements. If rules are correctly formalized, and their formalization covers the standards requirements entirely, also **confidence** can be increased since uncompliant situations, in all the levels, would be spotted. Since we have modeled in detail the requirements provided in Table 1, we can consider the checking of the small process reliable. A software process can be checked for compliance with different standards. This specific aspect could potentially be beneficial since it promotes **process reusability**, i.e., a process engineer can take processes designed in previous projects, check their compliance status with the normative requirements of the new project and improve it, based on the violations reported. In the example, we saw that the software process model created for automotive could be used as a base for model a small portion of the design phase recommended in the rail sector.

As we see in Fig. 1, the adopted methodological approach for our automatic compliance checking vision, is tool supported. While the **maturity** of the methodology is high, its tool support still requires additional work. EPF Composer and Regorous have been tested separately and the bridge between them, namely, the transformations between the EPF Composer and Regorous, have been designed and implemented. The transformations, applied to the portion of the design phase recommended in the rail sector (See Sect. 4), are *correct* since they have generated a complete set of inputs that are compatible with Regorous schemas, making possible to check compliance. The transformation implementation, which is still in a prototyping stage, could be improved if techniques, such as Model Driven Engineering (MDE) are applied. We consider essential to further exploit the process modeling language agnosticism underlying Regorous methodology to be able to perform a future seamless integration of the tools required for our compliance checking vision.

6 Related Work

Automatic compliance checking of processes is one of the mechanisms that can provide benefits, as we have discussed above, to compliance management. In particular, researchers in the business and legal compliance context have explored potential formalisms to create compliance checking frameworks, such as the ones presented in [14] and in [15]. However, they are based on temporal logics, in which the modeling of normative requirements is still considered difficult. To model the rules more naturally, we have chosen Regorous, which underlying formalism called FCL, permits the modeling of deontic notions (i.e., obligations, prohibitions and permissions) which are the actual notions that describe normative requirements. Automatic compliance checking of safety-critical software processes has not been as explored as in business management. However, in [16], the authors presented initial steps of an approach for process reasoning and verification, which is based on the combination of Composition Tree Notations (CTN), a high-level modeling notation used for modeling process structure, and Description Logics (DL). DL is used to reason about the compliance of the process structure. Instead, our approach includes the accumulation of compliance effects that trigger new effects, focusing on the process behavior. Another difference we have included in our approach is the use of SPEM 2.0-compatible software process models, which may be preferred over other process modeling languages since it allows the creation of process method contents that can be reused in different kind of processes. SPEM 2.0-related community, to the best of our knowledge, has not addressed compliance checking. However, based on SPEM 2.0, some solutions for compliance management exists. In [3], compliance tables are generated. Compliance tables require the modeling of the standard's requirements, which should be mapped to the process elements that fulfill them. The modeling of compliance elements is also exploited in [17], in which the modeling of standards requirements is required to detect whether the process model contains sufficient evidence for supporting the requirements. The approach provides feedback to the safety engineers regarding detected fallacies and recommendations to solve them. In our case, we have also exploited not only the modeling of standard requirements, but also we have provided a mechanism to include rules within the standard's requirements, which facilitate the resolution of uncompliant situations after the automatic compliance checking is performed.

7 Conclusions and Future Work

In this paper, we defined the transformation necessary to automatically generate the models checkable for compliance in Regorous from SPEM 2.0-compatible process models. We also applied our transformation to a small portion of the software component design phase recommended in the rail sector and discussed aspects related to our findings.

To increase the maturity of the results shown in this paper, a proper plugin is going to be implemented to enable the push-button solution for the entire generation of the inputs required by Regorous. Also, as presented in [5], we need to further validate our approach and complete some tasks, i.e., the addition of the rule editor to facilitate the modeling of FCL rules, which currently is done manually, and the mechanism to back-propagate compliance results into EPF Composer. This work is expected to be partly delivered within the final release of the AMASS platform [18].

Acknowledgments. This work is supported by the EU and VINNOVA via the ECSEL JU project AMASS (No. 692474) [19]. We thank Guido Governatori for his guidance during the execution of this project.

References

1. Gallina, B., Ul Muram, F., Castellanos Ardila, J.: Compliance of agilized (Software) development processes with safety standards: a vision. In: 4th International Workshop on Agile Development of Safety-Critical Software (2018)
2. Castellanos Ardila, J.P., Gallina, B.: Towards increased efficiency and confidence in process compliance. In: Stolfa, J., Stolfa, S., O'Connor, R.V., Messnarz, R. (eds.) EuroSPI 2017. CCIS, vol. 748, pp. 162–174. Springer, Cham (2017). https://doi.org/10.1007/978-3-319-64218-5_13
3. McIsaac, B.: IBM Rational Method Composer: Standards Mapping. Technical report, IBM Developer Works (2015)
4. Governatori, G.: Representing business contracts in RuleML. Int. J. Coop. Inf. Syst. **14**, 181–216 (2005)
5. Castellanos Ardila, J.P., Gallina, B., Ul Muram, F.: Enabling compliance checking against safety standards from SPEM 2.0 process models. In: Euromicro Conference on Software Engineering and Advanced Applications (2018)
6. Object Management Group Inc.: Software & Systems Process Engineering Meta-Model Specification. Version 2.0. OMG Std., Rev, 236 (2008)
7. The Eclipse Foundation.: Eclipse Process Framework (EPF) Composer 1.0 Architecture Overview (2013). http://www.eclipse.org/epf/composer_architecture/
8. Governatori, G.: The Regorous approach to process compliance. In: IEEE 19th International Enterprise Distributed Object Computing Workshop, pp. 33–40 (2015)
9. Koliadis, G., Ghose, A.: Verifying semantic business process models in verifying semantic business process models in inter-operation. In: IEEE International Conference on Service-Oriented Computing, pp. 731–738 (2007)
10. IBM Corporation: Key Capabilities of the Unified Method Architecture (UMA)
11. Object Management Group: UML 2. 0 Diagram Interchange Specification (2003)
12. La Rosa, M., et al.: APROMORE: an advanced process model repository. Expert Syst. Appl. **38**, 7029–7040 (2011)
13. EN50128 BS: Railway applications - Communication, signalling and processing systems - Software for railway control and protection systems (2011)
14. Elgammal, A., Turetken, O., van den Heuvel, W., Papazoglou, M.: Formalizing and applying compliance patterns for business process compliance. Softw. Syst. Model. **15**, 119–146 (2016)
15. El Kharbili, M.: Business process regulatory compliance management solution frameworks: a comparative evaluation. In: 8th Asia-Pacific Conference on Conceptual Modelling, pp. 23–32 (2012)
16. Kabaale, E., Wen, L., Wang, Z., Rout, T.: Representing software process in description logics: an ontology approach for software process reasoning and verification. In: Clarke, P.M., O'Connor, R.V., Rout, T., Dorling, A. (eds.) SPICE 2016. CCIS, vol. 609, pp. 362–376. Springer, Cham (2016). https://doi.org/10.1007/978-3-319-38980-6_26

17. Ul Muram, F., Gallina, B., Gomez Rodriguez, L.: Preventing omission of key evidence fallacy in process-based argumentations. In: 11th International Conference on the Quality of Information and Communications Technology (2018)
18. AMASS Platform. https://www.polarsys.org/opencert/
19. AMASS: Architecture-driven, Multi-concern and Seamless Assurance and Certification of Cyber-Physical Systems. http://www.amass-ecsel.eu/

Ensuring Conformance to Process Standards Through Formal Verification

Edward Kabaale[2](✉), Lian Wen[1,2], Zhe Wang[1,2], and Terry Rout[1]

[1] Institute for Integrated and Intelligent Systems, Griffith University, 170 Kessels Road, Nathan, QLD 4111, Australia
{l.wen,z.wang,t.rout}@griffith.edu.au

[2] School of Information and Communication Technology, Griffith University, 170 Kessels Road, Nathan, QLD 4111, Australia
edward.kabaale@griffithuni.edu.au

Abstract. Software process standards and models encapsulate best practices and guidelines for engineering and managing software. These are usually prescribed in natural language. However, natural language based process specifications can be inconsistent and ambiguous that makes it difficult to monitor and verify if they have been fully implemented and adhered too in a given software project. Besides the process of defining and documenting the necessary evidence to comply with process standard requirements is often manual, time consuming and laborious. In earlier studies, we developed a translation scheme and meta-model for consistent and uniform software process formalisation. In the current study, we leverage the formal process specification to develop a two-step formal process verification approach; first we extract process requirements from the standard documents and translate them into logical axioms. We then augment these axioms with additional information in a process verification ontology. This ontology is then utilised in conformance verification of a performed process. We demonstrate the feasibility of our approach with software requirements analysis process and a case study.

Keywords: Process · Standards · Ontology · Verification

1 Introduction

Software process management is a systematic and continuous endeavor to define, assess and improve processes that are used to produce quality software products and services within the constraints of time, budget and schedule [1]. The process perspective to software development is premised on the manufacturing principle that product quality is influenced and evolved by the process used to produce it [1]. To systematise software development and ensure interoperability, consistency, and repeatability; software process standards such as ISO/IEC 12207 [2], ISO/IEC 29110 [3] are widely adopted as a source of universally accepted best

I. Stamelos et al. (Eds.): SPICE 2018, CCIS 918, pp. 248–262, 2018.
https://doi.org/10.1007/978-3-030-00623-5_17

practices and guidelines to support the design, implementation and improvement of software processes. However, software process standards are usually prescribed in natural language that makes it difficult to implement, monitor and verify such processes in practice [4]. Given that software standards are typically multi-paper documents and vebrose, they are likely to be ambiguous and inconsistent which impedes their automated analysis and verification. Novice users may find them hard to implement and verify in projects [5]. Despite, some efforts making software standards more applicable and accessible even to very small entities (VSE); for example ISO/IEC 29110 with deployment packages[1], still considerable time and resources are needed to understand, implement and verify thier conformance [6].

The process of verifying the extent to which the implemented process is in conformance with a process reference model (PRM) is referred to as process compliance [7] and accomplished through *process assessment* or appraisal [8]. Process assessment is the disciplined evaluation of the organisational processes against a set of criteria defined in a process assessment model (PAM) to determine the capability of the organisational processes to perform within the constraints of quality, cost and schedule [8]. During process assessment, the emphasis is placed on two measures, i.e., organisational process conformance to the PRM and the effectiveness of the organisational processes (process capability) to achieve organisational business objectives [8]. Where as a process capability assessment studies individual processes and thier attributes, a conformance assessment on the other hand, can study fulfillment of a standard's requirements [9,10]. Therefore, Process assessment provides a way to verify conformance to a standard like ISO/IEC 29110, if such a standard is considered a set of requirements [10]. The main stream assessment methods such as ISO/IEC 15504 (aka SPICE) that is transiting to ISO/IEC 330xx [11] describe guidelines that standards compliant processes should follow namely; (i) defining processes in terms of purpose and outcomes, (ii) use of objective evidence to prove conformance to the defined criteria. When assessing software process implementations, the main stream assessment methods are however, complex, resource intensive and unaffordable to many software companies [12].

To overcome the above challenges, formal approaches to process modeling and verification have been proposed in previous studies [4,7,12–14]. These increase confidence and trustworthiness in the evidence used for process compliance [15] and enable the use of automated analysis and verification techniques in software process [17]. A formal process specification also enables compliance and certification to process standards and reference models [18]. However, we couldn't use the available approaches for the task at hand for various reasons; The approach by [7] employs first order logic (FOL), to formalize and verify standards compliant software development. FOL is a proven and necessary expressive formalism. However, its major drawback is its undecidability that leads to inefficiency in terms of computational costs. Other approaches are not expressive enough for the task at hand.

[1] http://profs.etsmtl.ca/claporte/english/vse/vse-packages.html.

Essentially ontology approaches are an application of formal methods into the semantic web where web resources are formally specified using logical notations and rigorously verified using ontology reasoning engines [14]. In recent years, Description Logics (DLs) [16] based ontologies have been widely accepted as an important means for representing and formalising knowledge in different domains including software process engineering (see, e.g., [17,19]). DLs are a decidable fragment of FOL that provides a rich and flexible modeling language that underpins the web ontology language (OWL)[2]; a W3C standard for developing ontologies in the semantic web. DLs come with an unambiguous, standardised semantics and a wide range of tools that can be used to develop, validate, integrate and verify formal models of software processes. Moreover, DLs are supported by a variety of optimised inference engines[3] that can be utilised to support both consistent process implementation and querying the process space by logical expressions, e.g. in conformance checking.

In earlier studies [20,21], we developed a translation scheme and metamodel for consistent and uniform process formalisation. In the current study, we leverage such a formal process specification for process verification since formal models are basically a set of domain theorems that are amenable to formal proving through reasoning [14]. Therefore in this paper, we extend our earlier work, with a formal process verification approach where two levels of verification can be performed to ensure the correctness of a process specification, i.e., the ontology and instance verification levels. The former ensures the correctness of the process specification itself, and the latter ensures the conformance of a process instance to the standard process. Moreover, ontology reasoners can be used to fully automate these formal verification activities. Consequently, we develop a process verification ontology where we treat the problem of conformance to standard processes as *instantiation* with a case study. The paper is structured as follows: In Sect. 2 we provide preliminaries about process management and improvement, a formal foundation about description logic and ontologies while we present an overview of our approach in Sect. 3 and a feasibility study of this approach based on software requirements analysis process. Simultaneously, we provide challenges for further development and evaluation of the approach in Sect. 4 concludes the paper.

2 Background

2.1 Process Management and Improvement

Software process management is the use of process engineering concepts, techniques, and practices to explicitly monitor, control, and improve the software process [1]. The objective of software process management is to enable an organization to produce software products according to a plan while simultaneously improving the quality of its products [1]. A process is a *set of interrelated or*

2 https://www.w3.org/OWL/.

3 http://owl.cs.manchester.ac.uk/tools/list-of-reasoners/.

interacting activities which transforms inputs into outputs [2]. We limit ourselves to defining a process in terms of its purpose and outcomes [8]. Processes be technical or management are an inherent part of software engineering (SE), so is process assessment which is a foundation step for process improvement [29]. Organisations use process assessment models (PAM) such as ISO/IEC 330xx [11] to evaluate and change their processes in light of achieving business objectives and supporting process conformance to standard processes [10]. A PAM is a two dimensional representation that describes processes in terms of objective evidence that may be identified to demonstrate process implementation. PAMs generally comprise sets of practices and descriptions of work products that serve as indicators of process performance and process capability dimensions of the assessment framework [2]. The process dimension of a PAM describes processes drawn from one or more PRMs, in SE, these processes can be drawn from ISO/IEC 12207, ISO/IEC 29110 among others. The PRM provides a list of processes to be verified and their descriptions with a common terminology and scope for process assessments. In a PRM, processes are described in terms of purpose and outcomes. According to [9,10] conformance assessment may utilize PRM in evaluating achievement of the process outcomes. We use software requirements analysis (SRA) process from ISO/IEC 15504-5 [22] as a running example in this paper.

Process Purpose: *The purpose of the Software requirements analysis process is to establish the requirements of the software elements of the system.*

Process Outcomes:

- *PO1: The requirements allocated to the software elements of the system and their interfaces are defined;*
- *PO2: Software requirements are analysed for correctness and testability*
- *PO3: The impact of software requirements on the operating environment are understood*
- *PO4: Consistency and traceability are established between the software requirements and system requirements*
- *PO5: Prioritization for implementing the software requirements is defined*
- *PO6: The software requirements are approved and updated as needed*
- *PO7: Changes to the software requirements are evaluated for cost, schedule and technical impact*
- *PO8: The software requirements are baselined and communicated to all affected parties*

Accordingly, SRA process outcomes can be achieved by implementing *base practices* and evidencing their implementation through availability of *work products* produced. These are also referred to as the process performance assessment indicators for the process dimension in the process assessment model. The base practices and work products for software requirements analysis process drawn from [22] are shown in Tables 1 and 2 respectively.

ISO/IEC 33020 [23] defines an ordinal scale for the evaluation of process capability based upon six defined capability levels. It characterises the extent to which

Table 1. SRA process base practices

No	Base practices	Process outcome achieved
BP1	Specify software requirements	PO1, PO2, PO5
BP2	Determine operating environment impact	PO3
BP3	Develop criteria for software testing	PO2
BP4	Ensure consistency	PO4
BP5	Evaluate and update software requirements	PO6, PO7
BP6	Communicate Software requirements	PO8

Table 2. SRA Process process work products

No	Work product	Process outcome evidenced
WP1	Communication record	PO8
WP2	Change control	PO7
WP3	Traceability record	PO4
WP4	Analysis report	PO2, PO3, PO7
WP5	Interface requirements	PO1
WP6	Software requirements	PO1, PO2, PO4, PO5 and PO6

the process outcomes are achieved. The outcome achievement is behaviourally aggregated to the process attribute which in turn is transformed to an ordinal scale as shown in Table 3 and aggregated to determine a given capability level [24]. We use this rating scheme in a *conjugate* way [24] to determine the extent to which the process outcomes are achieved.

2.2 Description Logics and Ontologies

Ontologies are engineering artefacts that are an explicit formal specification of a shared conceptualisation [25]. Web Ontology Language (OWL)[4] is an ontology modeling language designed and standardised by W3C for modeling ontologies in the semantic web. OWL is underpinned by DL for its formal semantics [16] that enables expressed knowledge to be reasoned on by human and artificial agents. An OWL DL ontology is mainly composed of two main components; The Terminological knowledge represented in the TBox (Class Level) and the Assertional knowledge forming the ABox (Instance Level). The TBox defines the intensional knowledge by which a concrete world can be described in form of classes, properties and the respective axioms that define the constraints on the conceptual schema. The ABox on the other hand, represents assertional knowledge that describes some particular situation that instantiates the TBox. Although in DL, only the Tbox is commonly referred to as an ontology and the

[4] https://www.w3.org/OWL/.

Table 3. The rating scale of process outcomes (cited from ISO/IEC 33020 [23])

Acronym	Achievement of the defined Outcome
Not achieved (**N**)	There is little or no evidence of achievement of the defined outcome in the assessed process
Partially achieved (**P**)	There is some evidence of the approach to, and some achievement of, the defined attribute in the assessed process
Largely achieved (**L**)	There is evidence of a systematic approach to, and significant achievement of, the defined outcomes in the assessed process. Some weakness related to this attribute may exist in the assessed process
Fully achieved (**F**)	There is evidence of a complete and systematic approach to, and full achievement of, the defined outcome in the assessed process. No significant weaknesses related to the outcome exist in the assessed process

combination of the TBox and ABox is referred to as the knowledge base (KB), in this work we use both ontology and knowledge base interchangeably. In the scope of our solution, the actual process implementation will be treated as the ABox while the process standard will be coded as the TBox.

Ontology modeling in the semantic web, follows an open world assumption (OWA) where anything is permissible unless explicitly prohibited. In others, OWA semantics assume incomplete information by default, i.e., missing information is treated as unknown rather than false. If any information is not declared in the ontology, it is not taken to be false as is the case in database systems that follow a closed world assumption (CWA) [26]. DL Axioms are used to constrain classes, properties and individuals that classes can admit. Where as axioms in an OWA semantics are used for inference purposes, in this study, we would like such axioms to behave more like integrity constraints [26] in the presence of process instance data (ABox) that needs to conform to the standard process in the TBox (ontology) through the verification process using an ontology reasoner such as Pellet [27]. Indeed, whereas inference is useful for reasoning over the domain knowledge, when dealing with process conformance, the assessor wants to verify that the presented objective evidence in form of e.g., artefact such as SRS is indeed validated and baselined.

3 Overview of the Approach

In this section, we present our approach that includes translation of natural language process to formal specification (DL language), capturing process standard requirements as DL axioms consisting of base practices, work products and process outcomes. We also present a process instance in a form of an ABox that we verify against the DL Axioms in the TBox using a reasoner such as Pellet.

The consistency of which represents conformance to the standards requirements or non conformance. Figure 1, gives a high level view of the process verification approach presented in this section.

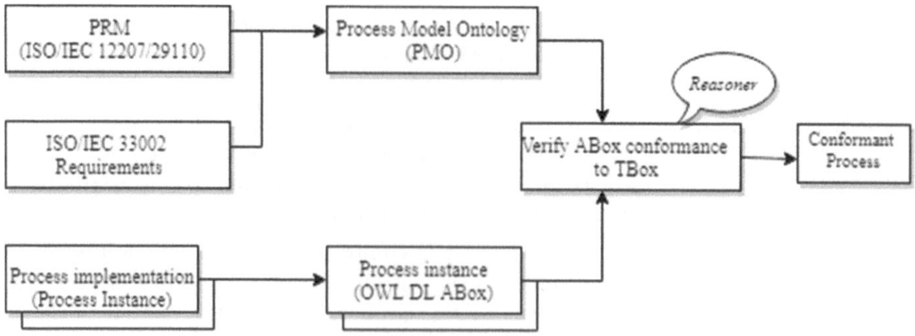

Fig. 1. Process verification architecture

3.1 Constructing the Process Model Ontology (PMO)

In [29] a conceptual framework for ontology usage in process assessment is provided. In this framework a number of ontologies are proposed such as PRM ontology, measurement and process ontology. In the current study, we mainly develop a process model ontology (TBox)consisting the PRM and PAM, and the process ontology as the process instance (ABox) which we use for process verification. A well known ontology construction approach recommends investigating available upper ontologies and extracting reusable concepts from them before developing domain specific ontologies. We refer to the upper ontology developed for ISO software engineering standards [28] that provides an ontological base for all ISO present and future standards. This ontological infrastructure provides an ontological base for various standard domain ontologies that are specific to a given domain such as process management. We also make use of concepts and properties in earlier developed ontologies for the SE domain such as the Software Lifecycle Ontology (SLO) and Software Implementation Process Ontology (SIP) developed in the ALIGNED project[5] that we reuse in our ontology development following guidelines suggested in [29]. The ontology we develop is in conformance with the guidelines prescribed for process descriptions in ISO/IEC TR 24774 [30]. The PMO ontology is defined via the concepts and roles that describe the process in terms of objective evidence that prove process performance in an organisation.

A key concept of the ontology is Process that is defined through its intended purpose and evidenced by the achievement of the process outcomes. Process

[5] http://aligned-project.eu.

outcomes are sufficient and necessary conditions to achieve the software purpose. To achieve the ProcessOutcomes, Practices (i.e., base and generic) are performed to produce WorkProducts. WorkProducts are also inputs to the Practices that are used to achieve the ProcessOutcomes. WorkProducts are used to prove that the practices are being implemented and ProcessOutcomes are being achieved. For instance, in our running example, the SRS a type of work product can be used to prove that the software requirements analysis process was carried out. The ontology is further augmented with DL axioms to constrain the class behaviours and the instances that can be admitted by the ontology.

3.2 Representing Standard Requirements as DL Axioms

Generally standards can be considered as a set of requirements (rules) prescribing what should be done in order to achieve the process outcomes [31]. ISO/IEC 33002 constrains processes in a PRM to be defined in terms of purpose and outcomes. Where a set of process outcomes is necessary and sufficient to achieve the process purpose. In order to achieve the process outcomes, ISO/IEC 15504-5 [22] specifies base practices to be implemented with work products providing evidence that the base practices are being performed and the outcomes are being achieved. Where as conformance assessment may utilize the PRM in evaluating the achievement of process outcomes [10], there is no guarantee that individual process outcomes are being achieved. To overcome this situation, we extract the process requirements from the standard documents in form of *if...then* statements made up of three major components; practices, work products and process outcomes that are translated into DL axioms. These constitute statements such as; *If a given base practice is implemented and evidenced by a work product then a related process outcome should be achieved.* These are illustrated with a set of SRA process outcomes, practices and work products identified in Sect. 2 we slightly adapt the outcome numbering from ISO/IEC 15504-5 to PO1..., for uniformity through out the example illustrations in this paper.

1. If `SRA` has software requirements that are specified in a `SRS`, then outcome `PO1` is achieved

$$SRA \sqcap \forall hasSR.(\exists specifiedIn.SRS) \sqsubseteq achieve.\{PO1\} \tag{1}$$

2. If `SRA` has `TestingCriteria` for software requirements that is developed and recorded in an `AnalysisReport`, then outcome `PO2` is achieved

$$SRA \sqcap \forall hasSR.((\forall hasTestingCriteria.Developed) \sqcap \exists recordedIn.AnalysisReport) \sqsubseteq achieve.\{PO2\} \tag{2}$$

3. If `SRA` has the impact of software requirements on the operating environment that is determined and recorded in analysis report, then outcome `PO3` is achieved

$$SRA \sqcap \forall hasSR.((\forall hasImpact.Determined) \sqcap \exists recordedIn.AnalysisReport) \sqsubseteq achieve.\{PO3\} \tag{3}$$

4. If SRA has consistency of system requirements (SSR) to software requirements that is ensured and recorded in a traceability record, then outcome PO4 is achieved

$$SRA \sqcap \forall hasSR.((\exists consistencyEnsuredBetween.SSR) \sqcap \exists recordedIn.AnalysisReport) \sqsubseteq achieve.\{PO4\} \quad (4)$$

5. If SRA has software requirements that are prioritised and documented in SRS, then outcome PO5 is achieved

$$SRA \sqcap \forall hasSR.(\exists prioritisedIn.SRS) \sqsubseteq achieve.\{PO5\} \quad (5)$$

6. If SRA has software requirements that are evaluated and approved by the customer and updated in SRS, then outcome PO6 is achieved

$$SRA \sqcap \forall hasSR.(\exists evaluatedWith.Customer \sqcap \exists updatedIn.SRS) \sqcap \exists recordedIn.AnalysisReport \sqsubseteq achieve.\{PO6\} \quad (6)$$

7. If SRA has changes to the requirements that are evaluated for cost, schedule and technical impact and recorded in change control record and analysis report, then outcome PO7 is achieved

$$SRA \sqcap \forall hasSR.(\forall hasChange.Evaluated \sqcap \exists recordedIn.(ChangeControl \sqcap AnalysisReport) \sqsubseteq achieve.\{PO7\} \quad (7)$$

8. If SRA has software requirements that are communicated to all parties who will use them and recorded in a communication record, then outcome PO8 is achieved.

$$SRA \sqcap \forall hasSR.(\exists communicated \sqcap recordedIn.CommunicationRecord) \sqsubseteq achieve.\{PO8\} \quad (8)$$

To determine the extent to which the process outcomes are achieved, we follow the process rating scheme from ISO/IEC 33020 as shown in Table 3. Since SRA process has eight process outcomes, we base our rating scheme on the achievement of these outcomes as shown in DL axioms (9)–(13). Given a SRA process if two but less than four Process Outcomes are achieved this will be ranked as the process not being achieved.

$$NotAchieved \equiv SRA \sqcap (\geqslant 2 \sqcap < 4) achieve.ProcessOutcomes \quad (9)$$

Given a SRA process if four but less than six process outcomes are achieved, then the process will be ranked as partially achieving its purpose.

$$PartiallyAchieved \equiv SRA \sqcap (\geqslant 4 \sqcap < 6) achieve.ProcessOutcomes \quad (10)$$

Given a SRA process if six but less than eight process outcomes are achieved, then the process will be ranked as largely achieving its purpose.

$$LargelyAchieved \equiv SRA \sqcap (\geqslant 6 \sqcap < 8) achieve.ProcessOutcomes \quad (11)$$

Given a SRA process and it achieves all its eight process outcomes, then the process will be ranked as fully achieving its purpose.

$$FullyAchieved \equiv SRA \sqcap (\geqslant 8)achieve.ProcessOutcomes \tag{12}$$

Achieving process outcomes to the level of largely or fully achieved status, helps to build process performance attribute (PA1.1) that forms capability level one of the assessed process.

$$CapabilityLevelOne \equiv \exists hasProcessAttribute \cdot (PA1.1 \sqcap hasRating \cdot (LargelyAchieved \sqcup FullyAchieved)) \tag{13}$$

3.3 DL ABox Construction (Moodle SRA Process Instance)

As an implementation process instance, we adapt and give a detailed analysis and verification of the moodle e-learning system software requirements analysis process suggested in [32]. In this case study, we only highlight and summarise activities related to SRA process in Table 4, for other software implementation processes, interested readers can refer to [32]. In a moodle SRA process, a moodle community starts by communicating with the core team for performing a *feature voting activity*. The features could be about functional requirements (*req1*) or performance requirements (*req2*). In Moodle, there are four activities to be executed in order to vote and select a feature and develop a requirement specification for the selected feature(s). They are *feature voting activity, road map development, developing the requirements specifications* and *suggestions, discussions and agreements about the requirements specification.* At each end of a successful execution of these activities, a work product is produced. For example the *roadmap list* is developed after successful completion of voting process for selecting and prioritizing the features with the highest number of votes. The roadmap is used to guide the implementation of selected features. In Moodle, *software requirements specification (SRS) documents* are to be created for each of the feature added to the roadmap. The final work product in moodle SRA process are the suggestions and discussion on the *SRS* document that the entire community provides and agrees to, based on the specification released earlier. Due to space constraints, we only provide summarised process evidence for the first two TBox axioms (1–2) in form of DL ABox identified during Moodle development process in Table 6. The ABox for the remaining TBox axioms (3–8) can be constructed in the same way.

3.4 Process Verification

During software process verification, the object that is checked and verified is the process instance against the standard process using objective evidence from the organisation that indeed shows the process was carried out by the organisation. A process instance (PI) is defined to be a singular instantiation of a process that is uniquely identifiable and about which information can be gathered in a

Table 4. Moodle SRA process terminology

Moodle concept	Abox concepts
Moodle software requirements analysis process	*mSRA*
Software requirements	*SR*
Moodle software requirements specification	*mSRS*
Requirement examples	*req1* and *req2*
Roadmap	*rm*
System requirements	*ssr*
Moddle community	*mc*
Open source forums such as blogs, email	*openforum*

Table 5. Moodle SRA process evidence

Process outcome	Moodle SRA process evidence
PO1	Moodle roadmap created
PO2	Feature voting process
PO3	Feature voting process
PO4	-
PO5	Moodle SRS created
PO6	Moodle SRS is discussed and agreed upon
PO7	Moodle SRS discussions and agreement
PO8	Requirements are communicated through open forums and road map

Table 6. Moodle process instance (Abox)

Instance	Relations	Process outcomes
SRA(*mSRA*)	hasSR(*mSRA, req1*)	achieve(*mSRA, P01*)
SR(*req1*)	hasSR(*mSRA, reg2*)	
SR(*req2*)	specifiedIn(*req1, mSRS*)	
SRS(*mSRS*)	specifiedIn(*req2, mSRS*)	
SRA(mSRA)	hasSR(mSRA, req1)	achieve(mSRA, P02)
SR(req1)	hasSR(mSRA, req2)	
SR(req2)	hasTestingCriteria(req1, tc1)	
Developed(tc1)	hasTestingCriteria(req2, tc2)	
Developed(tc2)	recordedIn(tc1,rm	
TestingCriteria(tc1)	recordedIn(tc2, rm)	
TestingCriteria(tc2)		
AnalysisReport(rm)		

repeatable manner [22]. In this case study, we take moodle SRA process as a process instance about which information has been gathered and summarised in a form of an ontology ABox in Table 6. From this example, we can use an ontology reasoner such as pellet to verify automatically if moodle process (ABox) is conformant to the SRA process represented in the TBox axioms (1)–(8). If the moodle process achieves the rating of largely or Fully achieved, then it can be ranked as a performed process (see axiom (13)). Process performance is the process attribute that helps to build capability level one of the assessed process [2]. Therefore moodle process achieves its purpose and is classified at capability level one see Fig. 2. An ABox inconsistency with the TBox axioms can vary the process ratings (DL Axioms 9–12) based on the process outcomes achieved. Based on the analysis results in Table 5, there was no moodle process evidence to support the achievement of SRA process outcome PO4, i.e., *consistency and traceability are established between software requirements and system requirements.* Given our rating scheme for process outcome achievement in axioms (9)–(12), moodle process SRA process is rated as largely achieved.

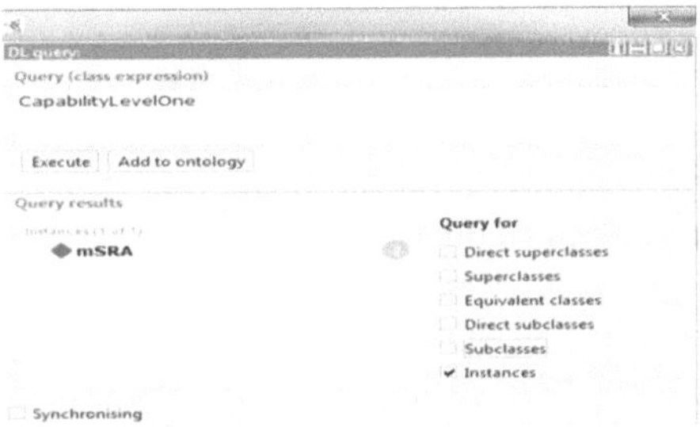

Fig. 2. Inferred mSRA process as an instance of CapabilityLevelOne

In order to test our process verification approach and the inferencing services offered by ontologies, we have implemented the ontology in Protege[6], a free open source editor for building and storing ontologies based on OWL standard. Protege integrates different reasoners such as pellet as well as different visualization schemes that we have used in our approach. DL facilitates different reasoning services both at the ontology and instance level. In our software process verification example, we used them both for consistency and process conformance checking via the DL query tab in protege see Fig. 2.

4 Conclusion and Future Works

In this paper, we proposed a formal approach to software process analysis and verification using Description logic based ontology. This paper is a significant

[6] https://protege.stanford.edu/.

extension to our previous works [20,21] by providing a more systematic, consistent and practical approach to translate software processes into DL ontology so that they can be formally reasoned and verified by using ontology reasoners, thereby automating the conformance approach through formal verification. We have represented software process standard requirements as DL axioms argumenting them with other process information in a PRM ontology (DL TBox). We also represented the moodle e-leaning system case study as a DL ABox specifying the evidence derived during moodle software development. Using ontology reasoners we are able to automatically perform confirmatory verification of process implementation (moodle case study) and establish that moodle case study is classified at capability level one. This means that the moodle process is able to achieve its process purpose through process outcome achievement. Ontology reasoners enable the process to be automated improving the efficiency, effectiveness and reduce on human errors in process assessments and improvement.

Future work includes extending the approach to the capability dimension of the PAM. We also intend to further evaluate the developed ontology using competency questions. These can be drawn from process assessment questionnaires and translated to SPARQL[7] queries to derive more information from the ontology. Automating the process parsing software process requirements from textual descriptions (natural language standards) into DL axioms is another area for future work. This is done manually at the moment and without a predefined approach. We could systematise it through the use of natural language process techniques. Secondly, we plan to develop a graphical user interface (GUI) to support users during process analysis and verification. This tool will be based on the features highlighted in [29]. The tool should integrate all the formal model definitions and verification steps proposed in this paper. We also intend to carry out more case studies in industry.

References

1. Kitson, D., Humphrey, W.S.: The role of assessment in software process improvement. Technical report CMU/SEI-89-TR-3, Software Engineering Institute (1989)
2. ISO/IEC FDIS 12207:2017 - Systems and software engineering - Software life cycle processes (2017)
3. ISO/IEC TR 29110-5-1-2:2011 - Software engineering Lifecycle profiles for VSEs: Management and engineering guide: Generic profile group: Basic profile (2011)
4. Wen, L., Tuffley, D., Rout, T.: Using composition trees to model and compare software process. In: O'Connor, R.V., Rout, T., McCaffery, F., Dorling, A. (eds.) SPICE 2011. CCIS, vol. 155, pp. 1–15. Springer, Heidelberg (2011). https://doi.org/10.1007/978-3-642-21233-8_1
5. Golra, F.R., Dagnat, F., Bendraou, R., Beugnard, A.: Continuous process compliance using model driven engineering. In: Ouhammou, Y., Ivanovic, M., Abelló, A., Bellatreche, L. (eds.) MEDI 2017. LNCS, vol. 10563, pp. 42–56. Springer, Cham (2017). https://doi.org/10.1007/978-3-319-66854-3_4

7 https://www.w3.org/TR/rdf-sparql-query/.

6. Boucher, Q., Perrouin, G., Deprez, J.-C., Heymans, P.: Towards configurable ISO/IEC 29110-compliant software development processes for very small entities. In: Winkler, D., O'Connor, R.V., Messnarz, R. (eds.) EuroSPI 2012. CCIS, vol. 301, pp. 169–180. Springer, Heidelberg (2012). https://doi.org/10.1007/978-3-642-31199-4_15
7. Emmerich, W., Finkelstein, A., Montangero, C., Antonelli, S., Armitage, S., Stevens, R.: Managing standards compliance. IEEE Trans. Softw. Eng. **25**(6), 836–851 (1999)
8. Rout, T.P., El Emam, K., Fusani, M., Goldenson, D., Jung, H.-W.: SPICE inretrospect: developing a standard for process assessment. J. Syst. Softw. **80**, 1483–1493 (2007)
9. ISO/IEC 17000: Conformity assessment Vocabulary and general principles. International Organization for Standardization, Geneva (2004)
10. Varkoi, T.: Process assessment in very small entities-an ISO/IEC 29110 based method. In: 7th International Conference QUATIC. IEEE (2010)
11. ISO/IEC JTC1/SC7 WG10: Transition from ISO/IEC 15504 to ISO/IEC 330xx, Working Document (2017)
12. Proença, D., Borbinha, J.: A formalization of the ISO/IEC 15504: enabling automatic inference of capability levels. In: Mas, A., Mesquida, A., O'Connor, R.V., Rout, T., Dorling, A. (eds.) SPICE 2017. CCIS, vol. 770, pp. 197–210. Springer, Cham (2017). https://doi.org/10.1007/978-3-319-67383-7_15
13. Wen, L., Rout, T.: Using composition trees to validate an entry profile of software engineering lifecycle profiles for very small entities (VSEs). In: Mas, A., Mesquida, A., Rout, T., O'Connor, R.V., Dorling, A. (eds.) SPICE 2012. CCIS, vol. 290, pp. 38–50. Springer, Heidelberg (2012). https://doi.org/10.1007/978-3-642-30439-2_4
14. Thaddeus, S., Kasmir Raja, K.: Ontology for software Engineering Process Automation (2006). Accessed http://www.researchgate.net/publication/278241783
15. Castellanos Ardila, J.P., Gallina, B.: Towards increased efficiency and confidence in process compliance. In: Stolfa, J., Stolfa, S., O'Connor, R.V., Messnarz, R. (eds.) EuroSPI 2017. CCIS, vol. 748, pp. 162–174. Springer, Cham (2017). https://doi.org/10.1007/978-3-319-64218-5_13
16. Baader, F., Calvanese, D., McGuinness, D., Nardi, D., Patel-Schneider, P.F. (eds.): The Description Logic Handbook: Theory, Implementation and Applications. Cambridge University Press, Cambridge (2003)
17. Wang, S., Jin, L., Jin, C.: Represent software process engneering metamodel in description logic. In: Proceedings of World Academy of Science, Engineering and Technology, vol. 11 (2006). ISSN 1307–6884
18. Diebold, P., Scherr, S.: Software process models vs. descriptions: what do practitioners use and need? J. Softw. Maint. Evol. Res. Pract. **29**, e1479 (2017)
19. Morales-Trujillo, M., Oktaba, H., Hernandedez-Quiroz, F., Escalante-Ramirez, B.: Towards a formalisation of a framework to express and reason about software engineering methods. Comput. Inform. **37**(1), 109–141 (2018)
20. Kabaale, E., Wen, L., Wang, Z., Rout, T.: Representing software process in description logics: an ontology approach for software process reasoning and verification. In: Clarke, P.M., O'Connor, R.V., Rout, T., Dorling, A. (eds.) SPICE 2016. CCIS, vol. 609, pp. 362–376. Springer, Cham (2016). https://doi.org/10.1007/978-3-319-38980-6_26

21. Kabaale, E., Wen, L., Wang, Z., Rout, T.: An axiom based metamodel for software process formalisation: an ontology approach. In: Mas, A., Mesquida, A., O'Connor, R.V., Rout, T., Dorling, A. (eds.) SPICE 2017. CCIS, vol. 770, pp. 226–240. Springer, Cham (2017). https://doi.org/10.1007/978-3-319-67383-7_17
22. ISO/IEC 15504–5:2012 - Information technology - Process assessment An exemplar Process Assessment Model, International Organization for Standardization and International Electrotechnical Commission Std. (2012)
23. ISO/IEC DIS 33020 - Information technology Process assessment Process measurement framework for assessment of proecess capability (2013)
24. Jung, H.W.: Investigating measurement scales and aggregation methods in SPICE assessment method. Inf. Softw. Technol. **55**(8), 1450–1461 (2013)
25. Guarino, N.: Formal ontology in information systems. In: Proceedings of FOIS98, Trento, Italy. IOS Press, Amsterdam (1998)
26. Motik, B., Horrocks, I., Sattler, U.: Bridging the gap between OWL and relational databases. In: WWW 2007 (2007)
27. Pellet: OWL 2 Reasoner for Java. http://clarkparsia.com/pellet/
28. Gonzalez-Perez, C., Henderson-Sellers, B., McBride, T., Low, G.C., Larrucea, X.: An ontology for ISO software engineering standards 2) proof of concept and application. Comput. Stand. Interfaces **48**, 112–123 (2016)
29. Tarhan, A., Giray, G.: On the use of ontologies in software process assessment: a systematic literature review. In: EASE (2017)
30. ISO/IEC TR 24774 - Software and systems engineering - Life cycle management - Guidelines for process description (2007)
31. Nash, E., Wiebensohn, J., Nikkil, R., Vatsanidou, A., Fountas, S., Bill, R.: Towards automated compliance checking based on a formal representation of agricultural production standards. Comput. Electron. Agric. **78**, 28–37 (2011)
32. Krishnamurthy, A., O'Connor, R.V.: Using ISO/IEC 12207 to analyze open source software development processes: an e-learning case study. In: Woronowicz, T., Rout, T., O'Connor, R.V., Dorling, A. (eds.) SPICE 2013. CCIS, vol. 349, pp. 107–119. Springer, Heidelberg (2013). https://doi.org/10.1007/978-3-642-38833-0_10

Specification and Deployment of a Semantic Database for System Configuration Management

Ricardo Eito-Brun(✉)

Universidad Carlos III de Madrid, c/Madrid 124, 28903 Getafe, Madrid, Spain
reito@bib.uc3m.es

Abstract. During the system lifecycle, the evolution of the configuration of the different system components must be recorded, and their coherence and consistency must be kept and reported. In the case of complex systems whose components are built by different companies, configuration data integration becomes complex due to the lack of well-defined industrial standards and tools.

This paper reports a case study conducted on a company working on the aerospace sector. A solution based on semantic web technologies and standards was developed for managing system configurations, support CM reporting and auditing. The proposed solution is based on the definition of an ontology using as a basis the European Space Agency CM standards for systems engineering. The proposed solution provides the flexibility needed to accommodate additional customer specific requirements on CM and reporting. It also facilitates report generation and data exchange between different companies participating in the development of system's components.

Keywords: Configuration management · Ontologies · Configuration reporting Information management · System engineering · RDF

1 Introduction

Configuration management (CM) is a critical process in system engineering. In complex engineering projects, strict control procedures are needed on the different items that constitute the hierarchical arrangement of the system's components and subcomponents. Several international standards define the rules for the CM process that includes the identification of configuration items, both HW and SW, change control, configuration reporting and auditing [1].

INCOSE Systems Engineering Handbook [2] defines Configuration Management as "the discipline of identifying and formalizing the functional and physical characteristics of a configuration item at discrete points in the product evolution for the purpose of maintaining the integrity of the product system and controlling changes to the baseline." The baseline, a key concept on CM, refers to the set of requirements, both technical and managerial, that are sufficiently mature to be accepted and that are placed under change control by the project. The definition of clear baselines is a must

I. Stamelos et al. (Eds.): SPICE 2018, CCIS 918, pp. 263–271, 2018.
https://doi.org/10.1007/978-3-030-00623-5_18

have for the development of any system and software engineering activities due to several reasons:

- Baselines must be defined and agreed between the involved parties, as they represent the target requirements and specifications to be implemented and validated in the final product or service.
- The evolution of the baselines must be managed to ensure that any change request is properly recorded, analyzed and that an informed decision is taken on its implementation. Baseline evolution and changes must be subject of impact analysis studies to ensure that the project costs are properly estimated and avoid regression issues.

The CM process involves four main activities:

- Identification of the configuration items, components and work products that compose the baselines at different points in time.
- Control of the changes requested and implemented in the configuration items maintaining the integrity of baselines.
- Reporting the configuration status data to all the parties involved in the project: design and manufacturing engineers, support staff, end-users, customers, etc.
- Auditing the configuration management process and the product, to ensure that the delivered product is compliant with the reported configuration. Configuration audits involve (a) verifying that the delivered product meets the functional and non-functional requirements stated in the applicable baseline, and (b) verifying that the product is built on the set of components that are agreed and that are reported in the product configuration. The terms "functional configuration audit" and "physical configuration audit" are used to refer to these two types of configuration checks. They are a means to ensure the consistency between the proposed and the actual configuration, and to assure the integrity of the product with respect to its written specifications.

In systems engineering projects, CM process start at the early beginning, with the identification of the system components and its subsequent subdivision into subcomponents (List of Configuration Items); At the design phase, the initial structure is refined and specified with the definition of the Configuration Item Data List (CIDL); This configuration evolves until the final construction and validation of the systems, referred to as As built configuration (ABCL). At the operation and maintenance phases, any change in the system configuration must be properly recorded and managed to ensure the integrity and the safety characteristics of the system.

This evolution is common to different industrial sectors. As this study is focused on the CM requirements in the Aerospace industry, the European Space Agency (ESA) standards, European Cooperation for Space Standardization (ECSS) have been used as a reference to develop our case study.

ECSS standards include a specific standard for configuration and information management: ECSS-M-ST-40C Rev. 1. (9 March 2009) [3]. This standard defines CM as "the process for establishing and maintaining a consistent record of a product's functional and physical characteristics compared to its design and operational requirements.", and indicates that CM must be applied throughout the entire life cycle of the product. The specific objectives of CM declared in this standard refer to the need of knowing at any time the technical description of the product, recording its evolution by keeping traceability data, ensuring the consistency of the interfaces, providing an accurate representation of the products it describes, identifying the current configuration baseline, and reporting any discrepancy detected during its production and the product known limitations.

To achieve these objectives, the CM standard not only defines a set of process requirements that companies must fulfill. It also defines a set of CM work products or reports that describe the current configuration of the product at different stages during its development. ECSS-M-ST-40C establishes these work products in a set of Document Requirements Definitions (DRDs) that are published as annexes to the standard..

2 Configuration Data Management. The Requirements

The main DRDs in the ECSS-M-ST-40C standards aimed to report the product configuration are the following ones:

- Configuration Item List
- Configuration Item Data List (CIDL)
- As-built Configuration List (ABCL)
- Software Configuration Files (SCF)
- Configuration Status Accounting Report (CSAR)

These work products respond to different needs during the system engineering life cycle.

The aim of the Configuration Item List is "to provide a reporting instrument defining the programme or project items subject to configuration management process."; this document shall contain, for each configuration item, data regarding its identification (derived from the product item code), models, name, category (developed or non-developed), supplier and applicable specification.

On the other hand, the CIDL "is generated from the central database giving the current design status of a configuration item (CI) at any point of time". The CIDL must incorporate - for each CI – its related documentation and data items, including: references to customer specifications and interfaces, design documentation (verification plans, special instructions or procedures for transportation, integration, and handling. lower level specifications, drawings, test specifications and procedures, user manuals), as well as the list of changes not incorporated yet into the baseline and the planned or existing deviations with their status.

ABCL is another relevant CM work product that reports "the as-built status per each serial number of configuration item subject to formal acceptance". Data to be collected in the ABCL include the breakdown obtained from the equivalent section in the CIDL completed with the information specific to each manufactured recurrent unit: (a) serial number, (b) lot or batch identification and (c) references to problem reports and related waivers. The ABCL must also report all the discrepancies between the product design (as-designed configuration reported in the CIDL) and the configuration of the final, manufactured product.

The other work products cited in the list above are the SCF and the CSAR. The SCF reports the configuration of software-specific products, and includes: (a) documents applicable to the delivered software version, (b) the list of all the files making up the software (source, binary data and configuration files), (c) other items needed to develop, modify, generate and run the software, (d) installation instructions and (e) changes and known problems.

The CSAR on the other hand provides a snapshot generated at a given time with the status of all the documents that are part of the product configuration. It incorporates data about the documents and drawings and their status, RFDs and RFWs, change proposals and Review item discrepancies (RID).

Additional document types are defined as part of the standard DRDs for other data items that affect the evolution of the product configuration. These document types include the (a) change requests and change proposals, and (b) request for deviations (RFDs) and request for waivers (RFWs). In the case of these two documents, both of them inform about deviations or departures with respect to the approved requirements in the product baseline, being the difference that the RFDs inform of an anticipated, planned departure, and the RFWs inform about an actual departure that exists in the product being delivered. The standard also requests the preparation of a Configuration Management Plan, and establishes an exchange data package for reporting the configuration of the product in XML format (this is the Technical Data Package description in the annex L of the ECSS standard).

All these DRDs respond to the different CM requirements exposed in the ECSS standard. An analysis of CM requested documentation and work products permit the identification of the data to be recorded and maintained during the product life cycle. The DRDs provides guidelines on the management and maintenance of a complex set of related data about product requirements and product characteristics. But CM processes and work products cannot be understood in isolation from other engineering activities. For example, the identification of the configuration items that is done with the creation of the Configuration Item List must consider the product structure defined in the Product Tree, a document type that is defined in the annex B of the ECSS standard with code ECSS-M-ST-10C Rev. 1, dedicated to Project Planning and Implementation. Other processes that use the data identified during the CM activities are those related to Integrated Logistic Support (ILS) activities. These activities must collect additional data for the items that constitute the physical configuration of the product. ILS documents and data closely related to CM work products include the inventory lists, that provide a list of all the procured items and components that will be used to build the product, and the obsolescence data report that informs about planned discontinuities on the manufacturing process of procured components, potential alternatives, announced end-of-life, etc.

3 Configuration Data Management. The Challenge

Configuration data management may be complex, in particular in the case of small entities not having at their disposal specific software-based solutions built to manage these processes. Even in those cases in which specific tools are in place, different issues may be observed:

- Different Client companies may impose different requirements regarding CM reporting.
- Tools using rigid, relational-based structures may impose constraints on the capability of relating CM data with data and information entities related to different processes, like project management or ILS.
- CM processes require keeping a live link between configuration items, documents and records.

In a typical scenario, companies are using different software-based solutions for keeping all the data items and informational entities that are handled in the configuration activities. The most frequent problem arises with the document management tools used to keep document data. As previously indicated, CM reports require the explicit management of the relationships between configuration items and their related documentation. At the design level, the identified set of configuration items that compose the product must be related to their specifications, design documents, operation and user guides, etc. As the project evolves and items are procured, additional documents are collected and generated, and must be linked to the procured components, e.g., declarations of compliance, RFWs, problem reports, etc.

The standard functionalities provided by document management systems makes difficult to handle these links and relationships. Document management tools are not well-suited to handle hierarchical metadata schemas and non-documentary entities (like the Configuration Items that make up the product tree). Document management tools demonstrate a good performance managing metadata and properties linked to documents, but they have some limitations when managing metadata for entities that do not correspond to documents.

The development of custom software solutions to support configuration management using a relational database may become difficult, as the design of a data model may fail to predict the identification of all the relationships between data items that may be needed to support the engineering and managerial processes around Configuration Items: ILS, engineering, quality, inspections, etc. The development of a custom tool should also consider the need of exchanging data with other potentially existing tools used for document, inventory or requirements management. The availability of these tools, serving different purposes and used to handle partial sets of data consumed by the CM processes makes the development of custom-solutions complex.

CM data management challenges may be summarized as follows:

- Information about different entities must be recorded, being difficult to define a frozen schema of properties and metadata, as different standards require different metadata.

- The CM processes need to handle data for entities that are also used in other engineering processes, like Quality Assurance or ILS. Due to that, may be necessary to link data properties to entities and configuration items beyond those initially requested by the CM standards.
- Configuration items are grouped and nested together building different configurations. Higher level configuration items are made up of lower-level configuration items, and the final product configuration results of complex hierarchical arrangements of existing items, both developed and procured. CM data management must provide an efficient method to support the aggregation of configuration items into larger components.
- Metadata must be collected and managed for documents containing the information related to configuration items, and the links between documents, documents grouped into baselines and individual configuration items must be kept.
- Metadata about documents, developed items, procured items (including Commercial Off-The Self – COTS – or open source) may be spread into separate, heterogeneous applications, and must be harvested and reconciled to provide an accurate view of the product configuration and related data.
- As the product life cycle evolves at different stages (design, production, etc.), additional relationships must be managed to keep these snapshots. This also affects the maintenance and operations period, where changes in the initial as-built configuration must be recorded into logbooks describing the different interventions completed by the operation/maintenance staff, their rational, items replacements, execution of tests, etc.

All these challenges may be summarized into two core requirements: a configuration data management solution should support the easy aggregation of new data for new items incorporated into the inventory process, and the addition of relationships between all the represented items (configuration items, documents, deviations, waivers, requirements, etc.).

At the same time, the configuration data management solution should provide mechanisms to avoid data integrity problems, to name a few:

- having the components with the same serial number deployed into different higher level recurrent units,
- having as-built configurations that go against the declared as design configuration without an approved RFD deviation, or
- having RFWs not linked to any nonconformity report.

4 Proposed Solution Based on Semantic Technologies

To support the management of CM data, a solution has been designed based on semantic web technologies and standards. In particular, an ontology has been designed using the RDF/OWL modeling language and a repository was fed with sample data from two real aerospace projects.

The ontology has been modeled with the TopBraid software tool, also used to build the initial testing data set. The purpose of the implementation was to assess the feasibility of using these technologies to streamline the management of CM related data, including both the inventory of hardware components and software COTS, and their aggregation into higher-level configuration items. The analysis of the standards and the interaction with two experienced CM managers led to the definition of a set of competence questions that the ontology was expected to answer [4, 5]. This allowed the initial identification of the main classes, properties and relationships.

The ontology schema included classes for the following items:

- Configuration Item (CI), further divided into two subclasses for HW CIs SW CIs. SWCI class was also divided into different subclasses to distinguish between reused items, both commercial (SW-COST) and open source, and developed items.
- Properties were defined and allocated to classes by means of their domain and range. The definition of the properties included those needed to keep information about different aspects of both the configuration items and recurrent units, like: item number, identifiers and description, quantities, part and serial numbers, model, manufacturer type code, acquisition and replacement values, date of entry into the inventory, date of purchase or production, estimated cost of dismantling the asset, status (in progress, accepted by the Contracting Authority, rejected,…), life duration in months, custodian, contract number, related WBS Code, current and planned physical location, method of disposal clearances with regard to international security regulations, etc.
  - In the case of SWCIs, requirements derived to the need of maintaining data about the software licenses (commercial, open source, etc.), and their validity or expiry periods were also considered.
  - Properties were also applied to keep the relationships between the different individuals of the classes.
  - Properties reflected the fact that higher level CIs are the result of aggregating several lower-level CIs in the Product Tree (is_part_of and the inverse property is_composed_of).
  - Other properties were used to indicate that a specific item is a recurrent element of a specific CI type, for example, the hard disk with serial number "PHD531O0I0" is a recurrent unit of the model with part number "652605-B21".

Additional properties were declared to establish relationships between work packages in the project work breakdown structure (WBS) and the items (recurrent units) recorded in the inventory, or to establish a relationship between configuration items and recurrent units with documents, problems or waivers. The allocation of SWCIs to HWCIs was also supported with additional properties (is_deployed_at and deploys).

The proposed ontology does not try to model the different configuration management documents defined in the standards used as a reference. Instead of that, the purpose of the ontology is to allow the capture of all the configuration management data that are requested in the ECSS standard. The DRD in the ECSS standards were analyzed to identify specific data requirements to be supported by the ontology and the outputs that should be obtained via SPARQL queries for the generation of the requested reports.

One of the characteristics of the proposed solution is that data maintenance is not constrained by a restricted data model. This means that data can be easily uploaded for the different items by adding triples to the data set. Data about the different individuals can be completed at a later stage, as data are provisioned and collected. For example, if one data about a recurrent hardware unit is missing at a given time, it can be easily reported later just by adding a new triple to the repository. In a similar way, in case it is necessary to record or update a relationship between items (for example when replacing a HWCI from a higher-level CI with a new one), it is just necessary to tag the existing triple as obsolete and add a new one. For those relationships between items that are subject of having validity periods, additional classes were created to keep track of these relationships and add starting and ending time tags for the relations. This happened with the information about the as-built configuration of HW items, where some HWCIs may be replaced at a given time with a different unit in response to faults or following the recommendations of the obsolescence plan. The proposed model also provided the flexibility needed to relate the different identifiers used for items in the CM processes. For example, the standards refer to different identifiers for inventory items, CIs, or logistic data items, being possible to have different IDs for the same unit or item. In these cases, the possibility of indicating that an individual is the same as another provides an easy way to get all the related data together.

For validating the proposed solution two tasks were completed using real configuration data from two different projects. First of all, the existing documents (CIDL, ABCL, inventory list and logistic data) were processed to generate a set of triples according to the proposed schema. The incorporation of these data led to some minor adjustment in the proposed schema of properties and classes. Later on, a set of SPARQL queries were defined to extract data from the triple store. These queries were also defined by analyzing the reporting requirements stated in the set of CM documents.

5 Conclusions

As main conclusions of this study, it may be stated that:

- The approach based on the maintenance of data using semantic web standards for data modeling frees the people working on CM data maintenance of the constraints related to the use of predefined, restricted databases.
- The solution avoids the complexity of building specific applications and complex interfaces with other tools used to manage project data (e.g. work packages) and documents. For example, document metadata can be easily exported from a document management tool and incorporated into the semantic data set, and later related to the CIs by adding a new triple.
- For end-users keeping the configuration management data, they just need to be provided with a view of the schema (classes, properties) and a simple interface to define the triples that will be later translated into RDF/OWL statements and

uploaded into the data set. The use of the identifiers they are used to apply (for example the serial numbers for the recurrent units or the part numbers for the models) as the distinctive part of the URIs for each individual, reduce to a great extent the potential complexity of the proposed approach. This also helps avoid potential mistakes when registering the data, for example, by alerting to the user when he is trying to upload one statement for an item not previously registered in the data set.

- Perhaps one of the most challenging difficulties was the extraction of the data from the data set in the layout requested by the ECSS DRDs. At this point, the flexibility of the SPARQL language and the possibility of running different searches to gather data in tabular format provided an adequate solution. After a quick introduction to SPARQL, CM staff acquired the necessary competences to build predefined queries for solving data reporting requirements.

References

1. Thayer, R.H.: Glossary software engineering. IEEE Softw. **20**(4), 97-93 (2003). https://doi.org/10.1109/ms.2003.1207487
2. INCOSE: Systems Engineering Handbook: A Guide for System Life Cycle Processes and Activities, 4th edn. 304 p. (2015). ISBN: 978-1-118-99940-0
3. ESA: ECSS-M-ST-40C Rev. 1. Space Project Management. Configuration and Information Management. ESA-ESTEC. ECSS Secretariat (2009)
4. Corcho, O., Fernández-López, M., Gómez-Pérez, A., López-Cima, A.: Building legal ontologies with METHONTOLOGY and WebODE. In: Benjamins, V.R., Casanovas, P., Breuker, J., Gangemi, A. (eds.) Law and the Semantic Web. LNCS (LNAI), vol. 3369, pp. 142–157. Springer, Heidelberg (2005). https://doi.org/10.1007/978-3-540-32253-5_9
5. Park, J., Sung, K., Moon, S.: Developing graduation screen ontology based on the METHONTOLOGY approach. In: Fourth International Conference on Networked Computing and Advanced Information Management NCM 2008 (2008)

SPI and Agile

Adopting Agile in the Sports Domain: A Phased Approach

Jennifer Callan-Crilly[1(✉)], Alan Moynagh[1], Özden Özcan-Top[1], and Fergal McCaffery[1,2]

[1] RSRC and Lero, Dundalk Institute of Technology, Dublin Road, Dundalk, Ireland
{jennifer.callancrilly, alan.moynagh, ozden.ozcantop, fergal.mccaffery}@dkit.ie
[2] STATSports Group, Newry, Ireland

Abstract. Sports Science is a new and evolving industry. There is a great potential in this domain which will be realised by capturing and analysing the performance data of the elite athletes and displaying all relevant information to them for better decision making and performance improvement. Establishing reliable systems to achieve performance monitoring in the sports science domain require hardware sensors, firmware and software algorithms work coherently. Such complex systems having also cyber-physical characteristics would bring their own challenges. In this paper, first we present the challenges related with the domain and the development environment based on our experiences in the STATSports Company. Then, we discuss how we adopted agile software development practices to overcome these challenges in a phased approach.

Keywords: Sports science · Agile software development · Agile adoption Scrum · Distributed teams · Feature Driven Development · GPS tracking

1 Introduction

Software engineering is different than the other engineering disciplines due to its essential and accidental difficulties [1]. The Agile Manifesto [2] has been established with a set of values and principles in 2001 by a group of software engineers in search of a better approach to software development. Agile software development (ASD) methods focus on customer satisfaction by offering continuous delivery of quality software at time-boxed intervals. They promote communication and collaboration between the development team and all stakeholders throughout the life of the project. ASD welcomes change during the development with implementation of specific practices such as product backlog grooming, sprint planning, face-to-face communication, automated testing, continuous integration etc. Reviews of the process at the end of each short cycle allow the team and stakeholders to continuously refine and improve their product and process [2].

Due to these benefits observed in the field [3, 4, 5], we aimed to adopt agile software development practices in the STATSports company, performing at the elite athletes domain to monitor performance data of the athletes and presenting analysed performance information. Sport Scientists use this information to monitor fatigue

I. Stamelos et al. (Eds.): SPICE 2018, CCIS 918, pp. 275–288, 2018.
https://doi.org/10.1007/978-3-030-00623-5_19

levels, appraise performance and assess injury risk. The detailed level of the data collected means that it can be classed as medical data and additional processes are needed to offer adequate data protection and ensure safety. The major reasons for agile adoption in the company are to improve communication between distributed development teams, produce quality software, promote customer involvement, offer stakeholders transparency throughout the development process, improve delivery of new software, increase data security and ensure traceability from design to release. The purpose of this paper is to present the domain and development related challenges and describe how we improved the development environment by adopting the agile software development practices.

The remainder of the paper is structured as follows: In Sect. 2, we present the background which includes a brief literature review on agile software development and the characteristics of the sports science domain. In Sect. 3, we present the challenges specific to the STATSports company which were identified with MDevSPICE® based process assessment. In Sect. 4, we provide the solutions developed for the organization which were adapted using a phased approach. Finally, In Sect. 5, we conclude and present the future work.

2 Background

In this section we provide a brief background on agile software development and the characteristics of the organization that we have performed the agile adoption.

Agile Software Development

Agile software development methods are designed around four core values; *Individuals and Interactions over processes and tools, Working software over comprehensive documentation, Customer collaboration over contract negotiation and Responding to change over following a plan* [2]. While all of the above is valued within the agile process, it is the factors listed first which are considered most important [2]. These core values have been incorporated in a number of agile approaches which are widely used in software development. Crystal Methodologies [6], Dynamic Systems Development Method (DSDM) [7, 8], Feature Driven Development (FDD) [9], Extreme Programming (XP) [10] and Scrum [11, 12] are among the most common approaches and are implemented across a number of different industries and domains [4, 5]. We focused on these five ASD Methods when assessing a best fit model for STATSports.

Agile Software Development promotes regular intense communication throughout the Software Development Life Cycle (SDLC), this offers transparency to all stakeholders and allows for more accurate risk assessment as the project progresses [13]. The small timeboxed iterations or sprints used in the agile process mean that after a short time working software is produced and validation and verification are carried out frequently. This process improves the quality of the code produced by reducing bugs and ensures the system is delivered as expected by the customer. Agile practices also reduce the maintenance effort after product release [1, 2]. The Agile approach chosen greatly depends on the environment in which the software is to be developed, a detailed look at the characteristics of the project is needed to determine a suitable approach [14, 15].

Although there are large number of studies in the literature regarding agile development methods in various domains, we were unable to find any publications relating directly to the very new Sports Science domain. To get an understanding of the challenges and successful application of agile development methods in the Sport Science domain, we examined publications relating to safety critical domain and mobile medical device software as they would be subject to similarly restrictive regulations which maybe challenging to implement within an agile development lifecycle. Research suggests that it is entirely possibly to implement agile practices within safety critical domain as many of the iterative practices offer repeated opportunities for risk assessment, verification and validation [4, 5, 16, 17].

Characteristics of the Organization and the Projects
STATSports was founded in 2007 and launched its first product, a performance tracking device for elite sports clubs. GPS Tracking along with other instruments provided by the device allow the tracking of movement for a given player. The product consists of three components, hardware, firmware and software. The first product of the company had been very successful but rapid advances in sports science meant that the company needed to evolve to offer the most up to date analysis information to its clients. STATSports' new product, is designed to produce more detailed data and will calculate additional metrics offering a better experience with its superior real time functionality.

The field of Sport Science involves the study of physiology, psychology, anatomy, biomechanics, biochemistry and bio kinetics. Physics theories are applied to the movement of the body which is captured by a number of small highly sensitive sensors imbedded in the device. The Software is developed to extract data from the sensors, it is then passed through a calculation engine where algorithms produce metrics and statistics. These can then be viewed through the software for individuals and on a team level.

The data produced by the device and software is considered highly sensitive performance information data or Electronic Personal Health Information (ePHI), strict data security requirements have been specified to ensure compliance with the General Data Protection Regulations (GDPR) which come into effect in May 2018 [18]. The company is also striving to obtain HIPAA compliance (The Health Insurance Portability and Accountability Act of 1996). On obtaining HIPAA compliance, the device will be counted among a small group of non-medical devices worldwide which adhere to these data security standards [19].

3 Challenges

The product consists of hardware, firmware and software components, all three of which are developed in different locations; hardware component is developed in the Republic of Ireland, the firmware team is located in Romania and the software team is based in Northern Ireland. Dependency between the three components is incredibly high and a lack of process across all departments caused many road blocks and delays. We assessed the challenges of the project under two categories; Development Challenges and Domain Challenges. The development challenges were specified based on an MDevSPICE® assessment which took five business days, performed by two assessors. MDevSPICE® is a process capability assessment model for medical device software process assessment [20].

Development Challenges

- There was no single point of contact for gathering new requirements/requirement changes in the organization. The organization's Sport Scientists were directly contacting developers and demanding features to be developed. This resulted in developers' receiving different tasks from multiple sources and it was difficult to understand which new features should be prioritized.
- Software, hardware and firmware departments demonstrated an Ad-Hoc approach to development, developing features as they were suggested by various stakeholders. A major challenge was that new requirements and features were constantly introduced throughout development.
- The organization operates in a hardware led software development environment yet no documentation relating to design decisions existed within the hardware department.
- The firmware team who develop embedded software for the organizations' products produced infrequent emails regarding changes made in new firmware versions. Small adaptations in firmware could completely change the way the software communicated with the device causing existing software to stop working and unnecessary hours of debugging by the software team to determine the cause.
- There was no shared code repository meant that each team was looking at their piece of the product in isolation.
- There was no formal traceability from system requirements to the testing and release phases.
- Poor communication between the distributed departments meant they followed separate Ad-Hoc development plans which led to development being out of sync.
- The software development team adopted a "Code and Fix" approach to development to ensure software delivery and responded to all requests without evaluating hardware and firmware requirements.
- Manual builds, poor code repository management and a lack of versioning meant that a number of versions of software were in production at the same time.
- The team spent a large amount of time post release bug fixing and performing maintenance.

Domain Challenges

- Complex computations and algorithms needed to transform scientific concepts into meaningful performance metrics from GPS and sensor data.
- The highly sensitive nature of the data recorded and captured meant that documentation of decisions and development lifecycle would need to be provided to satisfy strict regulations.
- Additional Data security measures needed to be implemented to comply with data processing and storage regulations.

The challenges listed above have led the company to search for alternative software development approaches. The decision was made to design and implement an agile software development life cycle to improve the continuous delivery of the new product and significantly reduce the number of bugs remaining in each release version. The method chosen must allow for change while offering opportunities to monitor and control. This project was a massive undertaking involving the development of several pieces of hardware which must integrate with firmware, and software (Apple/Windows) to produce accurate performance data. By introducing agile practices, we aimed to increase the transparency of the development process, reduce time to market, reduce bugs, reduce maintenance effort, increase data security and increase communication between all three development departments.

4 Adopting Agile

4.1 Choosing the Agile Methods and Practices to Implement

With a clear understanding of the development environment and the challenges involved, we needed to decide on an agile approach for the development of the new product. The complexity of the project with many custom algorithms and it's scientific application domain ruled out DSDM as research suggests it is best suited when applied in a business domain and is less effective when used in engineering or scientific applications [7, 21, 22]. The Crystal's stretch to fit model looked promising with four different levels of implementation to match the complexity level of any project yet problems had been noted when applying across a distributed team due to the core value of Osmotic Communication [6, 21, 23]. Having reviewed numerous publications and assessed the domain, FDD was chosen as the agile approach most suited to this project [9, 24, 21]. The new product needs to incorporate all the features offered by its predecessor along with new features identified by the Sports Science department. Visualising development by feature was already the preferred approach of the company so FDD was universally welcomed by the management. The FDD process model was followed, allowing a team made up of Business Stakeholders (IT, Management and Sports Scientists), the Senior Software Architect and Senior Developers to create an overall project model by defining the architecture and a high-level plan.

Creating a prioritised feature list allowed all three development departments to create a development roadmap and facilitated synchronized development planning. FDD improved the overall project planning and offered a clearer overview for all stakeholders. In order to offer full transparency to stakeholders throughout the development lifecycle it was decided that Scrum framework [25, 16, 12] should be applied in addition to a feature centric approach.

Scrum supports iterative development and promotes communication within the development team [3]. It encourages development cycles of between 1 and 4 weeks and facilitates frequent backlog grooming and requirements refining within each cycle (See Fig. 1). The defined roles within the Scrum process allow for close collaboration between departments and increase transparency throughout development. The role of Product Owner (PO) is crucial in Scrum, the PO decides what will be selected for development and when, they are also responsible for specifying requirements for all features. The PO needs to have a very good understanding of what is required by the system and must be available to the Development team throughout the process. The Scrum Master (SM) is a servant leader role within the Development team, the SM is there to ensure that scrum values and practices are followed within each sprint. The SM facilitates communication between the PO, Dev Team and Stakeholders during the development Lifecycle, removing impediments for the Dev Team is also an important part of this role [21, 11]. We decided to apply Scrum to FDD as a development management framework.

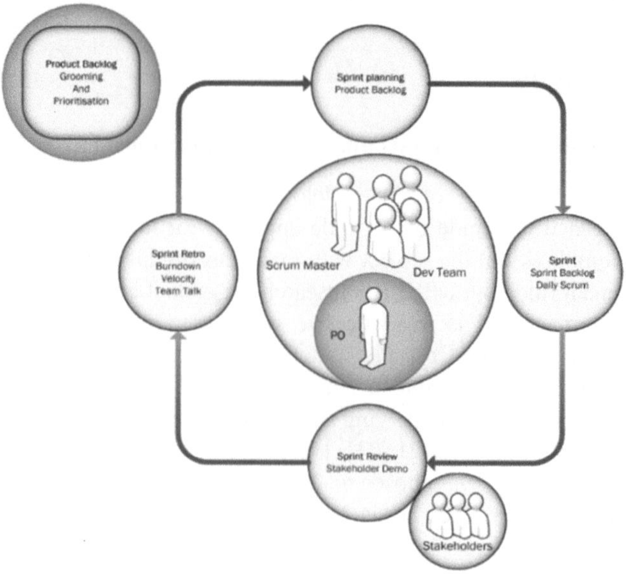

Fig. 1. Scrum iterative cycle

4.2 Implementing Agile

Changing to an Agile software development life cycle was a big undertaking.

It was decided to introduce agile methods' (FDD and Scrum) practices in phases to allow a gradual adoption and limit disruption to ongoing development activities (please see Table 1 for the practices adopted in each phase). The practices at Phase 5 are planned at this stage.

Phase 1 (3 Week Duration)

Communication within the development team was essential for the process to succeed, so it was identified as a priority for the first phase, the role of Scrum Master was assigned. the SM was to set up daily Stand-Up meetings for the development team. The team used these meetings to flag issues or concerns they had regarding impediments to development and team members were encouraged to offer advice and help. The first

Table 1. Phases of agile implementation and adopted practices for each phase

Areas to improve	Phase 1	Phase 2	Phase 3	Phase 4	Phase 5
Communication and team work					
Daily stand up	x				
Sprint review				x	
Sprint restrospective				x	
Pair programming			x		
Organisation & planning					
Jira	x	x	x		
Confluence		x	x		
Create feature list			x		
Develop by feature			x		
Requirements gathering		x	x		
Product backlog			x		
Estimation (Time)		x	x		
Estimation (Story points)			x	x	
Self-organisation	x				
Sustainable pace		x			
Definition of done					
Timeboxing		x			
Scrum master	x				
On-site customer					
Defining product owner		x			
Assigning product owner		x			
Product requirements specification			x		
Acceptance criteria			x		
Backlog grooming and prioritisation			x		
Acceptance testing			x		
Quality					
Unit tests		x			
Functional tests			x		
Regression tests				x	
Integration tests				x	
Commit process					x
Repository management					x
Code inspections					x
Continuous integration					x

week of Stand-Up meetings was a little uncomfortable for the developers but by the end of week 2 they had become more relaxed and accustomed to speaking in front of their colleagues. This open discussion and collective ownership of problems helped the team build trust and began to change the mind-set of the developers from individual to team.

Face to Face communication was improving in the team, but, there was little to no record of development tasks, a software development tool needed to be introduced to help the team plan and track their progress. Jira was chosen after researching available options, it offered a well-designed UI, allowed for a significant level of customisation and integrated with a number of development tools which we planned to introduce. Initially a Scrum board was created with an active empty Sprint, the developers created tasks and added them to the active Sprint as they started development. The initial workflow consisted of 3 swimlanes (To Do, In Progress and Done), User Stories and Tasks did not require estimation. In this gentle introduction to Jira, the developers became familiar with the application and gradually creating and logging their tasks became part of the development itself.

Phase 2 (2.5 Month Duration)

For the second phase there were three main goals: The first one was to bring a structure and create transparency in the development process. The second one was to allow the team time to familiarise themselves with management tools, Jira and Confluence, by introducing additional functionality gradually. Writing quality user stories, recording requirements and gathering efforts were the learning goals for this phase. Quality was the third consideration in this implementation with the introduction of unit tests as a mandatory task for developers.

Time-boxsprints were a very big change for both the development team and management. The sprints were set at one-week duration as they were operating in the improvement phase of an old product. A working week was agreed to be 32.5 h. The developers were instructed to only commit tasks to a sprint which they could complete in a working week. The short sprint duration offered the developers frequent opportunities to refine the process and with each new sprint they began to close the gap between committed and completed tasks. Time-boxed sprints allowed developers and Stakeholders gain a better understanding of the length of time required to complete a task or story. Starting with one-week iterations meant that developers had to place greater emphasis on requirements analysis to ensure any tasks chosen were concise and clear allowing for completion within the sprint. This left little room for ambiguity while gathering specifications and within three weeks began to show improvements in the requirements analysis process while also increasing the quality of the tasks and stories created.

Confluence [26] a document repository and project management tool by Atlassian was introduced to improve traceability and quality throughout the SDLC. All requirements being passed to developers needed to be recorded in a requirements document. Confluence was solely used by the developers at first, allowing them to complete requirements templates for upcoming features. The developers had to analyse the features they had committed to deliver from a different perspective, this allowed them to break down each feature into more manageable/deliverable pieces. During the requirements analysis and gathering process questions arose about implementation and requirements had to be refined. Features could evolve and change during this process. A greater transparency prior to development helped us to identify risks, for example, additional technologies needed to develop a feature, a lack of domain knowledge for the developer meant that research was needed before committing the tasks or stories to the sprint.

As mentioned in the first implementation phase above, the developers started to record their development tasks as user stories on a simple Scrum board. The purpose of this basic introduction was to get the developers using Jira to record their tasks as they developed. The tasks recorded contained minimal information and related to the technical implementation steps rather than describing the functionality. It was difficult to associate a task to a functional requirement. To improve this process and aid transparency for all stakeholders, we introduced a definition of User Story based on Bill Wake's INVEST approach [27] . Developers had to create a user story for small pieces of functionality, giving it a meaningful title, which was easy to read by non-team members. By adding readable stories to the backlog stakeholders could easily relate work items to a specific piece of functionality.

To improve the requirements analysis and gathering process, a Product Owner (PO) role was defined. The PO is the sole source of requirements specification for features. Only the specified product owner can request features and prioritise their delivery. An experienced senior Sports Scientist was picked to become the PO and all future feature requests had to be presented to the PO for approval.

Phase 3 (3 Month Duration)

The introduction of the Product Owner role had an immediate impact on the development process, fulfilling practices of both Scrum and FDD by creating a focused prioritised list of features for the new software. The PO is an experienced Sports Scientist who had worked closely with the clients and has a very detailed understanding of the clients' needs. The established relationship with the sports clubs meant that clarification on any suggested feature was easily obtained and this removed any delays in development.

Through the coaching of the Scrum Master, the Product Owner has developed a template on the Confluence tool for a detailed prioritised backlog. For the prioritization of the items, we specified the following process: One member of the development team sits down with the PO to detail a new feature through the product requirements template. The template records the goals, assumptions, business value, and user stories necessary to complete the requested feature. The product owner also specifies the Acceptance Criteria at this stage allowing the developer to understand what is necessary for delivery. Once all Users Stories for a feature have been completed, the template is then used to auto generate User Stories to the Development Backlog in Jira. The PO then reviews the backlog and prioritises the User Stories to be included in the next sprint. Only the stories with a priority of High or Highest are considered for the sprint. Development by feature is now possible as Senior Developers, Stakeholders and the Product Owner has a detailed feature and user story list. At this phase, the sprint duration was changed to a two-week cycle, marking the end of a legacy product maintenance phase and the beginning of development for the company's new product.

Although the stories and tasks were being created, they had no assigned unit of measurement. Estimation using story points following the Fibonacci sequence (1, 2, 3, 5, 8, 13, 21) was chosen. One in the Fibonacci sequence represented a story which required little effort and low risk while 21 represented a very difficult and possibly risky story. All stories were pointed by individual developers at first and they were instructed how to use the outliers to determine a story's estimation. Story point estimation was a difficult concept for the developers to grasp. After four weeks of confusion regarding story points estimation and most developers swinging wildly from over estimation to under estimation, it was decided to revert to effort estimation. Developers felt that they had a better understanding of how long something would take them to complete rather than using the more abstract scale. The developers looked at the tasks and committed to what they felt could completed within 32.5 h (per week). The Tasks/Stories were time tracked and within two weeks estimations were almost in line with completion rate.

Pair programming was also tried in this phase but, it was unsuccessful due to the small size of the development team. In a development team of five, it was unrealistic to have two developers working on the same piece of functionality. Developers also felt that they lost interest in the feature when they were not coding it themselves. This practice was stopped after two weeks.

The introduction of a Quality Assurance (QA) role allowed functional and acceptance test cases to be written once a feature was detailed in the Confluence tool. The TestRail [28] tool was introduced to record and manage test cases allowing a quality assurance person to create Test Runs for each sprint. The results of the tests can be linked directly to each Jira user story allowing full transparency of bug creation and fixes.

Phase 4 (4 Month Duration)

By Phase 4, the developers had become comfortable using the project management tools and had embraced all the adoptions made to date. It was time to fully implement Scrum with the introduction of regular structured Sprint Review and Retrospectives meetings. All the Stakeholders, the Product Owner and the Development Team had started attending the bi-weekly Sprint Review meetings where the development progress was demonstrated to all parties. The Sprint Review meeting was also used to clarify upcoming development functions (features and stories) and to adjust backlog prioritisation when necessary. The Retrospective meetings were a chance for the development team to examine their performance during the recent sprint and to identify the positive and negative factors influencing delivery. It also gave the developers an opportunity to refine the process by highlighting practices which they felt did not work in the development environment, pair programming was universally disliked by the team. The Retrospective meetings were very new to the team at this phase, the first couple of meetings produced little feedback as developers struggled to vocalise their experiences within the sprint. The Scrum Master facilitated these sessions and changed the format for each meeting to establish the optimum set up for the team. Novel approaches were employed using games and Lego to get the development team thinking and talking about ways to improve the overall process. "The Retrospective Game" [29] is an engaging fun way to gather feedback from your team, based on the popular game "Cards against Humanity" [30] but tailored for a development environment, it offers Object, Context and Feedback cards. The Object card relates to a random character (the president, an alien), the Context card relates to the development lifecycle (Sprint, Release, Development Team) and the Feedback cards which contain positive and negative statements prompt the players to fill in the blanks. The game creates a relaxed environment in which the team can create hilarious yet relevant feedback on things done well during the sprint and areas in need of improvement.

Within the "Legospective" normal retrospective questions where prosed to the developers but instead of vocalising their responses they were asked to visualise and build a Lego construct to represent their views. 15 min was allotted for consideration and construction and once completed each developer introduced their creation explaining its significance to the recent sprint. After five consecutive retrospective meetings, the team began to become familiar with the format and started to produce valuable actionable feedback to improve the overall software development approach. The PO role also intensified during this stage with the SM and PO working closely to ensure that weekly backlog grooming was carried out. Regularly refining and reprioritising the backlog allowed the development team to easily plan for up-coming sprints by allowing the creation of sprint backlogs and estimating the delivery of features more accurately.

The development team was now accurately estimating user stories through time tracking as Story Points estimation had proven difficult for them to visualise in the earlier stages of agile adoption. The decision was made to reintroduce estimation by Story Points as it offers a better reflection of the overall effort and value of each story [31]. After two sprints with the introduction of the Planning Poker Game [32], the developers started to feel confident in estimating the user stories based on the Fibonacci sequence.

With comprehensive user stories defined, detailed functional and behavioural requirements for the software and explicit acceptance criteria, the QA tester started to develop functional integration and acceptance tests which run during the sprint. During each test run, a QA can define a bug relating to a particular user story directly to the development board for the developer to fix. The introduction of the TestRail tool added another level of traceability to the development process.

Having created and executed a number of successful Functional and Acceptance Test Suites, the QA could now identify tests to be included in ongoing regression suites. The tests were identified and created which would offer a significant level of code coverage with the fewest test runs. Once full testing processes where in place, the team created their Definition of Done, a user story is Done when it has been coded and unit tested by a developer and has successfully passed all functional, integration, regression and acceptance tests by a QA. Only on successful completion of all tests, a user story is moved to the Done column on the sprint board.

5 Conclusion

There were many challenges involved in adopting an Agile Software Development approach within the Sports Science domain. The domain in which the company operates requires additional documentation and planning to satisfy strict data security regulations while also needing flexibility and agility in development to allow for changing requirements. A number of factors needed to be considered while assessing the development environment, a distributed development team comprising of Hardware, Firmware and Software departments needed a process which would work remotely and suit all three disciplines.

In this paper, we identified the challenges related with the domain and the development environment. Following this, we described how we adopted FDD and Scrum methods in four phases in the organization. A tailored FDD combined with Scrum approach was chosen as the SDLC that suited to the current strategic approach of the company. We had to find a balance that would suit the company and all three departments for this project and future development. We achieved full traceability within the development process which was an essential requirement for the domain.

The phased-based introduction of agile practices was a slow, yet a steady process, offering all stakeholders the opportunity to familiarise themselves with agile practices gradually. Selecting a small number of practices for introduction in each phase allowed us to monitor the process and assess the suitability of each practice within the development environment. In this way, we could identify the practices which were unsuited to the development team and adjust the time spent on each phase according to the complexity of implementation.

Adopting FDD, Scrum practices and the use of project management tools allowed the development team to plan, capture requirements, refine requirements, capture decisions, implement solutions and perform verification and validation in two-week cycles. Adopted approach has improved the communication between all three development teams and offered transparency to all stakeholders. We created an agile culture within the company which offers comprehensive yet lightweight documentation and allows for change while meeting strict development guidelines for safety critical software.

The main contributions of the paper are the presentation of how we tailored the agile practices in the company, the order that we introduced the practices to the teams, the practices that were resisted by the team and the solutions to overcome such challenges.

As future work, we plan to adopt a repository management strategy to ensure the quality and maintainability of the code base. A defined branching model for both local and remote repositories, the introduction of pull requests rather than a code and push policy and a commit process detailing the compulsory comment format will be established. Repository management roles will be assigned to specific developers within the development team ensuring that each commit is reviewed and inspected before being merged to the development branch for integration and regression testing. Only on successful testing will the development branch be merged to the release ready master branch by a designated repository manager. Our experiences regarding these new adoptions are planned to be shared as well.

Acknowledgement. This research is supported by the Science Foundation Ireland Research Centres Programme, through Lero - the Irish Software Research Centre (http://www.lero.ie) grant 10/CE/I1855 & 13/RC/2094.

References

1. Brooks, F.P.: No silver bullet. IEEE Comput. **20**(4), 10–19 (1987)
2. Kent, B. et al.: Agile Manifesto (2002). http://agilemanifesto.org/principles.html

3. Trektere, K., McCaffery, F., Lepmets, M., Barry, G.: Tailoring MDevSPICE® for mobile medical apps. In: Proceedings of the International Conference on Software and System Process - ICSSP 2016, no. Md, pp. 106–110 (2016)
4. Trektere, K., Regan, G., Caffery, F.M., Flood, D., Lepmets, M., Barry, G.: Mobile medical app development with a focus on traceability. J. Softw. Evol. Process. 29(11) (2017)
5. McHugh, M., McCaffery, F., Coady, G.: An agile implementation within a medical device software organisation. In: Mitasiunas, A., Rout, T., O'Connor, Rory V., Dorling, A. (eds.) SPICE 2014. CCIS, vol. 477, pp. 190–201. Springer, Cham (2014). https://doi.org/10.1007/978-3-319-13036-1_17
6. Cockburn, A.: Crystal Clear: A Human-Powered Methodology for Small Teams. Addison-Wesley, Boston (2004)
7. Stapleton, J.: DSDM, Dynamic Systems Development Method: The Method In Practice. Cambridge University Press, Cambridge (1997)
8. Sani, A., Firdaus, A.: A review on software development security engineering using dynamic system method (DSDM). Int. J. Comput. Appl. **69**(25), 37–44 (2013)
9. Bauer, M.: FDD and project management. Cutter IT J. (2004). http://www.martinbauer.com/Articles/FDD-and-Project-Management. Accessed 07 Jun 2018
10. Beck, K.: Embracing change with extreme programming. Computer **32**(10), 70–77 (1999)
11. Sutherland, J., Schwaber, K.: The Scrum Papers : Nuts, Bolts, and Origins of an Agile Process, Origins, pp. 1–202 (2007)
12. Khmelevsky, Y., Li, X., Madnick, S.: Software development using agile and scrum in distributed teams. In: 2017 Annual IEEE International Systems Conference (SysCon) (2017)
13. Dybå, T., Dingsøyr, T.: Empirical studies of agile software development: a systematic review. Inf. Softw. Technol. **50**(9–10), 833–859 (2008)
14. Ayed, H., Vanderose, B., Habra, N.: Supported approach for agile methods adaptation: an adoption study. In: Proceedings of the 1st International Workshop on Rapid Continuous Software Engineering - RCoSE 2014, pp. 36–41 (2014)
15. Rai, P., Dhir, S.: Impact of different methodologies in software development process. Int. J. Comput. Sci. Inf. Technol. **5**(2), 1112–1116 (2014)
16. Özcan-Top, Ö., McCaffery, F.: How does scrum conform to the regulatory requirements defined in MDevSPICE®? In: Mas, A., Mesquida, A., O'Connor, Rory V., Rout, T., Dorling, A. (eds.) SPICE 2017. CCIS, vol. 770, pp. 257–268. Springer, Cham (2017). https://doi.org/10.1007/978-3-319-67383-7_19
17. McHugh, M., McCaffery, F., Casey, V.: Software process improvement to assist medical device software development organisations to comply with the amendments to the medical device directive. IET Softw. **6**(5), 431 (2012)
18. General Data Protection Regulation (GDPR) – Final text neatly arranged. https://gdpr-info.eu/. Accessed 28 Mar 2018
19. About HIPAA.com – HIPAA.com. https://www.hipaa.com/about/. Accessed 28 Mar 2018
20. Lepmets, M., McCaffery, F., Clarke, P.: Development and benefits of MDevSPICE, the medical device software process assessment framework. J. Softw. Evol. Process **28**, 800–816 (2016). https://doi.org/10.1002/smr.1781
21. Abrahamsson, P., Salo, O., Ronkainen, J., Warsta, J.: Agile software development methods: review and analysis, p. 112. Espoo, Finland. Technical Research Centre of Finland. VTT Publications (2002)
22. Moreira, M.E.: Being Agile: Your Roadmap to Successful Adoption of Agile. Apress, New York (2013)
23. Dilamani, M.T.: A short review on crystal clear methodology and its advantages over scrum, the popular software process model (2014)

24. Goyal, S.: Major Seminar On Feature Driven Development, p. 22 (2007)
25. Umbreen, M., Abbas, J., Shaheed, S.M.: A Comparative approach for SCRUM and FDD in agile. Int. J. Comput. Sci. Innov. **2015**(2), 79–87 (2015)
26. Atlassian: Confluence - Team Collaboration Software| Atlassian. https://www.atlassian.com/software/confluence. Accessed 14 Apr 2016
27. Wake, B.: INVEST in Good Stories, and SMART Tasks. http://xp123.com/articles/invest-in-good-stories-and-smart-tasks/. Accessed 17 Aug 2003
28. Test Case Management and Test Management Software Tool - TestRail. http://www.gurock.com/testrail/. Accessed 14 Jun 2018
29. The Retrospective Game - The Feedback Game That's Fun and Does Good – theretrospectivegame. https://theretrospectivegame.com/. Accessed 10 Feb 2018
30. Cards Against Humanity. https://cardsagainsthumanity.com/. Accessed 15 Jun 2018
31. Radigan, D.: Secrets to agile estimation and story points|Atlassian. https://www.atlassian.com/agile/project-management/estimation. Accessed 14 Jun 2018
32. Planning Poker: Planning Poker.com - Estimates Made Easy. Sprints Made Simple. https://www.planningpoker.com/. Accessed 14 Jun 2018

Systematic Mapping Study on Process Mining in Agile Software Development

Sezen Erdem[1(✉)], Onur Demirörs[2,3], and Fethi Rabhi[3]

[1] ASELSAN INC, Ankara, Turkey
erdem@aselsan.com.tr
[2] Computer Engineering Department, Izmir Institute of Technology, Izmir, Turkey
demirors@metu.edu.tr
[3] School of Computer Science and Engineering, University of New South Wales, Sydney, Australia
f.rabhi@unsw.edu.au

Abstract. Process mining is a process management technique that allows for the analysis of business processes based on the event logs and its aim is to discover, monitor and improve executed processes by extracting knowledge from event logs readily available in information systems. The popularity of agile software development methods has been increasing in the software development field over the last two decades and many software organizations develop software using agile methods. Process mining can provide complementary tools to Agile organizations for process management. Process mining can be used to discover agile processes followed by agile teams to establish the baselines and to determine the fidelity or they can be used to obtain feedback to improve agility. Despite the potential benefit of using process mining for agile software development, there is a lack of research that systematically analyzes the usage of process mining in agile software development. This paper presents a systematic mapping study on usage of process mining in agile software development approaches. The aim is to find out the usage areas of process mining in agile software development, explore commonly used algorithms, data sources, data collection mechanisms, analysis techniques and tools. The study has shown us that process mining is used in Agile software development especially for the purpose of process discovery from task tracking applications. We also observed that source code repositories are main data sources for process mining, a diversity of algorithms are used for analysis of collected data and ProM is the most widely used analysis tool for process mining.

Keywords: Process mining · Agile software development · Process discovery

1 Introduction

Process mining is a relatively young research discipline that sits between computational intelligence and data mining on the one hand, and process modeling and analysis on the other hand [1]. The aim of process mining is to discover, monitor and improve executing processes, by extracting knowledge from event logs readily available in

I. Stamelos et al. (Eds.): SPICE 2018, CCIS 918, pp. 289–299, 2018.
https://doi.org/10.1007/978-3-030-00623-5_20

information systems. Although it has received great attention during the last few years, the idea of reconstructing processes using the stakeholder footprints is not new. Many groups have been working on techniques on process mining over the last two decades. Earlier studies are around application of process mining in the context of workflow management systems. The studies of Cook and Wolf [2, 3] are the pioneers of the works on application of process mining techniques in the field of software development process. There are various methods and algorithms in the field of process mining proposed for different purposes such as rediscovering business processes, conformance checking, process enhancement, software development and social networks analysis [4–10]. Akman and Demirors [11] studied the applicability of process discovery algorithms for software organizations. As the capabilities of information systems and features of CASE tools are improved, it has become possible to record the footprints of each stakeholder in software development processes which leads to increase in the maturity of process mining techniques.

As the benefits of large scale process centric improvement approaches questioned more [12], Agile software development methods have increased their popularity in the software development field. Today prominent percentage of software organizations develop software using agile methods [13]. Agile software projects are generally developed by small teams and in short iterations. Agile methods are more lightweight, more people centric and leave less traces when compared with the traditional approaches such as waterfall [14]. Agile approaches such as Scrum and XP also suggest a set of practices and rules for developers. However, their application in the field is left to the agile teams. Process conformance validation is one of the key challenges in agile software development [15] together with the agile maturity of their practices [16]. Process mining techniques have the potential to be used to discover agile processes followed by agile teams to determine the conformity. They can also establish the necessary evidence for assessing or measuring the agility of organizations.

There are case studies, researches on applicability, systematic literature reviews and mappings on process mining on software engineering in the literature [44–46]. However these studies do not provide evidence and a general understanding on their usability in the Agile software development context.

In order to understand the applicability and usage of process mining in agile software development, we have searched the literature systematically with the aim for determining the state of the art on process mining in agile software development. Our goal is to find out usage areas of process mining in agile software development, explore commonly used methods, algorithms and techniques, data sources, data collection mechanisms, analysis techniques and tools.

Both process mining and Agile Software Development are hot topics. Usage of process mining in agile software development is an interesting topic to research. The aim of this paper is to find out the studies on application of process mining in agile software development process. The contributions of this study will be creating awareness about researches on the subject and highlight the usage areas process mining in agile software development. Also we can create a base for our further research activities and prepare a road map for our studies.

The paper is structured as follows. The design of our research and the method that we followed for the systematic mapping are described in Sect. 2. Findings obtained from the analysis of selected publications that we performed to answer our research questions are summarized in Sect. 3. Finally, our conclusions are in Sect. 4.

2 Research Method

A systematic literature mapping is a mechanism used to contextualize a particular area of interest through identification, assessment and interpretation of the set of research works which describe such an area [17]. Systematic mapping studies adopt rigorous planning, follow repeatable and well-defined processes, and produce unbiased and evidence-based outcomes [18]. We have conducted a systematic mapping study to achieve our goals for identifying the answers to the research questions we set in advance. The questions are derived based on a preliminary research on process mining in software engineering and also in agile software development. Also the aim of process mining and the fundamentals explained in Process Mining Manifesto [1] lead us to generate these questions.

The guidelines for performing a systematic literature mapping mentioned by Kitchenham [17] are followed in our study quality assessment.

Research questions to address in this mapping are as follows:

Q1. What are the different categories of research areas concerned with process mining associated with agile software development?
Q2. What are the different purposes of using process mining in Agile Software Development processes?
Q3. Which agile teams' footprints are utilized by proposed methods in the agile process mining context?
Q4. What are the techniques and methods of process mining used for Agile Software Development processes?
Q5. How do current process mining techniques use these footprints?

Springer Link, IEEE Xplore, ACM Digital Library, Google Scholar and Science Direct repositories are selected as data sources. Search terms are determined, and the same search terms are used for all data sources. The searches are full-text searches and the terms are searched in the title, abstract and body of the paper.

Search Terms:

- "Process mining" AND "Agile"
- "Process mining" AND "Agile Software"
- "Process mining" AND "Agile Software Development"
- "Process mining" AND "Agile Software Lifecycle"
- "Process mining" AND "Scrum"
- "Process mining" AND "Extreme Programming"
- "Mining" AND "Agile event logs"
- "Mining" AND "Scrum event logs"

We performed the study selection in two phases. In the first phase, the search results are evaluated via reading the title and abstract part. The relevance of studies with process mining in software development, especially agile methodologies, is the main concern for study selection. Relevant studies are selected for final evaluation. In the final evaluation part, entire paper is read and evaluated based on a control list containing study selection criteria. Inclusion/Exclusion criteria for paper selection is as follows:

Inclusion Criteria:

- Article reporting software process mining related study in agile software development context.
- Written in English
- Published in a journal, conference or workshop,
- Full-text is available.

Exclusion Criteria:

- Article that is not utilizing process mining in agile software development,
- Article that is not entirely in English,
- Partially available or unreachable articles
- Article that is published as a short study and not as a full study.

References of the selected papers are also checked to find the related papers to increase the results set size before the selection process is completed.

The list of papers are cross checked by the authors to validate paper selection criteria. Papers which are found related by all authors are selected for data extraction and analysis.

Data about the methods applied in the field of process mining, the tools used, and the results of the applied methods are collected. Collected data is analyzed to generate classifications to extend the analysis.

3 Results

Process mining is a growing research area and there are many works on algorithms, methods, tools and applications in business process management field. There are also special studies on the field of software development which are referred to as software process mining. The application of process mining algorithms and methods in the field of software development is also a rapidly growing research area but overall, there are not many studies on the application of process mining in agile software development.

Although there are more search keywords in the design of search process, the results drive us to similar paper sets. So search keywords are analyzed and only four of them which produce most relevant results are selected for reporting. The numbers of publications associated with the keywords in the target data sources are given in Table 1.

After applying the inclusion and exclusion criteria to the search results, the number of publications related with process mining in the field of agile software development decreases considerably. The different numbers of publications after the study selection process are given in Table 2.

Table 1. Search results

Search Term/Databases	Springer Link	IEEE Xplore	ACM Digital Library	Google Scholar	Science Direct
"Process mining" AND "Agile"	196	2	3	1750	49
"Process mining" AND "Agile software development"	12	14	1	220	3
"Process mining" AND "SCRUM"	17	9	0	209	0
"Process mining" AND "Extreme programming"	17	6	1	151	3

Table 2. Selected search results

Search Term/Databases	Springer Link	IEEE Xplore	ACM Digital Library	Google Scholar	Science Direct
"Process mining" AND "Agile"	6 [19–24]	1 [25]	1 [31]	15 [19, 21, 25, 27, 28, 31–40]	1 [3]
"Process mining" AND "Agile software development"	2 [19, 20]	5 [25–29]	1 [31]	9 [19, 27, 32, 34–39]	0
"Process mining" AND "SCRUM"	1 [19]	3 [25–27]	0	5 [19, 27, 31, 32, 38]	0
"Process mining" AND "Extreme programming"	1 [20]	1 [30]	1 [30]	4 [27, 28, 39, 40]	0

Search results of Google Scholar database include some of the papers from our other search databases. So the number of publications obtained from Google Scholar database is higher when compared with other databases. However, some of the papers appear only in the search results of Google Scholar database.

Selected publications are analyzed to search for answers to our research questions.

Q1. What are the different categories of research areas concerned with process mining associated with agile software development?

Selected publications can be categorized into three subgroups according to the application area of process mining in agile software development.

- Application of process mining in agile business processes: The studies [22–24, 27, 33] in this classification are not directly related with agile software development. Agile business processes are able to act immediately to changes in real time. Application of process mining in agile business processes may lead us to generate methods of application of process mining in agile software development area.
- Usage of process mining in agile software development: These articles focus on developing software using process mining techniques. The aim is to characterize

user interaction with the software, to understand which features are used and to find out sequence of operations. Event logs generated during usage of applications are analyzed via process mining algorithms and the findings are used for developing software in an agile manner [31, 34, 38].

- Usage of process mining for discovering/conformance checking of agile software development processes: Process mining is used for discovering the application of agile software development processes by agile teams/organizations. The aim is not only process discovery but also conformance checking and enhancement are in the scope [19–21, 25, 26, 28–30, 32, 35–37, 39, 40]. In the second research questioned we decomposed the different purposes.

Q2. What are the different purposes of using process mining in Agile Software Development processes?

Classification of publications according to purpose of usage is given in Table 3.

Table 3. Purpose of usage

Purpose of usage	Publications
Process discovery	[19, 21, 25–30, 32, 33, 35, 39]
Process conformance check	[19, 32, 36, 37, 40]
Process improvement/enhancement	[19, 21, 25, 36, 37, 40]

Process discovery is the most commonly used area of process mining [1, 8]. Our work also has shown that process mining is used mostly for process discovery to reveal the processes that were actually executed in organizations. Event logs generated during process executions are analyzed to extract real processes.

Process mining has also usage in process conformance checking. Agile methodologies such as Scrum, Extreme Programming (XP), Agile Unified Process (AUP), have prescriptions to follow. Also the artifacts defined in agile methodologies (product backlog items, tasks, bugs etc.) have states and workflow of these artifacts are predefined by agile methodologies. After process discovery, the results are compared with the predefined models to check process conformance.

Another usage area is process improvement and enhancement. Actual executed processes are analyzed to find out bottlenecks and delays in actual executions. Best practices of actual executions are put in evidence for the benefit of organizations.

Q3. Which agile teams' footprints are utilized by proposed methods in the agile process mining context?

The data sources that contains footprints of agile teams can be classified into three groups. The classification is given in Table 4.

Table 4. Process Mining Data Sources

#	Data source	Publications
1	Issue tracking applications such as Microsoft TFS and JIRA are valuable data sources. State changes of work items generate data for analyzing the real process. The order of events, timestamps, and team member changing the state can be queried to generate data for analysis	[19, 32, 39, 40]
2	Software repositories such as version control systems, source code configuration control systems and bug tracking systems. Mining software repositories reveal data about the real process executions	[26, 29, 36, 37, 39]
3	Communication channels between agile team members are another potential source for collecting data about the executed process. Analysis of e-mails between the agile team members is a research topic for extracting process data. The aim is to build a set of workflow models that represent the processes laying behind the agile teams' activities	[21, 25]

Q4. What are the techniques and methods of process mining used for Agile Software Development processes?

Process mining algorithms used in analysis in selected papers are given in Table 5.

Q5. How do current process mining techniques use these footprints?

Our work has shown us that analysis are conducted by using noninvasive techniques to collect the data. Data collected in event logs are queried for transforming into the format that can be fed to process mining tools. Collected data should be transformed into a format that process mining tools can understand to conduct the analysis. Most commonly used format is eXtensible Event Stream (XES) [43]. There exist many tools with process mining capability. ProM is a popular and powerful tool for process mining. It has many plug-ins and serves a high number of alternative to run analysis. Majority of the selected studies make use of ProM or extension of ProM for analysis [19, 21, 22, 25, 29, 32, 35, 38–40]. Disco is another process mining tool used in analysis [19, 39].

Table 5. Techniques and methods

Algorithm	Publications
MINERfull algorithm [41]	[21, 25]
Fuzzy miner [6]	[29, 38, 39]
Genetic mining algorithm [5]	[19]
Heuristic mining algorithm [42]	[19, 22, 38, 40]
Alpha algorithm [8]	[19, 32, 38]

4 Conclusions

There are numerous research studies on process mining algorithms, methods and tools but our study has shown that application of process mining in agile software development processes is a research area that requires more work to be done. Usage of process mining in agile software development have significant potential for agile teams and organizations to increase their success and agility. However the mapping study has shown us that there is not so much work on application of process mining in agile software development context.

We were able to identify 25 papers in this study. Most of these papers are published in the last decade. This shows that software process mining in agile software development has an increasing research trend in recent years.

We observe that process mining is mainly used for discovering actual processes. Organizations want to see what is going in real life and what the bottleneck in their processes are. But this does not mean that process discovery is the sole interest area of process mining. Process conformance checking and process enhancement are other types of process mining having significant usage areas.

We have also observed significant challenges reported for applying process mining in agile contexts. Data collection and event log creation are non-trivial issues in agile software development processes. Due to the nature of agile software development, finding structured event logs to mine the process is a challenging problem. Concept drift is another challenging issue since process improvement is a continuous activity in agile approaches through the iterations.

Agile approaches value individuals and interactions over processes and tools which frequently lead to development processes which are not formalized. Agile approaches are lightweight, more people centric and leave less traces behind when compared with traditional methods. Since development process is often not formalized, agile teams feel themselves freer to determine the sequence of events and the techniques which may result in inconsistency, instability, and unpredictability. Interpretation of agile method rules differently by the teams in an organization may lead to interoperability problems between the projects of the organization. Agile methodologies such as Scrum, Extreme Programming (XP), Agile Unified Process (AUP) have prescriptions to follow in order to achieve real agility. Process mining can be the right tool to extract the actual processes followed by agile teams. It can be valuable and help to visualize consistency, stability, interoperability and repeatability problems.

References

1. van der Aalst, W.: Process mining manifesto. In: Daniel, F., Barkaoui, K., Dustdar, S. (eds.) BPM 2011. LNBIP, vol. 99, pp. 169–194. Springer, Heidelberg (2012). https://doi.org/10.1007/978-3-642-28108-2_19
2. Cook, J.E., Wolf, A.L.: Automating process discovery through event-data analysis. In: Proceedings of 17th International Conference on Software Engineering, pp. 73–82 (1995)
3. Cook, J.E., Wolf, A.L.: Discovering models of software processes from event-based data. ACM Trans. Softw. Eng. Methodol. (TOSEM) **7**(3), 215–249 (1998)

4. Weijters, A.J., van der Aalst, W.M.P.: Rediscovering workflow models from event-based data using little thumb. Integr. Comput. -Aided Eng. **10**(2), 151–162 (2003)
5. de Medeiros, A.K., Weijters, A.J., van der Aalst, W.M.P.: Genetic process mining: an experimental evaluation. Data Min. Knowl. Disc. **14**(2), 245–304 (2007)
6. Günther, Christian W., van der Aalst, Wil M.P.: Fuzzy mining – adaptive process simplification based on multi-perspective metrics. In: Alonso, G., Dadam, P., Rosemann, M. (eds.) BPM 2007. LNCS, vol. 4714, pp. 328–343. Springer, Heidelberg (2007). https://doi.org/10.1007/978-3-540-75183-0_24
7. Schimm, G.: Mining exact models of concurrent workflows. Comput. Ind. **53**(3), 265–281 (2004)
8. van der Aalst, W.M.P.: Process Mining: Data Science in Action. Springer, Heidelberg (2016). https://doi.org/10.1007/978-3-662-49851-4
9. Hindle, A.: Software process recovery: recovering process from artifacts. In: 2010 17th Working Conference on Reverse Engineering, Beverly, MA, pp. 305–308 (2010)
10. van der Aalst, W.M.P., Song, M.: Discovering Social Networks from Event Logs. BETA Working Paper Series, WP 116, Eindhoven University of Technology, The Netherlands (2004)
11. Akman, B., Demirörs, O.: Applicability of process discovery algorithms for software organizations. In: 35th Euromicro Conference on Software Engineering and Advanced Applications, SEAA 2009, pp. 195–202. IEEE (2009)
12. Uskarcı, A., Demirörs, O.: Do staged maturity models result in organization-wide continuous process improvement? Insight from employees. Comput. Stand. Interfaces **52**, 25–40 (2017)
13. Garousi, V., Coşkunçay, A., Can, A.B., Demirörs, O.: A survey of software engineering practices in Turkey. J. Syst. Softw. **108**, 148–177 (2015)
14. Beck, K., et al.: Manifesto for Agile Software Development (2001)
15. Brhel, M., Meth, H., Maedche, A., Werder, K.: Exploring principles of user-centered agile software development. Inf. Softw. Technol. **61**(2), 163–181 (2015)
16. Ozcan-Top, O., Demirörs, O.: Assessment of agile maturity models: a multiple case study. In: Woronowicz, T., Rout, T., O'Connor, Rory V., Dorling, A. (eds.) SPICE 2013. CCIS, vol. 349, pp. 130–141. Springer, Heidelberg (2013). https://doi.org/10.1007/978-3-642-38833-0_12
17. Kitchenham, B.: Guidelines for performing systematic literature reviews in software engineering. EBSE Technical Report EBSE-2007-01. Keele University (2007)
18. Barn, B., Barat, S., Clark, T.: Conducting systematic literature reviews and systematic mapping studies. In: Proceedings of the 10th Innovations in Software Engineering Conference (ISEC 2017), pp. 212–213. ACM, New York (2017). https://doi.org/10.1145/3021460.3021489
19. Erdem, S., Demirörs, O.: An exploratory study on usage of process mining in agile software development. In: Mas, A., Mesquida, A., O'Connor, Rory V., Rout, T., Dorling, A. (eds.) SPICE 2017. CCIS, vol. 770, pp. 187–196. Springer, Cham (2017). https://doi.org/10.1007/978-3-319-67383-7_14
20. Capodieci, A., Mainetti, L., Manco, L.: A case study to enable and monitor real IT companies migrating from waterfall to agile. In: Murgante, B. (ed.) ICCSA 2014. LNCS, vol. 8583, pp. 119–134. Springer, Cham (2014). https://doi.org/10.1007/978-3-319-09156-3_9
21. Di Ciccio, C., Mecella, M., Scannapieco, M., Zardetto, D., Catarci, T.: MailOfMine – analyzing mail messages for mining artful collaborative processes. In: Aberer, K., Damiani, E., Dillon, T. (eds.) SIMPDA 2011. LNBIP, vol. 116, pp. 55–81. Springer, Heidelberg (2012). https://doi.org/10.1007/978-3-642-34044-4_4

22. Montani, S., Leonardi, G., Quaglini, S., Cavallini, A., Micieli, G.: Mining and retrieving medical processes to assess the quality of care. In: Delany, S.J., Ontañón, S. (eds.) ICCBR 2013. LNCS (LNAI), vol. 7969, pp. 233–240. Springer, Heidelberg (2013). https://doi.org/10.1007/978-3-642-39056-2_17
23. Brander, S., et al.: Refining process models through the analysis of informal work practice. In: Rinderle-Ma, S., Toumani, F., Wolf, K. (eds.) BPM 2011. LNCS, vol. 6896, pp. 116–131. Springer, Heidelberg (2011). https://doi.org/10.1007/978-3-642-23059-2_12
24. Schönig, S., Gillitzer, F., Zeising, M., Jablonski, S.: Supporting rule-based process mining by user-guided discovery of resource-aware frequent patterns. In: Toumani, F. (ed.) ICSOC 2014. LNCS, vol. 8954, pp. 108–119. Springer, Cham (2015). https://doi.org/10.1007/978-3-319-22885-3_10
25. Di Ciccio, C., Mecella, M.: Mining artful processes from knowledge workers' emails. IEEE Internet Comput. **17**(5), 10–20 (2013)
26. Jankovic, M., Bajec, M.: Comparison of software repositories for their usability in software process reconstruction. In: The International Conference on Research Challenges in Information Science, pp. 298–308 (2015)
27. Caldeira, J., e Abreu, F.B.: Software development process mining: discovery, conformance checking and enhancement. In: 10th International Conference on the Quality of Information and Communications Technology (QUATIC), pp. 254–259. IEEE (2016)
28. Astromskis, S., Janes, A., Mahdiraji, A.R.: Egidio: a non-invasive approach for synthesizing organizational models. In: Glinz, M., Murphy, G.C., Pezzè, M. (eds.) Proceedings of the International Conference on Software Engineering (ICSE), Zürich. IEEE (2012)
29. Poncin, W., Serebrenik, A., van den Brand, M.G.J.: Process mining software repositories. In: CSMR, pp. 5–14. IEEE (2011)
30. Ceravolo, P. et al.: An ontology-based process modelling for XP. In: Software Engineering Conference, Tenth Asia-Pacific Conference, pp. 236–242 (2003)
31. Rubin, V., Lomazova, I., van der Aalst, W.M.P.: Agile development with software process mining. In: Proceedings of the 2014 International Conference on Software and System Process (ICSSP 2014), pp. 70–74. ACM, New York (2014)
32. Zayed, M.A., Farid, A.B.: The discovery of the implemented software engineering process using process mining techniques. Int. J. Adv. Comput. Sci. Appl. **1**(7), 279–286 (2016)
33. Schönig, S., Cabanillas, C., Jablonski, S., Mendling, J.: Mining the organisational perspective in agile business processes. In: Gaaloul, K., Schmidt, R., Nurcan, S., Guerreiro, S., Ma, Q. (eds.) CAISE 2015. LNBIP, vol. 214, pp. 37–52. Springer, Cham (2015). https://doi.org/10.1007/978-3-319-19237-6_3
34. Astromskis, S., Janes, A., Mairegger, M.: A process mining approach to measure how users interact with software: an industrial case study. In: Proceedings of the 2015 International Conference on Software and System Process (ICSSP 2015), pp. 137–141. ACM, New York (2015). http://dx.doi.org/10.1145/2785592.2785612
35. Sunindyo, W.D., Moser, T., Winkler, D., Biffl, S.: Foundations for event-based process analysis in heterogeneous software engineering environments. In: 2010 36th EUROMICRO Conference on Software Engineering and Advanced Applications, Lille, pp. 313–322 (2010). https://doi.org/10.1109/seaa.2010.52
36. Chen, N., Hoi, S.C.H., Xiao, X.: Software process evaluation: A machine learning approach. In: 2011 26th IEEE/ACM International Conference on Automated Software Engineering (ASE 2011), Lawrence, KS, pp. 333–342 (2011). https://doi.org/10.1109/ase.2011.6100070
37. Chen, N., Hoi, S.C.H., Xiao, X.: Software process evaluation: a machine learning framework with application to defect management process. Empir. Softw. Eng. **19**, 1531 (2014). https://doi.org/10.1007/s10664-013-9254-z

38. Olson, K.: Process Mining Concepts for Discovering User Behavioral Patterns in Instrumented Software. All Regis University Theses. 842 (2017). https://epublications.regis.edu/theses/842
39. Mittal, M., Sureka, A.: Process mining software repositories from student projects in an undergraduate software engineering course. In: Companion Proceedings of the 36th International Conference on Software Engineering (ICSE Companion 2014), pp. 344–353. ACM (2014). http://dx.doi.org/10.1145/2591062.2591152
40. Thomson, C., Gheorghe, M.: Using process mining metrics to measure noisy process fidelity. In: Budgen, D., Turner, M., Niazi, M. (eds.). Proceedings of the 13th International Conference on Evaluation and Assessment in Software Engineering (EASE 2009), pp. 132–135. BCS Learning & Development Ltd., Swindon (2009)
41. Di Ciccio, C., Mecella, M.: Mining constraints for artful processes. In: Abramowicz, W., Kriksciuniene, D., Sakalauskas, V. (eds.) BIS 2012. LNBIP, vol. 117, pp. 11–23. Springer, Heidelberg (2012). https://doi.org/10.1007/978-3-642-30359-3_2
42. Weijters, A.J.M.M., van der Aalst, W.M.P., Alves de Medeiros, A.K.: Process mining with the HeuristicsMiner-algorithm. In: BETA Working Paper Series WP 166. Eindhoven University of Technology, Eindhoven (2006)
43. 1849-2016 - IEEE Standard for eXtensible Event Stream (XES) for Achieving Interoperability in Event Logs and Event Streams. https://standards.ieee.org/findstds/standard/1849-2016.html
44. Chavada, V.N., Kumar, P.: A survey paper on process mining. Int. J. Adv. Res. Comput. Sci. Softw. Eng. **5**(2) (2015). ISSN: 2277 128X
45. Dong, L., Liu, B., Li, Z., Wu, O., Babar, M.A., Xue, B.: A mapping study on mining software process. In: 2017 24th Asia-Pacific Software Engineering Conference (APSEC), Nanjing, pp. 51–60 (2017). https://doi.org/10.1109/apsec.2017.11
46. Maita, A.R.C.: A systematic mapping study of process mining. Enterp. Inf. Syst. (2017). https://doi.org/10.1080/17517575.2017.1402371

A Comprehensive Evaluation of Agile Maturity Self-assessment Surveys

Ozan Raşit Yürüm[1(✉)], Onur Demirörs[2,3], and Fethi Rabhi[3]

[1] Informatics Institute, Middle East Technical University, Ankara, Turkey
oyurum@metu.edu.tr
[2] Department of Computer Engineering, İzmir Institute of Technology, İzmir, Turkey
onurdemirors@iyte.edu.tr
[3] School of Computer Science and Engineering, University of New South Wales, Sydney, Australia
f.rabhi@unsw.edu.au

Abstract. Agile methodologies are adapted by growing number of software organizations. Agile maturity (also called agility) assessment is a way to ascertain the degree of this adoption and determine a course of action to improve agile maturity. There are a number of agile maturity assessment surveys in order to assess team or organization agility and many of them require no guidance. However, the usability of these surveys are not widely studied. The purpose of this study is to determine available agile maturity self-assessment surveys and evaluate their strengths and weaknesses for agile maturity assessment. An extensive case study is conducted to measure the sufficiency of 22 available agile maturity self-assessment surveys according to the seven expected features: comprehensiveness, fitness for purpose, discriminativeness, objectivity, conciseness, generalizability, and suitability for multiple assessment. Our case study results show that they do not satisfy all of the expected features fully but are helpful in some degree based on the purpose of usage.

Keywords: Agility assessment · Agility surveys
Agile maturity self-assessment · Agile maturity self-assessment surveys
Self-assessment

1 Introduction

As traditional development approaches did not produce the desired effects [1, 2] agile approaches became popular [3] specifically in largely growing SMEs [4]. This popularity has also increased the coverage and depth of agile methodologies in line with the agile manifesto [5]. Today, there are different agile software development methods, proposing different ways of achieving agile values and principles. The most popular

O. R. Yürüm—This study has been supported by Turkish Scientific and Technological Research Council of Turkey (TUBITAK), Project 113E528.

I. Stamelos et al. (Eds.): SPICE 2018, CCIS 918, pp. 300–315, 2018.
https://doi.org/10.1007/978-3-030-00623-5_21

agile software development methods are Extreme Programming [6], Scrum [7], Feature Driven Development [8], Adaptive Software Development [9], Dynamic Software Development Method [10], Crystal [11], Rational Unified Process [12], Kanban [13], and Lean Software Development [14]. Each of these methods includes different practices and techniques to increase the agile maturity (e.g. agility) of an organization. Even though the underlying practices and techniques are quite different, all of these methods focus on agile values and principles and organizations frequently utilize a number of them to obtain desired benefits.

Proliferation of agile methods led to proliferation of assessment approaches for measuring agility of organizations. Assessment approaches in agile adoption frameworks [15–17] and agile maturity models [18–24] require expert judgement; therefore, professional assessors must perform assessments. It can also take a substantial amount of time depending on the size of the project or projects and detail level of the assessment required. There are also self-assessment techniques that can be used by teams or organization. It takes less time, it is cost effective and have the potential to provide much needed feedback directly to the team. Hence, agile maturity self-assessment surveys can play a crucial role for improving agile maturity. These self-assessment models are frequently called surveys and they are in the form of checklists, questionnaires, tests, or software tools.

In the existing literature, a limited number of surveys were examined in depth by independent researchers. In existing comparisons, generally two surveys which are Comparative Agility and Thoughtworks are discussed [25–28]. In addition, several outdated agile maturity assessment surveys such as Thoughtworks Agile Assessment survey [29] and Nokia Test [30] are compared. We have also compared a subset of these models by means of a case study [31]. Nevertheless, there is no study that examines all available surveys in a systematic way.

The purpose of our study presented in this paper is to extend our exploratory evaluation study [31] to all the surveys available in the literature. Our previous work has evaluated 8 self-assessment surveys while this paper includes results of 22 surveys. This study aims to provide two significant contributions. First, based on the results software organizations will be better equipped to be able to determine the most suitable survey for their needs. Secondly, the results will also depict potential areas of improvement. For this purpose, we applied all the surveys in a medium-sized software company and systematically evaluate the surveys in terms of the expected features identified in [31]: comprehensiveness, fitness for purpose, discriminativeness, objectivity, conciseness, generalizability, and suitability for multiple assessment.

The rest of this paper is organized as follows: In Sect. 2, we provide a review of literature. In Sect. 3, we describe the case study design and conduct. In Sect. 4, we present findings obtained during the case study in detailed way. Finally, in Sect. 5, we provide a conclusion and future work.

2 Related Work

The interest in agile methods led researchers or organizations to develop agile assessment approaches to assess and measure the adoption degree by evaluating a set of practices with respect to these methods. Agile assessment approaches can be categorized into three categories: (1) agile adoption frameworks, (2) agile maturity models, (3) agile self-assessment surveys.

Agile adoption frameworks were developed to guide organizations in order to adopt agile practices. Some of these frameworks [15–17] include assessment techniques as well. Assessment approaches of the adoption frameworks usually rely on expertise and cannot be performed quickly. As a result, as Jalali emphasizes that they are not used by any organization or team except their creators [27].

Agile maturity models, also known as agile reference models are developed as baselines for guiding agile transformation. Similar to process based assessment models (e.g. CMMI (Capability Maturity Model Integrated) [32] and ISO/IEC 15504 [33]) they are used for improving and assessing agility of organizations. Agile maturity models developed based on these process assessment models are [18–24]. As Lappanen depicts these models are not mature and require further work to be usable in practice [34]. The latest and most complete model is AgilityMod [21]. It has been developed coherently with agile values and principles, based on the meta-model of ISO/IEC 15504 process assessment model and validated through a number of case studies.

Agile maturity self-assessment surveys, on the other hand, are used for assessing the health of team or organization in specific time range [35]. So, there are many surveys consisting of checklists, questionnaires and tests today such as Karlskrona Test, Nokia Test, 42-Point Test, and Scrum Master Checklist [36]. They are also attracted the attention of researchers who are interested in agility assessment. Chronis analyzed 4 of the surveys which are SAFE Team, Comparative Agility, 42-Point Test, and Thoughtworks [25]. The study concludes that they do not yield similar results and a measurement tool which satisfies the needs of one team may not be suitable for other teams. There is still work to be done in order to find a universal tool for measuring agility. Leppanen in a different study states that the most significant problem of the surveys is the predefined practice expectations and difficulty of adapting to various agile software development methods [34]. Some of the surveys on the other hand try to understand agility instead of measuring agility [37]. There are also studies focusing on features related to automation of the surveys [38, 39].

In summary we can state that although there are a number of agility self-assessment surveys and a few studies related with evaluation of surveys there are no studies in the literature that evaluates all the available surveys systematically by means of a case study in a software organization.

3 The Case Study

This section explains the design and conduct of the case study. Case study was selected as a research method in order to observe the usability of existing agile maturity self-assessment surveys. Case study enables us to examine a contemporary phenomenon within its real-life context [40]. Thus, it suits best in evaluating surveys for agility assessment of software organizations.

In this study, there is one main research question having seven sub-questions regarding the expected features of a survey (C1: Comprehensiveness, F: Fitness for purpose, D: Discriminativeness, O: Objectivity, C2: Conciseness, G: Generalizability, S: Suitability for multiple assessment).

RQ 1: To what extent do surveys cover the features that are identified in our previous study [33]?

RQ 1.1: Do the surveys meet agile practices in AgilityMod? (C1)
RQ 1.2: Are the surveys fit for purpose? (F)
RQ 1.3: Are the surveys discriminative enough to determine the agility? (D)
RQ 1.4: Do the surveys have objective questions? (O)
RQ 1.5: Do the surveys have concise questions? (C2)
RQ 1.6: Can the survey be used for all kinds of agile methods? (G)
RQ 1.7: Are the surveys suitable for multiple assessment? (S)

3.1 Design of the Case Study

In the design of our case study, we adopted the following strategies:

Survey Selection Strategy
We planned to benefit from scientific papers and search engines in order to find agile maturity self-assessment surveys. Therefore, IEEE, ScienceDirect, Web of Science and Scopus were determined to find surveys in scientific papers. In addition to the scientific papers, commercial surveys were also planned to be investigated. Two research key sets which are {Agile Assessment, Agility Assessment} and {Survey, Test, Questionnaire} were determined to identify existing agile maturity self-assessment surveys. The criterion for selection from those identified surveys is the availability of agile maturity self-assessment surveys.

Case Selection Strategy
Our strategy was to select an organization having results about their agility assessment. So, we planned to perform assessment on an organization in which assessors had already assessed its agility. The reason for choosing such an organization was that we were able to access to evidences about weaknesses and strengths of the organization related to its agility. Therefore, an organization, which had already assessed by professional assessors according to AgilityMod reference model would be selected. In addition, we planned to select a different organization from the organization in our previous exploratory case study.

Data Collection Strategy
In order to record data, we use a spreadsheet consisting of aspects and practices of AgilityMod, a form consisting of 7 expected features and assessment reports. The assessor having experience on agility assessment based on AgilityMod reference model was expected to match each question with the practices in AgilityMod and fill the form during the assessment. At the end of the assessment, the assessment report is obtained

about the agility of the organization. We also planned to examine this assessment report in terms of expected features.

Data Analysis Strategy

Our plan was firstly to write the number of questions for each practice after finishing the assessment. Then, we aimed to calculate the number of covered practices according to existence or absence of a question for each practice in order to determine comprehensiveness. The following table shows an example analysis about the determination of comprehensiveness.

Table 1. Example analysis for comprehensiveness.

Aspect OR Aspect Attribute	**Number of Question per Practice**								**Covered / Total**
Exploration (E.A.)	P1	P2	P3	P4	P5	P6			3/6
	1	**1**	0	0	**1**	0			
Construction (C.A.)	P1	P2	P3	P4					2/4
	1	**2**	0	0					
Transition (T.A.)	P1	P2	P3	P4	P5	P6			3/6
	0	**1**	0	**1**	**1**	0			
Management (M.A.)	P1	P2	P3	P4	P5	P6	P7	P8	7/8
	2	**3**	0	**1**	**4**	**2**	**5**	**3**	
Iterative	GP 2.1.1	GP 2.1.2							2/2
	9	**9**							
Simple	GP 2.2.1	GP 2.2.2							2/2
	2	**2**							
Technically Excellent	GP 3.1.1	GP 3.1.2							1/2
	5	0							
Learning	GP 3.2.1	GP 3.2.2	GP 3.2.3	GP 3.2.4					2/4
	8	0	**1**	0					
Total Practice (over 34)									**22/34**

AgilityMod [21] has 4 aspects and 4 aspect attributes. The aspects are Exploration, Construction, Transition and Management. The aspect attributes are Iterative, Simple, Technically Excellent, and Learning. Each aspect and aspect attribute have certain number of practices. There are totally 34 practices in AgilityMod. Therefore, Table 1 shows distribution of number of questions per practice and number of practices covered by a survey with questions.

In order to find the objectivity and conciseness, we concentrated on distribution of concise and objective questions in each practice. Then, we would determine objectivity and conciseness of the survey according to number of "Largely Achieved", and "Fully Achieved" practices. The following formula shows how objectivity is calculated for each survey.

$$Objectivity = (\#\,of\,FA\,Practices + \#\,of\,LA\,Practices)/(\#\,of\,Total\,Covered\,Practices)$$

Table 2 shows an example about the analysis of results in terms of objectivity.

Table 2. Example analysis for objectivity.

Rating	FA	LA	PA	NA	Objectivity (Total)	Objectivity (Percentage)
# of Practices	10	5	5	2	15/22	68.2

The same formula is used for determining the conciseness of the surveys.

$$Conciseness = (\#\,of\,FA\,Practices + \#\,of\,LA\,Practices)/(\#\,of\,Total\,Covered\,Practices)$$

Table 3 shows an example about the analysis of the results in terms of conciseness.

Table 3. Example analysis for conciseness.

Rating	FA	LA	PA	NA	Objectivity (Total)	Objectivity (Percentage)
# of Practices	18	4	0	0	22/22	100.0

In order to find sufficiency of other features, we decided to develop a case description for each case. We would evaluate the case description and form including seven features with content analysis. That is, we would match the findings with the criteria, and then rate each criterion for a survey according to 4-point scale.

Validation Strategy

After performing assessment with each survey, we planned to prepare assessment reports and discuss the results with an expert of both process improvement and agile software development methodologies.

3.2 Conduct of the Case Study

According to literature review, 22 available self-assessment surveys shown in Table 4 were determined for main case study. Table 4 shows available agile maturity self-assessment surveys with their name, owner, type, and number of questions they include.

The organization that we selected for the case study is one of the leading media companies in Turkey with its 17 million unique visitors on its various internet platforms. An ongoing online video platform project including 9 software developers, 2 graphical user interface designers, 2 business intelligence analysts, 1 tester and 8 content providers was assessed according to AgilityMod reference model. The evidence was collected from two project managers, a software team leader, and a graphical

Table 4. List of agile maturity self-assessment surveys.

Name	Survey owner	Type	Number of Questions/Items
42-Point Test [41]	Kelly Waters	Yes/No	42
Agile 3R Model of Maturity Assessment [42]	PhaniThimmapuram	5 point likert scale	11
Agile Assessment [43]	Piotr Nowinski	Yes/No	66
Agile Karlskrona Test [44]	Mark Seuffert	Multiple Choice	11
Agile Maturity Self-assessment [45]	Bryan Campbell &Robbie Mac Iver	Multiple Choice (2 Option)	6
Agile Maturity Self-Assessment Survey [46]	Eduardo Ribeiro	Yes/No	26
Agile Team Evaluation [47]	Eric Gunnerson	Yes/No	17
AgileTest [48]	ACM	5 point likert scale	14
Agility Questionnaire [49]	Marcel Britsch	6 point likert scale	60
Borland Agile Assessment [50]	Borland	7 point likert scale	12
Cargo Cult Agile Checklist [51]	Stefan Wolpers	Yes/No	25
Comparative Agility [52]	Mike Cohn and Kenny Rubin	5 point likert scale	65
Corporate Agile 10-point Checklist [53]	Elena Yatzeck	5 point likert scale	10
Depth of Kanban [54]	Christophe Achouiantz	5 point likert scale	69
IBM's Scaled Agile Framework © (SAFe™) Team Self-Assessment [55]	IBM	Yes/No, 5 point scale, Multiple Choice, Open Question	38
Maturity Assessment Model for Scrum Teams [56]	MarmamulaPrashanth Kumar	5 point likert scale	15
SAFe Team Self Assessment [57]	Scaled Agile	5 point likert scale	25
Scrum Checklist [58]	Henrik Kniberg	5 point likert scale	80
Scrum Master Checklist [59]	Michael James	5 point likert scale	42
Scrum Self Assessment [60]	Cape Project Management	Yes/No	60
Team Barometer [61]	Jimmy Janlén	Yes/No	16
The Art of Agile [62]	James Shore	Yes/No	46

user interface designer via interviews. The assessment results based on AgilityMod reference model showed that exploration and construction aspects of the organization were in first levels while its transition and management aspects were not implemented.

During this study, agility assessment was performed again with each available agility assessment survey in the light of assessment results and the evidence collected from the organization. Since we reached 22 agility assessment surveys, we performed 22 different assessments with the same organization in different time periods.

As mentioned in data collection part, we took notes in a form according to seven evaluation criteria and examined each question to match them with the practices in AgilityMod. After finishing the assessment, we obtained an assessment result based on related survey if the survey supports to generate assessment result.

We analyzed the forms, the spreadsheets, the assessment results, and case descriptions as mentioned in data analysis part in case study design section. Then, we rated each agility assessment surveys using the same rating approach [63] defined in ISO/IEC 15504 in terms of each expected feature. After rating, the results were presented to an expert who has more than 10 years' experience on process assessment and 2 years' experience on agile software development.

3.3 Validity Threats

The survey-based assessments were performed by one of the authors of this paper. He has assessment experience based on AgilityMod [21], CMMI [32] and ISO/IEC 15504 [33] since 2014. However, he had not taken active role on the previous assessment process of the selected case based on AgilityMod reference model. Therefore, there was a possibility to assess agility of the case incorrectly. In order to avoid this possibility, he examined the expert-based case study results and evidences in a detailed way before starting the case study with each agile maturity survey. Since he has enough experience on agility assessment process, it was easy to understand and adopt the expert-based case study results. In addition, after performing survey-based assessments, the results were discussed with an expert of both process improvement and agile software development methodologies in order to eliminate any bias of the assessor. We selected all possible agile maturity assessment surveys since our aim was a comprehensive evaluation. Although the evaluation is performed based a single case as the properties are related with the surveys not with the case it is unlikely to find further insight through replication. In terms of construct validity, which refers to the degree of measuring what is expected to measure, we selected an organization having enough number of indicators for agility assessment so that we can evaluate the measurement capability of the surveys.

3.4 Limitations

This study is limited to the agile maturity self-assessment surveys published on the time where the case study was performed. After that time, it is possible that new versions of the surveys have been developed by their owners. In addition, new agile maturity self-assessment could have been published during this study. However, we only take into account the surveys obtained at the end of literature review.

4 Results

The assessment results obtained at the end of the case study for each agile maturity self-assessment survey according to seven features are shown in the following Table 5.

Comprehensiveness
Assessment results show that there is no survey that can be called fully comprehensive. In other words, the surveys do not focus on all agility aspects. Many of them concentrate on management aspects only and exploration, construction, and transition

Table 5. Case study results.

Survey/Criteria Legend FA: Fully achieved LA: Largely achieved PA: Partially achieved NA: Not achieved	Comprehensiveness	Fitness for purpose	Discriminativeness	Objectivity	Conciseness	Generalizability	Suitability for multiple assessment
42-Point Test [41]	PA	PA	PA	FA	LA	FA	LA
Agile 3R Model of Maturity Assessment [42]	PA	PA	LA	PA	LA	FA	FA
Agile Assessment [43]	LA	PA	LA	LA	LA	FA	FA
Agile Karlskrona Test [44]	PA	PA	LA	FA	FA	FA	NA
Agile Maturity Self-assessment [45]	PA	PA	LA	PA	PA	FA	NA
Agile Maturity Self-Assessment Survey [46]	PA	PA	NA	PA	FA	FA	NA
Agile Team Evaluation [47]	PA	PA	NA	PA	LA	FA	NA
AgileTest [48]	PA	PA	NA	LA	FA	FA	NA
Agility Questionnaire [49]	PA	PA	LA	LA	LA	FA	NA
Borland Agile Assessment [50]	PA	PA	NA	PA	LA	FA	NA
Cargo Cult Agile Checklist [51]	PA	PA	LA	FA	LA	PA	NA
Comparative Agility [52]	LA	LA	LA	LA	FA	FA	NA
Corporate Agile 10-point Checklist [53]	PA	NA	NA	PA	NA	FA	NA
Depth of Kanban [54]	PA	LA	FA	FA	FA	PA	NA
IBM's Scaled Agile Framework © (SAFe™) Team Self-Assessment [55]	PA	PA	PA	LA	NA	FA	FA
Maturity Assessment Model for Scrum Teams [56]	PA	PA	LA	PA	LA	FA	FA
SAFe Team Self Assessment [57]	PA	PA	PA	LA	PA	FA	NA
Scrum Checklist [58]	LA	PA	NA	FA	FA	PA	NA
Scrum Master Checklist [59]	PA	PA	NA	LA	PA	PA	NA
Scrum Self Assessment [60]	LA	PA	LA	FA	FA	PA	NA
Team Barometer [61]	NA	PA	PA	NA	NA	FA	FA
The Art of Agile [62]	PA	LA	FA	LA	PA	PA	NA

aspects are not well covered by the surveys. In addition, the surveys generally focus on specific aspect attributes such as iterative and learning whereas they disregard the attributes related to simplicity and technically excellence. There are four surveys that we call largely comprehensive. These surveys are Comparative Agility, Scrum Self-Assessment, Scrum Checklist, and Agile Assessment. While Comparative Agility and Agile Assessment include Likert type questions, Scrum Self-Assessment and Scrum Checklist include true/false questions. They include sufficient number of questions for more practices when compared to others. Team Barometer is the least comprehensive survey as most of the questions focus on same practice that is "support collaborative work and shared responsibility" of the learning aspect.

Fitness for Purpose
Even though the surveys claim that they are developed with the aim of assessing agility of a team or an organization, there is no survey that meets fully the feature "fitness for purpose". They do not generate assessment results that include the improvement opportunities and suggestions. The purpose of the assessment is to guide the organization for continuous improvement as well as identifying problems. Almost all of the surveys focus to identify problems only. Therefore, many of the surveys are partly suitable for assessment purpose. There are only three surveys that largely achieve fitness for purpose. While The Art of Agile does not give the details about the improvement opportunities, Comparative Agility and The Depth of Kanban do not provide improvement suggestions to increase the agility level of the organization. The common positive property of these three surveys is to support reporting of the assessment. Corporate Agile 10-point Checklist does not meet the feature "fitness for purpose" at least partially. It does not include assessable items or questions. Furthermore, it does not support showing any improvement opportunity or improvement suggestion.

Discriminativeness
Assessment results show that Depth of Kanban and The Art of Agile surveys achieve discriminativeness fully. In these surveys, there are defined agility levels that show the agility degree of an organization based on the specific scoring range. Both surveys include four agility levels. In The Art of Agile, three of them are defined with colors: Red, Yellow, Green while one of them indicating 100 percent agile is not defined with any color since color also shows risk level of the organization. In Depth of Kanban, the level names are different. These levels are "Necessary for Sustainable Improvements", "Improving Sustainably", "Excellence" and "Lean". All of these are indicated with colors in radar chart. In addition, both survey results include areas or features that yield more specific results about the agility of the organization. In Depth of Kanban, these are related to 7 properties of Kanban: Visualize Effects, Improve, Feedback Loops, Explicit Policies, Manage Flow and Limit WIP. In The Art of Agile, these are based on phases of Extreme Programming: Thinking, Collaborating, Releasing, Planning, and Developing. There are also some practices to increase the agility in both surveys. Apart from these surveys, less than half of the surveys are largely discriminative. Comparative Agility, Agile Karlskrona Test, Agile Maturity Self-Assessment, Cargo Cult Agile Checklist, Agile 3R Model of Maturity Assessment, Maturity Assessment Model for Scrum Teams, Scrum Self-Assessment, Agility Questionnaire, and Agile Assessment are achieved largely in terms of discriminativeness. They do not include either agility level for the organization or scoring for areas/aspects of agility. The remaining are either partially achieved or not achieved. The general reason of not meeting discriminativeness fully is the missing comprehensive assessment methods in the surveys.

Objectivity
Approximately quarter of the surveys, include measurable questions that lead to objectivity: 42-Point Test, Agile Karlskrona Test, Cargo Cult Agile Checklist, Depth of Kanban, Scrum Self-Assessment, Scrum Checklist. The scaling type of most of these surveys is true/false. They are generally checklists or marked as true or false. Only Agile Karlskrona Test has multiple-choice questions. From other surveys, Comparative

Agility, Scrum Master Checklist, The Art of Agile, Agility Questionnaire, SAFe Team Self-Assessment, IBM's Scaled Agile Framework © (SAFe™) Team Self-Assessment, Agile Test, Agile Assessment are largely objective. Many of them include questions that are subjective such as "the team is more productive" or "the team produces higher quality products". Other surveys except Team Barometer are partially objective. They use words leading to subjective answers such as "good", "better", and "well". Team Barometer does not include sufficient questions related to practices that it covers in term of objectivity since it focuses on the ideas of team members about their team's agility.

Conciseness

There are eight surveys that meet conciseness fully. These surveys are Comparative Agility, Agile Karlskrona Test, Depth of Kanban, Scrum Self-Assessment, Scrum Checklist, Agile Maturity Self-Assessment Survey, Agile Test, and Agile Assessment. They are asking one-question at a time. In addition, the lengths of the questions are short enough to be easily comprehended. While 42-Point Test, Borland, Cargo Cult Agile Checklist, Agile 3R Model of Maturity Assessment, Maturity Assessment Model for Scrum Teams, Team Agile Evaluation, Agility Questionnaire, and SAFe Team Self-Assessment are achieved largely in terms of conciseness, Agile Maturity Self-Assessment, Scrum Master Checklist, The Art of Agile are partially achieved. Most of these include questions that ask two different things at once. An example from 42-Point Test is the item "Software is tested and working at the end of each sprint/iteration." Testing software and delivering working software are two different things that need to be considered separately. The other example is "Team members trust each other and are motivated to deliver sprint deliverables" from Agile 3R Model of Maturity Assessment. Trusting each other and being motivating are two different things. Their general property is that they are asked at once with a conjunction such as and, but etc. The remaining three surveys which are Team Barometer, IBM's Scaled Agile Framework © (SAFe™) Team Self-Assessment and Corporate Agile 10-point Checklist have not achieved conciseness even partially. They usually include more than one question for each item.

Generalizability

Most of the surveys focus on generic methods rather than focusing on one specific method. Apart from six surveys that are partially generalizable, others are suitable for assessment in the context of variety of agile methodologies. From the surveys, six of them focus on only one agile software development method. These surveys are Cargo Cult Agile Checklist, Depth of Kanban, Scrum Master Checklist, Scrum Self-Assessment, The Art of Agile, and Scrum Checklist. That is, they are not generalizable to all agile software development methodologies. Four of them, which are Cargo Cult Agile Checklist, Scrum Master Checklist, Scrum Self-Assessment, and Scrum Checklist, are based on Scrum, while Depth of Kanban is based on Kanban and The Art of Agile is based on Extreme Programming. In other words, these surveys are developed to be compatible with only one specific agile software development method. They are partially applicable to other methods since all agile software development methodologies share same principles.

Suitability for Multiple Assessment
Five of the surveys are fully suitable for multiple assessment. That is, they give each member a chance to rate each item. According to ratings of each team member, average rating value is determined for each item. Then, this value is used in determining the agility of the organization for the specific area. In addition, the analysis of multiple assessment is performed and depicted in detail in the assessment result. The fully achieved surveys are Team Barometer, Agile 3R Model of Maturity Assessment, Maturity Assessment Model for Scrum Teams, IBM's Scaled Agile Framework © (SAFe™) Team Self-Assessment, and Agile Assessment. 42-Point Test survey is largely suitable for multiple assessment. It allows each team member of an agile team to fill the survey and it gives superficial information about the result. However, it is not possible to get detailed analysis from the survey. Other surveys do not support multiple assessment. They are suitable for single agility assessment. In other words, only one person can perform self-assessment. with most of the surveys.

5 Conclusion

In this study, twenty-two available agile maturity self-assessment surveys are evaluated by means of a case study in terms of Comprehensiveness, Fitness for Purpose, Discriminativeness, Objectivity, Conciseness, Generalizability, and Suitability for Multiple Assessment. The case study results support the results of our previous study in the way that none of the agile maturity self-assessment surveys has fully satisfied the expected features. We found that, comprehensiveness, and fitness for purpose are the most problematic features that are not fully achieved by any of the surveys. While four surveys are largely comprehensive, three surveys are largely fit for the purpose. Only Comparative Agility meets largely both features. We also found that there are a number of surveys that are generic enough to be used by a variety of agile methodologies and there are also some surveys that enable multiple assessment.

From twenty-two surveys, Comparative Agility and Agile Assessment had six features which are largely or fully achieved. However, both surveys also have significant improvement opportunities. Comparative Agility meets only two features, which are conciseness and generalizability completely. This survey is largely comprehensive, fit for the purpose, discriminative, and objective. Nevertheless, it need to focus on more practices, establish ways to suggest practices for improvement, should have agility level definitions and more measurable questions. In addition, it needs to be improved to support multiple assessments. Like Comparative Agility, Agile Assessment also has significant improvement opportunities. Especially, it has serious deficiencies about fitness for purpose.

When all surveys are examined, it is seen that almost all of them have at least one fully achieved feature depicting how this feature can be implemented. For example, IBM's Scaled Agile Framework © (SAFe™) Team Self-Assessment is a good example for multiple assessment. Or some surveys can be used by organizations who adopt specific agile methodology. For example, while Depth of Kanban is more useful for organizations implementing Kanban, Scrum Self-Assessment is more useful for organizations implementing Scrum when compared to others. Comparative Agility is suitable for organizations to measure their agility from generic perspective. In other words, organizations can select the most suitable survey according to their priorities based on the results of this study. Organizations should consider that each survey has certain limitations even though they have some good features.

As a further research, we are planning to increase the number of case studies. In addition, we are planning to measure the effects of self-assessment surveys on success of organization's agility by using some of them repetitively over a long term period. We hope this study will establish a baseline for improving the usability of available surveys and lead to the development of new surveys.

References

1. Uskarcı, A., Demirörs, O.: Do staged maturity models result in organization-wide continuous process improvement? insight from employees. Comput. Stand. Interfaces **52**, 25–40 (2017)
2. Uskarcı, A., Demirörs, O.: Causes of continuity and participation problems in process improvement with staged maturity models. Commun. Comput. Inf. Sci. **526**, 177–178 (2015)
3. Garousi, V., Coşkunçay, A., Betin-Can, A., Demirörs, O.: A survey of software engineering practices in Turkey. J. Syst. Softw. **108**, 148–177 (2015)
4. Garousi, V., Coşkunçay, A., Demirörs, O., Yazici, A.: Cross-factor analysis of software engineering practices versus practitioner demographics: an exploratory study in Turkey. J. Syst. Softw. **111**, 49–73 (2016)
5. Beck, K., et al.: Manifesto for Agile Software Development (2001). http://www.agilemanifesto.org/
6. Beck, K.: Extreme Programming Explained: Embrace Change, 1st edn. (1999)
7. Schwaber, K., Sutherland, J.: The Scrum Guide, July 2014
8. Palmer, S.R., Felsing, J.M.: A Practical Guide to Feature-driven Development. Prentice Hall PTR, So Paulo (2002)
9. Highsmith, J.: Adaptive Software Development: A Collaborative Approach to Managing Complex Systems. Dorset House Publishing, New York (2000)
10. Wells, T.: Dynamic Software Development: Managing Projects in Flux. CRC Press LLC, Florida (2003)
11. Cockburn, A.: Crystal Clear: A Human-Powered Methodology for Small Teams. Addison-Wesley Professional, Boston (2004)
12. Kruchten, P.: The Rational Unified Process: An Introduction, 3rd edn. Addison-Wesley Professional, Boston (2004)
13. Stellman, A., Greene, J.: Learning Agile: Understanding Scrum, XP, Lean, and Kanban. O'Reilly Media Inc., Sebastopol (2014)
14. Poppendieck, M., Poppendieck, T.: Lean Software Development: An Agile Toolkit. Addison-Wesley Professional, Boston (2003)
15. Qumer, A., Henderson-Sellers, B.: A framework to support the evaluation, adoption and improvement of agile methods in practice. J. Syst. Softw. **81**(11), 1899–1919 (2008)
16. Sidky, A., Arthur, J.: A disciplined approach to adopting agile practices: the agile adoption framework. Innov. Syst. Softw. Eng. **3**(3), 203–216 (2007)

17. Sureshchandra, K., Shrinivasavadhani, J.: Adopting agile in distributed development. In: Proceedings of the 2008 3rd IEEE International Conference on Global Software Engineering ICGSE 2008, pp. 217–221 (2008)
18. Packlick, J.: The agile maturity map a goal oriented approach to agile improvement. In: Proceedings of the Agil 2007, pp. 266–271 (2007)
19. Patel, C., Ramachandran, M.: Agile maturity model (AMM): a software process improvement framework for agile software development practices. Int. J. Softw. Eng. **2**(1), 3–28 (2009)
20. Ambler, S.: The agile scaling model (ASM): adapting agile methods for complex environments. Environments 1–35 (2009)
21. Ozcan-Top, O., Demirörs, O.: A reference model for software agility assessment: AgilityMod. In: Rout, T., O'Connor, R.V., Dorling, A. (eds.) SPICE 2015. CCIS, vol. 526, pp. 145–158. Springer, Cham (2015). https://doi.org/10.1007/978-3-319-19860-6_12
22. Türetken, O., Stojanov, I., Trienekens, J.J.M.: Assessing the adoption level of scaled agile development: a maturity model for scaled agile framework. J. Softw. Evol. Process **29**(6), e1796 (2016)
23. Yin, A.P.G.: Scrum Maturity Model. Technical University of Lisbon (2011)
24. Nawrocki, J., Walter, B., Wojciechowski, A.: Toward maturity model for eXtreme programming. In: Proceedings of the 27th EUROMICRO Conference, pp. 233–239 (2001)
25. Chronis, K.: Measuring Agility: A Validity Study on Tools Measuring The Agility Level of Software Development Teams. University of Gothenburg (2015)
26. Gandomani, T.J., Nafchi, M.Z.: Agility assessment model to measure Agility degree of Agile software companies. Indian J. Sci. Technol. **7**(7), 955–959 (2014)
27. Jalali, S., Wohlin, C., Angelis, L.: Investigating the applicability of agility assessment surveys: a case study. J. Syst. Softw. **98**, 172–190 (2014)
28. Nafchi, M.Z., Zulzalil, H., Gandomani, T.J.: On the current agile assessment methods and approaches. In: 2014 8th Malaysian Software Engineering Conference MySEC 2014, pp. 251–254 (2014)
29. Thoughtworks: Agile Assessment (2010). https://www.agileassessments.com
30. Sutherland, J.: ScrumButt Test aka the Nokia Test (2009). http://jeffsutherland.com/ScrumButtTest.pdf
31. Yürüm, O.R., Demirörs, O.: Agile maturity self-assessment surveys: a case study. In: 43th Euromicro Conference on Software Engineering and Advanced Applications (SEAA) (2017)
32. CMMI Product Team: CMMI® for Development, Version 1.3 CMMI-DEV, V1.3. Software Engineering Institute, Carnegie Mellon University, Pittsburgh, Pennsylvania (2010)
33. ISO/IEC: ISO 15504-5 Information Technology - Process Assessment - Part 5: An exemplar Process Assessment Model (2006)
34. Leppanen, M.: A comparative analysis of agile maturity models. In: Pooley, R., Coady, J., Schneider, C., Linger, H., Barry, C., Lang, M. (eds.) Information Systems Development: Reflections, Challenges and New Directions, Information Systems Development, vol. 1, pp. 329–343. Springer, New York (2013). https://doi.org/10.1007/978-1-4614-4951-5_27
35. Diebold, P., Ostberg, J.-P., Wagner, S., Zendler, U.: What do practitioners vary in using scrum? In: Lassenius, C., Dingsøyr, T., Paasivaara, M. (eds.) XP 2015. LNBIP, vol. 212, pp. 40–51. Springer, Cham (2015). https://doi.org/10.1007/978-3-319-18612-2_4
36. Nebe, K., Baloni, S.: Agile human-centred design: a conformance checklist. In: Yamamoto, S. (ed.) HIMI 2016. LNCS, vol. 9734, pp. 442–453. Springer, Cham (2016). https://doi.org/10.1007/978-3-319-40349-6_42

37. Guillot, I., Paulmani, G., Kumar, V., Fraser, S.N.: Case studies of industry-academia research collaborations for software development with agile. In: Gutwin, C., Ochoa, S.F., Vassileva, J., Inoue, T. (eds.) CRIWG 2017. LNCS, vol. 10391, pp. 196–212. Springer, Cham (2017). https://doi.org/10.1007/978-3-319-63874-4_15
38. Adalı, O.E., Özcan-Top, Ö., Demirörs, O.: Evaluation of agility assessment tools: a multiple case study. In: Clarke, P.M., O'Connor, R.V., Rout, T., Dorling, A. (eds.) SPICE 2016. CCIS, vol. 609, pp. 135–149. Springer, Cham (2016). https://doi.org/10.1007/978-3-319-38980-6_11
39. Yürüm, O.R., Top, Ö.Ö., Demirörs, O.: Assessing software processes over a new generic software process assessment tool. Coll. Econ. Anal. (43), 1–30 (2017)
40. Yin, R.K., Case study research design and methods. **26**(1) (2003)
41. Waters, K.: How Agile Are You? (Take This 42 Point Test) (2008)
42. Thimmapuram, P.: Agile 3R Model of Maturity Assessment (2015). https://www.scrumalliance.org/community/articles/2015/march/agile-3r-model-maturity-assessment
43. Nowinski, P.: Agile Assessment (2016). https://nowinskipiotr.wordpress.com/2016/04/29/agile-assessment/
44. Marberg Consulting: Karlskrona Test Online (2008). http://mayberg.se/learning/karlskrona-test-online
45. Campbell, B., Mac Iver, R.: Agile Maturity Self-Assessment. http://www.robbiemaciver.com/documents/presentations/A2010-Agile_Maturity_Self-Assessment.pdf
46. Ribeiro, E.: Agile Maturity Self-Assessment Survey (2015). https://www.scrumalliance.org/community/articles/2015/december/agile-maturity-self-assessment-survey
47. Gunnerson, E.: Agile Team Evaluation (2015). https://blogs.msdn.microsoft.com/ericgu/2015/10/05/agile-team-evaluation/
48. ACM: Agile Test (2016). http://www.acm-software.com/agile-test/
49. Britsch, M.: Assessing your Client's Agility - An Agility Questionnaire (2014). http://www.thedigitalbusinessanalyst.co.uk/2014/07/Agile-Questionnaire.html
50. Borland: Borland Agile Assessment 2009 (2009). http://borland.typepad.com/agile_transformation/2009/03/borland-agile-assessment-2009.html
51. Wolpers, S.: Cargo Cult Agile: The 'State of Agile' Checklist for Your Organization. https://age-of-product.com/cargo-cult-agile-state-agile-checklist-organization/
52. Cohn, M., Rubin, K.: Comparative Agility (2008). https://comparativeagility.com/
53. Yatzeck, E.: A Corporate Agile 10-point Checklist (2012). http://pagilista.blogspot.com.tr/2012/12/a-corporate-agile-10-point-checklist.html
54. Achouiantz, C.: Depth of Kanban - A Good Coaching Tool (2013). http://leanagileprojects.blogspot.com.tr/2013/03/depth-of-kanban-good-coaching-tool.html
55. DevOps Community: IBM's Scaled Agile Framework © (SAFe^{TM}) Team Self-Assessment (2015). https://www.ibm.com/developerworks/community/wikis/home?lang=es#!/wiki/W54ecb028c53d_48b0_9d5e_4584a00489d3/page/IBM%E2%80%99s%20Scaled%20Agile%20Framework%20%C2%AE%20(SAFe)%20Related%20Webcasts
56. Kumar, M.P.: Maturity Assessment Model for Scrum Teams (2014). https://www.scrumalliance.org/community/articles/2014/july/maturity-assessment-model-for-the-scrum-teams
57. Scaled Agile: Team Self-Assessment - Scaled Agile Framework (2008). http://www.scaledagileframework.com/?wpdmact=process&did=NjEuaG90bGluaw==
58. Kniberg, H.: The Unofficial Scrum Checklist (2010). https://www.crisp.se/wp-content/uploads/2012/05/Scrum-checklist.pdf
59. James, M.: An Example Checklist for ScrumMasters (2007). http://scrummasterchecklist.org/pdf/ScrumMaster_Checklist_12_unbranded.pdf

60. Cape Project Management: Scrum Self Assessment (2015). http://www.agileprojectmanagementtraining.com/Agile-Self-Assessment/quiz.html
61. Janlén, J.: Team Barometer (Self-Evaluation Tool) (2014). http://blog.crisp.se/2014/01/30/jimmyjanlen/team-barometer-self-evaluation-tool
62. Shore, J., Warden, S.: The Art of Agile Development. O'Reilly Media Inc., Beijing (2008)
63. ISO/IEC: ISO 15504-2 Information Technology - Process Assessment - Part 2: Performing an Assessment (2003)

Agile Usage in Embedded Software Development in Safety Critical Domain–A Systematic Review

Surafel Demissie(✉), Frank Keenan, Özden Özcan-Top, and Fergal McCaffery

Regulated Software Research Center, Dundalk Institute of Technology and Lero, Dundalk, Ireland
{surafel.demissie, frank.keenan, ozden.ozcantop, fergal.mccaffery}@dkit.ie

Abstract. Safety critical embedded software is a software that needs to provide correct functionality to avoid loss of human life. Embedded software controls much of the functionalities in Medical, Automotive, Aerospace and Cyber-Physical-Systems. The development of embedded software is different from ordinary software development as such development needs to be coordinated with the hardware development. Additionally, regulation processes and audits are also in place before placing the products to market. The objectives of this study are to understand the challenges of embedded safety critical software development, to investigate agile practices which have been in use in the domain, the factors affecting agile implementation in embedded safety critical software development. We have performed a systematic review to achieve these objectives. Our review has identified challenges related to hardware development, team-based communication and regulation process. This paper outlines the result of the systematic review.

Keywords: Agile software development · Embedded · Automotive Medical · Mechatronics · Aircraft · Safety-critical Software development challenges

1 Introduction

Nowadays embedded systems (ES) are everywhere from home appliances, wearable devices and electric cars to control systems in complex plants. By 2020, there will be 50 to 100 billion devices that will be connected through the advancement of internet of things (IOT) and embedded systems [1].

ES are composed of two basic components: hardware and software. The hardware component contains microprocessor or microcontroller, memory, input output (I/O) interfaces as well as the user interface. The software in ES is 'embedded' inside the hardware and provides control functionalities. Unlike commercial software that focus on algorithm and data processing, embedded software is often written for the specific hardware.

I. Stamelos et al. (Eds.): SPICE 2018, CCIS 918, pp. 316–326, 2018.
https://doi.org/10.1007/978-3-030-00623-5_22

Having hardware and software components to constitute the overall ES, the development of ES is characterized by simultaneous development of hardware and software. This is known as co-design [2]. A typical ES design life-cycle, as defined by Berger [3], has hardware and software development processes in parallel. Such development processes are dependent on one another and testing of one unit will require stubs of the other, and this can be challenging [4].

ES can be simple control units as in printers and cameras or safety critical systems like automobiles and medical devices. Given their criticality, evidence through highly-regulated process is required. For example, in the medical domain, depending on their geographical location companies need to provide evidence that they went through the desired process to get the approval by the regulatory bodies. In the European Union, medical devices must have the CE mark [14]. This process includes satisfying standards such as medical device quality management standard (EN ISO 13485:2003) [15], medical device risk management standard (EN ISO 14971:2009) [16] and the medical device product level standard (IEC 60601-1 [17]).

Modern ES functionalities are getting complex, and most of these functionalities are relying on the embedded software. For example, infusion pumps today contain tens of thousands of lines of code [5], and this number will go higher for recent premium class automobile which contains close to 100 million lines of software code [6]. With the increasing of complexities, safety critical domains are calling for a better software development practice. For example, in the medical domain, [7] report that complexity is exceeding software maturity, and the industry is not taking full advantage of well-known techniques for engineering software.

The development of safety critical ES must deal with challenges at high level concerning certification and regulation and technical challenges associated with ES at a lower level.

One approach that may offer assistance is agile methods (AM) [8] which has been a hot topic in safety critical domains in recent times. Agile methods recommend a high degree of expert customer involvement, ability to incorporate changing requirements and short development cycles producing working software. There are numerous agile methods including Scrum [9], eXtreme Programming (XP) [10], DSDM [19] and DevOps [11]. Previous studies of agile implementation in safety critical domains report both benefits and challenges. ES has also been reported to benefit from AM [20–22]. But as in safety critical domains, agile implementation in embedded systems also reported to have challenges particularly due to the hardware and software dependency.

The purposes of the study are to reveal the challenges of embedded safety critical software development in practice, to investigate the agile practices which have been in use and the factors affecting agile implementation in the embedded safety critical software development. We performed a systematic literature review to achieve these purposes. The review included 30 studies from Automotive, Medical, Aircraft, Aerospace and Mechatronics. The existing literature covers agile usage and challenges in the safety critical domain and ES themes separately, the review we performed focuses on agile usage on safety critical ES. The rest of the paper is structured as follows: In Sect. 2, we provide the followed review protocol. In Sect. 3, the results of the review are given. Then, we discuss the results for each research question in Sect. 4. Finally, in Sect. 5 we conclude the review.

2 The Review Protocol

The systematic literature review has been performed following a review protocol, which defines the research questions, selected digital libraries, search strings, inclusion and exclusion criteria and data extraction procedure. The review protocol was defined in the guidance of [12, 13].

2.1 Research Questions

In this research, the following research questions have been defined:

- RQ1: What are the challenges related to agile implementation specifically in embedded safety critical domains?
- RQ2: What agile practices have been used in embedded safety critical domains?
- RQ2.1: How are agile practices extended to address the challenges of embedded safety critical domains?

2.2 Search Strings

The following search strings have been selected and arranged to address the research questions above. In some cases, the search strings have been adapted to suit some of the specific requirements of the digital libraries that were selected in this review.

```
("agile" OR "scrum" OR "XP" OR "extreme programming" OR
"test driven development" OR "TDD" OR "lean" OR "DevOps"
OR "feature driven development") AND
("embedded" OR "embedded system" OR "embedded software")
AND ("Safety critical")
```

Additionally, we have applied the snowballing technique to avoid missing any relevant studies [19]. We used the following the digital libraries for the search process (Table 1):

Table 1. Digital libraries

Digital libraries
IEEE Xplore
ACM Digital library
Google scholar
ScienceDirect
SpringerLink

2.3 Inclusion/Exclusion Criteria

The following inclusion and exclusion criteria were defined for the review:

Inclusion Criteria

- Studies on agile implementation for embedded software and embedded system development.
- Studies on agile implementation for embedded safety critical systems.

Exclusion criteria

- Studies discussing general agile software development practices (non-embedded).
- Studies that are not in the safety critical domain.

2.4 Data Extraction

After defining the inclusion and exclusion criteria, a data extraction template has been defined on tabulated format on spreadsheet with contents of year, author/title, agile practices, domain, challenges, implementation detail and summary.

3 Results

The search process has been performed applying the keywords on each digital library. All of the search results from each database have been recorded on a spreadsheet. The initial search resulted in a total of 292 studies. In addition to the spreadsheet, we have used the Mendeley[1] tool to manage the organization of the studies. The first screening results (292 studies) have been imported on Mendeley. Each study has been analyzed based on the inclusion and exclusion criteria.

After analyzing individual studies and removing the duplicates, the final screening resulted in a total of 30 studies. The stages of the review process have been discussed and analyzed by senior researchers in this study.

The numbers of the studies found from each digital library after the first and second screening are shown on Fig. 1 below.

The studies which passed the inclusion criteria have been categorized in two groups:

- Studies that report agile implementation for embedded at a general level without specifying safety critical domain. These studies are S7, S12, S13, S14, S16, S17, S18, S20, S21, S22, S23, S24, S25, S26, S27, S28 and S29.
- Studies that address the safety critical domain with the embedded software characteristic. These studies are S1, S2, S3, S4, S5, S6, S8, S9, S10, S11, S15, S19 and S30.

In the tables below, we provided two classifications: the first one is based on the research type of the studies and the second one is based on the safety critical domain. In the first group, most of the studies are the case studies and experience reports. The

[1] https://www.mendeley.com/.

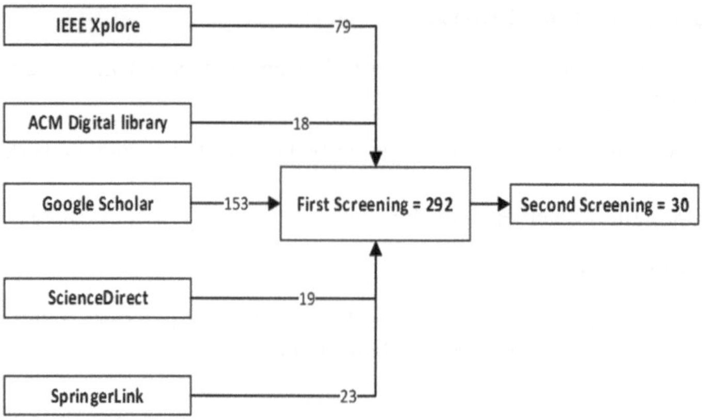

Fig. 1. Screening results

previous systematic reviews such as S22, S26, and S27 have also been identified. S26, which also addressees the previous review S22, report the result of a review that includes agile implementation with respect to embedded software, hardware and integrated circuit. This review concludes that most of the previous reports are case studies and experience reports and there is lack of rigorous empirical research on the actual benefits of agile methods in the embedded domain. A review by S22 addressed the implementation of agile methods in embedded software development. Study S28 performs a mapping of the principles of the agile manifesto to embedded system development. Table 2 summarizes the studies that have been categorized in the first group based on their types:

In the second group, a total of 13 studies have been identified to be in safety critical domain. Some of the domains are cyber-physical systems, automotive, medical/healthcare, aircraft and mechatronics. Table 3 shows the volume of studies that has been identified from each domain. The majority of these studies are case studies and experience reports. Some of the studies such as S1, S5 and S8 address agile implementation for safety critical systems without addressing embedded systems characteristics. On the other hand, studies such as S2, S3, S4, S6, S9, S10, S11, S15, S19 and S30 address safety critical embedded systems and software.

3.1 Agile Practices and Implementation

The majority of the studies implement a combination of agile practices. In the reports such as S4, S13, S20, S21, S22 Scrum is used with combination of XP. In S4, a combination of the practices such as unit tests, adaptive planning, iterative and incremental approach have been used. S20 implements the combination of Scrum and XP practices. Practices such as sprint planning meeting, Daily Scrum, Sprint review (retrospective), Unit Test, Test First and Pair Programming.S14 discusses the implementation of Scrum with acceptance criteria. This study stated that practice such as acceptance criteria can be used to define the aim of each of the stakeholders to manage geographically separated teams and collaboration.

Table 2. Studies on ES

Type	Empirical study	Case study	Experience report	Systematic review
Studies	S29	S7, S14, S17, S18, S21, S23	S12, S13, S16, S20, S24	S22, S26, S27, S28

Table 3. Domain specific publications

Domain	Publications	Embedded
Cyber-Physical systems	S11	x
Automotive	S3, S19, S30	x
	S1	
Medical/Healthcare	S5	
	S4, S9, S15	x
Mechatronics	S8	
	S2	x
Safety critical (not specific) Aircraft	S10	x
	S6	x

In S11, Scrum method has been extended for cyber-physical systems (CPS) known as 'Scrum-CPS'. This report proposes two sprints, design sprint and hardware sprint that synchronizes using the concept of Agile Release Train (ART) Additionally, Scrum has been combined with model driven software development, S6 and platform-based design approach, S21.

Study S23 improve the co-design processes using XP practices such as system metaphor, planning game, small release, testing, refactoring and pair programming.

The studies such as S18 and S25 have reported the implementation of TDD. Some of these studies addressed the need for tools support to effectively implement agile practices in the context of embedded systems.

Another study, S12 proposed a framework composed of Lean and Scaled Agile Framework using practices such as Two-Level Rolling Planning, Cadence, Synchronization, and Key Decision Points.

4 Discussions

In this review, we have investigated the challenges related to agile implementation specifically in embedded safety critical domains (RQ1). The results of our review showed that there are challenges related to agile implementation in safety critical embedded software development. One of the challenge that has been investigated in our review is hardware development which mostly cause long feedback loops. The long lead time of the hardware development affects agile implementation as hardware loops will be longer than the software development loops. As observed in S8, mechanical development also causes long feedback loops in the mechatronics domain.

Study S19 investigated the challenges of DevOps adoption in the embedded systems domain. The study categorizes the challenges in four groups, hardware dependency, limited visibility of customer environments with regard to configuring test environment, scarcity of tools and absence of feature usage data in system performance data.

In addition to hardware development, team-based communication challenge between diversified team members with domain specific knowledge is also investigated. Agile software development encourages team-based communication through practices such as cross-functional teams, pair programming and daily stand-up meeting. The implementation of such team-based practices in embedded safety critical domain has been reported to be difficult as a result of diversified team members with domain specific knowledge.

Standards and regulation process have been reported to affect agile implementation in safety critical embedded domain. Studies such as S5 and S10, states that standards require special attention as they set obstacles for continuous delivery.

Regarding agile implementation (RQ2), most of the studies report the implementation of more than one practice. The combination of Scrum and XP practices have been reported in most of the studies. Additionally, practices such as test-driven development and acceptance testing have been used with the combination of Scrum and XP. In addition to Scrum and XP, the recent trend has also shown the implementation of practices from DevOps, Lean and Scaled Agile Framework.

We have also investigated how agile practices have been extended to address the challenges (RQ2 -1). Our review has shown that agile practices have been extended, combined with other development technologies such as platform-based design approach and model driven development. Scrum has been extended to address the hardware-software designs. A combination of Lean and Scaled Agile Framework to address hardware-software development has also been investigated.

5 Conclusions

In this paper, we have discussed the result of the systematic review on agile usage in the embedded safety critical domain. The result of the review provides information for practitioners in this domain in understanding the challenges related to agile implementation and the way in which agile practices have been implemented to address the challenges. The majority of previous studies on agile implementation in embedded safety critical domains were case studies and experience reports. The result of the review has shown challenges such as hardware development, team-based communication and regulation process. The review has also shown that agile practices from Scrum and XP have been used in different variations and in combination with other development technologies. Additionally, the recent trend has also shown the implementation of practices from Lean, DevOps and Scaled Agile Framework. The embedded safety critical domain is looking for rigorous research to address the challenges related to agile implementation.

Acknowledgments. This work was supported with the financial support of the Science Foundation Ireland grant 13/RC/2094 and co-funded under the European Regional Development Fund through the Southern & Eastern Regional Operational Programme to Lero - the Irish Software Research Centre (www.lero.ie).

Appendix: Selected Studies

S1. Katumba, B., Knauss, E.: Agile Development in Automotive Software Development: Challenges and Opportunities. Prod. Softw. Process Improv. Profes 2014. 8892, 33–47 (2014).
S2. Eklund, U., Holmström Olsson, H., Strøm, N.J.: Industrial Challenges of Scaling Agile in Mass-Produced Embedded Systems. In: AGILE METHODS: LARGE-SCALE DEVELOPMENT, REFACTORING, TESTING, AND ESTIMATION. pp. 30–42 (2014).
S3. Manhart, P., Schneider, K.: Breaking the ice for agile development of embedded software: An industry experience report. Proc. - Int. Conf. Softw. Eng. 26, 378–386 (2004).
S4. Cordeiro, L., Barreto, R., Barcelos, R., Oliveira, M., Lucena, V., Maciel, P.: TXM: An Agile HW/SWDevelopment Methodology for Building Medical Devices. ACM SIGSOFT Softw. Eng. Notes. 32, 4 (2007).
S5. Laukkarinen, T., Kuusinen, K., Mikkonen, T.: DevOps in Regulated Software Development: Case Medical Devices. 2017 IEEE/ACM 39th Int. Conf. Softw. Eng. New Ideas Emerg. Technol. Results Track. 15–18 (2017).
S6. Mirachi, S., da Costa Guerra, V., da Cunha, A.M., Dias, L.A.V., Villani, E.: Applying agile methods to aircraft embedded software: an experimental analysis. Softw. Pract. Exp. 47, 1465–1484 (2017).
S7. Shatil, A., Hazzan, O., Dubinsky, Y.: Agility in a large-scale system engineering project: A case-study of an advanced communication system project. SwSTE2010 IEEE Int. Conf. Softw. Sci. Technol. Eng. 47–54 (2010).
S8. Eklund, U., Berger, C.: Scaling Agile Development in Mechatronic Organizations - A Comparative Case Study. In: 2017 IEEE/ACM 39th International Conference on Software Engineering: Software Engineering in Practice Track (ICSE-SEIP). pp. 173–182. IEEE (2017).
S9. Duffau, C., Grabiec, B., Blay-Fornarino, M.: Towards Embedded System Agile Development Challenging Verification, Validation and Accreditation: Application in a Healthcare Company. 2017 IEEE Int. Symp. Softw. Reliab. Eng. Work. 82–85 (2017).
S10. Axelsson, J., Papatheocharous, E., Nyfjord, J., Törngren, M.: Notes On Agile and Safety-Critical Development. ACM SIGSOFT Softw. Eng. Notes. 41, 23–26 (2016).
S11. Wagner, S.: Scrum for cyber-physical systems: a process proposal. Proc. 1st Int. Work. Rapid Contin. Softw. Eng. - RCoSE 2014. 51–56 (2014).
S12. Laanti, M.: Piloting Lean-Agile Hardware Development. Proc. Sci. Work. Proc. XP2016 - XP'16 Work. 1–6 (2016).

S13. Salo, O., Abrahamsson, P.: Agile methods in European embedded software development organisations: a survey on the actual use and usefulness of Extreme Programming and Scrum. Software, IET. 2, 58–64 (2008).

S14. Jie, J.L.H.: Industrial Case Study of Transition from V-Model into Agile SCRUM in Embedded Software Testing Industries. SIGSOFT Softw. Eng. Notes. 41, 1–3 (2016).

S15. Könnölä, K., Suomi, S., Mäkilä, T., Jokela, T., Rantala, V., Lehtonen, T.: Agile methods in embedded system development: Multiple-case study of three industrial cases. J. Syst. Softw. 118, 134–150 (2016).

S16. Punkka, T.: Agile Hardware and Co-Design Agile development – a brief intro. 1–8 (2012).

S17. Van Schooenderwoert, N.: Embedded agile project by the numbers with newbies. Proc. - Agil. Conf. 2006. 2006, 351–363 (2006).

S18. Smith, M., Miller, J., Huang, L., Tran, A.: A More Agile Approach to Embedded System Development. IEEE Softw. 26, 50–57 (2009).

S19. Lwakatare, L.E., Karvonen, T., Sauvola, T., Kuvaja, P., Olsson, H.H., Bosch, J., Oivo, M.: Towards DevOps in the embedded systems domain: Why is it so hard? Proc. Annu. Hawaii Int. Conf. Syst. Sci. 2016–March, 5437–5446 (2016).

S20. Greene, B.: Agile methods applied to embedded firmware development. Proc. Agil. Dev. Conf. ADC 2004. 71–77 (2004).

S21. Cordeiro, L., Mar, C., Valentin, E., Cruz, F., Patrick, D., Barreto, R., Lucena, V.: A Platform-Based Software Design Methodology for Embedded Control Systems: An Agile Toolkit. In: 15th Annual IEEE International Conference and Workshop on the Engineering of Computer Based Systems (ecbs 2008). pp. 408–417. IEEE (2008).

S22. Mingjuan Xie, M.S. and G.R.: Empirical Studies of Embedded Software Development Using Agile Methods : a Systematic Review. J. Inf. Syst. 2, 21–26 (2012).

S23. Chae, H., Lee, D., Park, J., In, H.: The Partitioning Methodology in Hardware/Software Co-Design Using Extreme Programming: Evaluation through the Lego Robot Project. In: The Sixth IEEE International Conference on Computer and Information Technology (CIT'06). pp. 187–187. IEEE (2006).

S24. Srinivasan, J., Dobrin, R., Lundqvist, K.: "State of the Art" in Using Agile Methods for Embedded Systems Development. 2009 33rd Annu. IEEE Int. Comput. Softw. Appl. Conf. 2, 522–527 (2009).

S25. Cordemans, P., Van Landschoot, S., Boydens, J., Steegmans, E.: Test-Driven Development as a Reliable Embedded Software Engineering Practice. In: Embedded and Real Time System Development: A Software Engineering Perspective. pp. 91–130 (2014).

S26. Kaisti, M., Rantala, V., Mujunen, T., Hyrynsalmi, S., Könnölä, K., Mäkilä, T., Lehtonen, T.: Agile methods for embedded systems development - a literature review and a mapping study. EURASIP J. Embed. Syst. 2013, 15 (2013).

S27. Bozheva, T., Hulkko, H., Ihme, T., Jartti, J., Salo, O., Van Baelen, S., Wils, A., consortium, I.-A.: Agile in embedded software development:
S28. Kaisti, M., Mujunen, T., Mäkilä, T., Rantala, V., Lehtonen, T.: Agile principles in the embedded system development. In: Lecture Notes in Business Information Processing. pp. 16–31 (2014).
S29. Ronkainen, J. and Abrahamsson, P. (2003). Software development under stringent hardware constraints: do agile methods have a chance? Extreme Programming and Agile Processes in Software Engineering, 2003, pp.1012–1012.
S30. Bosch, J. (2012). Applying Agile Development in Mass-Produced Embedded Systems Ulrik., 111(January 2016). Available from: http://link.springer.com/10.1007/978-3-642-30350-0

References

1. Perera, C., Liu, C.H., Jayawardena, S., Chen, M.: A Survey on internet of things from industrial market perspective. IEEE Access **2**, 1660–1679 (2015)
2. Wolf, W.: Hardware and software co-design. In: High-Performance Embedded Computing, pp. 383–432 (2007). Chapter 7
3. Berger, A.: Embedded Systems Design-An Introduction to Processes, Tools, and Techniques. CMP Books, CMP Media LLC, Lawrence (2002)
4. Teich, J.: Hardware/software codesign: the past, the present, and predicting the future. In: Proceedings of the IEEE, vol. 100 (2012). 1 Perera, C., Liu, C.H., Jayawardena, S., Chen, M.: A Survey on Internet of Things from Industrial Market Perspective. IEEE Access. 2, 1660–1679 (2015)
5. Jiang, Z., Mangharam, R.: High-confidence medical device software development. Found. Trends® Electron. Des. Autom. **9**, 309–391 (2015)
6. Infographic: How Many Millions of Lines of Code Does It Take. http://www.visualcapitalist.com/millions-lines-of-code/
7. Fu, K.: Trustworthy medical device software. Inst. Med. Work Publ. Heal. Eff. FDA **510**, 1–20 (2011)
8. Highsmith, J., Cockburn, A.: Agile software development: the business of innovation. Comput. (Long. Beach. Calif.) **34**, 120–122 (2001)
9. Schwaber, K., Beedle, M.: Agile Software Development with Scrum (2001)
10. Beck, K.: Embracing change with extreme programming. In: Archives of Disease in Childhood - Fetal and Neonatal Edition, vol. 92, pp. F83–F88 (2007)
11. Kim, G., Humble, J., Debois, P., Willis, J.: The DevOps Handbook: How to Create World-Class Agility, Reliability, and Security in Technology Organizations, DevOps Handb, p. 480 (2016). ISBN 194278807X, 9781942788072
12. Petersen, K., Vakkalanka, S., Kuzniarz, L.: Guidelines for conducting systematic mapping studies in software engineering: an update. Inf. Softw. Technol. **18**, 1–18 (2015)
13. Kitchenham, B., Charters, S.: Guidelines for performing systematic literature reviews in software engineering. Engineering **2**, 1051 (2007)
14. British Standards Online (America). http://www.bsiamerica.com/en-us/Sectors-and-Services/Industry-sectors/Healthcare-and-medical-devices/CE-marking-for-medicaldevices/

15. EN ISO 13485:2003 Medical Device: Quality Management Systems. Requirements for the Regulatory Process, 24 July 2003
16. EN ISO 14971:2009 Medical Devices.: Application of Risk management to medical devices, 31 July 2009
17. EN 60601-1 Medical Electrical Equipment.: General requirements for basic safety and essential performance. Collateral standard. Usability, 31 May 2010
18. Wohlin, C.: Guidelines for snowballing in systematic literature studies and a replication in software engineering. In: Proceedings of the 18th International Conference on Evaluation and Assessment in Software Engineering - EASE 2014, pp. 1–10 (2014)
19. Stapleton, J.: DSDM, Dynamic Systems Development Method: The Method in Practice (1997)
20. Manhart, P., Schneider, K.: Breaking the ice for agile development of embedded software: an industry experience report. Proc. Int. Conf. Softw. Eng. **26**, 378–386 (2004)
21. Kaisti, M., et al.: Agile methods for embedded systems development - a literature review and a mapping study. EURASIP J. Embed. Syst. **2013**(1), 15 (2013)
22. Salo, O., Abrahamsson, P.: Agile methods in European embedded software development organisations: a survey on the actual use and usefulness of Extreme Programming and Scrum. Softw. IET **2**(1), 58–64 (2008)

Industry (Short) Papers

An Enterprise SPICE Capability Profile for an ISO 9001:2015 Compliant Organization

Linda Ibrahim[1(✉)], Antanas Mitasiunas[2], and Robert Vickroy[3]

[1] Enterprise SPICE, Washington, DC, USA
rlibrahim@aol.com
[2] Institute of Informatics of Vilnius University, Vilnius, Lithuania
[3] ASK Advisors and Developers, Austin, USA

Abstract. This paper provides an Enterprise SPICE capability profile for an ISO 9001:2015 compliant organization. Assuming that an ISO 9001:2015 compliant organization would implement all requirements of ISO 9001, the author team assessed that assumed implemented process with respect to Enterprise SPICE processes and practices. The assessment results are presented in the paper. The results intend to indicate how Enterprise SPICE and ISO 9001 are complimentary to each other in improving performance across an enterprise.

Keywords: Enterprise SPICE · ISO/IEC 33071 · ISO 9001
Process improvement · Capability levels

1 Purpose

The purpose of this paper is to provide an Enterprise SPICE (ISO/IEC 33071) [1, 2] capability profile for an ISO 9001 (ISO 9001:2015) [3] compliant organization and, in doing so, indicate what additional Enterprise SPICE practices could help an ISO 9001 compliant organization improve its performance. It is hoped that ISO 9001 compliant organizations might investigate or implement Enterprise SPICE processes, as relevant to their business needs.

The paper seeks to address the following questions:

- Where does an ISO 9001 compliant organization stand in relation to Enterprise SPICE
- What additional Enterprise SPICE practices could help an ISO 9001 compliant organization improve
- How might Enterprise SPICE and ISO 9001 be used together in process improvement.

Why should we look into this topic when other research has addressed relationships between ISO 9001 and SPICE? With the exception of [4] most other studies have focused on software-specific models for comparison (e.g. [5–7]) whereas Enterprise SPICE is domain-independent, as is ISO 9001, and thus may provide additional insights for improvements across the enterprise.

I. Stamelos et al. (Eds.): SPICE 2018, CCIS 918, pp. 329–336, 2018.
https://doi.org/10.1007/978-3-030-00623-5_23

2 Background

Enterprise SPICE is an integrated enterprise-wide standard, published as ISO/IEC 33071, bringing together and harmonizing best practice from over 20 models and standards, including ISO 9001, into a single standard to provide efficient and effective guidance for process improvement. Enterprise SPICE users can reap the benefits of best practice guidance brought together from the most prominent models and standards into a single model. It is domain independent and can be used by any large, small, or very small enterprise that provides products and services to its customers. Each Enterprise SPICE process is described by a purpose statement, outcomes, and a set of base practices that support the achievement of outcomes and the fulfilment of the purpose. When used with the capability level definitions of ISO/IEC 33020 [8], (a measurement framework for process capability) it provides a path to continuous improvement from capability level 0 to capability level 5. Enterprise SPICE users select processes, according to their business needs, and do not need to address all processes at once.

ISO 9001 "specifies requirements for a quality management system when an organization: (a) needs to demonstrate its ability to consistently provide products and services that meet customer and applicable statutory and regulatory requirements, and (b) aims to enhance customer satisfaction through the effective application of the system, including processes for improvement of the system and the assurance of conformity to customer and applicable statutory and regulatory requirements" [3]. All ISO 9001 requirements, within the scope determined by the organization, must be met to achieve certification. ISO 9001 is intended for use by any organization of any size in any domain.

Enterprise SPICE and ISO 9001 can be successfully used together to help the enterprise. ISO 9001 helps set up a quality management structure, an organization that operates according to documented procedures, and that focuses on the customer. Enterprise SPICE helps by providing detailed best practice guidance to be included in the processes that are performed by the enterprise, and in the quality management system. Although they are implemented differently, e.g. certification vs continuous improvement, both standards are concerned with quality and process management.

3 Methodology

The author team made the assumption that an ISO 9001:2015 compliant organization would implement all requirements of ISO 9001. That assumed implemented process was used for assessment vs. Enterprise SPICE. Thus, we did not visit any specific organizations, but based our assessment assuming any ISO 9001 compliant organization would meet the requirements stated in the ISO 9001 standard. The authors, all experienced assessors/appraisers/auditors, proceeded to rate that virtual ISO 9001 compliant organization vs. Enterprise SPICE according to ISO 33020 [8] assessment requirements. Note that detailed assessments indicating which ISO 9001 clauses address which Enterprise SPICE practices, and the extent of implementation, were prepared for each Enterprise SPICE process. However, they are not included in this paper due to space limitations.

4 Results

This section summarizes assessment results and provides the Enterprise SPICE capability profile with assessment scope CL1 for an ISO 9001:2015 compliant organization. In the profile, PA 1.1 values F, L+, L−, P+, P− and N are defined in ISO/IEC 33020 [8]. Next, this section includes, for each Enterprise SPICE process, a summary of assessment results and suggestions where an ISO 9001 compliant organization might investigate or implement Enterprise SPICE processes to improve or expand its improvement program across the enterprise, as applicable.

4.1 The Capability Profile

See Table 1.

Table 1. Enterprise SPICE capability profile for ISO 9001:2015 compliant organizations.

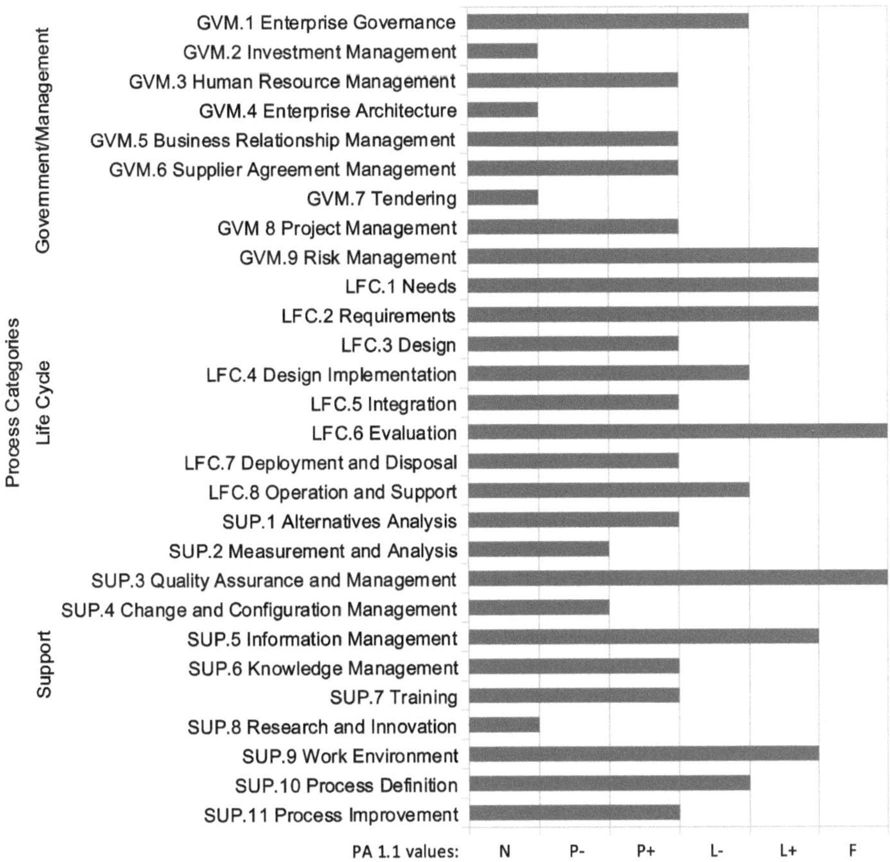

4.2 Brief Summary of Results for Each Enterprise SPICE Process

Governance/Management Category:

- **GVM.1 Enterprise Governance (L−):** ISO 9001 requirements cover many parts of Enterprise Governance, especially regarding establishing and communicating policy and objectives, and ensuring management review, but several additional practices need to be in place in relation to Enterprise SPICE. For example, the organization would need to establish and maintain a strategic vision, strategic plans, and tactical plans to accomplish the strategy.
- **GVM.2 Investment Management (N):** The Investment Management process is not addressed in ISO 9001. Thus, this process may be of interest to ISO 9001 compliant organizations concerned about managing their investments.
- **GVM.3 Human Resource Management (P+):** Several ISO 9001 clauses address part of Human Resource Management, such as identifying needed skills and competencies, ensuring persons are competent, and maintaining records of staff regarding skills. However, there is limited attention paid to establishing a strategy for human resource management, assessing staff performance, encouraging staff collaboration and teamwork, and staff motivation.
- **GVM.4 Enterprise Architecture (N):** ISO 9001 does not directly address Enterprise Architecture. It mentions changing and improving the Quality Management System, but there is no reference to the use of Enterprise Architecture standards, describing the current state, determining the desired state, and identifying benchmarks on the way to achieving that desired state.
- **GVM.5 Business Relationship Management (P+):** Several ISO 9001 clauses support Business Relationship Management practices, such as determining interested parties, creating service level agreements, and identifying value creation opportunities. However, attributes of business partners are not addressed, nor is there mention of establishing a service catalog.
- **GVM.6 Supplier Agreement Management (P+):** Several Enterprise SPICE practices are covered in ISO 9001 clauses including identifying and choosing competent suppliers and controlling changes to agreements. However, ISO 9001 does not directly address objectively reviewing estimates, establishing a supplier selection strategy, establishing a collaborative environment with suppliers, reviewing supplier processes and plans, and paying the supplier.
- **GVM.7 Tendering (N):** The Tendering process is not addressed in ISO 9001. Thus, this process may be of interest to ISO 9001 compliant organizations that pursue acquisition opportunities.
- **GVM.8 Project Management (P+):** The Project Management process applies to managing any product development or maintenance undertaking or managing service provision. Similarly, ISO 9001 addresses managing projects that provide products and services. However, Enterprise SPICE project management practices provide more detailed guidance.

- **GVM.9 Risk Management (L+):** The Risk Management process of ISO33071 elaborates on the newly added risk management depicted in ISO9001. Enterprise SPICE provides more best practices where more depth is necessary in that process.

Life Cycle Category:

- **LFC.1 Needs (L+):** ISO 9001 requirements cover many parts of the Needs process: identification of customers and stakeholders, communication and interaction with customers throughout the life cycle. Several additional practices need to be in place in relation to Enterprise SPICE: elicitation of customers and other stakeholders' needs, expectations, and measures of effectiveness.
- **LFC.2 Requirements (L+):** ISO 9001 clauses address many parts of the Requirements process: identification of all types of requirements to ensure that they satisfy established quality criteria. The requirements are not linked to the customer needs and expectations, the traceability, feasibility and verifiability is not required.
- **LFC.3 Design (P+):** Several ISO 9001 clauses address part of Design process. However, there is limited attention paid to establishing criteria for design alternatives, evaluation of alternatives against established criteria to select the architecture, structure, and elements for the product or services design, development interface specifications for selected products and service elements.
- **LFC.4 Design Implementation (L−):** ISO 9001 considers several aspects related to design implementation strategy and methods to be used. However, the establishing of standards and tools is not required, the constraints associated with the strategy are not required to be identified, the requirements to formulate solution components according to the implementation strategy are missing.
- **LFC.5 Integration (P+):** Several ISO 9001 clauses support Integration process. However, the requirements to develop an integration strategy and supporting documentation, to obtain integration facilities, personnel, and materials are absent.
- **LFC.6 Evaluation (F):** Almost all Enterprise SPICE practices are covered in ISO 9001 clauses including establishing and maintaining the tools, facilities, personnel, documentation, and environment needed to perform planned evaluations.
- **LFC.7 Deployment and Disposal (P+):** ISO 9001 considers several aspects related to Deployment and Disposal process. However, the requirements to identify functions and resources needed to ensure continuity during transition, establish and maintain continuity plans, to destroy, store, recycle the replaced product are absent.
- **LFC.8 Operation and Support (L−):** A number of Operation and Support process practices are addressed in ISO 9001. However, the core practices of this process are not addressed: operate the product or service in its intended environment according to agreed service levels, perform corrective and/or preventive maintenance by replacing or servicing product or service elements prior to failure.

Support Category:

- **SUP.1 Alternatives Analysis (P+):** There are some ISO 9001 requirements pertaining to Alternatives Analysis including determining and applying criteria for evaluation and selection of external providers and retaining documentation regarding their selection. However, several practices are not addressed including:

establishing an alternatives analysis strategy, selecting alternative analysis methods, identifying alternative solutions, and communicating analysis results.

- **SUP.2 Measurement and Analysis (P−):** Several ISO 9001 requirements address Measurement and Analysis practices to analyze and evaluate appropriate data and information arising from monitoring and measurement. However, the practices to define an appropriate measurement strategy to identify, perform and evaluate measurement activities and results, to collect, verify and validate measurement data and interpret results, to store measurement data in a repository are not addressed.
- **SUP.3 Quality Assurance and Management (F):** ISO 9001 requirements address Quality Assurance and Management practices to assure the quality of the product or service and of the processes used, and provide management with appropriate visibility into all relevant quality aspects.
- **SUP.4 Change and Configuration Management (P−):** Several ISO 9001 requirements address Change Management practices. However, the practices related to the configuration management are not required.
- **SUP.5 Information Management (L+):** ISO 9001 addresses many Information Management practices including establishing a strategy and requirements for information to be managed. However, information capability is not addressed including repository, tools, equipment, procedures for Information Management.
- **SUP.6 Knowledge Management (P+):** Several ISO 9001 requirements pertain to Knowledge Management, e.g. it is required to determine knowledge needed for operation of processes and to achieve conformity of products and services, to record knowledge items, and to disseminate knowledge assets. However, there are no requirements to establish a knowledge management strategy, establish a network of contributors, or assess or validate knowledge assets.
- **SUP.7 Training (P+):** Several Training practices are addressed in ISO 9001 including determining needed skills, ensuring persons are competent, evaluating effectiveness of training, and retaining training records. However, there are no requirements to establish a training strategy or a training plan. There is no attention given to establishing a training capability, delivery mechanisms, or preparing for training execution, and there is no mention of establishing a learning environment.
- **SUP.8 Research and Innovation (N):** ISO 9001 does not directly address Research and Innovation. It does have a requirement to determine and select opportunities for improvement, but this does not address innovation. An ISO 9001 compliant organization might consider establishing initiatives to: maintain new technology awareness, establish criteria for choosing innovations, prepare for innovation infusion such as piloting the innovation, and manage those innovations.
- **SUP.9 Work Environment (L+):** Several ISO 9001 requirements address Work Environment including understanding needs and expectations, establishing environment and infrastructure, and ensuring competency and qualification of personnel. However, work environment standards are not addressed, nor are the following: maintaining technology awareness, monitoring and inserting new technology to improve the work environment, ensuring work environment continuity, and testing and training for continuity and recovery.

- **SUP.10 Process Definition (L−):** Several ISO 9001 requirements address Process Definition process practices including establishing and maintaining the enterprise's set of standard processes. However, the practices to establish and maintain tailoring criteria and guidelines for the enterprise's set of standard processes, to establish and maintain the enterprise process asset library are not addressed.
- **SUP.11 Process Improvement (P+):** Several ISO 9001 requirements address Process Improvement practices including identifying issues arising from the organization's internal/external environment or organization's appraisals as improvement opportunities. However, the explicit practices to continuously and measurably improve processes capability are not required.

5 Summary, Conclusions and Future Work

This paper presents the Enterprise SPICE capability profile for an ISO 9001:2015 compliant organization. It indicates quality management areas that might be improved as well as additional processes that might be addressed in an ISO 9001 compliant organization in relation to the Enterprise SPICE standard, in accordance with its business needs. The paper includes brief summarizing narratives for Enterprise SPICE process assessment results indicating the strengths and improvement opportunities as related to each process. Some Enterprise SPICE processes are beyond the scope of ISO 9001, and have been indicated as such, for potential investigation by ISO 9001 compliant organizations.

Of the 28 processes of Enterprise SPICE, ISO 9001 ratings included: 2 rated as Fully implemented, 9 rated as Largely implemented (either L+ or L−), 13 rated as Partially implemented (either P+ or P−) and 4 rated as Not implemented. However only 2 Enterprise SPICE processes were rated as Fully implemented: Evaluation and Quality Assurance and Management.

Since Enterprise SPICE is much broader in scope than ISO 9001, there are several Enterprise SPICE processes that might benefit an ISO 9001 compliant organization. By looking more broadly at improvements across the rest of the enterprise beyond the quality management system, there are many opportunities to address best practices that have been integrated into Enterprise SPICE. In addition, since Enterprise SPICE includes all ISO 9001 requirements, a successful Enterprise SPICE assessment already addresses ISO 9001 certification requirements, and more.

Further work may include a study of the ISO 9001 Process Assessment Model (ISO/IEC TS 33073:2017 Information technology - Process assessment - Process capability assessment model for quality management) [9] in relation to Enterprise SPICE. Both ISO 9001 PAM and Enterprise SPICE are domain independent process assessment models for an organization's processes. The comparison of these two models could be done at the base practices level. The results of comparison could be presented as two Enterprise SPICE capability profiles established under the assumption that ISO 9001 PAM base practices are performed fully.

ISO 9001 PAM base practices consist of two subsets. One subset contains base practices that have associations with ISO 9001 requirements. The other subset contains additional base practices that have no associated requirements. A question is, do the additional base practices with no associated ISO 9001 requirements influence the Enterprise SPICE capability profile? Thus, one Enterprise SPICE capability profile could be established based on ISO 9001 PAM base practices that have associations with ISO 9001 requirements, and the other capability profile could be derived based on all ISO 9001 PAM base practices. Such capability profiles would demonstrate relations between ISO 9001 PAM and Enterprise SPICE and the extent of ISO 9001 PAM enhancement in comparison to ISO 9001 requirements.

Acknowledgments. The authors wish to thank Alec Dorling, Vicky Hailey, Ernest Wallmueller, and Wolfgang Daschner for their valuable comments on a preliminary version of this paper.

References

1. ISO/IEC 33071 Information Technology- Process assessment – An integrated process capability assessment model for Enterprise Processes (2016)
2. Enterprise SPICE Project Team: Enterprise SPICE An Integrated Model for Enterprise-wide Assessment and Improvement, Technical report – Issue 1. SPICE User Group (2010). http://www.enterprisespice.com
3. ISO 9001:2015 Quality management systems – Requirements (2015)
4. Ibrahim, L., Wells, C.: Guidelines for Using FAA-iCMM® v2.0 and ISO 9001:2000 in Process Improvement, Federal Aviation Administration, February 2004
5. Paulk, M.C.: A Comparison of ISO 9001 and the Capability Maturity Model for Software, Technical report CMU/SEI-94-TR-12, ESC-TR-94-12, July 1994
6. Jung, H.-W., Hunter, R.: The relationship between ISO/IEC 15504 process capability levels, ISO 9001 certification and organization size: An empirical study. J. Syst. Softw. **59**, 43–55 (2001)
7. Hailey, V.A.: A comparison of ISO 9001 and the SPICE framework. In: El Emam, K., Drouin, J.-N., Melo, W. (eds.) SPICE the Theory and Practice of Software Process Improvement and Capability Determination. IEEE Computer Society (1998)
8. ISO/IEC 33020 Information Technology- Process assessment - Process measurement framework for assessment of process capability (2015)
9. ISO/IEC TS 33073:2017 Information technology - Process assessment - Process capability assessment model for quality management

A Process Reference and Assessment Model for ECU Software Calibration Data

Paul Malcolm Darnell[1](✉) and Joe Walsh[2](✉)

[1] Modus SSE Ltd., 15 Dunblane Drive, Royal Leamington Spa, UK
pdarnell@modus-sse.co.uk
[2] Jaguar Land Rover Ltd., Abbey Road, Whitley, Coventry, UK
jwalsh82@jaguarlandrover.com

Abstract. There have been significant developments in process models for the development of embedded software over many years, culminating in the Automotive SPICE® process model. In automotive applications, there has been an increasing use of application parameters within the embedded software to allow for the parameterisation of generic solutions to specific vehicle applications. This paper proposes a process assessment model that can be applied to the parameterisation process, referred to as calibration. The process follows the framework of the Automotive SPICE® process model and links to the 'plug-in concept' therein described. It details an exemplar calibration process and defines specific outcomes and base practices. The steps within the processes will be familiar to professionals working in the field of calibration. The benefit of the process model is combining elements of industry best practice into a single process model.

Keywords: Calibration · Parameterisation · Automotive SPICE®
Process assessment model

1 Introduction

Since the 1990s, the importance of strong process in the field of embedded software has become increasingly recognised as a foundation for delivery of high quality, safe software. There are numerous exemplar process models, and the adoption and adherence to these is becoming essential as software complexity increases.

In 2002, ISO15228 [1] was published, covering Systems and Software Engineering - Systems Life Cycle Processes, followed by Automotive SPICE®[1] in 2005 [2]. These support increasing adoption of System Engineering within the automotive industry, but do not define processes for 'calibration'.

An example of calibration is parameterisation of software application parameters for a cruise control (CC) system. The software is likely to include a closed loop vehicle speed controller, consisting of proportional, integral and differential (PID) terms. The optimisation of the PID gain settings (application parameters) will be conducted once

[1] Automotive SPICE® is a registered trademark of the Verband der Automobilindustrie e.V. (VDA).

I. Stamelos et al. (Eds.): SPICE 2018, CCIS 918, pp. 337–344, 2018.
https://doi.org/10.1007/978-3-030-00623-5_24

the software and hardware (e.g. cruise control switches) are integrated as a system into the vehicle. This optimisation process is widely known as ‘calibration’.

A single Electronic Control Unit (ECU) can contain upwards of 60000 application parameters. Calibration of an ECU for a specific vehicle variant may take a large team of specialist engineers several years. Vehicle faults and warranty often occur due to incorrect calibration, whether it is due to misunderstanding stakeholder requirements, inadequate change management or configuration management, and so forth.

Automotive SPICE® defines an ‘Application Parameter’ as:

“a parameter containing data applied to the system or software functions, behavior or properties. The notion of application parameter is expressed in two ways: firstly, the logical specification (including name, description, unit, value domain or threshold values or characteristic curves, respectively), and, secondly, the actual quantitative data value it receives by means of data application.”

The process for planning, deriving, verifying and integrating the quantitative data values of the application parameters is not defined. Hence, an extension to Automotive SPICE® to include calibration is proposed.

2 Automotive SPICE Plug-in Concept

Automotive SPICE® introduces the ‘plug in concept’ (Fig. 1), depicting the fact that “A system is a construct or collection of different elements that together produce results not obtainable by the elements alone” [3].

The Automotive SPICE® concept includes elements consisting of hardware (e.g. sensors, actuators), software, mechanical (e.g. brake pads & cylinders), to form the system.

Logical definition of calibration data (e.g. data type, parameter name) is contained within the software. As described earlier, the calibration (i.e. definition of data values) usually occurs after system integration, which corresponds to SYS.4 within the Automotive SPICE process reference model (PRM).

Utilising the cruise control (CC) example, a system requirement for the cruise control system may be:

“The CC system shall maintain vehicle speed to target set speed +/−1 km/h*”.*

Qualification testing (SYS.5 in the Automotive SPICE PRM) to verify this requirement is satisfied can only occur following calibration of the CC system. This leads to the conclusion that the process of calibration is following SYS.4, and prior to SYS.5.

3 Calibration Process and Complexity

Calibration of data values is a significant task, and usually completed by cross functional teams at vehicle manufacturers and suppliers. There will be specialist engineers within these teams, each responsible for planning, calibration, integration, product release, quality assurance as so forth.

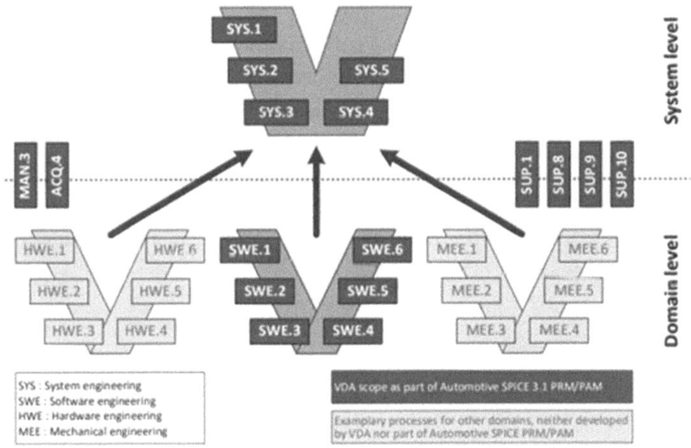

Fig. 1. Automotive SPICE® process plug-in concept

As an example, a power train ECU consists of technical domains such as sensor & actuator interfacing, combustion optimisation, emissions control, torque management, diagnostics, functional safety. The calibration of these domains is usually divided into tasks, termed 'work packages' (WPs). The sensor & actuator WP (e.g. the transfer characteristic for an air flow meter from voltage to air flow g/s) will have to be completed prior to the combustion WP (e.g. optimisation of fuel injection for a defined air flow), followed by the diagnostic WP (e.g. diagnosis of combustion faults).

Hence, the division of the system/software into WPs, the planning of WPs, verification of WPs, integration of completed WPs requires considerable planning. An example calibration process flow is shown in Fig. 2. It is an iterative process, with potential for frequent WP integration and verification events.

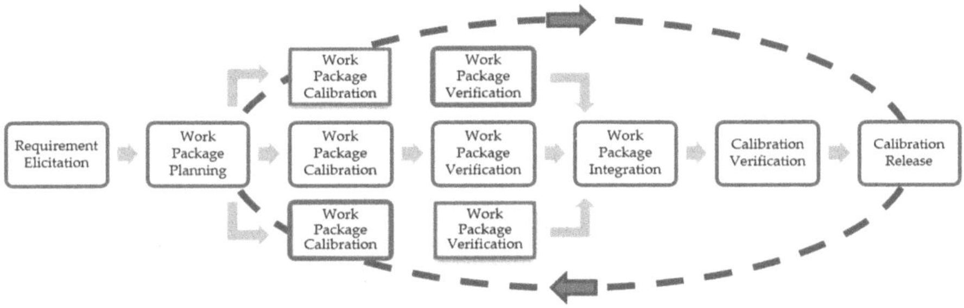

Fig. 2. Example calibration process flow

One of the drivers for the presence of high numbers of application parameters within automotive software, and especially within the power train domain, is the use of common technologies in different vehicle applications. For example, the same four cylinder engine may be installed in a variety of vehicle applications from small passenger car to large SUV. Rather than produce individual software variants for each application, it is more efficient to produce software that can deal with all of the potential variants and allow that software to be configured by calibration.

The magnitude and complexity of the calibration task has increased significantly over the last 15 years across all automotive domains. The number of application parameters that require calibration within a Land Rover power train ECU has increased from less than ten thousand in a 2005 model year (MY) gasoline four cylinder application to in excess of forty thousand by 2020MY in an equivalent application (Fig. 3).

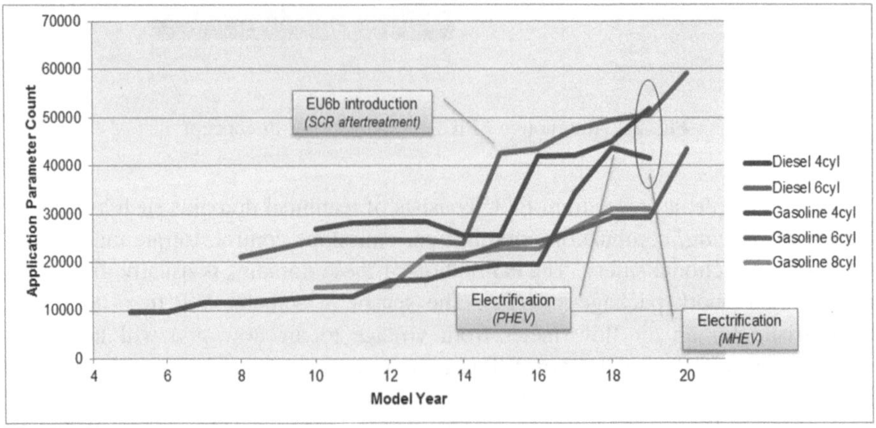

Fig. 3. Growth in number of application parameters in Jaguar Land Rover powertrain ECU

The number of application parameters continues to increase unabated, with substantial increases expected with the advent of Connected Autonomous Vehicles.

4 Why Is a Calibration Process Model Required?

The Automotive SPICE® process model provides a framework for creation of a strong, requirement based, software development process. Although it recognises the need to include application parameters within the software, it does not include the processes or base practices for ensuring that the quantitative data values of these application parameters are suitably managed. In the context of software that can be parameterised, the calibration of these application parameters has a significant effect on the functionality within the context of the overall system.

Engineers and project managers within any industry that relies on software that can be parameterised will recognise that many of the quality issues or error states that escape into the end user domain are not a consequence of software failures, but a consequence of the quantitative data values of the application parameters applied during the calibration process.

A recent example of such an escape, that may be attributed to the data values applied during the calibration process rather than the software development, is the fatal crash involving an Uber self-driving vehicle in Arizona in March 2018 [4]:

> *"the accident was caused by software that had been tuned [calibrated] to ignore objects in the road to weed out false positives such as plastic bags and other road debris. The software is suspected of having been dialed too far in the direction of ignoring objects in its path"*

A further example of the impact of the data values applied during the calibration process is the so called "Dieselgate" defeat device scandal that has affected parts of the automotive industry in recent years, with the Volkswagen Audi Group and Fiat Chrysler Automobiles allegedly using software strategies to circumvent emissions control requirements. In their detailed report [5], Contag et al. show that it is a combination of functionality in the software and the calibration of that functionality that led to the existence of the alleged defeat devices. In the case of some of the software aspects shown, it could be argued that the specific calibration of the various application parameters moves the software function from being an appropriate emissions control strategy to being a defeat device. As with most potential examples of this type of escape, the root causes have not been publicly confirmed by the manufacturers in question for either of the above examples.

A more mundane example of an escape would be a production intent calibration that was released into the manufacturing plant with an incorrect data value in the application parameter for the calibration part number.

Hence, there is a clear need for a Calibration Process Model.

5 Calibration SPICE

The concept development for the Calibration Engineering Process Group (CAL) (Fig. 4) came from the recognition that the existing Automotive SPICE® framework did not address specific escapes identified as part of product quality retrospectives within Jaguar Land Rover. The engineering teams were becoming increasing aware of the benefits and extendibility of Automotive SPICE®, and hence the logical step was to apply the philosophy of Automotive SPICE® to the calibration process.

The development of CAL was conducted by a team of technical experts, with experience in the field of calibration and Automotive SPICE®. There was a strong focus to maintain the structure and wording of Automotive SPICE®, even if this is less familiar to a calibration engineer (e.g. CAL.2 'Architectural Design for Calibration'). The expectation is that this approach better supports process experts and assessors to successfully deploy CAL, and that calibration engineers would adapt accordingly.

CAL consists of management of calibration requirements derived from system requirements, the sub-division of the overall calibration task into specific calibration activities, as well as the verification, integration and testing of the calibration. The subsequent sections provide high level overviews of each of the process areas for calibration engineering. In keeping with the Automotive SPICE® PAM, base practices and outcomes have also been identified and described for each of the process areas.

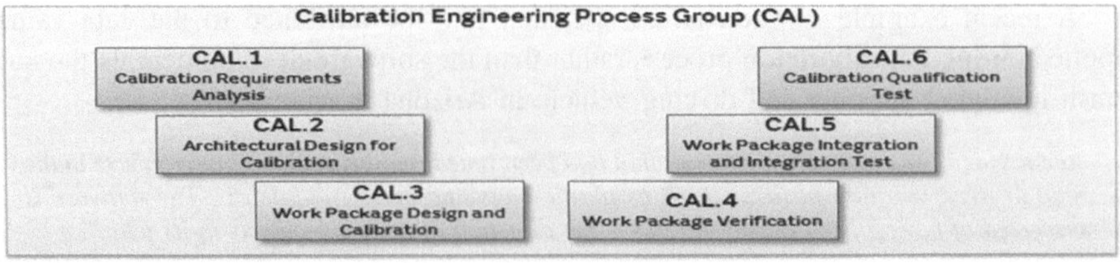

Fig. 4. Calibration engineering process group (CAL)

The 'Supporting', 'Management', 'Acquisition', 'Supply', 'Reuse' and 'Process Improvement' process groups within the Automotive SPICE® model are fully applicable to, and support CAL.

5.1 CAL.1: Calibration Requirements Analysis

This process deals with the identification of calibration requirements and constraints, including the decomposition of the calibration aspects of the system level requirements identified in Requirements Elicitation (SYS.1) and System Requirements Analysis (SYS.2). It is also concerned with the development of verification criteria associated with the calibration requirements and establishing traceability of the requirements to the system level requirements.

5.2 CAL.2: Architectural Design for Calibration

This process introduces the concept of sub-dividing the calibration task into a series of specific activities, referred to as work packages. The calibration requirements can be allocated to the individually identified work packages enabling traceability. This process also deals with establishing a strategy for how the calibration data is to be stored and managed, including configuration and variant management strategies.

5.3 CAL.3: Work Package Design and Calibration

There are several key elements within the process, including the allocation of specific application parameters from the software to the work package; defining the data collection methods and data analysis tools required; defining the plan to collect the data in line with the project plan; collecting, analysing and optimising the application parameter values; creating a calibration data file in a format adhering to the strategy and publishing a report describing the calibration.

5.4 CAL.4: Work Package Verification

This process defines the need for development of a work package verification strategy and regression test strategy. The process step also includes the work package verification activity and communication of the results of the verification.

5.5 CAL.5: Work Package Integration and Integration Test

The creation of the strategies for integration, and verification of the integration, of the individual work package outputs to create a holistic calibration that aligns with project plans are aspects of this process. The process also deals with the activities of performing the integration and integration testing.

5.6 CAL.6: Calibration Qualification Test

This process is focused on confirming that the integrated calibration meets the calibration requirements identified in the CAL.1 process within the context of the whole system. This includes identifying the appropriate level of evidence to confirm that the calibration meets the requirements and the creation of regression tests to allow future updates of the calibration to be re-verified in a consistent manner.

5.7 Example of Process Outcomes and Base Practices

Detailed process outcomes and base practices for each process area within the Calibration Engineering process group have been developed. The seven process outcomes for CAL.3 are (1) the application parameter content of a work package is defined; (2) the methodologies, tools, facilities and test properties required are specified; (3) test data is generated according to the specified methods and analysed; (4) application parameter values are generated and optimised, and any trade-offs required are evaluated; (5) a calibration data file, containing the application parameter values, is produced; (6) calibration status is published for the associated calibration data file, indicating the maturity and robustness of the parameter settings; and (7) a test report, including summary of characterisation and optimisation analysis and details of any trade-off choices is created and filed.

Eleven individual base practices have been detailed to deliver the process outcomes of CAL.3. These include establishing data collection methods (CAL.3.BP2); specification of data analysis tools (CAL.3.BP3); evaluation of any trade-offs (CAL.3.BP6); and generation of the calibration data files (CAL.3.BP7).

As an example, CAL.3.BP6 is concerned with ensuring that any constraints or limitations that would prevent the optimal calibration settings for a specific work package are analysed and any trade-offs that are made are documented and reviewed with stakeholders.

6 Calibration Plug-in to Automotive SPICE

CAL fits primarily into at the System Level of the Automotive SPICE® plug-in concept, as the key purpose of calibration activity is to parameterise the software within the context of the system (Fig. 5, label ①). CAL can also be applied at the Domain Level to the parameterisation of the software in the context of the hardware and/or mechanical environment (Fig. 5, label ②).

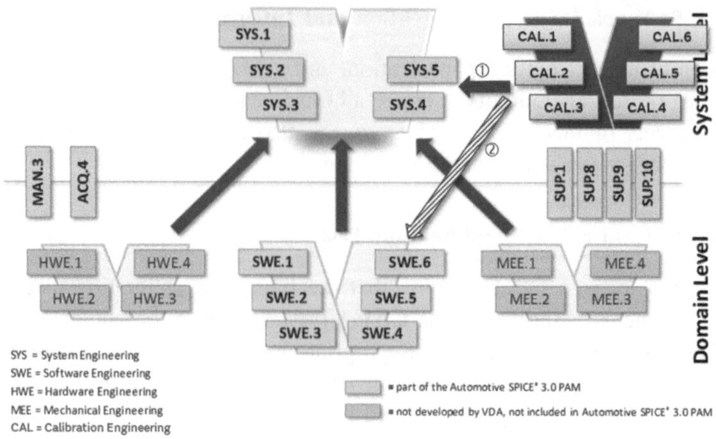

Fig. 5. CAL in context of automotive SPICE

7 Summary and Conclusions

The process of calibration has been described, and examples provided for issues relating to lack of calibration process control. Subsequently, a process reference and assessment model is developed for calibration engineering (CAL), and deployment of this model is proposed as a plug-in to Automotive SPICE®. All CAL process base practices and process work products are comprehensively defined. The authors seek wider collaboration and peer review, with the objective of formally publishing CAL.

The automotive industry, including manufacturers, suppliers, engineering service providers and tool vendors, will benefit from the introduction of CAL. It may support manufacturers to improve their calibration processes and assess supplier capability, tool vendors to develop and market product features, process auditors to seek new opportunities, and consultancies to provision training services.

Ultimately, the vehicle owner will benefit through improved quality and safety.

References

1. International Organization for Standardization, ISO/IEC/IEEE 15288:2015 Systems and software engineering - Life cycle processes (2015)
2. Automotive Special Interest Group. Automotive SPICE, 9 June 2018. http://www.automotivespice.com/
3. International Council on Systems Engineering (INCOSE), 9 June 2018. https://www.incose.org/about-systems-engineering
4. Ramey, J.: News article “Fatal Uber crash likely caused by autonomous driving software error, report says”. http://autoweek.com/article/autonomous-cars
5. Contag, M., et al.: How They Did It: An Analysis of Emission Defeat Devices in Modern Automobiles. https://cseweb.ucsd.edu/

An Ontology to Support TMMi-Based Test Process Assessment

Eda Gülçin Çiflikli[1] and Ahmet Coşkunçay[2,3](✉)

[1] ICterra Information and Communication Technologies, Ankara, Turkey
edaciflikli@gmail.com
[2] Department of Computer Engineering, Ataturk University, Erzurum, Turkey
ahmet.coskuncay@atauni.edu.tr
[3] Bilgi Grubu Ltd., Ankara, Turkey
ahmet.coskuncay@bg.com.tr

Abstract. TMMi, as a process reference model, introduces a collection of best practices that helps organizations improve their testing processes. Developing ontology of any process reference model help to clarify the structure of the knowledge, enable knowledge sharing, and enable interoperability. This study presents an ontology-based testing process assessment infrastructure to track conformance to TMMi as the process reference model. In this study, the TMMi model, SCAMPI-A method, and organizations are specified by the TMMi Assessment Ontology which is coded in a formal language and the ontology's application for assessment is described.

Keywords: TMMi · SCAMPI · Test process assessment · Ontology OWL

1 Introduction

Process reference models like CMMI and SPICE has become widely used with the intention of achieving higher quality. These models claim to bring benefits in cost, schedule, productivity, customer satisfaction, and return on investment within software development practices [1]. Although they cover all processes in software development, reference models that focus on improving or assessing specific processes within software development have emerged such as SMmm for maintenance [2], R-CMM for requirements engineering [3], MCM for measurement [4], and SA-CMM for acquisition [5]. In software testing, some of the most well-established process reference models are Test Maturity Model integration (TMMi), Test Process Improvement (TPI) Model, and Metrics Based Verification and Validation Maturity Model (MB-V2M2) [6].

Existing reference models are mostly textual. Representations of the models with clear rules and relations would improve their understandability. Also, software engineers that are more inclined to read graphical representations (i.e. models) would benefit from visual representation of the reference models and the assessments based on these models. Moreover, the tools supporting software process improvement do not usually interoperate with other tools. Interoperation would result in a benchmark of assessments based on reference models and knowledge sharing.

I. Stamelos et al. (Eds.): SPICE 2018, CCIS 918, pp. 345–354, 2018.
https://doi.org/10.1007/978-3-030-00623-5_25

There is not much evidence regarding the benefits of using ontologies to support implementing software process reference models [7]. However, commonly accepted uses of ontologies include enabling people and software reach a shared understanding and reusing domain knowledge [8]. Based on intuition, this would suggest that ontologies would contribute in establishing a shared understanding of the reference models, reusing the assessment outputs and outcomes, and enabling interoperability between tools supporting process improvement.

In the scope of this study, an ontology to support TMMi based assessments is developed with the intention of creating a mapping infrastructure between TMMi model and outputs generated by an organization as a consequence of implementing and assessing software testing processes. With a successful mapping, it can be an opportunity for an organization to consolidate their test process improvement efforts. The other purpose is to share TMMi assessment domain knowledge in a visual way since TMMi is mainly described as text in natural language. For these purposes, the study identifies and formally defines the concepts and their relationships that are necessary to perform a TMMi-based assessment.

Next section gives background information about TMMi model, TMMi-based assessments, and ontologies. Third section describes related studies on use of ontologies for defining software process reference models and performing assessments. Forth section specifies the TMMi Assessment Ontology and the three independent ontologies it is composed of. In fifth section, we describe an example use of the TMMi Assessment Ontology for an assessment in a real organization. Last section discusses the conclusion of the study and future works.

2 Background

TMMi is a guideline and reference model that was developed as a complementary model to CMMI by TMMi Foundation. It addresses software quality and test issues, which are briefly covered in CMMI, to support organizations with evaluating and improving their testing processes to achieve more effective and efficient software testing. TMMi has a claim to improve not only the testing processes but also the software quality, test engineering productivity, and cycle-time effort by doing so [9].

TMMi inherits several concepts from CMMI such as the maturity level, process area, goal, and practice. It has a staged architecture in which the highest maturity for an organization to achieve is the level 5. Each stage consists of process areas that an organization is required to implement. In order to achieve one maturity level, an organization should satisfy all process areas of that maturity level and the lower maturity levels.

Specific goals describe the unique characteristics that should be implemented in order to satisfy the process areas, whereas the generic goals describe characteristics that should be present across all process areas. In order to determine whether a process area is satisfied, associated specific and generic practices associated with the goals are expected to be performed.

The possible formal assessment methods to conduct a TMMi assessment are TMMi Accredited Assessment Method, TMMi Assessment Method (TAM) and The Standard CMMI Appraisal Method for Process Improvement (SCAMPI) A [10].

In this study, SCAMPI-A is selected due to it being a more commonly used method and being familiar to the organization where the validation is performed. SCAMPI-A is essentially designed for CMMI; however, it is recognized as a method to perform TMMi assessments. It provides benchmark-quality ratings which enable to identify the strengths and weaknesses of an organization, prioritize improvement plans by focusing on correcting weaknesses that are most beneficial to fix, derive maturity level ratings, and identify risks relative to maturity determination [11].

SCAMPI-A is used to decide practice implementation and goal ratings based on collected objective evidence. There are two types of objective evidence: Artifacts and Affirmations. Artifacts can be considered as a concrete output of either a model or a consequence of implementing a model practice whereas Affirmations are statements used to judge implementation or lack of implementation of a model practice. Based on collected artifacts and affirmations, the practice is characterized as Fully Implemented, Largely Implemented, Partially Implemented, Not Implemented or Not Yet.

Ontology is a formal representation of domain knowledge. More specifically, it is a formal explicit description of concepts and their relations in a specific domain [8]. An ontology can help to clarify the structure of the knowledge by machine-interpretable common vocabulary definitions, enable knowledge sharing, and build specific knowledge basis to make domain assumptions explicit [12]. Ontologies are usually defined with formal languages that are based on first-order predicate logic, frame-based languages, or description logic-based languages [13].

3 Related Work

Although, there are some studies presenting process reference model based ontologies, when it comes to TMMi and assessments based on it, there are no related studies. Tarhan et al. [7] also did not reported any studies related to TMMi related ontologies. However, there are some studies that shall be discussed and learned from.

Ryu et al. [14] presented an ontology for MND-TMM (Ministry of National Defense-Testing Maturity Model) in OWL language. In this work, only top-level concepts of MND-TMM are defined in order to share knowledge and help organizations improve their testing processes. The detailed ontology structure for the MND-TMM is stated to be under development. Gazel et al. [15] provides an ontology for both continuous and staged representations of CMMI-Dev and developed an Eclipse Plugin for supporting CMMI based assessments. The plugin is suggested to present an integrated infrastructure for process improvement and CMMI based assessment activities.

Soydan et al. [16] presented a CMMI-SW ontology. In this work, only staged representation of CMMI-SW model is defined in OWL and its possible use cases are explained. An ontology for CMMI-ACQ in presented by Sharifloo et al. [17]. It is implemented based on SUMO which is an upper ontology and is available for use in different applications to be developed in the future.

Software Process Ontology (SPO) by Liao et al. [18] is an ontology for software processes in conceptual level. The study briefly discusses how to extend SPO with concepts that belong to continuous representation of CMMI and ISO/IEC 15504 models as an example. A web-based process assessment tool is claimed to be under development, which will be used to collect data to develop a benchmark of software processes after being fully implemented.

4 Structure of the TMMi Assessment Ontology

TMMi Assessment Ontology is composed of three separate ontologies including a TMMi ontology, a SCAMPI-A ontology and an Organization ontology as in Fig. 1. It is developed in Web Ontology Language (OWL) by using Protégé platform. For the users to easily comprehend the mapping between the documents and concepts, the numbered tags within the documents were inherited into the ontologies (e.g. PA2.1). Also, some abstract classes (e.g. Level_2_Process_Area) were created for proper categorization. For instance, the "Test Policy and Strategy" process area is defined as "PA2.1_Test_Policy_And_Strategy" class and it is a sub-class of "Level_2_Process_Area" class.

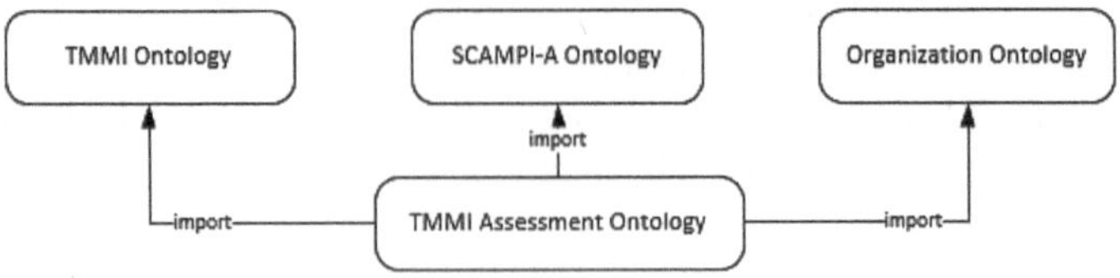

Fig. 1. The TMMi Assessment Ontology structure

4.1 TMMi Ontology

The TMMi Ontology includes 4 top level classes: Maturity_Level, Process_Area, Goal and Practice. There are 3 top level object properties as consistOf, achievedBy and satisfiedBy. The top-level classes and their relationships are shown in Fig. 2.

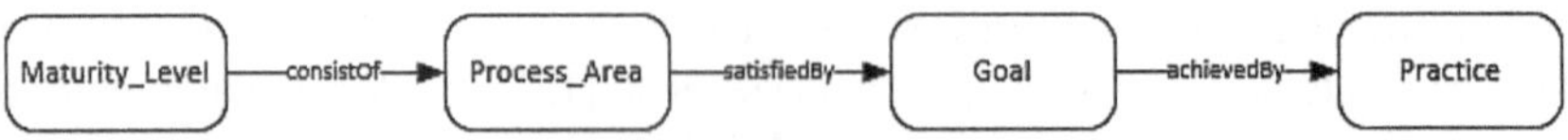

Fig. 2. The relationship between top level classes of TMMi ontology

In order to represent the staged foundation of TMMi, higher maturity levels are defined as subclasses of lower maturity levels as shown in Fig. 3. For instance, Maturity_Level_5_Optimization is a subclass of Maturity_Level_4_Measured, which denotes that an organization rated as maturity level 5 would inherit the properties of maturity level 4.

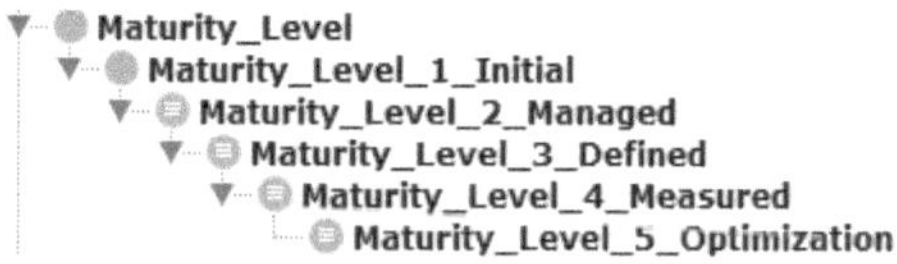

Fig. 3. The class hierarchy of "Maturity_Level" class of TMMi ontology

Process_Area class consists of subclasses to categorize process areas according to the maturity levels they belong to as shown in Fig. 4. A similar structure is applied for Goal class as shown in Fig. 5.

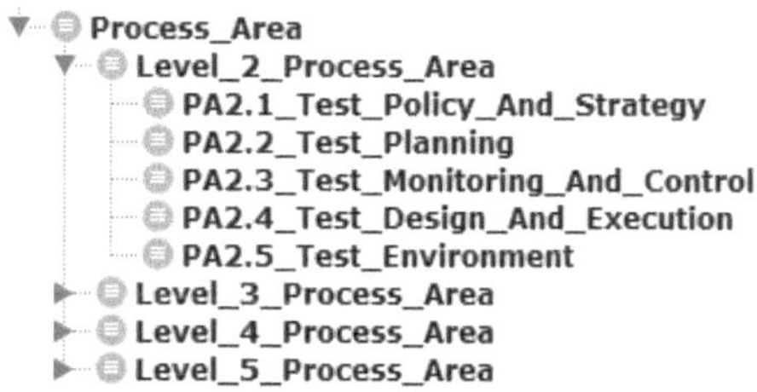

Fig. 4. The class hierarchy of "Process_Area" class of TMMi ontology

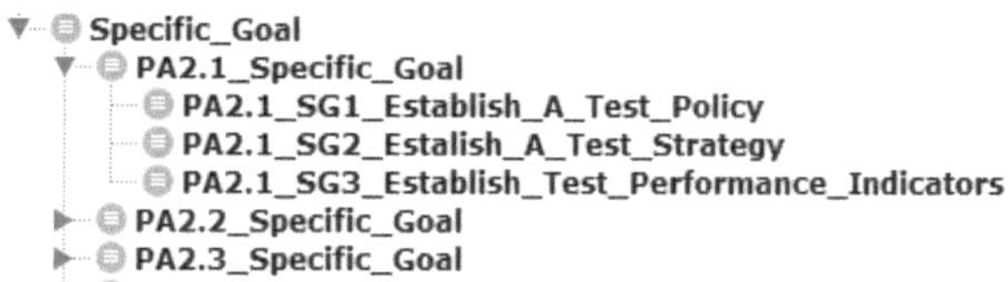

Fig. 5. The class hierarchy of "Specific_Goal" class of TMMi ontology

In the TMMi Model [9], applicability of the generic goals is determined by the targeted maturity level. For achieving maturity level 2, only generic goal 2 is applicable for all the process areas belonging to maturity level 2. However, for maturity level 3, both generic goal 2 and generic goal 3 are applicable for process areas of both maturity level 2 and maturity level 3. Therefore, generic goal 3 is defined as a subclass of generic goal 2 as shown in Fig. 6.

Fig. 6. The class hierarchy of "Generic_Goal" class of TMMi ontology

Each level in the Goal class hierarchy has more specific "achievedBy" relationship with the related class under Practice class hierarchy.

4.2 SCAMPI-A Ontology

As it is shown in Fig. 7, there are 6 top-level classes and 4 object properties identifying their relationships in SCAMPI-A Ontology. Although all related concepts of SCAMPI-A method are defined, only the assessment outputs of Conduct Appraisal Phase will be sufficient for assessment purposes in the scope of this study.

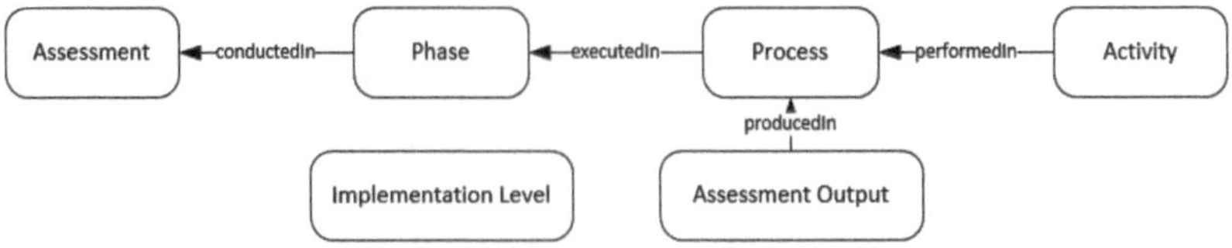

Fig. 7. The top-level classes and their relationships of SCAMPI-A ontology

Implementation_Level class does not have a relationship with other classes, however it is defined in SCAMPI-A ontology since it is needed for assessments and used in TMMi Assessment Ontology.

In SCAMPI-A method, each assessment process generates outputs, but the same assessment output may be revised and updated in several processes. Therefore, Assessment_Output class is grouped according to phases. Only "Objective_Evidence" and "Recorded_Rating_Decisions" outputs are used in mapping to the integrated TMMi Assessment Ontology. The class hierarchy of Assessment_Output is in Fig. 8.

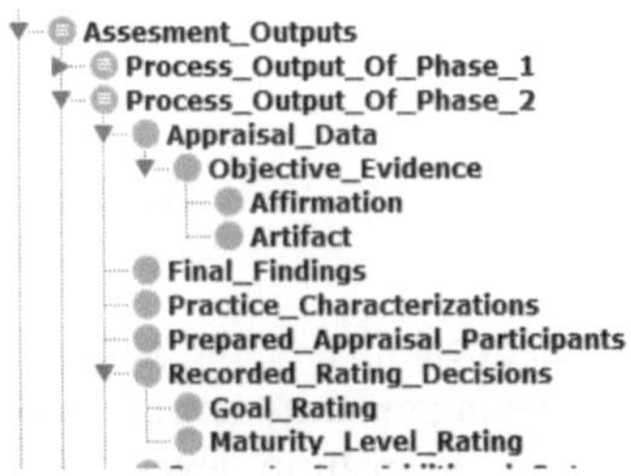

Fig. 8. Class hierarchy of "Assessment_Output" class of SCAMPI-A ontology

4.3 Organization Ontology

In order to establish mapping to the TMMi Assessment Ontology, the Organization ontology has three classes: Organization, Project, and Work_Product. Each organization, project, or work product can be defined as an individual to the related class during the assessments (Fig. 9).

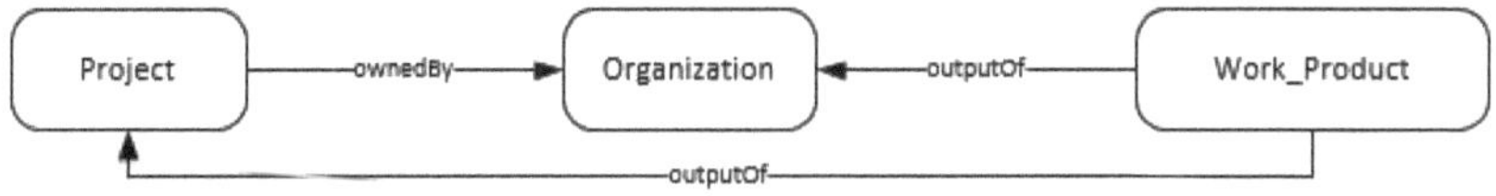

Fig. 9. The classes and their relationships of Organization ontology

4.4 TMMi Assessment Ontology

TMMi Assessment Ontology is composed of classes that are defined in the three imported ontologies described above. However, in order to complete the mapping, new object properties are defined to form relationships between classes across different ontologies. The top-level class hierarchy and relationships aggregated in TMMi Assessment Ontology can be seen in Fig. 10.

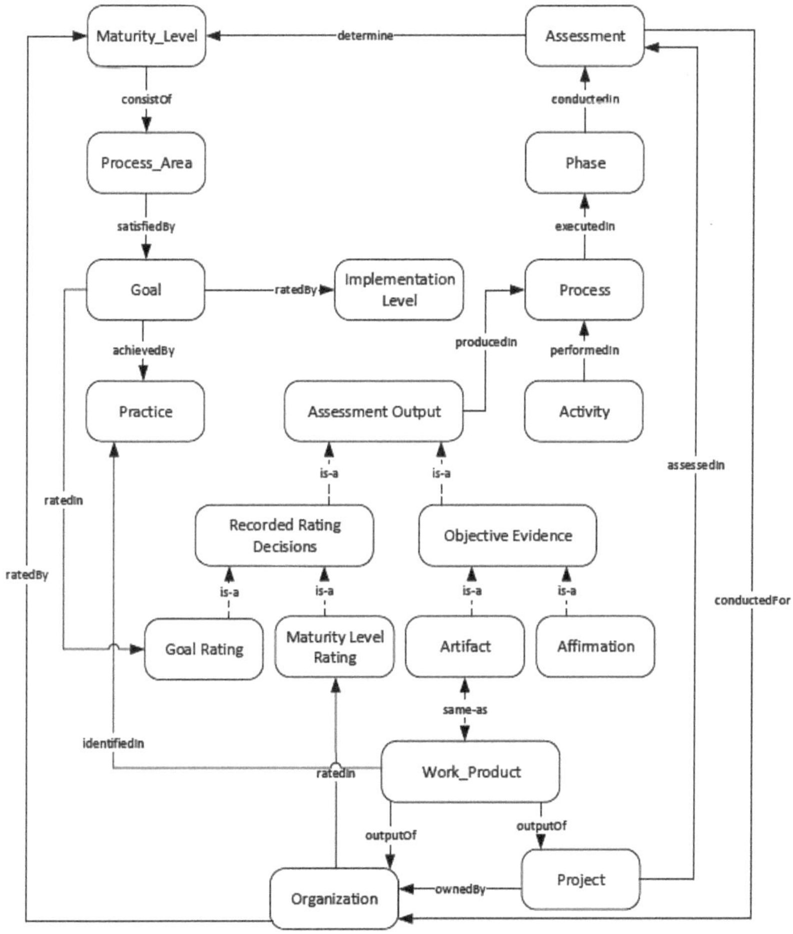

Fig. 10. TMMi Assessment Ontology top-level class hierarchy and relationships

5 An Example Usage of the TMMi Assessment Ontology

Figure 11 shows a part of an example usage of TMMi Assessment ontology. In the example, a TMMi based assessment was performed by following SCAMPI method in a real organization's software development project.

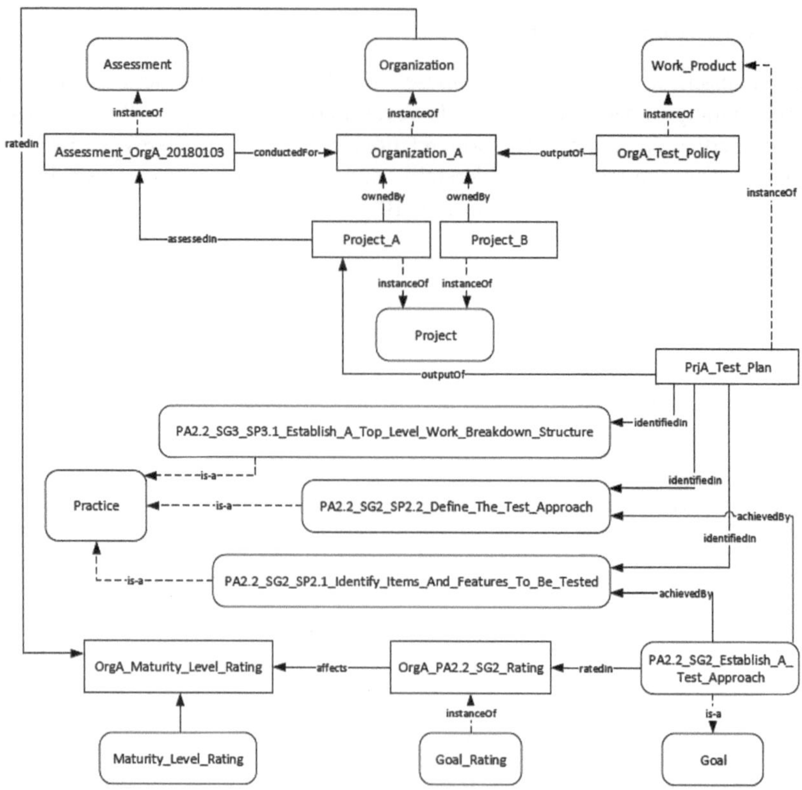

Fig. 11. Part of an example usage of TMMi Assessment Ontology

"Organization_A" is defined as an individual of the Organization class. The Organization_A has "Project_A" and "Project_B", which are defined as individuals of class Project. An assessment is conducted for Organization_A and only Project_A is in scope of the assessment. The assessment is recorded as an individual of Assessment class by the name "Assessment_OrgA_20180103". Project_A has a test plan called PrjA_Test_Plan, which is an individual of the class Work_Product. PrjA_Test_Plan indicates an objective evidence in Assessment_OrgA_20180103 for multiple specific practices which effects the achievement of Process Area 2.2 towards Specific Goal 2. The achievement of Process Area 2.2 towards Specific Goal 2 is rated in OrgA_PA2.2_SG2_Rating and the rating affects maturity level of the organization, OrgA_Maturity_Level_Rating, where both ratings (i.e. goal and maturity level ratings) identified in the assessment are shown via data properties tied to these individuals.

With that kind of a mapping, an organization, in this case Organization_A, can easily identify the state of each goal and which work products are identified in achieving that goal. Assume that Process Area 2.2 of Specific Goal 2.2 is rated as "Partially Implemented", then the Organization_A would become aware of that and need to improve their test approach by organizing their test process improvement efforts accordingly.

The resulting ontology, which includes assessment information via individuals created for Project_A of Organization_A, would be extended with other projects of the Organization_A or other organizations. This would result in the assessment information across different projects and organizations to be managed in the same repository while creating a linked structure of assessment data. The practitioners within the organization also confirmed that when proper tool support is provided, ontology supported testing process assessments would help referring the strengths and weaknesses, and work products identified in previous assessments in various contexts and projects.

6 Conclusion and Future Works

In this study, TMMi Assessment Ontology to support TMMi-based assessments is introduced. It integrates a TMMi ontology defining TMMi model information, a SCAMPI-A ontology defining SPAMPI-A method information, and an organization ontology specifying organization, their projects and work products. The ontology has a modular structure that would enable it to be extended and modified with additional process reference models and assessment methods. Furthermore, the three independent ontologies can be reused in other ontologies and applications.

The TMMi Assessment Ontology enables assessment data to be created via defining individuals of the classes and their relationships for TMMi-based assessments. In scope of an example assessment in a real organization, assessment data was defined and stored in the ontology. In practice, the ontology, which is a linked data environment for assessments, would be extended with more assessment data from other projects or organizations. This will enable assessors and practitioners benefit from data search, display, inference, and storage capabilities offered by the ontology.

Furthermore, the TMMi Assessment Ontology will improve the understandability of the domain knowledge included in TMMi model and SCAMPI method by people and machines. Also, it would enable semantic interoperability between assessment tools, where information would be exchanged correctly and completely, shared domain knowledge would be established, and assessment data would be used in linking data and benchmarking.

Although nearly all concepts of SCAMPI-A method are implemented, the TMMi Assessment Ontology is mainly designed to support execution of "Conduct Appraisal" phase. Therefore, "Plan and Prepare for the Appraisal" and "Report Result" phases may be a subject for another study, in order to make the infrastructure more usable and complete for supporting TMMi-based assessments.

References

1. Gibson, D.L., Goldenson, D.R., Kost, K.: Performance Results of CMMI-Based Process Improvement. Software Engineering Institute, Technical report CMU/SEI-2006-TR-004 (2006)
2. April, A., Huffman Hayes, J., Abran, A., Dumke, R.: Software maintenance maturity model (SMmm). J. Softw.: Evol. Process. **17**(3), 197–223 (2005)
3. Beecham, S., Hall, T., Rainer, A.: Defining a requirements process improvement model. Softw. Qual. J. **13**(3), 247–279 (2005)
4. Salmanoglu, M., Coskuncay, A., Yildiz, A., Demirors, O.: An exploratory case study for assessing the measurement capability of an agile organization. Softw. Qual. Prof. Mag. **20**(2), 36–47 (2018)
5. Cooper, J., Fisher, M., Sherer, S.W.: Software Acquisition Capability Maturity Model (SA-CMM) Version 1.02 (No. CMU/SEI-99-TR-002). Software Engineering Institute, Carnegie Mellon University, Pittsburgh (1999)
6. Farooq, A., Dumke, R.R.: Developing and applying a consolidated evaluation framework to analyze test process improvement approaches. In: Cuadrado-Gallego, J.J., Braungarten, R., Dumke, Reiner R., Abran, A. (eds.) IWSM/Mensura -2007. LNCS, vol. 4895, pp. 114–128. Springer, Heidelberg (2008). https://doi.org/10.1007/978-3-540-85553-8_10
7. Tarhan, A., Giray, G.: On the use of ontologies in software process assessment: a systematic literature review. In: 21st International Conference on Evaluation and Assessment in Software Engineering (2017)
8. Noy, N.F., McGuinness D.L.: Ontology Development 101: A Guide to Creating Your First Ontology. Stanford University (2001)
9. Veenendaal, E.: Test Maturity Model Integration (TMMi) Release 1.0. TMMi Foundation. https://www.tmmi.org/wp-content/uploads/2016/09/TMMi.Framework.pdf
10. TMMi Assessment Options. https://www.tmmi.org/assessment-options/
11. Software Engineering Institute: Standard CMMI Appraisal Method for Process Improvement (SCAMPI) A, Version 1.3: Method Definition Document (2011)
12. Chandrasekaran, B., Josephson, J.R., Benjamins, V.R.: What are ontologies, and why do we need them? IEEE Intell. Syst. **14**, 20–26 (1999)
13. Kalibatiene, D., Vasilecas, O.: Survey on ontology languages. In: Grabis, J., Kirikova, M. (eds.) BIR 2011. LNBIP, vol. 90, pp. 124–141. Springer, Heidelberg (2011). https://doi.org/10.1007/978-3-642-24511-4_10
14. Ryu, H., Ryu, D., Baik, J.: A strategic test process improvement approach using an ontological description for MND-TMM. IEEE (2008)
15. Gazel, S., Tarhan, A., Sezer, E.: An ontology based infrastructure to support CMMI-based software process assessment. Gazi Univ. J. Sci. **25**, 155–164 (2012)
16. Soydan, G.H., Kokar, M.M.: An OWL ontology for representing the CMMI-SW model. In: Workshop on Semantic Web Enabled Software Engineering (2006)
17. Sharifloo, A.A., Motazedi, Y., Shamsfard, M., Dehkharghani R.: An ontology for CMMI-ACQ model. IEEE (2008)
18. Liao, L., Qu, Y., Leung, H.K.N.: A software process ontology and its application. In: Workshop on Semantic Web Enabled Software Engineering (2005)

Permissioned Blockchains and Smart Contracts into Agile Software Processes

Sofia Terzi(✉) and Ioannis Stamelos(✉)

Aristotle University of Thessaloniki,
University Campus, 54124 Thessaloniki, Greece
{sofiaterzi, stamelos}@csd.auth.gr

Abstract. Since 2009 when Bitcoin was introduced, followed by the evolution of permissioned and permissionless blockchain networks as we know of them today, the technology of distributed ledgers is continuously changing to satisfy the markets interest into them. Alongside, software development methodologies are also evolving in order to incorporate the businesses and users demands. The broad use of internet in everyday tasks and services such as Backend as a Service, Database as a Service, Infrastructure as a Service, Platform as a Service and Software as a Service have formed the software processes that are adopted to produce the final product. Blockchain changes drastically the way software is developed and companies producing software must adapt quickly by changing their software processes accordingly to avoid obstacles and pitfalls coming of that, in order to incorporate this new technology but also follow techniques, which will produce sustainable software.

Keywords: Blockchain · Smart contracts · Software processes
Software development · Agile

1 Introduction

The software industry has faced many challenges during the past decades due to the invasion of computers in our everyday tasks taking place between business-to-customer (B2C), business-to-business (B2B) and business-to-government (B2G) which resulted in increased demand for quick development. The emergence of new software development techniques and processes such as agile methods provided the needed flexibility, became popular and are since being adopted, mainly by small to medium business entities (SMEs), as the most suitable software development process methods for cases where the initial requirements change rapidly [1]. The agile manifesto welcomes change even late in the development process [2] and this is a necessity when technologies as blockchain emerge, promising to reshape how assets are being exchanged between mistrusted parties by removing the intermediary and bringing decentralized applications allowing peer-to-peer interactions to take place. Furthermore, much research on software processes improvement resulted to establish standards and proved their value for the development of new software, with ISO/IEC 15504 (SPICE) [3] and Capability Maturity Model Integration (CMMI) [4] being dominant among software development companies. The paper will try to explain how permissioned blockchains

I. Stamelos et al. (Eds.): SPICE 2018, CCIS 918, pp. 355–362, 2018.
https://doi.org/10.1007/978-3-030-00623-5_26

and smart contracts come into the picture of software development processes. Additionally, it will explore if it is possible to incorporate the necessary techniques to improve and preserve the achieved software process maturity levels when traditional and agile software development methodologies are used along with permissioned blockchains. This paper is the result of best successfully applied practices during the development of software projects from the first of the two authors, who has more than three years of intensive experience in the software development industry, including blockchain technologies.

2 Software Development Methodologies

2.1 Agile Methodology

Software industry's most common agile methodologies such as SCRUM model, utilize iteration development and are known to have in focus the delivery of some form of the product to the customer as soon as possible, in order to receive feedback and incorporate this information into the next stages of development. This close collaboration with the customers and openness to specifications redefinition many times leads to continuous design with almost no freezing features until the latest stages of the final product [5]. Less planning in the beginning to serve flexibility is a natural outcome from agile management's philosophy, and at the initial stage of requirements gathering and analysis the result is to overlook or even ignore some of the key features. However, these key features will come into foreground at later stages and will have to be implemented. The implementation of such features many times require the adoption of new technologies, and this is the case software houses face with the blockchain technology.

2.2 Traditional Methodology

Traditional software development methods such as the waterfall model were tested for many years and leading software development companies still use them especially on critical projects [6]. The phases of requirement analysis, design, coding, testing, deployment and maintenance have this predefined particular order and no phase can start unless the preceding stage has been completed and verified. This makes it difficult to adopt new technologies at any stage later than the design phase, even if these new technologies might solve problems that otherwise is hard or even impossible to solve with existing technology. It is profound that projects which follow this life cycle and have passed the design stage and moved to the code phase are obliged not to use the blockchain technology even for problems that are impossible to solve with current technologies, such as immutability and assets exchange with no intermediaries.

3 Blockchain Technology

Bitcoin was introduced by [7] as a blockchain technology that made possible to perform transactions between trustless networks without a trusted intermediary. After the success of the Bitcoin, many other cryptocurrencies made their emergence with Ethereum technology [8] becoming popular especially due to its capability to utilize smart contracts. Smart contracts are computer programs that represent promises in a digital form including protocols within, that bind specific actions of the parties involved concerned to these promises [9]. Public blockchains as Bitcoin and Ethereum face drawbacks because no single entity controls who can enter or leave the network. Time and energy expensive algorithms have to run on the participating machines in order to achieve consensus, which means that all nodes globally have the same set of records at the same order on their ledger until that point in time. The main feature of blockchains, which no technology provided before, is immutability. The way blockchains are built with every block connected to the previous one forming a merkle tree, plus the facts that blocks are only appended at the end of the ledger forming a write-only data structure and that the ledger is distributed among all participants who verify and apply each transaction, is what makes blockchains immutable.

However, a problem for businesses arose because of the public distributed ledger; transactions are completely transparent to everybody. This eliminates businesses' competitive advantages, because they do not want to present all of their business information to everybody. That lead to the development of private permissioned blockchains, where the addition or removal of participants is controllable, and transactions are visible only to the participants of this network [10]. Because of the immutability of the ledger, the utilization of smart contracts on permissioned blockchain networks seems ideal. These computer programs became popular because they prove the exact terms agreed between the parties, although there is no legal enforcement of the agreement between strangers and there is no guarantee who will be responsible if there is a coding error that results in losses for either party [11].

4 Software Processes

We have to understand that blockchain is a tool, not a standalone solution. This dictates that software companies with established software processes who want to include blockchain solutions have to modify their development processes accordingly. We argued why blockchains and smart contracts seem to fit well with the agile methodology, but many small software companies have ignorance how to apply process improvement models, and also the existing software processing models must be altered to include good agile processes inside the process framework [12]. There is also evidence that most SMEs are skeptical to invest in software process improvement models primarily because this demands resources, commitment and the return of investment is many times not obvious [13]. If we add to all these the continuous change blockchain technology faces because of its immaturity at this early stages of adoption, then a satisfying level of standardization for permissioned blockchain development processes seems nearly impossible. Nevertheless, next we will try to specify the best practices we followed based on some of the agile manifesto pillars [2] that are important to apply and companies should consider following in order to achieve the minimum set of rules and guidelines needed when developing blockchain solutions.

- Early and continuous delivery: This principle must be followed at all times without any exceptions. Blockchain business solutions will usually include smart contracts. Smart contracts will perform actions if their conditions are met or if they are called directly by the user automating the agreement between participating parties, but if they are not deterministic or well-formed then losses for all or some parties are inevitable. Early delivery and testing will spot any omissions or misconfigurations. Close collaboration with the customer and/or specialized advisers such as lawyers, insurers, finance managers etc. will provide the development team with the necessary guidelines and suggestions to correct the discrepancies, if any.
- Expect changes at all stages: Changes while developing blockchain solutions are expected, maybe more than any other project the development team has faced, because the changes on blockchain technologies are frequent. They can vary from the usual ones, such us customer demanded changes in specifications, to technological factors. This is the reason team meetings should be scheduled very often to exchange knowledge and best practices, because the technology is new to every member of the team. Business permissioned blockchains such as Hyperledger, are mostly open source projects with stable editions counting only a few months of existence. Bugs are present and corrected as soon as possible, but they make the development process from hard, to impossible, in some special cases. New features are also introduced frequently and provide quick and stable solutions, and the custom code solutions developed from scratch by the developers have to be removed to preserve compatibility with future blockchain versions affecting the total code.
- Produce working software: A careful research for each candidate blockchain technology must be made, with enough time to identify the pros and cons for each one. If a wrong choice is made, it is likely to delay or cancel the project if the needed features are not supported by the chosen blockchain technology. Private permissioned blockchains is a new technology and not all of them provide the same capabilities. There are few common features among them but there are no standards, and almost every feature is subject to change at any time. This means that the blockchain technology version to choose must support all the features needed to deliver working software at the time the initial decision is made. Some solutions might seem more promising than others but are less tested or have limited support and this must be taken under serious consideration.
- Promote sustainable development: Sustainability is crucial for software applications. There are few times a blockchain application being developed not being used for a long time after. Besides, this is the purpose of a blockchain, to keep its records immutable forever. Likewise, blockchains came to stay. Smart cities, energy sector, insurance market, financial services, internet of things in all areas, agriculture, governments just to name a few, have recognized opportunities and benefits from the use of distributed ledgers and search ways to take advantage of the new possibilities they provide. By choosing a blockchain technology that uses a well-known

language such as JavaScript or Python, developers can focus more to what has to be done than how this can be done. They can design better the architecture and contribute to the sustainability of the final application.

Figure 1 below shows the steps to build successful sustainable software including drastic steps such as changing the blockchain technology at early stages in case the early delivery of the software is impossible even before the acceptance phase. Standard agile methodology is represented with black color whereas changes introduced by blockchains and smart contracts are represented with red color.

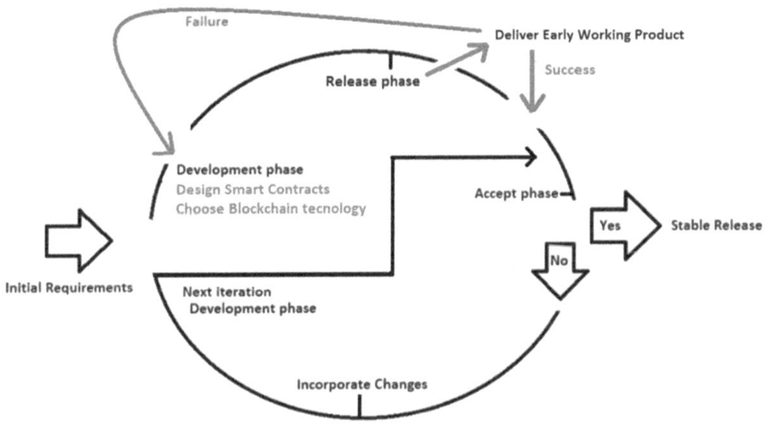

Fig. 1. Blockchain technology with agile methodology for sustainable software (Color figure online)

If smart contracts were carefully designed, the incapability to produce the early working software is a strong indication that the chosen technology is not suitable for the needed functionality. We can conclude from this circle that a new step between the release and accept phase is introduced, which represents the difficulties and restrictions that might be faced by the new blockchain technology and has to be confronted drastically and early.

5 Software Processes Improvement

It has proven to be important and sometimes indispensable for software companies undertaking critical projects to prove their maturity level for software development through a standardized process such as ISO/IEC 15504 or CMMI. Although ISO/IEC 15504, formerly known as Software Process Improvement and Capability Determination (SPICE) model, was introduced initially without maturity levels, after a revision new capability levels were documented. Compared to CMMI maturity levels a direct match between them is obvious [14, 15] which confers prestige to both these industry leading models. Next, we give directions for blockchain development processes and try to spot the possible pitfalls and the specific process areas that are expected to be affected, to help companies who want to conform to standard software process improvement techniques achieve their goal. We believe that the discussion that follows applies on all software process improvement models, including SPICE.

Software development houses should use open source technologies, the leading blockchain technologies not by accident are open source projects and are free to use and contribute. For requirements management processes attention should be given tracking the change requests, no changes that cannot be fulfilled with the chosen blockchain technology shall be accepted. The measurement and analyses processes might be tricky because measurement objectives will not be clear at first and are expected to change during the development phases. Metrics must be set from the beginning but only for what is meaningful, such as the total code lines for smart contracts or the total services each smart contract is allowed to call. Smart contracts are computer functions and they must follow the best practices for function's total code lines and embedded services, so it is very important to establish the objectives and select the measures and analytic techniques to measure performance on specific smart contracts. In addition, some classic measurements as write performance are off topic, because there are big performance gaps compared to the database systems [16]. Although security must be a priority, has to be designed along with other tools and hardware, such as proxies, firewalls and gateways. All these make the project planning of high importance; risks will be high for effort and cost, and there must be a flexible risk management plan for the development phases. Risk management obviously needs to assess the dangers that are coming from customer requirements change, development team inexperience, incorrectly designed and deployed smart contracts and technology rapid changes. Because blockchain technology is likely to change before the final product is delivered, the software company might face excessive pressure from the customer to incorporate this new technology, which may cancel much of the effort put on the current technology leading to delivery delays. To minimize the risks, the software company should focus to develop a product specifically for the requested solution with no or little add-ons because of the unknown outgrowth of distributed ledgers. Continuous monitoring against the project plan and corrective actions must be integral parts of the risk management plan.

The process and product quality must assure that the program components and especially smart contracts are in alignment with the defined requirements. The decision analysis has to evaluate the distributed ledger technologies and the alternatives, and then decide which technology to choose. As argued in this paper the risks are many and private permissioned blockchains are suitable for certain solutions only. If verifiability, transparency, privacy, integrity, redundancy and a trust anchor are the desired properties then a private permissioned blockchain is a good candidate but more questions have to be answered positively. More specifically if there is a need to store the state, if there are multiple writers and if all of them are known and trusted and last but not least if online processing at all times is feasible [17]. The project management processes must include close collaboration with stakeholders in order the smart contracts to be tailored to the customer's needs and to follow the essential standards for its terms and actions.

For organizational process definitions an agile lifecycle model has to be defined and take under consideration the strengths and weaknesses of the development team to establish special action plans if flaws are identified. Part of these established plans must be the organization's training before and during the development for aspects that span from development to law matters. For the product integration, thorough tests must take place to certify that smart contracts behave as expected as they make a blockchain system responsive and automatic. These tests must include mainly the back-end behavior but also the front-end components [18]. These processes are essential for both the customers and the organization to prove the product's fullness and expected behavior and make sure an unobstructed acceptance and deployment will follow. Causal analysis for permissioned private blockchains has to be further researched because of few examples in the market, but with a quick view, companies should focus to the outcome analysis before defining the causes. Keeping detailed documentation is vital at any stage. Blockchain agile methodology gives little attention to detailed documentation but practices that were tested must be defined and outcomes will reveal the causes of successes and failures. Future projects will rely heavily on this detailed documentation of projects that utilized these new technologies. The organizational performance management will completely rely at first on developers estimation about time needed to complete the project and the difficulty level. Thus, meetings between developers and managers are necessary to be frequent during the complete development process to exchange knowledge obtained gradually and perform managerial interpretation, to suggest improvements along with plans on how to deploy these improvements. If a software company follow the processes described above, it is expected to establish at least the minimum needed points level for the nine ISO/IEC 15504 process attributes [3] and be eligible for SPICE certification.

6 Discussion

Software process improvements are very important even if new technologies make it more difficult for the software companies to define certain methods for every development phase. As the maturity of blockchains increases and more services are standardized, teams that follow software process improvement methods will adapt more quickly and will make better choices for successful development, even if this includes to switch the blockchain technology for another which will serve better the customer's needs and the company's goals. We tried to comprise in this paper guidelines that will help development teams escape pitfalls, but we also acknowledge that distributed ledger technology is evolving and we have limitations such as scarce information and few permissioned private blockchain cases implemented and published since now. This research was mainly focused on technical aspects of blockchain implementations; future research should be made from the managerial perspective. Distributed ledgers, blockchains and smart contracts are here to stay and software processes will be reformed from these technologies. We strongly believe that this research will contribute this reform to be smoother and successful for the software development companies.

References

1. Wiley Online Library: Agile Software Development. Software – Practice and Experience, pp. 41:943–41:944 (2011)
2. Manifesto for Agile Software Development. http://agilemanifesto.org/iso/en/principles.html. Accessed 16 July 2018
3. Wikipedia: ISO/IEC 15504. https://en.wikipedia.org/wiki/ISO/IEC_15504. Accessed 16 July 2018
4. Wikipedia: Process area (CMMI). https://en.wikipedia.org/wiki/Process_area_(CMMI)#Maturity_Levels:_CMMI_for_Development. Accessed 16 July 2018
5. Serrador, P., Pinto, J.K.: Does Agile work? — A quantitative analysis of agile project success (2015)
6. Vijayasarathy, L.R., Butler, C.W.: Choice of software development methodologies do organizational, project, and team characteristics matter? IEEE Softw. **33**, 86–94 (2016)
7. Nakamoto, S.: Bitcoin: A Peer-to-Peer Electronic Cash System. https://bitcoin.org/bitcoin.pdf. Accessed 16 July 2018
8. Ethereum: A Next-Generation Smart Contract and Decentralized Application Platform, https://github.com/ethereum/wiki/wiki/White-Paper. Accessed 16 July 2018
9. Szabo, N.: Smart Contracts. http://www.fon.hum.uva.nl/rob/Courses/InformationInSpeech/CDROM/Literature/LOTwinterschool2006/szabo.best.vwh.net/smart.contracts.html. Accessed 16 July 2018
10. Christidis, K., Devetsikiotis, M.: Blockchains and Smart Contracts for the Internet of Things (2016)
11. Giancaspro, M.: Is a 'smart contract' really a smart idea? Insights from a legal perspective. Comput. Law Secur. Rev. **33**(6), 825–835 (2017)
12. Schweigert, T., Nevalainen, R., Vohwinkel, D., Korsaa, M., Biro, M.: Agile maturity model: oxymoron or the next level of understanding. In: Mas, A., Mesquida, A., Rout, T., O'Connor, R.V., Dorling, A. (eds.) SPICE 2012. CCIS, vol. 290, pp. 289–294. Springer, Heidelberg (2012). https://doi.org/10.1007/978-3-642-30439-2_34
13. Galinac, T.: Empirical evaluation of selected best practices in implementation of software process improvement (2009). https://doi.org/10.1016/j.infsof.2009.05.002
14. Peldzius, S., Saulius, R.: Comparison of maturity levels in CMMI-DEV and ISO/IEC 15504 (2011)
15. Ehsan, N., Perwaiz, A., Arif, J., Mirza, E., Ishaque, A.: CMMI/SPICE based process improvement, pp. 859–862 2010. https://doi.org/10.1109/icmit.2010.5492803
16. Dinh, T.T.A., Liu, R., Zhang, M., Chen, G., Ooi, B.C., Wang, J.: Untangling blockchain: a data processing view of blockchain systems. IEEE Trans. Knowl. Data Eng. **30**(7), 1366–1385 (2018)
17. Wüst, K., Gervais, A.: Do you need a Blockchain? IACR Cryptology ePrint Archive 2017, p. 375 (2017)
18. Wikipedia: Front and back ends. https://en.wikipedia.org/wiki/Front_and_back_ends

Author Index